Commitment, Voice, and Clarity

Commitment, Voice, and Clarity

An Argument Rhetoric and Reader

Janet Marting

University of Akron

NTC Publishing Group
Lincolnwood, Illinois USA

Executive Editor: John T. Nolan
Sponsoring Editor: Marisa L. L'Heureux
Cover and interior design: Ophelia M. Chambliss
Cover art: Fred Otnes/The Stock Illustration Sources, Inc.
Production Manager: Rosemary Dolinski

ISBN 0-8442-5905-5 (student text)
ISBN 0-8442-5906-3 (instructor's edition)

Published by NTC Publishing Group
© 1996 NTC Publishing Group, 4255 West Touhy Avenue
Lincolnwood (Chicago), Illinois 60646-1975 U.S.A.
Manufactured in the United States of America.
Library of Congress Catalog Card Number: 94-80057

5 6 7 8 9 ML 0 9 8 7 6 5 4 3 2 1

CONTENTS

Chapter 4

Strategies of Argumentation

Chapter 5

The Researched Paper   99

PART 2   READINGS FOR DISCUSSION
            AND ANALYSIS

Chapter 6

Education

Viewpoints

Arguments

Chapter 12

The Power and Politics of Language

Chapter 13

Matters of Equality

Arguments

PREFACE

As surely as students are asked to write narratives and expressive essays in most first-year composition classes, they are also asked to write argument and persuasive essays—and for good reason: The hallmark of an "educated" person is her ability to offer a perspective or viewpoint on a subject and to support it convincingly. At least that is the call from educators, parents, the media, and other people who decry the preparedness of students universities are turning out these days.

Not surprisingly, the selection of textbooks on argumentation is growing larger each year. Many offer advice on how to write a research paper; some are compendia of examples of argument essays; still others begin by advancing the principles of Aristotle's or Toulmin's logic; and many address "big issues," such as abortion, capital punishment, euthanasia, animal research, and so on, frequently offering pro and con perspectives.

While many of these books may work well for students who already are well versed in writing convincingly about ideas, they pose significant problems for inexperienced writers. *Commitment, Voice, and Clarity: An Argument Rhetoric and Reader* breaks from the tradition set forth in most of the argument rhetorics and readers currently on the market. This book emphasizes the connection between experience-based writing (which most students are practiced in and comfortable with) and idea-based writing (which is often a stumbling block for many students) by providing an explanation and examples of how a personal experience essay can be the springboard for both informal and formal argument papers.

Chapter 1, "Understanding Argument," begins with a discussion of key terms and examines the many reasons for writing argument papers. Then, the chapter explores the difficulties that can ensue when writing about facts and values. A discussion of myths and misconceptions addresses often-held notions concerning writing about ideas. By shattering these misconceptions, I hope to free students to write freely and openly about their beliefs. The aim of this chapter is to help students understand the importance of writing about ideas and to show them the many examples of argumentative writing in their lives.

The second chapter is the heart of the book. "From Experience-Based to Idea-Based Writing" demonstrates several ways in which students can move from writing about personal experiences and observations to writing about ideas and values that are rooted in those experiences and observations. Thus, when writing argument papers, students will see how to draw on events and ideas from their own lives. Examples of personal experience, viewpoint, and argument papers show students the differences between experience-based and idea-based writing. The writing of idea-based papers need not be a kind of discourse devoid of student interest and meaning. If anything, it can be the natural outgrowth and extension of personal experience writing.

Chapter 3, "Writing Viewpoint and Argument Papers," thoroughly discusses the writing process as it relates specifically to argument papers. Prewriting, writing, revision, editing, and proofreading strategies are described, as well as audience and counterarguments. A separate discussion of voice offers students information on ways to achieve the style or tone they want in their writing. This chapter offers eight examples (with descriptions) of different introductory paragraphs that demonstrate ways students can interest their readers. The chapter ends with a checklist for writers and readers. Throughout this chapter, students are given plentiful exercises that allow them to put the information they read into actual practice, so that by the end of the chapter, they will have written, revised, edited, and proofread an entire paper.

Chapter 4, "Strategies of Argumentation," covers both Aristotle's and Toulmin's logic and offers lucid explanations of the methods by which students can argue their stances. The three appeals of logos, pathos, and ethos are also presented, as are the ways to employ sound logic and a suitable tone to create convincing arguments. Students are given ample opportunities to practice their understanding of all the strategies of formal logic through a series of structured exercises throughout the chapter.

The last chapter in the rhetoric, "The Researched Paper," begins with a discussion of why and how to use outside sources and where to begin a library search. It then addresses the use of primary and secondary sources in the writing of argument papers, with special attention to taking notes, summarizing, paraphrasing, and using correct MLA and APA documentation. Helpful information on ways to introduce sources into a paper and how to avoid plagiarism is also provided.

The second part of the book, the reader, consists of forty-eight argument essays that are models of the kind of writing discussed in the first part of the book. These selections are grouped in eight appealing, thought-provoking, and timely topics: education, work, sports and leisure, popular culture, the family, values and human nature, the politics of language, and discrimination. Each reading is followed by discussion questions that ask students to analyze what they have read, based on the tools of argumentation discussed in the rhetoric portion of the text. Not only are the readings models of what argument writing looks and sounds like, the writing topics that appear at the end of each chapter encourage students to try their own hand at writing argument papers.

My goal in both parts of this book has been to offer students understandable, commonsensical information on ways to write argument papers; to show students ways to establish believability in their papers and to integrate outside sources to support their own thinking; and to provide a wide selection of appealing and challenging essays that will motivate students to move beyond personal experience essays to examine their own observations and ideas in engaging and convincing argument papers.

ACKNOWLEDGMENTS

Working on this text has given me the opportunity to clarify my beliefs about the writing and the teaching of argumentation. Thanks to Faun Bernbach Evans and Michael Keller, who offered clear and sensible advice.

I am especially grateful to my editors, John T. Nolan, for believing in and supporting my work and for his helpful suggestions; and Marisa L. L'Heureux, for her invaluable assistance in helping me to develop this text and for her insights, encouragement, and friendship.

Finally, thanks to my family, Bill and Chelsea, for their loving patience and understanding.

Janet Marting

PART 1

A GUIDE TO WRITING VIEWPOINTS AND ARGUMENTS

CHAPTER  1

UNDERSTANDING
ARGUMENT

What We Mean When We Talk about Argument

What is the first thing that comes to mind when you hear the word *argument*? Most people would agree with you if you said disagreement, quarrel, fight, tiff, spat, or dispute. Powerful emotions are suggested by those synonyms too, such as anger, outrage, fury, wrath, hate, annoyance, displeasure, disbelief, and exasperation. Clearly, for many people, the word *argument* has negative connotations.

Think for a moment of some situations in which arguments occur. Children argue about which toy belongs to whom; baseball players argue with umpires about whether a player was safe or out; and teenagers argue with parents about curfews on school nights. I'm sure you can add other instances to this list. The point is that situations in which we find ourselves arguing can occur frequently as we deal with people whose ideas do not mesh with our own. In fact, arguing might be seen as an expected part of growing up, of testing boundaries, and of standing up for one's most fervent beliefs.

When referring to argument so far in this discussion, I've used the more popular connotation of the term, something with which most people are familiar—and would probably prefer to avoid, since it can lead to a standoff in which one party is "right" and the other "wrong," with both sides reluctant to hear each other out. You are exposed to less confrontational spoken arguments when advertisements, commercials, or salespeople try to convince you to purchase one product rather than another. You also hear arguments whenever people express their perspectives on topics as diverse as which candidate should be elected to office, what type of exercise is the most beneficial for weight reduction, or what breed of dog is the best for apartment dwellers.

The term *argument* is used in this book to signal something that is far different from the explosive connotations discussed in the beginning of this chapter. When you read the word *argument* in this text, the term applies to the *writing* of argument papers.

What We Mean When We Talk about Writing Argument Papers

The origins of the term *argument* are far different from the popular connotation of the word. First introduced by Aristotle (384–322 B.C.), "argument" dealt with appeals or strategies for proving ideas and for trying to persuade others to share similar perspectives. Thus, in the traditional sense, argument is a formal approach to asserting a point persuasively and attempting to prove it.

Whether you are aware of it or not, written forms of argumentation are a part of your life. You compose written arguments in your college classes, in a job setting, and even as a concerned resident of your town or city. Every time you write a paper or take an exam, argument takes the form of your trying to prove to your teacher that you can support a stance you have taken or that you have learned the course material; at your job, you may write reports and proposals for your boss assessing current marketing strategies and suggesting new ones; you may write letters to the editor of your newspaper or to your state senator in which you support legislation on tax reform or increased funding for education.

Argumentation affords you the opportunity to present your specific point of view, discuss your ideas, and convince others to consider, if not adopt, your own perspective. Because we do not live in a world in which people always agree with each other, argumentation is an essential way by which we present written debates of our ideas—all in an attempt to reduce disagreements or dissension among people. And the more convincing the argument, the more successful you will be in having others adopt your perspective.

The first step in writing good arguments is commitment to the topic; however, arguments are not won because you are a committed and passionate speaker or writer. Good argumentation depends on your knowing *how* to argue—the ways in which you can present sound, convincing, and compelling cases for your beliefs. By reading examples of argument papers and writing your own, you can sharpen your skills in how to at least prove to your audience that you have thoughtfully, thoroughly, and logically presented your position. In this sense, then, written arguments are far different from spoken arguments, with their explosive connotations, which were presented earlier in this chapter.

Arguments deal with perspectives, points of view, stands, or ideas that are debatable and refutable. Many of the papers you write and exams you take in your college courses require you to use the elements upon which good arguments are based: a clear and strong idea backed by ample, believable evidence. At the center of good arguments is strong, sound thinking; immutable logic that develops and supports ideas; and awareness of opposing perspectives, or counterarguments. Clear, reasoned examinations of or deliberations on topics are at the heart of argument papers. Whether you are writing a term paper, an essay exam, a company proposal, an editorial, or any other piece of writing in which you are asked to take a stand and support it, traditional argumentation can help you to make your case.

Unlike many spoken arguments, the writing of argumentation offers you the opportunity to think carefully about a topic, develop your ideas, introduce and synthesize pertinent sources that support your thinking, employ sound logic to make your ideas convincing, and present your thinking clearly and forcefully. As a writer, you have the chance to carefully consider the audience for whom you are writing, organize your ideas to create the greatest impact, select sources that will help support your ideas, and revise your writing until you achieve the effect you want.

Another way to look at argument papers is that they answer the question *why*. That is, after offering your understandings of an issue, you must back them up with your reasons, or rationale. Thus, in arguments the question *why* is answered with a full examination of "because…"

The goal of argument papers is not to show how many sources you have amassed in your research, but to show your audience that you have thought critically and analytically about an issue or topic and that you have generated a carefully considered perspective you want your audience to take seriously. Argument papers do not necessarily end up with one side being right and the other wrong. Most issues worthy of examination are not that simple and clear-cut. No matter what perspective you take on an issue, however, a thorough, reasoned examination of the topic requires you not only to acknowledge that opposing perspectives exist, but to discuss them as a strategy for strengthening your own stance. Chapter 3, "Writing Viewpoint and Argument Papers," presents ways in which you can effectively address counterarguments.

All of the reading selections in *Commitment, Voice, and Clarity* are models of argument writing. While many include personal experience or observation, they are pieces of writing that predominantly offer *ideas* backed by supportive evidence and logical reasoning. There is no doubt that knowing the tools of argumentation—clearly presenting and logically supporting your ideas—will benefit you in many of the academic courses you take and in many of the writing projects you will undertake outside the college environment.

Viewpoints

An element of argument with which you are probably familiar is *viewpoints*. *Attitude, perspective, slant, outlook, position,* and *standpoint* are synonyms for *viewpoint*. Students posit viewpoints when they discuss the value of certain required courses in the college curriculum; architects offer viewpoints when they discuss the most innovative way to bring lighting into a building; sociologists offer viewpoints when they discuss the ways in which gentrification affects the elderly in old, run-down neighborhoods. Writers of op-ed columns in newspapers and magazines posit their viewpoints on topics and issues of current interest; so too do editorial writers and people who send letters to the editor of a newspaper or magazine.

Much like arguments, viewpoints are a means by which you can offer your perspectives on issues. Often, viewpoints arise from *observations*. Some examples of viewpoints that are the result of observation are that drivers have become increasingly aggressive in recent years; people claim to dislike the use of profanity but continue to swear as much as ever; advertising for events and holidays such as Halloween, Thanksgiving, Christmas, and Easter starts earlier and earlier each year; the greeting card industry seems to be creating new holidays (e.g., Grandparents' Day, Secretaries' Day, Sweetest Day, In-Laws' Day) to bolster their sales; salesclerks in stores and servers in restaurants are increasingly solicitous of their patrons. The list continues as long as you look around, observe daily phenomena, and *discuss the idea* that underlies your observation.

Unlike personal experience essays, however, viewpoints deal with *ideas* and not just with descriptions or narratives of "what happened to me." Unlike arguments, viewpoints do not necessarily have to be on issues or topics that are debatable or arguable; unlike opinion, they are more than personal preferences, but are thoughtful, idea-based reactions to events, situations, or occurrences that are observable in daily life. One difference between viewpoints and arguments is that viewpoints are aimed at more public and wide-ranging audiences and situations. Arguments, on the other hand, are geared toward academic or professional audiences and situations. Although the rhetoric portion of *Commitment, Voice, and Clarity* offers explicit instruction and discussion of argumentation, implicit in the information is viewpoint or any writing that is idea-based.

Differences among Personal Experience, Viewpoint, and Argument

To distinguish among writing about personal experiences, viewpoints, and arguments, let's use as an example the topic of the ways in which new technologies affect our lives. Suppose you have had unsuccessful experiences using answering machines, computers, and VCRs. You choose to write a paper in which you describe the time you made a blithering idiot of yourself when leaving a message on someone's answering machine; the time you lost three days' worth of work when trying to copy some files from your computer to a disk; and the time you had to call a VCR repair person to show you how to tape one show while watching another. Your nerve-wracking and anxiety-producing experiences made for a humorous paper that not only fulfilled the requirements of a personal experience essay in one of your composition classes but also relieved you of much frustration in the process.

Let's say in another paper you examine the idea that, despite your problems learning how to leave clear and succinct messages on answering machines, transfer certain files from computer to disk, and program your VCR, you have come to realize that using such new technologies is the way to do business in the real world. It may be scary and intimidating at first, but it represents what the latter part of the twentieth century demands of most people. This is an example of a viewpoint paper. Although it may include personal examples to help illustrate your main point, they are not the paper's principal focus; rather, your paper deals with a perception or observation that your personal experiences generated. Such a paper is appropriate for informal papers in college courses and for the commentary or editorial sections of newspapers and magazines.

When asked to write an argument paper for a college sociology class, you choose to pursue the topic of new technologies being not only frustrating but having a real downside to them, so much so that you decide to argue that people should rethink their reliance on them. In such a paper, you address the disadvantages of new technologies, the ways in which the world seemingly shuts down when new technologies fail. Some of your examples include people becoming less social when their interactions are with answering machines and voice mail rather than real, live human beings; university courses that cannot be added or dropped because the computer is down; airline travel that cannot be booked when the travel agent cannot access the airline's computer; and many people being drawn into excessive television watching because they can tape shows while away from home and watch them later instead of interacting with family and friends. The net result is that, despite the way in which the new technologies have revolutionized our lives, we have lost some of our freedom and human interaction in the process. You come to the conclusion that we need to rethink whether the new technologies, despite their helpfulness, are changing the characters of their users in the process. Thus, using descriptions of your personal experiences with technology as a starting point, your argument takes viewpoint one step further in overtly proposing refutable ideas that emerge from personal anecdotes and observations about them.

Let's consider one more example of the ways in which argument can be distinguished from personal experience and viewpoint. In a letter to your friends back home or in a personal experience essay for a composition class, you decide to describe the ingenious ways in which students at your school cheat when writing papers and taking exams. Your essay provides vivid details of students handing in papers that they or their friends have written in other courses; writing mathematical formulas on the palm of their hand or on gum and candy bar wrappers to refer to during the actual test; or hiring someone to take the multiple-choice exam in "monster" courses in which the professor lectures to three hundred students and doesn't recognize most of his or her students.

When writing a viewpoint or commentary about current trends on college campuses for your composition course or for your school newspaper, you choose the topic of cheating on campus. Using personal experience and observation as springboards, you write a paper in which you offer your perspectives on how the ways in which to cheat have become increasingly creative and how students seem relentless in devising new techniques and strategies to avoid writing papers and studying for exams. Your viewpoint results in a scathing observation on what you have witnessed at your school. Although the basic premises of the viewpoint can be refuted—those in any idea-based paper can—a writer who disagrees with your perspective would have to use his or her own observations or contentions to write a paper that posits the idea that cheating at colleges is not as pervasive and epidemic as you deem it to be.

For an argument paper on academic cheating in the 1990s, the previous descriptions of what you have witnessed and your viewpoint on the crisis in the classroom provide the impetus for you to write a paper that argues that colleges need to take new measures to guard against students' flagrant plagiarism of papers and cheating on exams. You might argue that it is the professors' responsibility to tailor-make paper topics in their courses to cut down on possible "recycling" of papers or to institute different ways to conduct exams to reduce the likelihood of students cheating. Another possibility might be to argue that it is the students' responsibility to rethink their behavior and to examine why they are in school in the first place. Or you might choose a combination of ideas: the responsibility rests on the faculty, on the administration, *and* on students.

In the preceding discussion of these three types of papers, we have moved from personal experience's descriptions and stories, to the observations and viewpoints that those descriptions and stories suggest, to a paper that argues who you think is responsible for remedying the problem. Each paper—personal experience, viewpoint, and argument—progressively relies less on experience-based descriptions or anecdotes and becomes increasingly more idea-based or idea-focused. While the line between viewpoint and argument papers is sometimes thin, viewpoints rely on observation and are less directed to an academic or professional audience than to a wide range of readers. Arguments, on the other hand, deal with ideas that are refutable, and argument papers are typically directed to specific audiences.

OPINIONS

Whether you agree or disagree with them, *everyone* has opinions. Opinions range from whether chocolate ice cream is tastier than vanilla, or whether hunter green is a more soothing color than wedgewood blue, to whether summer is a better season than winter. Because these examples are based solely on personal preference or individual taste, they cannot be argued or debated. Thus, they tend to be unsuitable topics for papers.

There is nothing wrong with having opinions. As John Milton wrote, "Opinions are but knowledge in the making." The point is that opinions are a starting point. All thinking can be said to begin with an opinion, but viewpoints and arguments examine the idea more thoughtfully and thoroughly than opinions ever can.

Think whatever you want, but if you are trying to write a paper that examines an idea, it is wise to keep in mind that you should choose an issue that you can support, back up, or provide some rationale for—beyond stating that "It's just my opinion" or "It's the way I feel." After all, if that's your only defense, why shouldn't your reader say, "So what?" and dismiss your opinion entirely? Can you imagine the futility and frustration of trying to discuss an issue with someone whose only defense is "It's just my opinion" or "That's just the way I see things"? Claiming it is "just an opinion" without fully discussing and supporting it not only ends a conversation prematurely, it ignores the critical thinking behind the formation of ideas. It is tantamount to a child answering a parent's questions with a shrug and a "Because."

PERSUASION

Think of all of the ways in which persuasion manifests itself in your daily life: Your friends try to persuade you to party instead of study; your parents try to convince you to stay in school instead of taking a year off to travel; Nike tries to convince you that its product is preferable to Reebok's; public service announcements try to convince you not to drink and drive, to stop smoking, and to have safe sex; a myriad of health agencies try to persuade you to donate money to their organization; telemarketing firms try to persuade you to buy anything from vinyl siding and a new roof to basement waterproofing and house insulation. And all of this before you have even left your home to begin the day's work! Suffice it to say, persuasion is so common a part of our lives that it is easy to overlook its pervasive and powerful role.

What, however, influences and determines the decisions you finally make? Do you attend the party or do you study? Do you stay in school or take the year off? Do you purchase Nike athletic shoes or Reeboks? Do you agree to be the designated driver, stop smoking, and have safe sex, or do you live dangerously? Do you donate to the American Cancer Society or to the American Lung Association? Do you have a new roof put on your house or do you postpone home improvements? Most importantly, what reasons and evidence convince or persuade you to make your decisions? What would it take to persuade you to make a different choice?

Persuasion can be seen as an extension of opinion, a by-product of viewpoint, and a goal of argumentation. To illustrate this point, let's say your friends think that you should join them at a party next Saturday night. Their observation—or viewpoint—is that you have lived in the library all week, burying your head in books, and need a break from studying. Because they want you to adopt their perspective, they argue their position by citing reasons: taking a break from studying will clear your head and be refreshing; you haven't participated in any social events in weeks; they miss your companionship; they know of a party at which a good band will be playing and the beer is free; all of your friends will be there; and so on. Your friends' goal is for you to join them in attending a fun get-together. How well they argue their case determines whether you continue studying or join them. Thus, persuasion—in this case, the goal of argumentation—is the result of your friends' successfully arguing their stand by voicing their opinion and offering their observation or viewpoint.

Chapter 4, "Strategies of Argumentation," provides detailed information on and discussion of ways to successfully argue positions.

ARGUING ABOUT FACTS

While all good arguments are backed by strong support, it is important to avoid trying to argue about facts that have long been proven and are undisputed. Some examples are: February lasts 28 days, except for leap years; 2 plus 2 equals 4; red is a primary color; Santa Fe is the capital of New Mexico; the pope is Catholic. There is simply no point in writing about facts that are not in question, are not bona fide issues, and are impossible to debate. Again, any reader can rightfully dismiss whatever you can generate by saying, So what? What's your point?

Viewpoint and argument papers need to demonstrate a perspective, take a stand, advance a specific idea, or prove a point. Writing about already proven facts amounts to little more than reinventing the wheel. Why bother?

ARGUING ABOUT VALUES

Arguing about values involves arguing about personal judgments. Because many values, especially ones that involve aesthetics and morals, are based solely on matters of personal tastes, preferences, or biases, they are often very difficult to defend. For an example that deals with aesthetics, you might believe that contemporary sculpture is not "real" art but rather an eyesore. How can you support your value judgment when others think such sculpture is magnificent? Do you say that "beauty is in the eye of the beholder" as your support? But what happens when your audience does not concur with that reason? To make your argument more convincing, you must define the basis of your standards (e.g., real sculpture is crafted from clay, stone, and metals, not by gluing together junkyard scraps and hanging a title over the piece to explain its meaning or purpose).

An example of arguing about value judgments might be that you judge euthanasia an immoral and unethical solution for suffering patients in the last stages of terminal illnesses. Issues that deal with morality are difficult and complex, to say the least. This particular case involves arguing ethical, religious, philosophical, and medical beliefs. As with the example that involves aesthetics, you must define the basis of your standards before you can effectively argue your position.

Complex issues involve complex thinking. Successfully arguing some issues, especially those that involve moral and ethical judgments, requires not only that you establish the standards on which you are basing your claim, but that your audience agrees with those standards and with your rationale or reasoning. It is little wonder that volumes have been written on issues such as abortion, capital punishment, euthanasia, and animal research and experimentation.

SUBJECTS VERSUS TOPICS

When you write argument papers, it is necessary to distinguish between subjects and bona fide topics. As you probably learned in previous composition courses, topics must be narrow enough for you to consider thoroughly and thoughtfully. The same holds true for the writing of viewpoint argument papers. The papers you will write in this course (and read in Part 2 of this book) aren't "about" a topic as much as they are answers to or examinations of questions you raise. No matter what topic or issue you choose to write about, you should be able to provide a brief declarative statement that summarizes the stance you are taking in your paper. For example, it is insufficient to say, "My paper is about MTV." What about MTV? a reader might ask. If you were to say, "My paper discusses how MTV is an effective way to present today's popular music," you are narrowing the topic and addressing a specific question that can be addressed in a paper.

If you are unable to pose a declarative statement that summarizes the stand you want to take in your paper, chances are you have not yet narrowed the subject matter into a workable topic. Here's another example of a subject that needs focusing: "My paper is about the O. J. Simpson trial." But what about the trial? Look at the many different questions or topics that can emerge from the subject of the Simpson trial: whether the prosecution and defense selected a partial or an impartial jury; whether the media influenced the case so much that it became a circus; whether big money won the case; whether the jury should or should not have been sequestered; whether all of the evidence should or should not have been admissible; whether the police were correct or incorrect in obtaining the evidence; whether Simpson should or should not have testified. The list continues. The point is that writing "about" something might produce many pages, but chances are they will be pages of unfocused writing that does not successfully center on one point, let alone prove anything. Papers need to address narrowed topics, not large and unwieldy subjects.

EXPANDING YOUR WRITING REPERTOIRE

Just as there are many different modes of transportation, there are many different modes of writing. If, for example, I want to visit a friend who lives in the western part of my state, I would drive there by car; if, however, I want to attend a conference on the West Coast, the most convenient way of getting there would be to fly, given that I live in the Midwest and time is at a premium; and if I want to take a romantic excursion with a loved one, chances are I would choose a ride in a hansom cab or an evening sailboat outing.

In much the same vein, if I want to express my innermost feelings in writing, I might write a poem or an entry in a journal; if I want to relate to others an unusual experience that happened on my vacation, I would probably write a personal, expressive essay; if I wanted to offer my perspective on the parking problems on the campus where I teach, I would write a letter to the editor of the university newspaper or to the head of the parking office on campus.

We have many different kinds of writing in our repertoire. Some may be appropriate for some situations, but simply unsuitable for others. (Can you imagine the reaction of the head of parking at a university if he or she were to receive a journal entry or a poem?) It is important to understand, however, that no matter what kind of writing you do, it should reflect your own thinking and character. We will explore more about this in Chapter 2, when we discuss ways to move from personal experience-based to idea-based writing.

Writing viewpoint and argument papers allows you the chance to focus exclusively on ideas in your writing. It expands your writing repertoire and gives you a forum in which to closely examine your ideas. In the next section, you will discover some additional reasons for reading and writing viewpoint and argument papers.

REASONS FOR READING AND WRITING
VIEWPOINT AND ARGUMENT PAPERS

What is the purpose of reading and writing argument papers? The following list offers five important reasons:

- *These kinds of papers can be seen as a natural outgrowth of, or the next step after, writing personal, expressive essays.* While writing about personal experiences is an important part of your writing background or repertoire, writing viewpoint and argument papers is a way to address the *consequences* of those experiences. Chapter 2, "From Experience-Based to Idea-Based Writing," will fully explain this idea and show you examples of ways to achieve this in your writing.

- *It is a natural activity to express one's ideas.* When people see the hottest film of the summer, chances are they have some reaction to it. (If you don't believe me, try eavesdropping on the conversations of people leaving the movie theater!) When tuition increases at your college, chances are you will be inclined to protest the change—if not to college officials, then certainly to family and friends. Even when you take time to observe people as they go about their lives, you might have interesting perspectives to offer: Does people's reliance on elevators and escalators, cruise-control cars, and other modern conveniences indicate laziness? What trends have you noticed in the recent lineup of television shows? Do people seem to be working harder than ever and achieving less? Are children growing up faster these days? Do television and magazine advertising unfairly target certain groups? To what extent do you think the exercise and diet industries in America have gotten out of hand? Do you think that procrastination has been given a bum rap? The list can continue so long as you scrutinize what's happening around you. In fact, with further consideration, the preceding list of questions might well become the topics of viewpoint or argument papers.

- *Viewpoint and argument papers offer readers a way to learn about issues and topics with which they are unfamiliar.* Given that most people's lives are occupied primarily with working (in school and/or at jobs), reading provides an opportunity for you to learn about ideas and other people's worlds that you might not have encountered otherwise. It provides an interesting and valuable education without actually having to meet other people. For example, by reading a review, prospective moviegoers have a way to judge whether a new film is worth spending $7.00 and two hours to watch. Similarly, by writing viewpoint and argument papers, you can make your perspectives known to others. No longer can you assume that just because you hold certain views, others will automatically agree with you. Arguments challenge your thinking and that of your audience as well. You have the power to enlarge other people's worldview. Both you and your readers are thus the beneficiaries of such writing.

- *Writing viewpoint and argument papers is a way of doing business in this world, a way to exchange information, offer perspectives, and learn about different ways of seeing things.* Consider the frustration and utter exasperation of parents whose children's response to a question is "Because." While that answer is cute when uttered the first few times and is to be expected from children, it is obviously insufficient as people mature and the need for an exchange of ideas increases. Writing viewpoint and argument papers provides an opportunity to learn how to deal with the conflicting information we face daily (e.g., political campaigns, commercials, advertisements, editorials, sales pitches, etc.); it enables us to become wiser, more savvy, and better informed consumers, since we are knowledgeable about the ways in which arguments work.

- *It is a hallmark of education to be able to discuss, analyze, probe, debate, and explore the world of ideas.* Noble endeavors? Perhaps. But with the ever increasing importance that society places on education, it is a rich opportunity to hear others' ideas and to be heard as you express your own. Writing viewpoint and argument papers is a valuable form of communication; it is a way to learn from and about other people. Read on and see some of the ways in which arguments manifest themselves in our daily lives.

COMMON SOURCES OF VIEWPOINTS AND ARGUMENTS

Despite the belief that viewpoint and argument papers are restricted to the academic community, we frequently come in contact with viewpoints and arguments in what we read. Look around at what you read frequently or have seen published. Chances are you have come in contact with the kinds of writing on which *Commitment, Voice, and Clarity* is based. Here's a list with which to begin:

- newspaper editorials
- letters to newspaper and magazine editors
- opinion/editorial columns in newspapers and magazines
- film, concert, and book reviews
- essay exams
- responses to others' ideas

- advertisements and commercials
- proposals to change something with which people don't agree (e.g., course prerequisites, dorm visitation policies, city zoning rules, amendments to the constitution)
- letters of application for jobs and enrollment into universities (they make a case for why you should be hired or admitted into the school)

Just look around you—with your eyes and ears open—and you will find people expressing their viewpoints and engaging in argument with surprising regularity. It is not just the territory of the academic world, but it is the stuff of civilization when people exchange ideas and discuss topics and issues that have an impact on their lives. It can be an exciting enterprise because your perspectives, ideas, and reasoning are put to the test. Think of reading and writing viewpoint and argument papers as exercising your mind.

MYTHS AND MISCONCEPTIONS REGARDING VIEWPOINT AND ARGUMENT PAPERS

Part of generating possible sources and topics for viewpoint and argument papers involves shattering erroneous beliefs about what constitutes a viable topic for such writing. Myths and misconceptions do not encourage or motivate people to write: if anything, they deter people, putting up false and unnecessary roadblocks. Some of the most widely held misconceptions including the following:

- *The paper must be about only global, controversial issues* (e.g., abortion, euthanasia, capital punishment). While there is nothing wrong with these topics, they are huge and extremely complex issues for the relatively short papers you will be writing. A quick look through your library's holdings will reveal a number of writers who have written volumes on the topic. What new perspective can you offer on such an issue?

- *The paper must be backed by other people's research or documented sources; your own thinking isn't strong enough to establish believability.* Too often, we doubt our own thinking and turn to others to support what we have to say. There's nothing wrong in finding outside sources to support your ideas, but this is not always necessary when you write viewpoint and argument papers. Here we find a crucial distinction between viewpoint papers and researched argument papers: Whereas viewpoint papers do not typically include outside research to support their ideas, researched arguments obviously do. Both are valid and valuable kinds of writing. Just don't think that quoting other people is the surefire route to a strong piece of writing; outside sources should be ancillary to your own thinking.

- *The more statistics, the better.* Numbers seem to impress many people and are thought to be more powerful than words. Just as there's nothing wrong with using outside sources to support your own thinking, there's nothing wrong with using statistics—if the statistics are relevant to the point you are making and convincingly support your stance. It might help you to recognize several ideas about statistics: (1) in and of themselves, statistics prove nothing; and (2) numbers can be bent or skewed to serve whatever purpose. With enough digging around, chances are you can probably find some statistics that will fit your paper, but unless they are relevant to the point you are trying to make, they are unnecessary. Also, statistics cannot substitute for your own careful and thorough thinking.

- *The writing should sound formal, technical, clinical, and devoid of any individual voice and style.* While you might think that writing about ideas dictates that your prose should sound completely different from other kinds of writing, this perspective is not entirely accurate. While most of the writing about ideas is not necessarily as casual, informal, and personal-sounding as experience-based essays, it need not be dry, antiseptic, and boring. Chapter 3, "Writing Viewpoint and Argument Papers," discusses matters of voice and style.

- *In argument papers, one side must be right and the other wrong, and a pro/con approach is the only way to propose and support a stance.* As much as we would like for issues in our lives to be clear-cut, they are often anything but that. Ideas worth examining are often too thorny and complex to be reduced to a simple right-or-wrong way of thinking. By seeing only black and white, you risk missing out on the complexities and nuances of ideas, and your thinking becomes simplistic. Richness lies in the many shades that exist between black and white.

If you have any other ideas about the writing of idea-based papers that you think might be myths or misconceptions, ask your instructor about them now. Don't allow inaccurate perceptions to block or slow down your writing.

CLOSING NOTES

Now that you have read discussions of what we mean when we talk about argument, reasons for writing viewpoint and argument papers, common sources of this kind of writing that can enlarge your writing repertoire, and myths and misconceptions that provide roadblocks for many people, I hope you see viewpoint and argument papers in a new light. In the next chapter, you will read about ways to move from writing personal experience-based essays to viewpoint and argument papers. It is important to remember that all kinds of writing—personal-based and idea-based—are valuable. Practice the skills you have learned in all of your previous writing classes—as well as the ones you learn from this book—to make all of your writing interesting and believable.

Exercises

1. Working individually or in small groups with your classmates, list three subjects that are too unwieldy and unfocused for viewpoint or argument papers. Explain your reasons for choosing them.

2. Working individually or in small groups with your classmates, generate a list of five topics or issues that you think would be suitable for a viewpoint or an argument paper. Explain why you think your choices would be appropriate.

3. Using the topics you listed in the preceding question, pose a question that can be examined in an argument paper. Then provide a one-sentence statement that answers each question.

4. In small groups, discuss which myths and misconceptions have deterred you in past writing assignments. Try to remember how and when you came to believe such misconceptions. Feel free to add and discuss other myths that might not have been discussed in this chapter.

5. Recall a time when you wrote an essay for a class, a letter, or some other type of paper that could be seen as a viewpoint or an argument. In a one-page paper, describe what you wrote, how you made your case, and the outcome of your writing. If you could return to that piece of writing and make any changes, what would they be and how would they improve the writing?

CHAPTER

FROM EXPERIENCE-BASED TO IDEA-BASED WRITING

Differences Between Writing Experience-Based Essays and Idea-Based Viewpoint and Argument Papers

In previous writing courses, you probably had an opportunity to write essays that were based on personal experiences. Perhaps you were asked to describe an important person in your life or narrate the story of a particularly memorable experience. From such writing assignments, you no doubt learned about the importance of making your readers experience for themselves what you yourself once experienced; that is, your task was to re-create for your readers the person or event from your own perspective.

As we discussed in Chapter 1, when you write viewpoint and argument papers, you are exploring ideas instead of examining personal experiences. But just as in writing personal experience essays, you are responsible for making your readers see for themselves the reasons behind your thinking; again your goal is to re-create for your readers the ideas and supporting evidence that underlies your thinking.

When you wrote personal experience essays, one of the ways for you to achieve believability was to employ such techniques as the use of specific detail and/or dialogue. While *you* knew what you saw or what happened, you could not assume that your audience knew what you witnessed or what transpired. Readers, after all, are not capable of mind reading. Besides, because you chose a topic that was important to you, you didn't want readers to have to guess at or fill in what you left out. Thus, one of your goals as a writer no doubt was to *show* your readers what you witnessed, felt, and thought.

The same principle holds true for writing idea-based papers. You cannot assume that your readers will automatically know why you are interested in your topic, what you are thinking, and the reasons that support your main idea. As a writer, you are responsible for showing your audience why your ideas are important and credible.

One-Way versus Two-Way Communication

When you wrote personal, experience-based essays, your first audience was most likely yourself. Such is one of the purposes of personal writing: to record for enjoyment and even perhaps for posterity your reflections on personal topics. Only after satisfying those purposes did you consider an outside audience. Often when we write personal, expressive essays for ourselves, we fail to consider our readers. You might even have thought, "It's clear to me, so it should be clear to others." Thus, expressive-based writing originates as one-way communication: because it is composed for yourself first, audience is a secondary consideration.

Writing idea-based papers, however, involves two-way communication. The primary goal of two-way communication is to get the audience to see, if not adopt, a point of view; it requires you to write with your audience in mind. When writing about ideas, you cannot simply assume that others will understand your thinking or agree with your perspective because you put it down on paper. Why should they? What makes your perspective so important that others should take note? What makes your ideas so interesting that they will capture others' attention? And what makes your thinking convincing enough for others to take your perspective seriously?

While these issues might seem insurmountable, they really aren't. Nor should the challenge they pose be discounted. Sometimes, when faced with writing idea-based essays, you may be tempted to fall into habits that do anything but help make your case: you choose to write about lofty, complex, or abstract subjects; you substitute outside sources for your own thinking; or you write in a style that is overly stiff and formal. But just as the writing of experience-based essays requires you to look within and examine your own past, the writing of idea-based papers requires you to begin by looking within to your own hunches, observations, and perspectives. Along with looking within, it is also helpful to look outside yourself to the world in which you live and to take note of what you observe around you, as was discussed in the previous chapter.

Remember, too, that although the writing of experience-based essays and idea-based papers originates from the same place—your own experiences, reflections, and ideas—the two kinds of papers are different. The idea-based paper is a more analytical discussion of the events that the experience-based essay may suggest. The term *analytical* in this context means writing that makes judgments, finds associations, makes comparisons and contrasts, and shows the relationship between events.

The writing of idea-based papers need not be like a foreign and impassable territory. Just as you have experiences about which to write, so too do you have perspectives, observations, and ideas to explore. Instead of writing from the world of experience, however, you are writing from the world of ideas—that is, from the landscape of personal happenings you move into the landscape of the mind.

To prove my point about the plethora of ideas to which you already have access, just think about the last time you saw a movie or attended a concert. Chances are you left the event ablaze with reactions. Pretend you are a film or music critic. Did the movie or concert, for example, live up to your expectations? (This is an example of making a judgment.) Were the reviews of the film or concert consistent with your assessment of it? (This is an instance of finding associations.) Were the actors' or musicians' performances as strong as they were in previous films or concerts? (This is a means of comparing and contrasting.) You probably touched upon such questions when discussing the event with others.

A SAMPLE VIEWPOINT

What follows is an idea-based viewpoint concerning *Forrest Gump*, the popular 1994 movie that stars Tom Hanks. As you read, notice the way the author, Michael Douglas (no relation to the actor), muses on his reservations about the statement the film is making and the film's enormous popularity. Such is the stuff of viewpoint papers.

DUMP GUMP

Michael Douglas

1 America has fallen in love with Forrest Gump. Even columnists have. Frank Rich of the New York Times gushed about Forrest Gump on the Commentary page. Our own Regina Brett swooned, suggesting that all she ever needed to know she learned from good ol' Forrest.

2   Once again, Americans have revealed just how soft-hearted they are. We talk tough. Shake our fists at each other in traffic. Snarl at the waffling of Bill Clinton. Sneer at those on welfare.

3   In the end, however, we're devout sentimentalists. Look at the bottom line for *Forrest Gump*, the summer movie sensation, the story of an innocent, slow-witted boy from Alabama who goes from football star to war hero to megamillionaire businessman. Americans have already put up more than $100 million to see the show.

4   Excuse me. I don't want to spoil the fun. Nor do I want to take what is entertainment too seriously. All the fuss, however, has me a bit troubled.

After all, as sweet as Forrest is, as warm as he is, as refreshing as the contrast is between his simplicity and the complicated world, the movie contains at least the root of a disturbing message.

5   To be sure, Forrest Gump is successful. He is decent and works hard. He does what he's told. In many ways, however, he succeeds on dumb luck. In short, the movie suggests that others can make it all too easily. Be kind and willing, and things will go your way.

6   What the heck, Gump made it with an IQ of 75. Why study?

7   And yet, Forrest Gump, in effect, won the lottery—repeatedly.

8   Interestingly, the 1986 novel by Winston Groom, upon which the movie is based, offers a less sentimental portrait of Gump. Our hero, for instance, doesn't reach the promised land of having his own family. Then again, the book hardly captured the country's imagination.

9   Indeed, what's bothersome about the dumb luck aspect of *Gump* is its reinforcement elsewhere. A year of debate over health care, and one can't help but wonder whether Americans are waiting to "gump" our way to reform. That someone will run through the issue and luckily end up with a policy that reduces costs, extends coverage, ensures choice and promises that Dr. Welby will attend to each of our aliments.

10   Are we going to "gump" our way through Bosnia, running, running, running until Serbs and Croats and Muslims live together in peace, having listened to earnest American diplomats? What about Rwanda or Haiti? How about the budget deficit? Where is the Gump who can scoot through the thicket of federal spending and, luck have it, find the mix of spending cuts that everyone will cheer?

11   Fat chance.

12   Forrest Gump reminds me all too eerily of the worst aspects of the Reagan presidency: the Dr. Feelgood, free-lunch approach that tripled the federal debt in a decade and neglected pressing national priorities. Is it a coincidence that Reagan followed Jimmy Carter and *Forrest Gump* becomes a hit at a time when Bill Clinton rides low in the polls while tackling, too often ineptly, sticky issues such as welfare and health care?

13   I know, I know. You're saying, give us a break, Douglas. It's *only* a movie. And sure enough, the pursuit of happiness is about feeling good. Still, I'd like a break, too. Enough of Gumpmania. Yes, kids say wise things. They also grow up to discover the world is a lot more challenging and complex than they ever thought.

In this viewpoint, Douglas offers his observations that although they may talk tough, Americans are "soft-hearted." He also offers his judgment that not only is *Forrest Gump* unrealistic but "the movie contains the root of a disturbing message." Based on his experience seeing the film, his observations of the sensation the movie has created, and the associations he finds with current national and international affairs, Douglas's viewpoint shows us how opinion, experience, observation, association, and judgment combine to form an idea-based piece of writing.

One need not attend a movie or a concert—or, for that matter, do anything extraordinary—to find material about which to write. Equally rich possibilities exist in looking closely at and thinking about everyday experiences. Consider, for example, the last course you took that proved to be especially enjoyable or disappointing. If you discussed your reactions with classmates, friends, or family, no doubt you offered specific reasons to support your viewpoint. Similar processes of reaction and discussion of your opinion take place when, for instance, you read an article in a newspaper or a magazine that angers you or with which you are in total agreement. Perhaps some of you have even gone as far as to write a letter to the editor of the paper or magazine offering your own perspective.

Such is the material for idea-based writing. In short, you assume a stance and defend it. While many students have little problem coming up with ideas for experienced-based essays, they frequently overlook their daily interactions with the world, which can form the basis of writing about ideas. Whereas the personal-experience essays you have written *describe* actual people and activities, idea-based writing presents your reactions to or perspectives on what you saw. Expressive essays describe what you did at the Whitney Houston or Billy Joel concert; idea-based writing *explains* why it was a good or bad concert, what things about the actual event contributed to its success or failure. .

In short, personal expressive essays deal with actual events and your feelings about them; idea-based papers deal with *thinking*, or *analysis* of your perspectives. What is the connection or the relationship between these two kinds of writing? First, both center on your own experiences, observations, and thinking. The experience essay can serve as a springboard for the idea-based essay. A personal example can be the center on which you offer your viewpoint or argument; it can personalize an idea-based paper, catching your audience's attention and interest. However, viewpoints and arguments go further in gleaning observations, understandings, connections, and ideas from the personal, expressive example or essay. As such, personal experience *informs* the viewpoint or idea.

Here's another example of this notion. Let's say you write an experience-based essay about a particular course you have taken. In it, you describe the professor whose casual wardrobe (e.g., khakis, sports shirts, and sneakers), informal actions (e.g., sitting on the desk, sipping coffee, chatting with students before and after class), and teaching methods (e.g., asking open-ended questions, addressing popular topics germane to the course, asking for students' reactions) made the class an enjoyable and memorable experience. A paragraph from such a paper might read as follows:

> When I walked into Psych 101 on an unusually hot morning for so early in September, Professor Jackson was sitting cross-legged on the table at the front of the room. He kind of looked like a Buddhist monk meditating, except he was wearing a bright red polo shirt, worn khaki Dockers, and Nikes (no socks). As the students entered the class he greeted us with a friendly, "How ya doin," and as he read the class roll, he joked about our names: "Clarice Lincoln. Any relation to Abe?" After every two or three names, he would pause to sip from a huge mug of what he called his "adrenaline fix"—coffee. He even invited us to bring to class something to eat for breakfast, since it was an 8:00 a.m. class and most people didn't have time to eat breakfast. After finishing taking roll, he told us to call him by his first name, "Ernie." Then he welcomed the class to join him on an adventure he called "Psych 101, everything you ever wanted and didn't want to know about psychology but were afraid to ask."

Now let's say that you want to write another paper that proposes that a certain classroom environment is more conducive to learning than other environments. Some of the ideas that will support or prove your point are the importance of an approachable professor, one who addresses students as equals instead of as underlings, who knows how to interact with others, and who makes the classroom environment and course material pertinent and accessible to others. This is the stuff from which idea-based writing is formed: the culling of ideas from specific, detailed descriptions and seeing ideas that experiences suggest. A paragraph from such a paper might read as follows:

> One of the most important aspects of a successful classroom environment is the professor's attitude. For many students, listening to lectures in which a professor holds court or sermonizes and never asks for students' reactions is boring: students are forced to hear the beliefs of a professor who

seems to be as anonymous as the name on a book cover. Students can "click in to" learning when it is personalized, and that personalization can start with a professor who makes it clear to students that he is just another person, without airs or pretension. Such a professor is unafraid to admit to students that he does not have all of the answers and that he, too, is in class to learn from other people. Maintaining such an open and friendly environment is one way to encourage and motivate students to learn.

Part of the experienced-based paragraph's strength comes from its attention to detail and specific example. Instead of just telling us that Ernie Jackson is a likable, interesting professor, the writer shows us these things in the vivid picture she creates of the professor. Similarly, part of the effectiveness of this idea-based paragraph emerges from its discussion of the idea of openness and friendliness creating an atmosphere conducive to learning. Whereas the first example makes its point by specific details, the second makes its point by supportive reasoning.

A SAMPLE EXPERIENCE-BASED ESSAY

To show you another example of this distinction, the following personal-experience essay, "Forgetting Woodstock," by Stephanie Salter, describes some of her disappointing experiences at the concert twenty-five years ago.

25 YEARS LATER—
FORGETTING WOODSTOCK

Stephanie Salter

1 San Francisco: About 3 feet by 2 feet, it hangs on my office wall, the best thing I remember about Woodstock.

2   It's a large black-and-white photograph of a comely female hippie, sitting under the Woodstock poster that advertised "3 days of peace & music." A

college chum shot the photo in 1969 in Greenwich Village, not at the Woodstock Festival or anywhere near it.

3   That's why I like it.

4   I was at Woodstock. I hated Woodstock. I left Woodstock about 16 hours after it started and felt as if I had gone over the Berlin Wall.

5   We are fast approaching the 25th anniversary—August 15–17—of the rock festival that launched a brave new world, so the nation is awash in Woodstock nostalgia. Commemorative festivals are set for this weekend, the largest in Saugerties, N.Y. They only heighten the recollection and deepen the resultant sentimental doo-doo.

6   Lest I mislead, I don't think it's cool to remember Woodstock as I do. It's a drag. I mean, you saw the movie, read the Rolling Stone magazine testimonials. Maybe you know someone who wrote a doctoral thesis on what it meant. Woodstock was a big deal.

7   To say you were there, 25 years after the fact, still earns you a kind of badge of honor. (Although, as with Babe Ruth's 714th home run, an awful lot more people say they were there than could have been.) But, to say you were there and that you hated it and left on the second day—well, that earns you a lot of barely veiled contempt.

8   People hear I was at Woodstock (OK, sometimes at a party I'll let it slip), and they want to know who I saw perform.

9   I don't remember, I always say, which is the truth.

10   I cannot tell you whether I saw Joan Baez, Richie Havens or what. I could almost swear I didn't see Janis Joplin. I know I didn't see Jimi Hendrix. But I have no idea who I did see on that teeny-tiny little lighted stage so far down the muddy hill.

11   Wow, people always want to know, did you forget because you were really tripping out on acid?

12   I wish, I usually say, which isn't true. But it's close. If I had been on any kind of drug (stronger than the oregano-grade of grass my friends and I brought to the festival), I probably wouldn't have left Woodstock 16 hours after I got there.

13   If I had been tripping, maybe I wouldn't have noticed the mud. Maybe I wouldn't cared that it rained incessantly on a half-million kids who hadn't brought camping equipment. Maybe I'd have laughed off the fact that, despite the promises, there was no fresh drinking water, no toilet facilities, no "free rice kitchens." And there was no way to turn one's car around and get out of the Bethel-White Lake area.

14   But I wasn't tripping, and I did notice. I was so miserable, Jimi and Janis themselves could have strolled up to our car and said, "Hey, man, what do you wanna hear?" and it wouldn't have made any difference to me.

15   I haven't even mentioned the borderline dysentery I did bring back as a memento. Nobody at any cocktail party ever wants to hear about that.

16   Combing through the retrospectives written lately about Woodstock, I came across an ironic item. John Scher, the promoter of this weekend's big do in Saugerties, reminisced to the Chicago Tribune about his own Woodstock experience in '69: "I had a ticket in advance, and me and six of my friends were going to drive up early on Friday morning from New Jersey," he said.

17   "Two left early and got stuck in traffic. They called and said, 'Don't bother,' so I rolled over and went back to sleep. I've lived to regret it."

18   Scher missed Woodstock and regrets it. I made it and regret it. This weekend, while he tries to recreate it, I'm going to roll over and go back to sleep.

In the preceding essay, Salter describes why she hated Woodstock by citing all of the events or activities that she did not experience. The paper is expressive writing: the author examines Woodstock through her own personal experiences and observations.

A SAMPLE IDEA-BASED ESSAY

Now read the following essay, "Woodstock Lessons Are Just an Illusion," by Steve Love. As you read, notice that the principal emphasis is not a description of personal experiences at Woodstock; rather, Love discusses his observation or idea that the goals and spirit of Woodstock did not pan out.

WOODSTOCK LESSONS
ARE JUST AN ILLUSION

Steve Love

1   Woodstock lives because no one died during that long August weekend on Max Yasgur's farm in '69. We got by in the rain. We got along in an instant community that mushroomed to half a million.

2   It wasn't much. Just a big party, really. But it impressed some of us and shocked the adults.

3   They were running things then, and not very damn well, either.

4   In Chicago the summer before, they had felt compelled to beat in a few of our heads when we dared to point out they were killing our friends and brothers in Vietnam.

5   And for what?

6   Someone said go. So we went.

7   Woodstock was like that, too.

8   Only no one died.

9   In another few months they would have us turning our weapons on our own on a rolling hillside in Kent, a bucolic place of learning where the lesson was bloody and lasting and haunts us still.

10   Now, 25 years later, the graying Woodstock Nation looks back on the eve of a new Woodstock, a different festival on a different site in upstate New York.

11   This has been a summer of anniversary remembrances: D-Day. Neil Armstrong on the moon. The sinking of Camelot at Chappaquiddick. Nixon's resignation.

12   Now Woodstock.

13   Man, ain't it groovy?

14   Richie Havens thinks so.

15   He opened Woodstock.

16   In an afterword to photographer Elliott Landy's book titled *Woodstock Vision: the spirit of a generation,* Havens writes: "We had a different view of the world and we wanted people to know that the world wasn't as negative as most people thought—that there were a lot of positive things that we could make happen for the betterment of our planet and the world around us.

17   "The world wasn't gonna change overnight …(but) as far as I'm concerned, everyone now is a product of the Woodstock spirit."

18   Oh, yeah?

Why Such a Mess?

19   Then tell me this: If the essence of Woodstock was not sex, drugs and music but a commonality, a willingness to share and care for one another, why are we as much a mess as we were in '69?

20   And we are.

21   Look around.

22   The war has come home to us.

23   It's in our streets and homes.

24   We live in fear not of our long-standing foreign enemies but of our own citizens of the Woodstock Nation and of their children.

25   We protested until we stopped a war. Now we run things. A citizen of the Woodstock Nation has become president. But we do not know how to stop what is happening in Rwanda, Bosnia, Haiti. We don't even know if we should.

26   We do not care enough about each other to find a way—and there has to be a way—to pay for universal health care.

27   I mean, isn't health care free? It was at Woodstock. There were no tolls for those on bad trips. Doctors even delivered a baby.

28   But it was just one birth, not the birth of a nation or a new way.

29   If death had come to Woodstock as it did to Altamont Speedway during a subsequent California music festival, the image, the memories, would be darker.

30   The two most audible, lasting images from Woodstock, at least for me, were Jimi Hendrix's off-center guitar rendition of *The Star-Spangled Banner* and the songs that Janis Joplin ripped from her gut in a rasping, raging whisper.

31   Like Woodstock, it was illusion.

32   Neither the festival's good will nor Hendrix and Joplin survived.

33   Now, 25 years later, the reprise of promoter Michael Lang has drawn fire and damnation for a commercialism believed to have been lacking in the original.

34   Of course, the first Woodstock never was intended to be the free concert it became. Lang and his fellow promoters underestimated the response that clogged and closed the New York roads.

35   They lost control and then scrambled to recover, in the end standing before the Academy Award-winning cameras of Michael Wadleigh and laughing in the wake of their financial bath.

36   "People are really communicating with each other," promoters said. "This is really happening."

37   No denying Woodstock was a happening, but, unlike the president, those who see the mud and music as an epiphany may have been guilty of excessive inhaling.

38   In a Pepsi commercial on Woodstock redux, John Sebastian inquires of fellow performer Country Joe McDonald: "Remember when we did this 25 years ago?"

39   Country Joe looks hazy.

40   "No," he says.

41   Emotionally, if not geographically, Woodstock seems far removed even from its own citizens.

42   In that same Pepsi commercial, two little boys stand behind a fence and watch some older Woodstock Nation citizens cavorting and pulsating to the beat.

43   "Do you think they'll go skinny-dipping again?" one asks.

44   "I hope not," the other says.

45   Perhaps Woodstock's lasting benediction came from Sebastian.

46   "Love everybody around you," he said long ago, "and clean up a little garbage on the way out."

47   We citizens of the Woodstock Nation could do worse than that as we make our way to our exits.

Both the Salter and the Love papers deal with Woodstock; however, they are markedly different papers. The former describes experiences, whereas the latter examines ideas. Both deal with the 1969 music festival, but have different goals or aims: in reminiscing about her Woodstock experiences, Salter wants us to relive some of the time she spent there. Love, on the other hand, wants us to think about the failed ideas that Woodstock professed.

With idea-based or argument papers, you take a position and try to defend it: you try to show your readers some evidence or proof of the statements or claims you make. In many ways, the writing of viewpoint and argument papers is answering the question, *Why do I think that way?*, which any interested and curious reader has a right to ask. In fact, if a piece of writing proves to its audience that its author knows what he or she is talking about, a case can be made that the writing can be construed as an argument paper. Chapter 4 of *Commitment, Voice, and Clarity* focuses on ways in which you can organize, develop, and support your ideas.

Exercises

1.   Think about the writing you have done in high school and college courses. How much of it has been personal, experience-based essays and how much of it has been viewpoint and argument papers? Which do you prefer? Why?

2.   Working either individually or in small groups, make a list of five personal-experience essays you wrote in other courses. Then generate a list of idea-based topics that can emerge from those essays.

3. In his viewpoint, Michael Douglas takes exception to the popularity lavished on *Forrest Gump*. If you disagree with his perspective, write your own idea-based paper in which you explain your reasons for believing that *Gump* should not be "dumped." If you haven't seen that film, choose another one whose popularity you find deserving or undeserving.

CHAPTER 3

WRITING VIEWPOINT AND ARGUMENT PAPERS

Given your past writing experiences, chances are you already know—and use—some strategies or techniques that enable you to put words down on paper or on the computer screen. It is often helpful to review such strategies and to learn about others. Understand that there is no one fail-proof way to go about writing a first draft of a paper: different writers use different techniques, and writers use different techniques for the different kinds of writing they do. Because the focus of *Commitment, Voice, and Clarity* is the writing of idea-based papers, this chapter will discuss and demonstrate the writing process as it applies to viewpoint and argument papers.

No matter how experienced or inexperienced, successful or unsuccessful a writer you are, no matter what kind of writing you're composing, and no matter if you're using paper and pen or a computer, the process by which you generate ideas and a text falls under the heading of *languaging*: writing, reading, speaking, and listening. As much as we would like for writing to "just happen" on the page, the reality is that it doesn't: some amount of effort and activity is required. That activity might take the form of reading as a source of inspiration; talking to others as a brainstorming activity; listening to others as a way to stimulate your own thinking; and certainly writing something down as a starting point to see what you have to say. The point is that generating written prose begins with language activities, not by waiting for divine inspiration to strike with an already-formed paper.

What follows is a list of activities that can help you to generate a preliminary or "discovery" draft of a paper. Instead of trying just one technique, experiment with as many as you can. Chances are your writing will benefit from your using a wide array of strategies. You never know which will prove most helpful until you try.

PREWRITING STRATEGIES

Because the blank mind/page syndrome befalls most writers at some time in their lives, there's nothing like getting *something* down on paper to overcome writer's block. Even if you don't have any idea what you want to say in a paper or even what topic you want to write about, the following techniques will help.

Freewriting

Try *freewriting*, writing down whatever comes to mind without stopping to think or to worry about the exact word choice, correct grammar, spelling, logic, or anything else for that matter. The point is to keep writing, even if you have to repeat the last word or write, "I can't think of a thing to say." Try writing for ten minutes nonstop. Time yourself. Although it may be difficult to sustain ten minutes of writing nonstop, it's remarkable to see how much writing you can generate in just ten minutes. Freewriting allows you the freedom of not worrying about the conventions of written discourse; instead, it encourages and enables you to let hidden ideas surface. If nothing else, freewriting is a first step in getting *something* down—a wonderful solution if you are terrified of a blank page—and shows you what possibilities are available to you.

Here's the freewriting of Amanda, a first-year student:

Okay, I'm supposed to write a paper that gives my ideas about something. What ideas? Writing is so hard when I'm not sure what I want to say. How can I write a paper if I don't know what it's about. Okay. I'm supposed to just write until an idea surfaces. Yesterday when I was talking to Jill and Steve and Tina they were asking me what I thought I wanted to do when I graduate. I wasn't sure. I want to find a job that will be interesting and different. I mean I hate having to do the same thing day after day. I want to meet new people and I want to have some authority. I hate working for other people who I don't like. And I really want to make some big bucks so I can afford all of the things I see in the stores. Like a Corvette and a big house would be nice too. The problem is I don't know which jobs will give me what I'm looking for. Tina said something about how even if I got the job there'd still be problems. And then we got talking about, I'm not sure who started it, the problem women face in their jobs. Steve said that his mother who is really qualified and works hard is stuck in her job. She works really hard and is really qualified but she has gone as far up in her company as she can. Jill said that there's a word for that. I think she said it was a glass ceiling or something like that. I don't want that to happen to me. The women's movement took care of that I think. Or that's what a lot of people say. But if women are supposed to be equal how come Steve's mom is stuck? Then we started talking about how Tina was at the mall on Saturday and saw a fashion show that had clothes from her mother's generation. Mini-skirts and bellbottomed jeans. Yuck. I hate that. Mini-skirts are okay, I suppose. My dad has this photograph album that has pictures of him wearing beads and headbands and long hair. I can't believe my father was a hippie. He doesn't talk about it much. I think he kind of regrets not living all of his dreams he had when he was my age. I wonder what happens to people who have dreams but they give them up or something when they become adults. I mean when they finish school and have to go out to get a job. I wonder if that will happen to me. I have a lot of dreams. I think I do but sometimes I'm not sure. We don't talk about it much maybe because we're afraid of the future. Older people don't see how tough it is on us young kids. Why can't they just listen to us and find out what we think. It's like they don't care. But maybe they do and can't do anything to help. Oops, ten minutes are up so I'm gonna stop.

After freewriting, read what you came up with. If you find a topic that interests you, try *focused freewriting* for ten minutes. In this activity, you want to focus your attention exclusively on the one topic and try to generate as many ideas as possible on it. This activity frequently can produce the raw material for a paper, the discovery draft of what you "didn't know you knew." If you were unable to find an interesting topic, try freewriting again until you do.

When Amanda read her ten-minute freewriting, she discovered three possible directions or topics to pursue in a focused freewrite: the glass ceiling, why people don't act on their dreams, and the communication problem between parents and children. She thought the topic about lack of communication was written about "to death" and the topic about dreams was still "kind of dreamy." Because the topic concerning the glass ceiling interested her the most, she chose it for her focused freewrite, which follows:

The term *glass ceiling* is an interesting idea for what happens to lots of people in jobs. I'm not sure how many people it pertains to but I think that women are one big group. Let's see. I suppose other groups are also affected by it. Women for starters and maybe other minorities, although I don't think that women are considered a minority anymore. It probably applies to groups like blacks or chicanos and other ethnic groups. You think that there's no limit to what you can do in a job and how high up you can go in the job but then pow you hit the ceiling. You can't see it, that's where the glass part comes in. I wonder if it doesn't pertain to some men too, especially if other people want to keep them down. I'm not sure if you can prove there's a thing like the glass ceiling, it's not as though companies make the fact known, but you can research what business analysts have to say about it. I'm sure that journalists have reported on it, and if you ask women in high-up positions in big companies I'm sure they will tell you what they think. Because Steve when we were talking mentioned it about his mother I can talk to her. I'm sure she's ticked off enough to let me know what has happened to her, and maybe she can give me other names to contact. I can't think of anything else right now. Maybe I need to make a list of all the reasons for glass ceilings hurting women and other people and maybe a list of all the reasons why people think it's not a big thing and we should quit worrying and just get back to work. I think it's important because some day I might be hurt by it, especially if I get a job in a company and work hard thinking I will be promoted like all of the other workers, the male workers, and find out that I'm stuck. Then what will I do? It's just not fair, to me and to other people like me and it's probably not fair to men either, but they don't see it that way. Time's up.

As you can see from reading Amanda's focused freewrite, she has restricted her ideas to one topic, the glass ceiling, and generated a few ideas on sources to investigate for her paper: business analysts, her friend Steve's mother, and journalists' articles. Although Amanda originally thought the glass ceiling was a problem only for women, her freewriting suggests that other minorities are victims of it as well. This idea might also provide her with one direction to explore in her paper: whether, although the term "glass ceiling" usually connotes women in the workplace, it might also refer to other minorities whom corporations want to "keep down."

Listing

List making is another prewriting exercise from which you can benefit. This activity can produce an inventory of possible topics about which to write. After composing your initial list, try another list-making exercise. This time, however, focus your attention exclusively on the one topic that catches your interest from the first list. Much like focused freewriting, this second activity can uncover many of the ideas you may want to examine in your paper.

Here is an example of two lists that Steve, Amanda's friend, generated:

First list:

gun control

legal drinking age

motorcycles and helmets

should kids have to attend school?

should athletes be given special dorms?

holidays becoming too commercial

infomercials on TV

phone solicitors

(900) phone lines

kids having jobs while in school

guard dogs and metal detectors in schools

people's reliance on computers

warning labels on beer and wine

total ban on the sale of cigarettes

sports being too expensive for most kids

having to pay to play sports in school

the 2-point conversion in pro football

violence in sports

athletes' strikes

media coverage of court trials

Second list that focuses on infomercials:

how misleading they are

seem like real TV

can influence naive buyers

play up to lonely people

the danger of buying without examining

sounds too good to be true

the sellers resemble celebrities

no credit limits

who regulates them?

propose restricted hours so people can't buy 24 hours a day

enforce truth in advertising laws

stop the contests that lure unsuspecting customers

stop the entertainment aspect that might confuse buyers

As you can see, the second list posits specific arguments regarding infomercials: that they have restricted hours for airing, and refrain from offering contests and appearing to be entertainment shows. Some of the reasons that might support these stands appear at the beginning of the list. The writer of these lists is on the way to a discovery draft of an argument paper on infomercials.

Clustering

Clustering is a variation of list making. In this activity, you should write a key word in the center of a piece of paper (e.g., *diets*). Then, surround that initial word with other words that *diet* connotes (e.g., *healthy, fad, boring, time-consuming*). Surround those words with other words or ideas that come to mind (e.g., fad—grapefruit, liquid diet, three-day fasting, only certain kinds of food). The principal difference between clustering and lists is that when you create a cluster, the branching out of a word produces other words or ideas that can become a theme in the paper. This exercise should produce something that looks like a sunburst or a web; indeed, it is meant to be a bursting forth or a web of information you have stored in your head about this idea. From this starburst or web, you can see what raw material you have with which to form a topic for a paper.

Here is what clustering actually looks like. Jill spent ten minutes or so creating this starburst or web of terms:

Reading

Reading is too often overlooked as a helpful strategy for writing. How many times have you read something and been angered or inspired by it? Because reading and writing are so closely connected, it makes sense to look at reading as a source for writing. Don't letters to the editor of newspapers and magazines begin with someone reading something to which they want to respond? Reading is a way to enter the world of thinking and ideas. As participants in that world, you have the opportunity to generate your own thinking or ideas. After all, besides providing information and entertainment, what is the goal of writing if not to encourage others to "join the conversation" by offering their own thinking? Just think about the growing popularity of the discussion or conversation forums on computer services such as Prodigy, CompuServe, and America Online, in which people write back and forth exchanging information, viewpoints, and ideas about a host of topics. But most of the writing starts with reading.

Reading as a prewriting strategy requires you to read *actively*. Often when you read, it is to get the gist of the author's ideas. Perhaps you have learned to make check marks in the margins or to use a highlighter to mark the key points of the article or book. While you might have believed you were reading actively, to what extent were you and your own ideas interacting with the author's? To read actively, try reading with a pen or pencil in hand. Whenever you come across an idea you strongly believe in or disagree with, write your reactions in the margins. If you are confused by some part of the text, make note of that too. (If you are reading a text from the library or one that you have borrowed, write your reactions in a notebook, on a notecard, or enter them in a computer file, with the author's and text's name along with the specific page number in case you want to return to a notation later.) The point is that by reading and responding in this fashion, you are actively "conversing" with the text, generating your own ideas in relation to what you need, and writing them down for later use. Active reading is testimony to the connection between reading and writing: one activity helps to promote the other.

Speaking

Speaking offers yet another helpful brainstorming activity. It is unfortunate that speaking has been discouraged in many classrooms. Granted, it is probably best for students to listen to the instructor's lecture and to keep "on task," but often the exchange of one's thinking is as educational as the best laid-out teaching plans. Why? Because it makes learning an active, not a passive, process. Just think of the times when you were stuck on an assignment and called a classmate, friend, or family member to discuss your problem. After talking about the project for a few minutes, chances are your thoughts were clearer, and you had a

better idea of what to do. Speaking can bring about new ideas and solutions. Don't be reluctant to discuss your projects with your peers,
friends, and family. For that matter, don't be afraid to talk about your
ideas with your professor. Despite the adage, "Talk is cheap," in these
cases it really isn't.

To use speaking as a prewriting strategy, pretend that you are "taking
the minutes" of a discussion. That is, take notes when you are discussing
your ideas with others. Keep a written record of what was said and by
whom. When you review your notes, you might be able to see the ways
in which the groups' ideas evolved. Moreover, you will be able to expand
on the ideas generated by oral discourse and detect gaps in the thinking,
thereby having produced a discovery draft of a paper.

Listening

Just as speaking is a prewriting activity, so too is listening. While this
may be viewed as something of a passive activity, real listening is an
active process of hearing and making sure you understand what the
speaker is trying to communicate. In much the same way that reading is
a helpful strategy, listening also offers quiet time in which to receive
and reflect upon what you heard. Think about the last time you listened to a sermon, a lecture, or an impassioned speech and found your
head swimming with ideas generated by the speaker. Such is the power
of listening.

Real listening takes practice. To use listening as a prewriting activity, pay close attention to what you hear. If you do not understand something, ask for clarification. In Amanda's freewriting, she referred to a
conversation she had with three of her friends, one of whom spoke of his
mother's problem with the glass ceiling. Because Amanda was listening
to her friends, she was later able to remember the term, and the problems associated with the inequity, so she could choose that topic to investigate in a research paper. The point is, it pays to listen.

Exercise

To test the powers of languaging, read the following list of ten
questions:

1.   What upsets you about your school/town/country?
2.   What do you find curious about _____?

3. If you could take out a full-page ad in a local newspaper or a national magazine, or buy one minute of radio or television time, what would you say?

4. What current trends or fads are hopeful or discouraging?

5. Why are you interested in _____?

6. What do most people misunderstand about _____?

7. Why is _____an unappreciated musician/writer/artist?

8. What do you like/dislike about your generation?

9. What issues in education/work/sports/popular culture excite or trouble you?

10. If you want my opinion about _____, it's _____.

Choose the one question that interests you the most and try one of the previously discussed prewriting strategies (i.e., freewriting, focused freewriting, list making, or clustering). If you wish, you might want to think about the personal-experience papers you may have written in previous composition courses as springboards into idea-based writing. If so, these might provide additional possibilities to explore in your search for a viable topic. Other sources are ideas you glean from the readings that appear in Part 2 of this book, as well as the writing topics that appear at the end-of-chapter reading selections.

After completing the prewriting exercise on your topic, you are ready to try the other prewriting strategies of reading, speaking, and listening. Of course, if there are other prewriting strategies that have worked well for you in the past, use them. Understand that no one activity is a sure-fire answer to coming up with a topic for an argument paper, but the preceding techniques *are* activities that can aid you in sorting through ideas and discovering possible writing topics. By all means, don't wait for inspiration to strike; instead, do something to generate ideas to explore.

With some prewriting in hand, you are ready to begin shaping that raw material into a well-focused, well-supported, and well-reasoned paper. The next section of this chapter will show you how to do so.

SELECTING A TOPIC

In trying your hand at the prewriting activities, you will have produced, if nothing else, a starting point for your viewpoint or argument paper.

Put another way, you are at the starting gate. Remember that it is vital that you select a topic that you are interested in and committed to. Think of your topic selection like choosing a marriage partner: you will stay with the topic and the spouse for the long haul, not for a quick fix—all the more reason to choose a topic you like and are willing to work with.

At this point, it is important to generate a declarative sentence that captures exactly what point, issue, or main idea you are trying to argue. That statement will be a helpful reminder of exactly what you are arguing should you wander off the track. Remember that your paper should not be "about" a topic: it must take a stand and defend it. If you are unable to come up with such a statement, chances are your paper is not focused enough. It might be helpful to read one or more of the articles that appear in *Commitment, Voice, and Clarity* and generate a short declarative statement of exactly what the essay is arguing. As you read the essays, pay close attention to how the writers make their essay's direction clear to the reader. Take cues from the essays you read; they can provide a valuable source of information about the writing of argument papers.

Considering Potential Audiences

No matter what you write, you must consider to whom you are writing. Sometimes, the audience for your writing is obvious: most of the writing you do in school is going to be read by your teachers. When you write a letter to a family member or a friend, you obviously know your audience. But much of the writing you undertake is to an audience with which you are unfamiliar; that is, you cannot be sure of their perspectives on the issues about which you may be writing. Because you do not necessarily know all of your audiences, it is wise to ascertain whether you are writing to a sympathetic, unsympathetic, or neutral audience.

Part of preparing a strong defense is knowing who your audience is. Before going out on the playing field, football players know what team they are competing against. In fact, they have spent the preceding weeks preparing what strategies to use against their competition. Before politicians deliver speeches, they know the makeup of the audience so that they can best prepare their comments. Before teaching courses, instructors know the level of their students so that the course materials will be appropriate to the audience.

Thus, it is important to ask yourself what you know about your audience's beliefs on the topic. What assumptions can you make about their existing knowledge of the topic? How much background information do you need to provide? Different audiences require different approaches. When you don't know exactly who your audience is or what their beliefs may be, it is safest to take a neutral line of defense that emphasizes your thinking but also prepares for any reasonable disagreements with your position.

First, consider the audience's background. Let's say you have written a viewpoint that praises Top 40 radio stations for playing heavy metal and rap music. If you were submitting your viewpoint to *Rolling Stone*, your audience would be far more knowledgeable about your topic than if you were submitting your paper to, say, *National Review*, a conservative magazine. Thus, knowing your audience can aid you in deciding what approach to take in your writing and how much support of your ideas you will need. For the readers of *Rolling Stone*, you won't have to provide background information (e.g., definitions of "heavy metal" and "rap," or explanations of who various musicians are) as you would if you were writing for people who are unfamiliar with your topic. Be careful, however, not to take for granted your audience's predilections.

When writing for unsympathetic audiences, it is best not to sound condescending or belligerent (e.g., "I'm sure that you don't know a thing about today's music, so I'm going to teach you a few lessons to get you up to speed"). You do not want to alienate your readers: if anything, you want to show them how reasonable, logical, and thoughtful you are; the object is to gain their respect and approval. This, however, does not mean falsely complimenting or pandering to them (e.g., "The music you listen to is a delight to the ear, and every radio station should be sure to feature the songs you have come to know and love"). Let your thinking support your stance, and do not resort to the low blows frequently seen and heard in political campaigns.

When you are unsure of your audience, the best advice you can follow is to play it safe. Make sure that you picture your audience as intelligent and reasonable people; present your ideas clearly, thoughtfully, and thoroughly; and address supporting *and* opposing views of your topic. Show your readers why you are interested in and committed to your ideas: if you demonstrate that there is a real person behind your ideas, most people will be inclined to listen to you.

Chapter 4, "Strategies in Argumentation," will present additional information about ways to present your argument. No matter who your audience might be, however, you cannot be faulted for following the suggestions offered in the preceding paragraph.

Exercise

For the question you chose to prewrite on (see pages 44–45), identify three different audiences you could aim your paper at. Write a brief explanation of what you would do differently in each of the papers that reflects the audience to whom you are writing.

DRAFTING

While some writers compose their papers in one setting, others write them piecemeal. There is no one "correct" way to compose. Moreover, we have different composing strategies for the many different kinds of writing we do. When we write notes to friends or family, chances are we do not bother to revise them. When we write a take-home exam for a course, we employ different composing techniques than we do when we write an in-class essay exam. For the papers you write in this course and in others, however, the best advice may well be do to what is most comfortable and what works best for you.

Writing a draft of a paper is but a small part of the process. Chances are the discovery of a suitable topic takes as much time, if not more, than the actual composing of a first draft. For many writers, discovering a workable topic is the hardest part of writing a paper: much contemplating and reviewing of possibilities occurs as topics are bandied about. When you compose a rough draft, you have an opportunity to discover what you have to say. As such, it is fitting that the result is often termed the "discovery draft." Composing a rough draft can help you to bring together and start making sense of all of your brainstorming activities. Because the rough draft of a paper shows you the raw material with which you have to work, it is best to get everything down on paper or on the computer screen (if you compose on a word processor, make sure to save your work in a file for future reference). Don't worry about whether you've said it the best way possible or whether the spelling or punctuation marks are correct; there will be ample time later on in the writing process for you to address those concerns.

Remember that composing is messy work, whether you compose with pen and paper or on a word processor. Neatness does not figure into the writing of a rough draft. Nor should it because you are in the process of making sense of your thoughts, sorting out and getting down your thinking. Because you sometimes do not know what ideas you have to work with until they are written down, the purpose of the rough draft is to get those ideas written out so that you can take stock of the materials with which you can work.

LOOKING BOTH WAYS, OR DEFENSIVE WRITING

Now that you have generated a preliminary draft of an argument paper, it is time to consider ways to make your writing as convincing as possible. Isn't the point of writing argument papers—in fact, the goal of *all* writing—to persuade others that you know what you're talking about? The issue of proof confronts us almost daily in our lives: On exams, students have to prove to their instructors that they understand the course material; in court, the prosecuting attorney must prove to the judge and jury that the defendant is guilty; the physician must prove to her patient that a change in lifestyle will result in improved health; a pharmaceutical company must prove to the FDA that its newest drugs are safe. The list is endless. Suffice it to say that providing evidence to persuade your audience is a commonplace activity.

How do you go about proving or establishing credibility? Why should your audience trust your word against others'? Obviously, the first factor is what you say: the plausibility and strength of your idea and its support. But just as important as your supporting evidence, reasoning, and logic is the *way* you go about presenting your argument. First, let's consider the matter of ideas.

Some of you might think that all that is necessary to establish believability is to provide a clear thesis statement or claim, and then furnish three reasons to support the claim. But the task is not that simple. Writers of successful argument papers must be "defensive" writers. Think of it this way: Can a soccer, baseball, hockey, or basketball team win a game without a strong defense? Or can a tennis player win by virtue of only a strong serve? Obviously, the answer is a resounding No. What is required for any sports team or player to be successful is a successful offense *and* defense.

The same kind of thinking comes into play when people learn how to drive a car. "Defensive driving" is a cardinal rule in drivers' education classes: to avoid accidents, drivers have to look both ways, anticipate what other drivers might do, and respond accordingly.

The same advice holds true for writers. You need to pay attention to your offense *and* defense to establish a thorough and convincing argument. Sound thinking alone will not prove your point; it is necessary to anticipate what your opposition might say and take that into account in your writing. "Looking both ways" shows your readers that you have carefully considered all standpoints in developing your argument: opposing viewpoints are accounted for. This is important because it is a sign that you have considered that there *are* points of view other than your own.

An additional benefit that is derived from "defensive" writing is that by considering opposing perspectives, you may alter your own ideas in the process. Because you have the opportunity to see a wide range of perspectives on an issue, you may decide that what you once thought was immutable really isn't; that is, by examining others' ideas, you can challenge your own thinking.

You can no doubt relate to the following example of the importance of incorporating offensive and defensive thinking into your arguments. Recall a time when, as a teenager, you asked your parents to extend your curfew for the prom. While you were expected to be home at midnight on typical weekend outings, you wanted to stay out this one time until, say, five o'clock in the morning. Chances are you devised an arsenal of reasons for your parents' inevitable question, "Why?" Some of those reasons probably included the following: It's a special, once-in-a-lifetime occasion; all of your friends are staying out until 5:00 A.M.; your parents' friends have given them permission to stay out; you will all be together at an after-prom party; you will be chaperoned, so there's no chance of getting into trouble; there will be no liquor at the party, and so on.

By this time, chances are you had gotten your parents' attention, but perhaps hadn't yet convinced them to grant your request. What was your next step? You offered reasons that attested to your virtues as their child and as a student. Some of your additional reasoning might have been that you are an honors student, you have never broken a curfew, you never have to be reminded to do household chores, and your after-school and weekend job will finance the prom, not your parents.

In generating this list of reasons, what you had ostensibly done was to think of all of your parents' reservations about your staying out until 5:00 A.M. and address them in your reasoning. You had prepared both an offense and a defense in your argument. By thinking of your parents' objections and dealing with them in your reasoning, you prepared a complete—and, with some luck, successful—argument.

Being aware of and addressing opposing viewpoints is required of politicians, debaters, and anyone whose ideas might be met with disagreement. In the following paper, which argues why Prince is such a successful and important rock musician, Chris refutes the opposing stance that contends his reputation is unearned.

ONE WORD SUMS UP PRINCE: TALENT

So what's all this hype about Prince, you ask? Why is he so special? What makes him so great that many critics and listeners consider him one of the greatest musical artists of our time? To be honest, when Prince first came to my attention (in 1984, when I saw his "1999" video on MTV), I hated him. To me, he resembled a weak imitation of Michael Jackson, who was very popular at that time. And when I saw him prancing around on the stage wearing that purple se-quined jacket, numerous silk scarves, and those hideous purple-lace gloves, with his scroungy band, The Revolution, slithering around in the background, I was all the more turned off. In retrospect, I now realize that most musicians at that time wore gaudy, crazy outfits. It was a part of the act, a way to catch people's attention. Besides, what musicians wear is different from the music they write and per-form.

Times have changed, although my changed reac-tion to Prince didn't happen overnight. It took me a long time to realize that Prince did have some tal-ent. Being the Top 40 music buff that I was at the time, I listened to single after single, trying to see what others saw in his music. I gradually began to notice a change.

When Prince released <u>Sign O' the Times</u>, he had *real* artists by his side (as opposed to providers of background noise). The album explored a whole different type of music for him. No longer did his music sound typical with the typical guitar, the typical drums, and the typical drippy lyrics about some girl who some guy lusts after. He now incorporated instruments like tom-toms and a gong into his music, and his lyrics became more thought-provoking and meaningful. In fact, the first song on the album caught my attention because the lyrics do not talk about his sexual appetite as most of his previous lyrics did but talk about the troubles in the world and how civilization is being destroyed by physical abuse, crime, and drugs. For the first time, I really began to like Prince's music. In the years to follow, I found myself liking the musician more and more.

It took me a long time to realize what other people have known for years: Prince has talent. If this were not true, Prince Rogers Nelson (his legal name) would not have released fifteen albums, almost one a year. Most were successes, too. He had number-one albums in 1984 (<u>Purple Rain</u>), 1987 (<u>Sign O' the Times</u>), 1989 (<u>Batman</u>), and currently with his new band, The New Power Generation (<u>Diamonds and Pearls</u>). Some people criticize Prince for producing more albums than hits (only five albums were hits; the other ten weren't well received), but even five hit albums is admirable. How many other artists can come close to batting .333?

Do you laugh? Then how do you explain all of the number-one albums, not to mention thirty Top 40 singles in ten years? Sure, he had his share of failures along the line, such as with the <u>Under the Cherry Moon</u> soundtrack in 1989, but take into account that he has released nearly one album per year since 1978, and a few mishaps are to be expected. Or, how about the fact that in 1989 the National Academy of Recording Arts and Sciences presented Prince with the Merit Award, an honor for those musicians who not only make influential breakthroughs in music, but are able to inspire other new artists to do the same. This prestigious award has been shared by such greats as Paul McCartney and Quincy Jones. Even though that's his only major award to date, it is only a matter of time before he wins a Grammy or an American Music Award.

Many people have criticized Prince for snubbing his fans and hardly ever touring. In fact, the last time I remember him touring was in 1984. Of course, Prince fans would like to see him in person. But Prince is a songwriter and producer as much as he is a performer. Public appearances and tours would take valuable time away from his writing and producing albums, and such a musical genius can spare only so much time.

If you still think Prince isn't talented, think about how many people you know who can play perfectly and write music for over twenty different instruments without ever having taken many music classes at all. I admit that Prince doesn't have the sexiest or the most melodic voice around, and he often speaks the lyrics instead of singing them, but his versatility is astonishing: never have I heard a male artist lower his voice as he does in "When Doves Cry" or reach incredible highs as in "Kiss." Such a huge range in octaves makes him sound like two entirely different people.

If you think Prince is a musical genius, consider the skills he has with publicity. Prince knows the right time to be controversial (e.g., the widely banned Lovesexy album in 1988 and his nude picture on the jacket) and when to avoid the media and hype (e.g., his rapid exit offstage on the October 1991 Arsenio Hall show, which followed his "baring his bottom" on the MTV Video Awards). As a result of his timing, Prince is able to stay popular enough with the public that he will not be forgotten between albums, but at the same time, he is able to avoid the tabloids and publicists that many megastars find themselves consumed by and catering to.

While some people would say that Prince is an egocentric and selfish musician because he performs only the music he writes, I think that he shares his talent: it is because of Prince that many other artists hit it big. It is he who created, in 1985, the chart-topping, career-beginning song "Manic Monday" for the all-female group, the Bangles. More recently, he wrote "Round and Round" for the unknown fifteen-year-old, Tevin Campbell, as well as almost the entire <u>Please Hammer Don't Hurt 'Em</u> album for the rap star MC Hammer. Or, how about his part in helping boost Sinead O'Connor to stardom by writing the song, "Nothing Compares 2 U," which became 1990s number-one song? Finally, Prince is the musician who arranged, produced, and wrote most of the songs for the veteran Sheena Easton on her 1985 album, which generated the number-two hit, "Sugar Walls." In effect, Prince's genius is spread through the music scene.

Although people may criticize Prince for unsuccessfully trying to launch a film career with appearances in four movies, I applaud him for trying out new media. Prince isn't afraid of a new challenge, and tries to expand his talents to include more than the areas with which he is already a proven success.

It is too easy to find fault with musicians. After all, they are human. I know I found lots to hate about Prince until I gave his music a chance, and then I discovered how very underrated he is, so much so that I don't think people realize what talent he has and how he is using his gifts to the fullest. It took me years to see. I just hope it doesn't take others that long.

Writing defensively is an important part of achieving believability in your papers. Because Chris has addressed perspectives about Prince that oppose her own (also known as counterarguments), she has demonstrated to her audience that she has considered *both* sides of an issue, not just her own singular perspective. This is an essential part of writing a convincing argument.

Exercise

Using the prewriting you generated (see pages 44–45), make a list of the objections someone might have to your ideas. Consider all other possible reactions to your position or thinking.

As essential as acknowledging counterarguments and writing defensively is the next topic, revision, which is seen by composition theorists and writers alike as one of the most crucial parts of the writing process. Read on to discover why.

REVISION

Revision is an integral part of the writing process because it allows you to add to, delete from, and rearrange the material in your papers. Because time and distance can often promote objectivity, revision allows you to "re-see" your paper in a new light. Revision, then, encourages you to reflect on and reconsider your ideas. Because the act of writing frequently produces new insights and ideas, revision enables you to incorporate such new understandings into your paper. It also challenges you to consider the best way to convey your experiences and ideas to others. Thus, revision serves you as your vision grows. It also serves your audience because writing is a communicative act, and because clear, believable ideas are often not achieved in one draft, revision is the process by which you can produce a clear and understandable message.

Contrary to what some people think, there are no set numbers of revisions that a paper needs: while some papers need only two or three revisions, others would benefit from twelve or thirteen. One of the premises on which revision is based is that it is often impossible to get all of your ideas down in one draft because your pen or keyboard doesn't move as quickly as does your mind. Moreover, the act of writing produces ideas you might have previously been unaware of, and only by reading what you have written do you see additional ideas or possibilities to examine in your paper. In short, composing is too complex an activity to restrict to only one draft. To reject the notion of revision is to refute the belief that writing is a process of growth, one that requires time and repeated visits to the text.

In "Revision: The Maker's Eye," Donald Murray distinguishes between student writers and professional writers: after having completed a first draft, student writers think the job is done, whereas professional writers believe that they have just started the writing process and the real job of writing is ahead of them.

Revision is not the sign of an inexperienced or poor writer. Rather, good writing demands and deserves revision. It is imperative to allow ample time to revise: it is not a quick, fix-it-up part of the writing process. In fact, many writers view revision as one of the most satisfying parts of the composing process because it enables them to expand on their ideas, omit those that don't fit, and shape their thinking to make their writing as convincing as it can be.

The first step in revising your paper is to read it carefully. As you read, take notes in the margins or on a separate piece of paper to record your reactions (e.g., I need more reasons; this section doesn't fit; it's unclear what I'm talking about; good thinking). These notes can provide you with a game plan for your revision. Consider, too, the following questions: Did you include all of the reasons you originally intended to? If so, do they all belong in the paper? If not, why not? Look, too, for any holes, or material you have neglected to include, as well as any redundancies. By all means, include the material you find missing, and don't hesitate to delete repetitive information from your paper.

Then look at the paper's organization. Why did you choose to organize it the way you did? Would a different organization work better? Don't be afraid of cutting the individual paragraphs in your paper and playing around with rearranging them. This might show you new possibilities for the paper's organization.

Remember that revision often requires just as much, if not more, time as the actual writing of the first draft. But its challenges pay off in the rewards of a thoughtful, believable, and compelling paper.

Exercise

Reread your response to the question you chose to prewrite on (see pages 44–45). Add pertinent ideas you didn't include in the prewriting or discovery draft of the paper, delete extraneous information that does not apply to your paper, and experiment with rearranging the order of the paragraphs to achieve a more powerful effect. In other words, use the tools of revision described in the preceding discussion to make your paper more compelling.

VOICE

When you write papers, one of your concerns might be the way your paper "sounds." Occasionally we have had the opportunity to read essays and comment, "I like the way that sounds." This comment addresses the "voice" in the writing, the experience of "hearing" an individual person in the writing as opposed to reading what could be construed as generic, or anybody's writing. Not only someone's ideas, but the way they are rendered, can catch a reader's attention and contribute to the paper's appeal.

If you are writing about ideas, as opposed to personal experiences, how can you achieve an interesting voice in your writing? When writing about ideas, some people think that they must assume a voice that is markedly different from the one they use in their personal, expressive essays. The result is often an extremely stiff and formal sound, one that is full of jargon, pomposity, and unnecessarily lengthy, complex sentences. Along with losing their readers' interest, such writers also lose their own credibility. After all, who is inclined to be interested in and believe writing that sounds so artificial?

Much like other aspects of composition, there is no formula for putting voice or style into writing. The noted composition researcher and teacher Donald Murray believes that "voice is not a matter of cosmetics." The analogy I have used for years involves seasonings: Unlike the salt and pepper that you can sprinkle on your food to enhance its flavor, voice is not a spice that can be added after the fact. Rather, it is primarily an organic outgrowth of your thinking. If you are interested in and committed to your topic, that's a good beginning in interesting your audience. After all, if your paper doesn't interest you, why should others be interested in it? Passionate commitment to a topic often affects the tone or sound of writing. As Madeleine Kunin, the former governor of Vermont and the current Deputy Secretary of the U.S. Department of Education, reveals in *Living a Political Life,* "When I learned how to meld information with conviction *and* emotion I discovered my true public voice." Notice that commitment is not enough: information or ideas are an essential part of the picture.

When you address the issue of voice, it is often helpful to ask yourself what you want your writing to sound like. Pay careful attention to exactly what you wish to avoid or emulate in other people's writing. Choose a piece of writing you admire and read it aloud, slowly and clearly. Listen to the writing. Let your ears pick up what your eyes may have missed when you read silently.

It might be helpful to think of voice or style as the written equivalent of "body language"; that is, in spoken discourse the elements of voice are the gestures a person makes when speaking, the way the speaker positions himself or herself, his or her facial expressions. Voice is much like the directions that many playwrights include to direct readers, actors, and actresses in their interpretation of the lines. Why is voice an important part of written discourse? In spoken discourse, most people get bored when listening to monotonous, boring speakers. The same reaction applies to people reading writing that is bland and lacking in character, vitality, and personality. Most listeners and readers want to get a sense of the speaker or writer; they want to get some indication of a real person behind the words, not some cardboard, generic, or computer-generated maker of sentences. And that is the role that voice plays in writing. In sum, voice is the way the writer sounds on the page.

Using the First Person Singular

When you write idea-based papers, one of your decisions is whether you should use the first person singular, "I." Although the answer to that query rests on the degree of formality of the paper (you may want to check with your instructor), a good rule of thumb is that the more formal the paper, the less often the first person singular is used. Here, again, the issue of audience arises. Your decision of what voice to use in a paper should take into account who will be reading the paper. For the papers you write in this class (and in other university-level courses), however, the use of "I" is warranted as long as it does not overshadow the ideas in the paper.

The use of the first person singular is implicit in idea-based papers. Prefacing your statements with "I think," "I believe," or "I contend" is unnecessary because you are presenting *your* ideas, and your audience can assume that what you write are your thoughts, beliefs, or contentions. The use of the first person singular, however, can add emphasis to your ideas. If you choose to use "I" to preface your ideas, it should be used sparingly. Overusing it will amount to "crying wolf"; the effect you wish to achieve will be lost. What your readers should notice about your paper is its ideas: the thinking in the paper is the star attraction, not you as a writer or as a character in the piece.

In order to sound knowledgeable, sometimes student writers refer to themselves as "this writer" in their papers. While writers of formal research reports use this form of self-acknowledgement, it is extremely formal and is best avoided in the papers you write for this course and for most other university-level courses. Similarly, the use of the word "one" as a way to refer to yourself also smacks of unnecessary formality. Again, the use of the first person singular, "I," is preferable, as long as it is not overused (and, of course, overusing any word is best avoided).

Length and Variety of Sentences

Voice is a combination of elements in writing. One factor involves the length and variety of structure of the sentences in your writing. If you were to pick up a novel by Ernest Hemingway, you would notice a predominance of short, declarative sentences. This choice of sentence structure is markedly different from that of, say, Henry James, who is renowned for his very lengthy, often complex sentences that sometimes contain upwards of one hundred words.

What length and type of sentences should you strive to write in your own papers? Because exclusive use of any one length and type of sentence calls attention to itself and because you are writing idea-based papers and not fiction, it is probably best to try varying the length and type of your sentences. Remember, though, that complex ideas often require lengthier and more complex sentence structure. You might want to experiment with different lengths and types of sentences. Read your paper aloud as though you were delivering it to an audience. Listen to what you hear. Let your ear be the judge of what length and type of sentence provides the emphasis you want to achieve.

Look at the way Michael Douglas interjects short, declarative statements (and sometimes sentence fragments) in "Dump Gump," which you read in Chapter 2: "We talk tough. Shake our fists at each other in traffic. Snarl at the waffling of Bill Clinton. Sneer at those on welfare." These brief lines are in marked contrast to other longer, more fully developed statements Douglas makes: "Look at the bottom line for *Forrest Gump*, the summer move sensation, the story of an innocent, slow-witted boy from Alabama who goes from football star to war hero to megamillionnaire businessman."

Douglas also intersperses a series of questions later on in his viewpoint, questions that make his readers think and that he implicitly answers in his paper: "Are we going to 'gump' our way through Bosnia, running, running, running until Serbs and Croats and Muslims live together in peace, having listened to earnest American diplomats? What about Rwanda or Haiti? How about the budget deficit? Where is the Gump who can scoot through the thicket of federal spending and, luck have it, find the mix of spending cuts that everyone will cheer?"

Word Choice

Yet another way voice is achieved in writing is through the use of diction, or word choice, that helps contribute to the tone of the writing. Are the words unusually interesting, simple, cumbersome, or evocative of your topic? Have you chosen the best words to express your ideas? Mark Twain once stated that the difference between a correct and incorrect word is the difference between lightning and a firefly. In other words, word choice makes all the difference in the world.

Look at some of Stephanie Salter's word choices in "Forgetting Woodstock," which appears in Chapter 2. To mimic the language popular in the late 1960s, Salter writes that "I don't think it's *cool* [emphasis mine] to remember Woodstock as I do. It's a *drag* [emphasis mine]." Not only does this use of slang conjure up the spirit of Woodstock, the word choices add credence to her being part of the Woodstock generation. Salter also comes up with the term "sentimental doo-doo" to mock the nostalgia that Woodstock evokes in the Woodstock generation. In addition, she uses repetition as a way to emphasize the points she is making: " . . . maybe I wouldn't have noticed the mud. Maybe I wouldn't have cared . . . Maybe I'd have laughed . . . ."

How many times have you heard someone speak and been impressed with or turned off by his or her language? Understand that changing the specific words you use is not a surefire guarantee to achieving voice in writing. It *can* help, but it can also backfire when writers choose synonyms from a thesaurus that are not particularly accurate. Again, there is no set formula for acquiring a written voice: it is the amalgamation of many qualities in writing.

To help demonstrate this idea, look at the way Steve Love, in "Woodstock Lessons" in Chapter 2, allows his readers to listen in on his thinking process after he poses the question, "Then tell me this: If the essence of Woodstock was not sex, drugs and music but a commonality, a willingness to share and care for one another, why are we as much a mess as we were in '69?" He then slows his writing down (and his audience's reading) by posing five thoughts, each in their own paragraph: "And we are." / "Look around." / "The war has come home to us." / "It's in our streets and homes." / "We live in fear not of our long-standing foreign enemies but of our own citizens of the Woodstock nation and of their children."

Readers can almost hear Love thinking in that passage as he works through his ideas. Instead of posing a question followed immediately by an answer, Love allows readers to think along with him as he reaches his conclusions. Readers are able to see the writer's train of thought, the way in which he arrives at his understandings.

Parentheticals

Yet another way to achieve a sense of the writer's way of thinking is by what is called "parentheticals." Parentheticals are additions to sentences that emphasize the writer's point and/or provide information about his or her thought processes. A good example of a parenthetical appears in Steve Love's paper: "We do not care enough about each other to find a way—and there has to be a way—to pay for universal health care." The parenthetical is the information that appears within the dashes. Although not essential to the meaning of the sentence, the material within the dashes provides readers with a glimpse of the writer's convictions beyond the actual information that the sentence provides.

Parentheticals also take the form of writers referring to their own thought processes. Classic examples of this appear when writers begin their sentences with such precursors as "I think," or "It seems to me." Although logic would have it that all statements that writers make are their own thoughts, such inclusions momentarily slow down the dissemination of ideas in the paper. Parentheticals can do so by appearing at the beginning, middle, or end of a sentence.

Considerations Regarding Voice

Some of the questions that address style and voice in viewpoints and arguments (as well as in other kinds of writing in which you want to pay attention to sound) are as follows:

- *What kind of human voice do I want talking to my reader: emotional? erudite? detached? compassionate?* Because writing idea-based papers involves two-way communication, your choice of voice depends on the audience to whom you are writing.
- *How do I feel and think about my topic and what I am saying: interested? disinterested (as opposed to uninterested)? committed? analytical?* Because attitudes have consequences, it is important to realize that your answers to this question can often be reflected in your writing.
- *What do I want my readers to know about me and my thinking?* Because ethos is one of the appeals you can use to help make your viewpoint or argument convincing, it is important to

consider how much you want to reveal about yourself and your ideas. No matter how you answer this question, remember that your ideas are the main attraction in your writing, not you as a person or as a writer.

- *How can I choose words and sentence structure to reflect my beliefs and attitudes?* One of the joys—and frustrations—of writing is the many options you have in the way you phrase and present your ideas. Because one of the key components of the writing process is revision, you are not tied down to words and structures you used in a rough (or subsequent) draft of your paper. After all, nothing is carved in stone. If you are unsure which word or sentence structure to use, write down the alternative choices that you have. Ask yourself some of the preceding questions to help you decide which version is best for your paper.

Along with these questions are others that concern the organization and development of the paper. They, too, can contribute to the style and voice of writing:

- *Where do I want my paper to begin?* The answer to this question often depends largely on your audience: the more knowledgeable your audience is on the topic, the less background information you will have to provide.
- *Where in the world of ideas do I want to locate myself and my paper?* If you see your paper as addressing a little-known or often-ignored topic, you can be considered "breaking ground" on the topic. Conversely, if you have chosen a topic that is widely discussed and written about, your paper adds a voice to the conversation about the topic or issue.
- *What role do I want personal examples to play in my paper?* Personal examples can appear anywhere in a paper, but their placement and prominence can affect how your audience reacts to your topic. The more you rely on personal examples, the more your audience can say, "Well, that's just his or her experience." The interjection of personal examples, however, can personalize your paper, drawing your readers into your topic and justifying your stance.
- You may wish to present the strongest support of your claim first to capture your audience's attention, and then proceed to weaker reasons. Don't save your weakest reason for the end of the

paper, however. Because it will be the last supporting point your audience will read, it will tend to make a weak final impression.

- *Do I need to slow down at any point, back up to cover other necessary points, and reiterate critical ideas?* When you are presenting a particularly critical idea in your paper, it stands to reason to give it the attention it deserves. This does not mean that your writing should be redundant; rather, it indicates that some ideas—especially crucial, difficult, or complex ones—deserve additional attention. Sometimes, returning to previously made points can serve as a helpful transition to new ideas you are presenting.

- *Where do I want my paper to end?* The conclusion of your paper needs to tie up any loose ends, remind your audience of your stance, and discuss whatever unresolved questions may have arisen in your argument. If you have difficulty concluding a paper, you might try rereading the beginning of your paper to see how you can return to that beginning, thereby forming a completed circle.

- *What final image of my topic and myself as a writer do I want to leave with my readers?* In the ending of a paper, you have the opportunity to leave your audience with one final impression. What do you want your audience to remember about your paper and about you as a writer? No matter what your answers may be, the ending of a paper needs to be consistent with what preceded it: changing the voice or the style of a paper will only call attention to itself, either confusing your audience or damaging your credibility.

All of these questions are valuable to ask throughout the entire writing process. While you may think that writing is simply a matter of putting words down on the page, it is also a matter of listening to your writing and controlling how you make style and voice complement your ideas.

Exercise

Using the revised draft of your prewrite, rewrite at least one page of the paper, paying attention to matters of voice: change the length of your sentences, play around with using different words, recast the piece in a different person (e.g., first person instead of third person). In other words, experiment with some of the elements of voice described in the previous paragraphs. After you have experimented with voice in your paper, write a brief reaction to the new draft: What improvements do you see? What do you think needs to be returned to its original form? What does your paper sound like?

INTERESTING YOUR AUDIENCE

One final element in writing a readable paper involves how to interest your readers in what you are writing. After all, how can writers prove their arguments if readers are simply uninterested in what they have to say? As we discussed under the topic of voice, there are no hard and fast rules or formulas for interesting your audience. Of course, choosing an appealing topic is a good way to begin. But as well you know, what one reader will find interesting might well put another reader to sleep. There are, however, some techniques to engage your readers that might prove helpful. The following list offers samples from the readings in Part 2 of *Commitment, Voice, and Clarity* that demonstrate such techniques:

- *Present a paradox.* "It's an odd thing when a cartoon series is praised as one of the most trenchant and 'realistic' programs on TV, but there you are." From Josh Ozersky, "TV's Anti-Families: Married . . . with Malaise."

- *Make a bold assertion.* "The American family does not exist. Rather, we are creating many American families of diverse styles and shapes." From Jerrold Footlick, "What Happened to the Family."

- *Begin with a story.* "Three years ago I stood at my sink, washing dishes and listening to the radio. I was tuned to rock and roll so I could avoid thinking about the big news from the day before— George Bush had just nominated Clarence Thomas to replace Thurgood Marshall on the Supreme Court. I was squeezing a dot of Lemon Joy into each of the wineglasses when I realized that two smoothly radio-cultured voices, a man's and a women's, had replaced the music." From Patricia J. Williams, "Hate Radio."

- *Provide a list.* "Image #1: In the foreground a blonde, beautiful and voluptuous woman dressed in a body-clinging, bosom-revealing red dress; in the darkened background the silhouetted figure of a man lurks, sinister and predatory. Image #2: A virile young man with the currently fashionable two-day stubble of beard, bare chested, belt loosened, presses his body against that of a girl whose back is to the camera, clad only in jeans." From Claudia Boatright, "Mythogyny."

- *Describe a situation or scene.* "The tension in the large room is almost palpable. The air is tainted with the odor of sweat. The faces of the men and women are drawn and taut. Their bodies are twisted in postures of agonized thought, of supplication, of despair. The scene is not that of a torture chamber but of a roomful of students taking a final examination." From Page Smith, "Human Time and the College Student."

- *Offer a personal feeling.* "As I write I am feeling severely over-worked. The deadline for this column looms, and it looks as if I won't make it, although I know I will because I always have. But my writing isn't getting any faster, something I can't seem to change. I have fallen so far behind on so many things that my office—normally an organized clutter—is now so strewn with piles of papers and books that it's virtually inaccessible." From Robert J. Samuelson, "Overworked Americans."

- *Ask a question.* "What's good English to you . . . that you should grieve for it? What good is correct speech and writing, you may ask, in an age in which hardly anyone seems to know and no one seems to care? Why shouldn't you just fling bloopers, bloopers riotously with the throng, and not stick out from the rest like a sore thumb by using the language correctly? Isn't grammar really a thing of the past, and isn't the new idea to communicate in *any* way as long as you can make yourself understood?" From John Simon, "Why Good English is Good for You?"

- *State your credentials and interest in the topic.* "I am not a physician; I am not a psychologist; I am not a sociologist; indeed, I do not work in any aspect of health care. But I am a man who has lived all but eleven of his years on earth as a cripple . . . ." From Leonard Kriegel, "Claiming the Self."

Obviously, not all of these techniques are suitable for all papers, but they can suggest some options for the beginning paragraphs of viewpoint and argument papers. The goal is to catch your readers' interest, so much so that they are unwilling to put your paper down. If you can capture their attention, you have set the foundation on which to build a credible, convincing, and compelling argument. Understand, how-ever, that no matter how appealing its beginning, a paper must demon-strate sound logic throughout; no matter how catchy a paper's opening, interest and style do not supersede ideas and their support.

Exercise

Reread the beginning paragraphs of the revised draft of the paper you have worked on in this chapter. Rewrite the introduction, trying the one technique described in this section that best fits your paper. Remember that your goal is to interest your audience so that they will want to read on.

EDITING AND PROOFREADING

Editing is often confused with revision. Whereas revision deals with the content or the global areas of writing, editing involves matters of word choice, correctness (sentence structure, marks of punctuation, etc.), and proofreading. This is the very last stage of the writing process because you want to be satisfied with what you have to say and the way you said it before spending time on editing. An apt analogy is cleaning up the work site of a construction job after the carpenters, plumbers, and electricians have done their job. It wouldn't make much sense to wash the windows, polish the furniture, and wax the floors when the work crew is still making a mess. The same holds true for writing: it is wasted energy to edit a piece of writing while it is still undergoing revision.

Part of editing a paper also involves proofreading. While you proba-bly already know that proofreading a piece of writing is necessary before turning it in for a grade, you might find it an onerous task—and for un-derstandable reasons: after having spent days thinking of a topic, com-posing a rough draft, and revising a paper seemingly countless numbers of times, the last thing you want to do is to reread it carefully to check for mistakes.

Proofreading takes patience and perseverance—qualities you might not have allowed time for at the end of the project. Nonetheless, proof-reading is an essential last step in the writing process if others are to read your work, and you want to show it off in the best light.

To proofread a paper, try reading the paper aloud slowly and clearly, as if you were presenting it to an audience. Chances are you may be able to catch some errors when you have to read it in such a manner. When we read silently, we often read in chunks, skipping over words or phrases. Listen to your writing as you read aloud: you may be able to catch wordiness, unnecessary repetitions, and perhaps even lines that do not make sense.

Another strategy to help you slow down your reading process to check for misspellings or typographical errors is to read the paper backwards. As strange as this may sound, try it: start at the end of your paper and read backwards. Like trying to walk backwards, this activity cannot be accomplished as quickly as doing it forwards. Error detection becomes easier when you intentionally slow down the process.

Yet another proofreading strategy is to create a personal checklist of errors you frequently make in writing (e.g., the misuse of semicolons, comma splices, misspellings) and read your paper paying special attention to the entries on your checklist. This process may require you to proofread several times, paying special attention to one of the problems on each read-through. It is time-consuming work, but well worth it when you discover all of the errors you had overlooked. Remember that your audience are not mind readers: they can only go by what they see on the page in front of them. Moreover, when they read your writing, you are not looking over their shoulder, coaching them on the way you really intended the paper to be read.

Proofreading is a sign of respect for your topic (to show off its thinking); it is a sign of respect for your readers (they don't have to interpret the typographical errors, misspellings, omissions, and repetitions); it is a sign of your self-respect as a writer (that you present yourself in a convincing and trustworthy light).

Exercise

Think about the comments regarding matters of correctness (grammar) you have received on papers you have written in all of your classes. Generate a list of the three most frequent mistakes that your instructors have pointed out to you. Read the paper you have written and revised in this chapter's exercises, and proofread your paper once for each of the three errors. As you proofread, make whatever corrections you deem necessary. Then read your paper aloud to catch any errors you missed in the three proofreading sessions.

FINAL NOTES ON THE WRITING PROCESS

Although the writing process is broken down into the stages of brainstorming, drafting, revising, and editing, it is not as clean and linear a process as these four activities might suggest. Rather, writing is a recursive endeavor: It is often necessary and appropriate to return to any of the stages of the writing process at any time. This should not be considered a weakness or even something you should try to avoid. As much as we would like for writing to be a neat and compact activity, it actually isn't. Instead, writing is messy work.

Using the construction analogy offered in the preceding section, when a house is built, sometimes entire walls must be torn down and new ones erected (revision); sometimes builders must return to the architect for rooms to be redesigned, as in "going back to the drawing board" (brainstorming or prewriting); sometimes minor cosmetic changes are made in the final stage of the construction process (editing). But all of these changes are warranted when the finished product is improved because of them. Seeing a piece of writing through all of the stages of the writing process is the sign of a professional and committed writer. Your writing and your readers deserve nothing less.

WRITER/READER CHECKLIST

After you have written a paper, it is not uncommon to be blinded by what you have written. Because you are so close to your topic, it is sometimes difficult to view your paper objectively, the way your audience will. What follows is a list of questions to ask yourself when reading your own writing and when reading other people's argument papers. The more experience you have writing, the more you will internalize these questions and unconsciously take them into account while you are writing. In addition, the more experience you have reading argument papers, the more you will assume these questions as part of your responsibilities as a critical reader. Being an astute reader of argument essays will aid you in your own writing. Attending to this list of questions will make you write like a reader, and read like a writer: when writing argument papers, you will be aware of your readers' expectations or demands, and when you read other people's argument papers, you will be cognizant of the many factors that went into the writing of the paper.

- What is the point or central idea this paper is arguing?
- What is the goal of this paper?
- Is the idea for this paper arguable? Why or why not?
- Who is the potential audience for this essay? What leads you to your response?
- How does the writer establish herself as credible?
- What incidents or reasons are offered that support the paper's main idea?
- What are the strongest or most convincing ideas in the essay? What are the weakest? What can be done to strengthen the weaker arguments?
- Is there enough support to make this paper convincing? If yes, why? If not, why not?
- How does the essay address the "other side"? Does it demonstrate "defensive" writing?
- Does the essay stay on track or does it wander? Will readers understand the purpose of the wandering and does it add to the paper?
- What kind(s) of appeals does the essay make? Are they appropriate? Why or why not?
- Is the essay weakened by any flaws in logic?
- How does the essay capture your attention or draw its readers into it? What makes you care about this piece of writing?
- Do you hear a writer in the essay? If so, identify examples of voice in it. If not, how might the writer achieve voice?
- Can any part of the essay be shortened or omitted? Should any part be amplified or clarified?
- Is the essay weakened by any errors in grammar, punctuation, or mechanics and diction?

CHAPTER  4

STRATEGIES OF

ARGUMENTATION

ARISTOTELIAN LOGIC: THE STRUCTURE
OF ARGUMENT

When you write argument papers, your principal goal is to support or defend the stance you are taking. But you must have a clearly defined position before you can begin defending or supporting it. Chances are you have heard position or stance called a paper's thesis, generalization, claim, main idea, or controlling idea. All of these terms are synonyms for "stance" or "position" and are used interchangeably.

Classic argumentation dates back some 2500 years, when Aristotle tried to describe the ways in which people discover the truth: observing the world, choosing impressions, making inferences, and generalizing. By analyzing this process, Aristotle identified two basic ways or processes by which people reason: induction and deduction.

Inductive Reasoning

Let's begin the discussion of ways to support your stance with inductive reasoning because it is the kind with which most people are more familiar and more comfortable. "Induction" means building from specifics to a general conclusion. A scientific approach, induction involves gathering evidence or clues that point to a conclusion; the method moves from the particular to the general. We see people using inductive reasoning in a host of situations: a jury uses inductive reasoning when piecing together evidence that leads to its verdict; listening to a patient's symptoms, a physician uses inductive reasoning to diagnose the illness; even the popular game show "Wheel of Fortune" is based on players finding all of the letters that spell out the clue. Because one or two pieces of evidence are insufficient for the jury, physician, and contestants to reach a valid verdict, diagnosis, or answer to the puzzle, the more specifics that are introduced, the stronger or more believable the conclusion. Think of inductive reasoning as piecing together for your audience the parts of a jigsaw puzzle or assembling the building blocks that reveal the picture you want to create.

In your own lives, you use inductive reasoning daily. For example, let's say that last semester you enrolled in six courses, worked thirty hours a week at the university's computer lab, volunteered at the soup kitchen twice a week, coached your little sister's soccer team on Saturday afternoons, and studied Japanese in your spare time. All of this evidence clearly points to the conclusion that you tried to do too much in that semester. In such a case, you learn from reasoning inductively that your schedule was overwhelming. One or two pieces of this evidence (e.g., taking six courses and volunteering at the soup kitchen) probably would not have led to that conclusion, but as the evidence piled up, the conclusion became very obvious. Inductive reasoning leads to learning from experience: just as it takes touching a hot stove only once or twice for children to learn that the result can be painful, so too can you learn that engaging in five time-consuming activities in a given semester is overdoing it.

As amusing as the preceding example might be, it makes an important point about how to make a good argument using inductive reasoning: the greater the number of specifics, examples, or details, the greater *likelihood* that your conclusion will be strong and believable. Notice the emphasis on the word *likelihood*. Because inductive reasoning does not link your activities to your being overworked (maybe you cut all of your classes, surfed the Internet at the computer lab, ate free meals at the soup kitchen, etc.), the conclusion is not totally valid. Nonetheless, the more specifics, the closer your conclusion comes to achieving the greatest degree of believability. As you move from your specifics to your generalization, you are making what is referred to as an *inductive leap*. The smaller the leap between specifics and conclusion, the stronger your argument will be. Of course, you need to pay attention not just to the quantity but the quality of the specifics in your arguments. More information about "how much support is enough" appears later in this chapter.

Whether you first state your thesis, generalization, controlling idea, or claim and then proceed to the particulars that led you to that thesis is up to you. While there is no absolute formula or progression that the inductive method of argumentation must take, much depends on what you are arguing. Because most readers appreciate knowing at the outset what the point of the paper is, it's probably safest to first state your generalization or claim. Then your readers will be able to follow your support without having to wonder where it is going. However, suspending the generalization until the end of the paper sometimes adds to its tension or suspense. But again, the choice is up to you. As long as you achieve clarity in your progression of ideas, you will have fulfilled your obligation to present your case clearly, and your readers should be able to follow your line of thinking.

Here is another example of inductive reasoning: Lee has high blood pressure. Lee smokes a pack of cigarettes a day. Lee's favorite pastime is watching the home shopping network on television. Lee eats donuts for breakfast and is fifteen pounds overweight. Lee gets winded climbing two flights of stairs. Coronary disease runs in Lee's family. Therefore, Lee would benefit from exercising regularly and losing weight. Notice how the combination of seven pieces of information or reasons not only points to but supports the conclusion that Lee needs to change his eating behavior and exercise regime.

To help illustrate inductive reasoning in writing, take a few moments to read Laurence Steinberg and Ellen Greenberger's "Teenagers and Work," which appears in Part 2 (page 204). In the first paragraph, Steinberg and Greenberger refer to recent reports as a springboard for their raising the question they discuss—and the position they argue—in their article. In the next paragraph, the authors then cite the three principal reasons for their stance that teenagers should not hold outside jobs while attending school: their performance in school suffers, the rate of drug and alcohol use increases, and they develop poor attitudes toward work. The rest of Steinberg and Greenberger's paper discusses each of these reasons in depth; they also defend their position by discussing why the reasons against it, or counterarguments, are weak, thus strengthening their own stance. The authors' discussion of particulars or the support of their position proves their generalization or main point.

To illustrate another example of inductive reasoning, read Tom Weir's "Navratilova Is Ace of All Female Athletes" in Part 2 (page 251). In the first two paragraphs, Weir states the main idea he argues in the rest of the paper: Martina Navratilova is the "best female athlete of the century" because of her "set[ting] her gender's athletic standards for quantity, quality, consistency and impact." In this selection, however, Weir first discusses all of the reasons why he does not consider other female athletes for the title of "best" in the twentieth century. Only after Weir dismisses the competition does he cite his reasons for concluding that Navratilova deserves the title. Thus, the many particulars Weir offers support or prove his position that Navratilova is, indeed, the best.

Deductive Reasoning

In contrast to inductive reasoning, deductive reasoning begins with a generalization and works backwards to reach a conclusion. The root of deduction, *deduce*, means "to infer." Inferences show the connection between ideas, how one idea has an effect on or leads to another. Here is the basic formula of deductive reasoning: if this is true, then that follows. An example of an inference or deduction is as follows: from the way Margarita looks, she must have studied all night. As is the case with inductive reasoning, deductive reasoning uses specifics or particulars to help prove its conclusion, generalization, claim, or assertion. Because deduction must prove that one act causes or leads to another, deductive reasoning is always valid or true; no other conclusion could have been reached. This is the principal difference between deductive and inductive reasoning: whereas inductive reasoning suggests, but does not guarantee, a cause-effect relationship, deductive reasoning always proves the connection to be valid.

Also based on classical logic, the basic tool of deductive reasoning is the syllogism, which is the process by which you reason your argument. A syllogism consists of two premises (statements or assertions) and a conclusion (or generalization or claim): a major premise, a minor premise that is an example of the major premise, and a conclusion that is reached. Both premises, however, must be true.

Here's an example of a syllogism:

> MAJOR PREMISE: Students who study hard in college algebra
> will pass the course.
> MINOR PREMISE: I am a student taking college algebra.
> CONCLUSION: If I study hard I will pass college algebra.

Sounds good, but as well you know, this is not necessarily the case because despite studying hard, many students do not pass college algebra. While the minor premise is true (you are a student in the mathematics course), the major premise (studying hard will lead to a passing grade) is false: Studying hard does not guarantee good grades. Just because A equals B and B equals C does not mean that A equals C.

Here's an example of a syllogism in which both the major and minor premises are valid, true, *and* make sense:

> MAJOR PREMISE: Students at Midwestern State University are
> required to take twelve courses in their
> major.
> MINOR PREMISE: Sally is a civil engineering major at MSU.
> CONCLUSION: Therefore, Sally must take twelve courses in
> civil engineering.

In this example, both the major and minor premises are undisputable facts. Moreover, they make sense, thus making the syllogism plausible.

Here's another example of a syllogism:

MAJOR PREMISE: All babies need to be fed.
MINOR PREMISE: Fido needs to be fed.
CONCLUSION: Fido is a baby.

The major and minor premises in this example are true, thus making the syllogism valid. But Fido is a dog, not a baby. What's lacking in this syllogism is common sense. While the conclusion may be considered logically sound and valid because the major and minor premises are correct, the syllogism is untrue. In argumentation, the words *valid* and *true* are not synonyms. Although the logic in arguments can be valid, the conclusion must be convincing, and a believable conclusion is one that also makes sense.

Deduction shows the progression of reasoning in arguments; it examines the links between ideas and the reasoning that supports your thinking. Argument papers must demonstrate both a strong controlling idea *and* sound reasoning to support that idea. The first example of a syllogism on college algebra that you read was faulty because of its assumption that studying hard will guarantee a passing grade. As a writer of argument papers, you need to be aware of all the assumptions, or premises—stated or unstated—you make so that your arguments can be as strong as possible.

Read the following syllogism and consider the unstated premise or assumption:

MAJOR PREMISE: Ministers are respected people.
MINOR PREMISE: George Montgomery is a minister.
CONCLUSION: Reverend George Montgomery is respected.

In this example, the unstated premise or assumption is that ministers are respected people. If your audience does not believe that major premise to be true, you will have difficulty proving that Reverend Montgomery is respected.

To illustrate deductive reasoning in a written argument, take a few moments to read Paul Goodman's "A Proposal to Abolish Grading," which appears in Part 2 on page 187. At the very beginning of his argument, Goodman boldly states his thesis or claim: "Let half a dozen of the prestigious universities—Chicago, Stanford, the Ivy League—abolish grading, and use testing only and entirely for pedagogical purposes as teachers see fit." The rest of the paper links together his rationale for offering such a claim: Because testing and grading "hinders teaching and creates a bad spirit" and because grading and testing is conducted more for businesses and graduate schools than for students, it stands to reason that testing and grading should be abolished.

If we were to identify the syllogistic form that Goodman establishes in his argument, it would be as follows:

> MAJOR PREMISE: Testing and grading hinders teaching, creates a bad spirit, and is done for corporations and graduate schools.
> MINOR PREMISE: The purpose of education is not to compare students, but to pass on to students and foster in them real learning.
> CONCLUSION: Abandon testing and grading.

Thus, Goodman goes about arguing his point by linking together valid, true, and commonsensical statements that support his generalization or claim.

Before moving on to a discussion of the three appeals your arguments can take, try detecting and using inductive and deductive reasoning by completing the following exercises.

Exercises

1. Working with your classmates in small groups, select an idea you want to argue (e.g., the physical education requirement at universities should be dropped; students should be required to read a daily newspaper; on the transcript, the class average grade should be recorded along with the student's final grade) and choose at least two audiences to whom you want to argue your position (e.g., the university's officer in charge of academic affairs, your fellow classmates). Write two drafts of your argument, first using inductive reasoning and then using deductive reasoning. Then discuss which of the two strategies you think is more effective.

2. Recall a time when you tried to convince someone of your position on an issue. What kind of strategy did you employ, inductive or deductive reasoning? How successful were you in making your case?

3. Look through the readings in Part 2 and find one that uses
    inductive reasoning and one that uses deductive reasoning.
    Analyze each argument, state its thesis or claim, and then
    explain how the paper's conclusion is reached through
    inductive or deductive logic. Finally, examine why the type
    of reasoning the author used helped to advance his or her
    argument. Would a different type of reasoning have worked
    just as effectively?

Three Different Appeals: Logos, Pathos, and Ethos

Using an inductive or a deductive structure for your argument is one of
the steps in achieving a sound, convincing argument. Along with using
these two structures, you can achieve increased believability for your
argument by employing three different kinds of appeals. Based on Aristotle's classical logic, these three appeals are commonly known as *logos*,
pathos, and *ethos*. *Logos* appeals to your audience's sense of reason; *pathos*
to their feelings; and *ethos* to their belief in your credibility.

Logos, Greek for "word," refers to the logical thinking and reasoning
of your argument. Its main concern is the idea and the supporting evidence that proves your stance or claim. Without clear, sound, and well-
reasoned thinking, a paper has little, if any, chance of being convincing.
Logos is the "mind" of argument writing.

Pathos, Greek for "emotion," is the appeal that your argument makes
to your audience's feelings. You can advance your arguments by appealing to your audience's emotions because people are swayed not only by
ideas, but by what their emotions or feelings tell them. The appeal of
pathos also addresses your readers' values, interests, and imagination.
As such, it connects to your audience on a more "human" level than
logos. *Pathos* can thus be seen as the "heart" of writing.

Ethos, Greek for "character," refers to your credibility, trustworthiness, and believability as a writer. As we've already established, your
paper must demonstrate clear, sound thinking. But another way to
achieve credibility is for your readers to believe you are someone they
can trust. An ethical appeal is established by the way your paper sounds
(i.e., voice, tone), and helps to convince your audience that you and
your ideas should be taken seriously. This holds true not just for what
we read but for our daily business interactions, too. We often want to

believe in the company or the salesperson as much as the product; in fact, the two often complement each other. *Ethos* can be seen as the "voice" of argumentation.

To illustrate how these three appeals manifest themselves in everyday life, consider the following examples: When disputing an audit by the Internal Revenue Service, you would use *logos* or your ideas and reasoning to try to prove that your calculations are correct. When trying to convince your grandparents to buy you a new bicycle, you might employ *pathos* as you appeal to their feelings and emotions. When making a campaign speech for first-year senator to the student council, you draw on the appeal of *ethos* as you attempt to convince your classmates that you are a reliable and worthy candidate whom they can trust. Depending on the situation, each of these appeals can be used separately to create a convincing case.

The three appeals can also work together in a paper to create an impact on your audience. Consider the types of logic you might use in the following scenario: Let's say you decide to take a year off from school to travel and to get a firmer idea of what occupation or profession interests you the most. You want to persuade three markedly different audiences that your decision is wise: your best friends, your academic advisor, and your parents.

When you write to your best friends, you might describe how you feel you are missing out on experiencing the "real world" and remind them of the late-night talks in which they confessed to feeling similarly. You might emphasize your need to nourish another part of your life that can be found only outside the restricted academic setting: your need for adventure and spiritual awakening. Because you want to appeal to your friends' emotions, you use *pathos* to argue your stance.

When trying to convince your academic advisor that taking a year off is a wise decision, you might explain how taking a leave of absence is temporary, that you plan to make use of your formal education by putting it to the test in the real world, how you have been a model student thus far and can be entrusted with the responsibilities of learning outside the traditional academic setting. These are the appeals of *logos* and *ethos*: you are using logic and your reputation as a responsible, thoughtful person to argue your stance.

Attempting to convince your parents of your decision, you might choose to invoke arguments similar to those you used for your academic advisor and friends. You are appealing to their sense of reason, their emotions, and your trustworthiness. Thus, you use all three appeals to argue your case.

Because part of effectively arguing a position is predicated on knowing or playing to your audience, it is often helpful to put yourself in the role of your audience. Imagining the way they will think will enable you to choose which approach is the best to take. Depending on *what* you are writing and for *whom* it is being written, using any combination of the three appeals can help to strengthen your argument. Understand that you do not have to choose just one of the appeals to use in your writing. In fact, using a combination of the three can prove to be a fruitful strategy. What is most important to remember is that the success of the three appeals depends on your audience. It is essential to remember that your audience will not automatically agree with your thinking. Why should they? It is your responsibility to persuade them, and this is where the appeals of *logos*, *ethos*, and *pathos* can help you.

No matter who your audience is, remember that you have a host of different appeals in your repertoire. Much like the different styles of clothing you have in your closets, you can employ different styles or appeals in your writing to help create the desired effect. Knowing how and when to use different kinds of appeals not only gives you choices, but enables you to exert power or influence. Writing involves making choices, and selecting the kinds of appeals that will have the greatest impact on your audience is one of the powers of writing over which you have control.

Exercises

1. Working individually or in small groups, select a popular advertisement or commercial (e.g., Miller beer, Calvin Klein apparel, Pontiac Grand Am automobiles), and analyze the way it uses the appeals of *logos*, *pathos*, and/or *ethos*.

2. Pretend you are interviewing for a job you desperately want. Identify what the job is, who is interviewing you, and the appeals you use when trying to convince the interviewer that you should be hired.

3. Read Gary Engle's "What Makes Superman So Darned American," J. Clinton Brown's "In Defense of the *N* Word," and Shelby Steele's "Affirmative Action: The Price of Preference" in Part 2 and analyze the appeals the authors make to prove their points.

TOULMIN'S LOGIC

Along with Aristotelian logic—which deals with induction, deduction, *logos*, *ethos*, and *pathos*—is another kind of logic formulated by British philosopher and logician Stephen Toulmin. This model, discussed in his *An Introduction to Reasoning* (1979), is based on Toulmin's observation that all successful arguments are comprised of six parts: a claim, the grounds, a warrant, backing, qualifiers, and rebuttals.

The *claim*, like the conclusion in a syllogism, is the argument that someone is trying to prove. The claim is the thesis statement or controlling idea of the paper. The *grounds* are the support or the proof to support the claim. Without grounds, your readers have no reason to believe your claim. The *warrant*, according to Toulmin, is "how you get from your grounds to your claim." Often an obvious assumption, the warrant explains why the grounds support that claim. *Backing* substantiates your warrant, showing the reasons why the warrant is valid. Because writers should avoid making generalizations that discredit their arguments, *qualifiers* limit your claim to make it more plausible. Finally, *rebuttals* consider specific instances not accounted for in the qualifiers; they are the equivalent of "defensive" writing discussed in Chapter 3.

Here's an example of Toulmin's model of argument:

CLAIM: *The Lion King* is a good movie for children to see.
GROUNDS: It appeals to their imagination.
WARRANT: Good movies encourage children to use their imagination.
BACKING: Cognitive psychologists believe that promoting children's imagination is important in children's development.
QUALIFIER: Since most children enjoy situations that promote imagination.
REBUTTAL: Unless children are not old enough to understand the difference between reality and pretending.

It is important to recognize that all arguments, Aristotelian and Toulmin's, are based on the principles that claims, grounds, warrants, backing, qualifiers, and rebuttals reflect. However, Toulmin's method analyzes or dissects argument in greater detail than Aristotle's.

To contrast Toulmin's model with the Aristotelian syllogism, here's an example of how the preceding model would appear using classical logic:

> MAJOR PREMISE: Disney movies are directed to children who enjoy using their imagination.
> MINOR PREMISE: *The Lion King* is a Disney movie.
> CONCLUSION: Children who enjoy using their imagination will like *The Lion King*.

When you analyze an argument using Toulmin's logic as opposed to Aristotelian logic, you will immediately notice how the Toulmin method shows the often unstated or assumed transitions between ideas, and how the writer makes the leap from one idea to another. This method of analysis often proves helpful to writers when they want to make their arguments as airtight as possible and to readers who want to analyze the ways in which writers present their arguments.

Here is another example of an argument using Toulmin's logic:

> CLAIM: Restaurants should retain their smoking sections for their patrons.
> GROUNDS: Smokers have rights, too.
> WARRANT: It's unfair to discriminate against smokers.
> BACKING: Discrimination is against the law.
> QUALIFIER: Since most restaurants want to accommodate all groups of people.
> REBUTTAL: Unless there isn't adequate space to separate smokers from nonsmokers.

The preceding argument would look like this if it were presented as a syllogism:

> MAJOR PREMISE: Restaurants want to attract all groups of people.
> MINOR PREMISE: Smokers are a group of people who eat in restaurants.
> CONCLUSION: Restaurants should have smoking sections to accommodate customers who smoke.

Using Toulmin's Logic to Strengthen Your Writing

Because the claim states what your argument is trying to prove, it needs to be clear and succinct. Unlike inductive reasoning, whose claims can appear at the beginning or end of the argument, or deductive reasoning, whose claims appear at the end, Toulmin's claims should appear at the beginning to provide immediate clarification of exactly what you are arguing. Remember to distinguish between fact and inference, and define or clarify any vague or ambiguous language or ideas that your readers can misinterpret. Because your audience aren't mind readers, they need to know exactly what you mean by the words you use so that they can follow your argument and know precisely how you understand or see the issue. For example, let's say you are trying to prove to someone that the weather in San Diego is "perfect." What *you* understand to be "perfect" weather is sunny and temperatures in the low 70s. A person from, say, Colorado might see "perfect" weather as snowfalls of 12 to 18 inches every week and temperatures in the high teens. Thus, paying attention to defining your terms can help prevent any misunderstandings.

Because a successful argument requires convincing evidence to support its claim, you need to make sure that the evidence you offer applies directly to your claim. For example, if you want to argue that heavy metal is bad because it is unmelodic and unromantic, some people won't be swayed by such reasoning because melody and romantic music are unimportant to them. Additional reasons are needed to provide more convincing evidence to support your claim for that particular audience. It is important to gear the pertinent evidence that backs up your argument to your audience.

For arguments to be convincing, your claim and support need to be convincing. So too do the unstated assumptions or ideas that are taken for granted: if your audience doesn't agree with the unstated thinking that explains why your support is credible, they will not believe your argument. To illustrate this point, let's return to the previous example that analyzes smokers' rights using Toulmin's logic. Your claim is that all restaurants should have smoking sections, and one of your grounds is that smokers have rights. Your audience, however, needs to believe the unstated assumption or warrant that smokers should have rights. If your audience doesn't agree with that assumption, your support is shaky.

HOW MUCH SUPPORT IS ENOUGH?
HOW MUCH IS TOO MUCH?

Another essential part of believability—indeed a part of the kind(s) of appeals you choose—involves the development of your argument. How do you go about making your case not only plausible but convincing? So far, this chapter has discussed deductive and inductive reasoning; the appeals of *logos*, *ethos*, and *pathos*; and Toulmin's logic. At some point in the writing of argument papers, however, the questions of "How much support is enough?" and "How much is too much?" will arise. And just as there is no formula for creating voice in writing, there are no definitive answers to these questions. There are, however, some guidelines or safety checks to ensure your argument is as strong as possible.

After you have complete a draft of your paper and are unable to think of anything else to add, delete, or rearrange in the draft, it might prove helpful to put the paper away for a day or so (all the more reason not to procrastinate in choosing a topic and generating a workable draft of the paper, so that you will have the time to do this!). Distance can often create objectivity; that is, by not working closely on the paper for a day or so, when you return to it you will be able to detect gaps in your thinking, ideas that you might have overlooked in the first draft, or even new and better ways of presenting or arranging your ideas.

It also might prove helpful to outline your paper at this point in the writing process. A traditional way to outline a paper is to place each of your main ideas under a roman numeral. Under each main idea, place your reasons or support under capital letters. Put the specifics that back up your reasons in Arabic numerals. For a less formal approach to outlining a paper, try clustering, an idea that is described in Chapter 3 under "Prewriting Strategies" (page 41).

While some people prefer to outline their paper before actually writing it, they run the risk of following the outline so closely that they are reluctant to consider new ideas during the composing process. Outlining a paper after having written a good working draft enables you to check on whether you have stayed on track or have drifted from your topic. Outlines are also a useful way to see your paper in a nutshell.

Another strategy to use when addressing the development of your argument is to play devil's advocate or doubting Thomas. Pretend that you are your most fervent opposition: Attack the thinking in the paper ruthlessly and see how well the paper stands up to close, critical scrutiny. You might want to try this strategy with classmates, friends, or family.

How well does your paper fare? Be honest with yourself! Understand that by bouncing your ideas off other people and listening to their reactions, what you are doing is putting your paper in a room full of mirrors to see how its ideas reflect off other people. That is, you are allowing your paper to be viewed from various directions and in different lights. Subjecting your paper to a devil's advocate or doubting Thomas is a reality check for you as a writer. Although your readers might suggest additional ideas to examine and/or ways to go about discussing the issues you present, you are not obligated to follow their advice. Remember that it is *your* paper.

It is also helpful to reread your paper and see not only how many reasons you have to support your thesis statement, controlling idea, or claim, but if those reasons can be examined in greater depth to add to their power. Make sure that you give each of your reasons ample time to grow and explain itself. When writing, people sometimes are so anxious to get on to the next idea (lest they forget it) that they race through their reasoning. Part of writing a convincing argument paper involves slowing down enough to let your ideas grow. The argument paper is not a drive-through eatery (thesis statement, three reasons, and you're done); rather, it is a restaurant in which real dining takes place (perusing the host of possible topics, selecting a claim, and spending adequate time experiencing all of its components). Understand, however, that this does not mean padding your writing or adding unnecessary material. You want to add muscle to your paper, not fat.

Writing Convincingly: Sound Logic to Match Sound Thinking

In your quest to make others take your stance on issues seriously, it is very easy to fall into what are known as "logical fallacies," errors in logic that weaken your argument. The term "logical fallacies" indicates a contradiction: while the thinking may *seem* to be logical, upon close examination it is anything *but* logical. Instead of offering valid reasons to support your viewpoints, fallacies are evidence of unclear, incomplete, and simplistic thinking.

Although often unintentional, sometimes fallacies are written on purpose as a way to deceive people. Some advertisements, commercials, and politicians are renowned for using this tactic. For instance, miracle weight reduction programs use logical fallacies when they link weight loss with beauty, popularity, and wealth; in his famous

"Checkers Speech," the late President Richard M. Nixon tried to argue that he did not cheat by saying he was a family man, his wife wore a cloth coat (instead of an expensive fur), and his family loved their dog, Checkers.

Read the following explanations and examples of the most common logical fallacies. After the two examples of each fallacy, a brief discussion explains the faulty thinking of the first example. Try your hand at analyzing the faulty thinking in the second example. Then write your own example of the particular fallacy and explain why it is faulty. Notice how some of the fallacies overlap with—and are sometimes difficult to distinguish from—others.

Loose Generalization

Drawing conclusions based on stereotypes, this fallacy lacks any substantive evidence. A reliance on stereotypes indicates that no serious thought has been given to the subject. Moreover, stereotypes contribute to unfounded biases and prejudices. Loose generalizations detract from your credibility as a writer and from your ideas being taken seriously:

Blondes have more fun.

The French are romantic.

The notion of one group of people—in this case, blondes—having more fun (or more of anything, for that matter) than another is not only impossible to prove, it is fatuous and dangerous thinking because it is based solely on stereotypes. Upon what evidence can anyone say that blonds have more fun? Stereotypes do not prove anything.

Hasty Generalization

Arriving at a conclusion with insufficient evidence, this fallacy is related to the loose generalization and is one of the most common. The hasty generalization rushes to reach a conclusion before all of the evidence is in. You need to support any generalization you make—the bigger the generalization, the more support you need to back it up:

Asian-American students are the best mathematics students.

Students who don't live on campus miss out on all the activities that the university has to offer.

On what evidence are these statements based? What Asian-American students? What level students? In what situations? Too many unanswered questions detract from the statements' credibility.

Circular Reasoning

Restating in different words what has already been stated, circular or circuitous statements may sound impressive, but in actuality mean nothing. When you take a close look at circular reasoning, you will find it is nothing more than an obvious and unnecessary definition:

Dieting is boring because it requires reducing caloric intake.

Soccer is a violent sport because its players engage in overly aggressive behavior.

"Dieting" and "reducing caloric intake" mean the same thing. So, rephrased the sentence could read "Dieting is boring because it requires dieting," something that is not only repetitive, but obvious.

Cause-Effect

Claiming that one event caused another, this fallacy fails to establish a bona fide connection between its two parts. The cause-effect fallacy *assumes* a real connection exists. Claiming causality requires that one part actually affects or leads to the other:

Ours is not a wealthy neighborhood; all of its residents are hard-working people.

Because I failed the exam, my friends abandoned me.

The neighborhood in which people reside bears no relation to the residents' work habits. Financial status has nothing to do with the work ethic. Just as people who live in run-down neighborhoods can have a strong work ethic, so can people who live in $600,000 houses have a poor one.

Slippery Slope

This logical fallacy takes cause/effect one step further, causing a chain of events to occur. The connection between ideas becomes increasingly suspect in the slippery slope fallacy:

> Ours is not a wealthy neighborhood; all of its residents are hard-working people who would never support strip bars, liquor sales on Sundays, and adult videos in the stores.

> Because I failed the exam, not only did my friends abandon me, but I gained ten pounds, got into a car wreck, had a terrible argument with my parents, and lost my wallet.

Not only does people's financial status have little, if any, bearing on how hard they work, it does not necessarily have any relation to whether they approve of drinking laws and the renting of X-rated videos.

Non Sequitur

Latin for "does not follow"; the first part of the idea does not relate to the other. Not only do *non sequiturs* fail to make sense, they are sometimes unintentionally comical:

> James would be a great politician because he is an accomplished skier.

> I did well in high school because I color-coordinated my socks to my outfits.

Just because a person is successful in one area (skiing) does not mean he will be good in another (politics). The two fields have nothing in common. It's like comparing apples to oranges.

Either/Or

Offering just two choices or ways of thinking when the situation is more complex, this fallacy fails to take into consideration other possibilities, options, or shades of gray. It reduces thinking to simplistic levels:

> Love me or leave me.

> Either I learn how to use this computer or I throw it out the window.

Are there just two options? How about talking about the problems that precipitated this confrontational demand, changing one's behavior, even seeking marital counseling? Isn't the alternative of leaving a bit drastic?

False Authority

Using the opinions of "experts" to make its case, this fallacy draws attention away from the evidence and tries to support its point by citing a purported expert's opinion. This logical fallacy is often seen in commercials and advertisements in which celebrities pitch whatever product to the audience:

> My family doctor has been a practitioner for thirty years, and she thinks doctors who support euthanasia are murderers.

> Kathie Lee Gifford, a popular television celebrity, says that cruises are wonderful, so she must be right.

Just because your family doctor does not approve of euthanasia does not mean that she is right. Nor does it mean that others who support it are murderers. Moreover, the number of years she has practiced medicine does not strengthen her credibility on such a moral, ethical, philosophical, religious, and medical issue as euthanasia.

Ad Hominem

Attacking the person instead of the issue, this fallacy ignores the opposition's ideas and focuses exclusively on the opponent. Because it smacks of personal attack rather than a reasoned examination of ideas, using this strategy can often backfire, causing your audience to discredit you as a responsible writer and to discount your argument as plausible:

> Don't believe what John has to say; he's just a left-wing fanatic, a throwback to the 1960s, who meditates and eats health foods.

> Our mayor doesn't care whether the voters approve an increased restaurant tax because he is a millionaire who doesn't have to worry about money.

Just because John's political leanings are liberal and he meditates and eats certain foods does not make his ideas good or bad. In this sentence, John as a person is being attacked, not his ideas. Ignoring ideas solely on the basis of who said or wrote them indicates the reader or listener's shortcomings.

Bandwagon Thinking

Claiming that because everyone else agrees and that the other people must be correct, this fallacy is an appeal to the masses. Taken to the extreme, bandwagon thinking can resemble mass hysteria: at some soccer matches, mayhem has occurred because thousands of spectators have joined a dozen or so others who decided to charge onto the playing field and fight. The point is that just because others believe or act a certain way doesn't mean their thinking is correct and others should believe or act likewise. Bandwagon thinking was the basis of many parents asking their children, "If all of your friends jumped off a bridge, would you do it, too?"

Because everyone I have ever met enjoys vacationing in the Keys, I think I will like it, too.

The only reason I cheated on my federal income tax forms is that I know everyone else does, so why should I be the exception?

Just because everyone else likes something does not necessarily mean that you will also like it. How believable would you find the statement, "Because everyone I have ever met enjoys bungee jumping and eating rattlesnake meat, I think I will like the sport and the delicacy, too"?

Stacking the Deck

Disregarding one side of an argument and focusing exclusively on the other side of the argument, this fallacy exposes just half of the picture, thus slanting the perspective:

Ben & Jerry's Peanut Butter Cup ice cream is a healthy food because it is an important source of calcium.

I deserve to get a A in this course because it was my favorite subject, I really like the professor's teaching style, and I studied harder in this course than I did in all of my other courses combined.

Ice cream does provide a valuable source of calcium, but it is also very high in fat grams, especially peanut butter ice cream, whose fat content is derived from the cream and from the peanuts. Foods with high fat content are anything but healthy. Thus, ice cream is (unfortunately) not a particularly healthy food.

Appeal to Human Emotions

Exploiting readers' feelings of pity or fear to make a case, this fallacy draws solely on readers' *pathos* and not on *logos* or ideas. A case can be made that appealing to your audience's emotions is the most legitimate or logically sound of all the fallacies. Just think of all the times you donated your time or money to worthy causes because they appealed to your emotions as a caring, sensitive, and empathetic human being. Many legitimate health organizations capture people's attention by appealing to human emotions. Because the appeal to emotions has proven successful, dishonest organizations have used the same tactics (e.g., bogus organizations soliciting funds, especially in the holiday season when many people are more prone to contribute to the needy). Only the ones that back up their pleas with substantive reasons or evidence are *fully* believable:

> Because I was an orphan who was later adopted by a dysfunctional family, I'm sure you will give me a scholarship.

> As someone who wants to keep your neighborhood safe, you see the need to require curfews so that teenagers and vagrants can't roam your streets and scare unsuspecting citizens such as you.

The circumstances of a person's homelife are not reason enough on which to base the awarding of a scholarship. Many students are orphans, many have been adopted, and claiming a dysfunctional family is open to interpretation (what does that term really mean anyway?). None of these pertain to the basis on which scholarships are awarded. Are there other reasons why this person should be awarded a scholarship? How about academic excellence or achievement?

Ignoring the Question

Changing the topic before it is ever considered, this fallacy ignores the issue at hand and deflects its examination by changing the topic. Politicians and guilty people are renowned for this practice:

> Because trying to motivate students to spend as much time studying as they do playing involves extensive research, it's best to discuss what pastimes they enjoy the most.

> I can't account for my activities the night before the crime, but I must say that I think we must put a stop to the unnecessary government spending in Washington.

Why is studying students' pastimes the "best" call to action when "extensive research" is required? Why not just do the research? What purpose will be served by changing the topic?

Trivial Objections

Bringing up trivial details as a way to reject the major point or argument, this fallacy is nit-picking and looks to find fault. Focusing on the picayune, trivial objections are a combination of *ad hominem* and cause/effect fallacies. Their net result ultimately backfires and demonstrates your own short-sightedness and lack of logical, thoughtful thinking:

> Oscar would be a poor choice as company president. He dresses poorly and has a funny-sounding first name.

> I thought Mr. Snow was a fantastic teacher. He wore a purple tie to class every day.

Oscar's ability to run a company has no bearing on his attire and his name. There may be other reasons to think of Oscar as a poor choice (e.g., he lacks administrative experience, he doesn't know much about the particular company, his last two company presidencies ended with the firms declaring bankruptcy), but the ones cited are trivial and inconsequential.

Exercise

> To further test your ability to detect logical fallacies, read the following student editorial, which attempts to argue against required courses for university-level students. As you read, keep a list of all of the fallacies you notice; you will need it for the last part of the exercise, which appears at the end of the editorial.

        The faculty and administration at this school
really need to get their act together and get with
it. It's time these people look at the unrealistic

and old-fashioned curriculum requirements for graduation and entrance into graduate school. The times
have changed, but their attitudes haven't.

Requiring students to take so many courses that
have nothing to do with their major forces students
to perform like trained circus animals in order to
get a degree. Do the required courses have to be so
boring and time-consuming? Why should students be
forced to take phys ed courses when they get enough
exercise walking to and from classes? Why study history when it's not their major and every year there's
more facts to memorize when they'll never have to use
to them? As far as foreign languages are concerned,
my English instructor last semester told me that I
have my hands full getting all of the grammar rules
in English right, so why try another language? It
seems to me that as a paying customer I should have
the right to choose which courses I think are necessary to complete my education. When I pay for a meal
in a restaurant, I get to choose what I want to eat,
not the waitress or the cook or the owner. I think
the same logic applies to what courses I take at the
university. I am a consumer, and as the old expression goes, "the customer is always right." It's not
as though I won't be taking hard courses, they'll
just be in my major and be courses I will need in my
career.

The school administration and teachers may say
it's necessary for students to put in the time to
prove they can do the work. But this forces students
to resort to unethical means to complete all of the

assignments foisted on them. When forced to decide between doing the work, not completing the courses, or using unethical means, which do you think students choose?

The bottom line is that the unnecessary requirements force students to cheat. The administration knows this, but as long as students aren't caught in the act, the administration doesn't do anything about it. One of the common practices in my dormitory is recycling homework assignments. Everyone does because the ridiculous requirements force them to.

Students also lie about term-paper sources because the source they really need is not in the library. Besides, how many professors would bother to check? Some people buy research papers from companies that specialize in writing them, and some students hire other students to write their papers. What student wouldn't resort to this kind of behavior if it means passing or failing a course? Again, the unrealistic requirements are to blame.

The solution is simple: reduce the number and type of required courses so students can complete the work without having to cheat. Why does the administration have to throw so many hurdles in front of students if they really want us to graduate? Maybe they've forgotten their own school days. But times have changed and students don't like to devote all of their time to education when they have a life outside of school like working to pay for their education.

Really caring students can contribute to their chosen professions if they were given a chance. Why

deny them that chance because of some arbitrary curriculum requirements? Just because professors had to
take required courses when they were students doesn't
mean that the tradition has to be upheld. Too many
parts of university requirements are around because
of tradition. Tradition needs to consider the reality of today's world.

Courses need to reflect the needs of today's
students or there won't be any students left. Get with
the times and give students a break so they can get
their degrees and become working members of society.

> Take the list of fallacies you discovered in this editorial and catego-
> rize them by groups (e.g., hasty generalization, ignoring the ques-
> tion, cause-effect, *ad hominem*). Then write a letter to the writer
> explaining why these fallacies weakened his editorial.

TONE

While you were generating a list of logical fallacies that weaken this
argument, you no doubt noticed that the writer also uses a belligerent
and confrontational tone. This, too, detracts from his argument. What
reader, after all, can be sympathetic to a writer who puts down and vi-
ciously attacks the people about whom he is writing? A condescending
attitude is not only inappropriate but it diminishes the writer's credibility. And establishing credibility is a key to successful argument papers.
Additional information that is germane to tone is provided in Chapter
3 under the heading "Considering Potential Audiences" (page 46).

By assuming a vengeful tone—not to mention the plethora of logical
fallacies—the student who has tried to argue that required courses are
unnecessary has left himself open to people not taking his ideas and
himself as a writer seriously. Both his knowledge and his truthfulness
about the topic can easily be called into question or even dismissed.

One of the goals of argument papers is for your audience to be able to
see that you have thoughtfully considered and presented your ideas,
and that they have merit—even if your readers do not agree with your

stance. This involves respecting your audience's intelligence, not writing as though you are in a fit of rage and are fighting your readers. An even-handed, rational, and thoughtful tone—one that displays commitment, voice, and clarity—can strengthen your argument.

CHAPTER 5

THE RESEARCHED PAPER

The Whys and Hows of Using Outside Sources

Many university-level courses require students to write a research or term paper. For some students, just the thought of such an assignment conjures up images of voluminous notecards; long hours spent in dusty library stacks or staring at the computer monitor to locate possible sources; a marathon and sometimes last-minute scavenger hunt in the library; and then late nights spent pasting together the results of their search. The task often seems onerous, and one that many students would prefer to avoid.

For these students, the research or term paper is more of an exercise in finding the required number of sources and including a sufficient number of correctly cited and documented quotations than it is a way to engage other writers' thinking about an issue or topic.

It need not be that way, however. Notice the title of this chapter: the *researched* paper (instead of the research paper). The ways in which you perceive the role or function of outside sources is critical to the difference between a research and a researched paper. Although the researched paper requires library research in which writers summarize, paraphrase, and directly quote their sources, it is not just an exercise in finding outside sources and correctly documenting them. Rather, the use of outside sources could be viewed as being akin to inviting additional voices to enter the conversation. The principal concern should be your own ideas, and the outside sources should serve to buttress or support those ideas.

Think of the researched paper this way: it is the "written" version of a movie in which you are fully responsible for all of the facets involved in creating the final product. You are in charge of producing, directing, casting of sources, editing, and choosing the approach you want to take—in essence, becoming a "scribal" filmmaker. In short, *you* are determining the focus of the piece and directing the parts that will create the whole. It is *your* movie or paper; you pull together all of the available resources (much like in film, the producer/director selects the actors, actresses, camera angles, lighting and sound techniques) to produce the desired effect. The responsibility is tremendous, but so too are the opportunities to utilize outside resources to create a paper that accomplishes exactly what you want. It is *your* vision or ideas that are in the making: it is assuming control and power to make your ideas real and convincing to your audience. Despite the work involved in such orchestrating, it can also be enjoyable work because you are bringing in other sources to help prove your argument.

Another analogy to help show you what a researched paper is involves teaching. In your schooling, you might have had the opportunity to take a course in which the instructor was particularly adept at including the views of critics and students themselves into the discussion of whatever issue was under discussion. Although the instructor was in charge of the topic, the class was not a lecture restricted solely to his or her viewpoint. The instructor asked students to offer their own reactions and referred to the thinking of scholars on the topic. Instead of letting the class become a free-for-all in which everyone expressed his or her various ideas, however, the instructor skillfully found commonalities between the varying perspectives, found connections between the ideas, discussed opposing points of view, and at the end of class, tied up all of the viewpoints expressed—all to create a thorough picture of what was said in relation to his or her focus. In essence, the instructor offered a stand, and it was discussed, examined, and analyzed using the thinking contributed by outside sources and by class members. In retrospect, when you think about the way the instructor utilized perspectives other than just his or her own, the final result was probably more interesting, believable, and compelling.

One of the guiding principles of using outside sources in your own writing is that by interacting with thinking other than your own, you are ostensibly entering into the discussion of ideas on paper. You are acknowledging that you are not only aware of others' perspectives, whether they confirm or refute your own, but you are willing to become an integral part of the conversation. Such interaction is exciting. Surely you have discussed current events, reviews of movies, topics you are studying in your classes, etc., with others and felt as though you not only contributed to the conversation, but learned from and felt exhilarated by the exchange of ideas. This is one of the rewards of engaging other people's perspectives and of writing researched papers. Moreover, it shows that you are willing to acknowledge ideas other than your own. Not only will this activity be required in many of the university-level courses you take, it is often a part of work outside the academic setting, whether it be in writing reports, making presentations, or discussing ideas you have in the workplace. In sum, the act of research is the sign of an aware, mature, and educated mind.

PRIMARY AND SECONDARY SOURCES

When you begin your research, you will discover two kinds of research: primary and secondary. Primary research is information acquired from the actual source. This includes interviews, field notes, laboratory experiments that you conduct, and any other information that you secure firsthand.

Because conducting primary research can be very time-consuming and is most often performed in specialized, upper-division courses, most of the undergraduate courses you take will probably not require you to engage in firsthand research. Instead, your research most likely will be conducted with secondary sources.

Secondary sources are what other writers, theorists, and researchers have published on your topic. You can find such sources in newspapers, magazines, journals, and books—anything that has already been published. In fact, secondary sources are probably what you are most familiar with.

SELECTING AND EVALUATING SOURCES AS EVIDENCE

You will probably find many sources that you can use to substantiate your ideas, but you need to ascertain the credibility and the quality of the sources you choose. Much as when you are shopping for clothing, you don't want to grab the first item you see and use it. In selecting which sources to use, consider how recent they are. For example, if you are writing a paper about the detrimental effects of the workplace on workers, you don't want to restrict your choices to materials written in the 1950s; rather, look for the most recently written information on the topic. This will show your audience that you have scrupulously researched your topic and that your research is up-to-date, thus helping you establish yourself as a credible researcher. Also, if you have chosen a very timely topic, avoid using books as sources because many books take several years to be written, let alone published. Instead, check the periodical and newspaper indexes: these will provide you with the most up-to-date material on your topic.

Besides considering when your source was published, try to include material from the leading experts in the field. This, too, will add credibility to your argument. For example, if you were to write a paper whose topic deals with cognitive development, you might want to consult the works of Jerome Bruner or Bruno Bettleheim, the leading experts in the field. By using well-known experts as sources in your paper, you are showing your audience that you are knowledgeable about and familiar with the most influential writers on your topic. If you do not know who the experts are in the field pertaining to your topic, look for names of writers and/or researchers that are repeated in books and articles: these can often provide valuable clues to the important figures in the field. Also, consult your librarian—he or she should be able to assist you.

Try to vary the selection of the sources you use. That is, don't rely on just one writer or researcher. Too narrow a selection of sources might indicate that you haven't researched widely enough or found enough sources to support your stance. Just as you should aim for variety in the authors you use, so too should you try to avoid restricting yourself to just one magazine, journal, newspaper, or book. Branch out to indicate to your audience that you are well read on your topic. This includes, if possible, using books *and* articles as sources. The greater selection of sources you use, the more knowledgeable you will be on your topic; the more knowledgeable you are on your topic, the greater credibility you will achieve in your readers' eyes.

WHERE TO BEGIN: USING THE LIBRARY

Because your search for secondary sources will necessitate library research, it is a good idea to familiarize yourself with your school and public libraries. Most libraries have maps and general information pamphlets that can help show you where to find card catalogs and/or computers; magazine, journal, and book stacks; indexes and bibliographies; and whatever other resources are available to you. Some libraries even have self-guided or librarian-run tours to help introduce you to the physical layout of the facility and the available resources. Because there is often nothing more frustrating than spending valuable time trying to find where a certain journal, book, or computer is located, it's well worth the effort to get to know the library before you begin your research. In the long run, it will save you time and reduce your frustration in trying to find what you're looking for. Also, don't hesitate to ask the library's staff for assistance; that's what they are there for.

Because the task of researching a topic can be daunting ("Where do I begin? There's so much to look at. I don't know what I'm even looking for!"), it is easier to have a clearly defined research question before you start searching for outside sources than to have no idea what you want to write about. Entering the library thinking that a good, researchable topic will tap you on the shoulder or call for you from the stacks is unrealistic. If only that were the case!

Although wandering through the library and searching its holdings can sometimes help in your finding topics about which to write, it is more time-consuming than if you enter the library having *some* idea of what direction you want to take. Moreover, when you do not have a defined research question before you begin your library search, it is easy to become frustrated when you are unable to find suitable sources for your paper. Another danger of not having a bona fide topic is that you will jump at the first sign of a possible subject and not choose a narrow enough research topic, or you may even select one in which you are not really interested.

Card Catalogs

A search for suitable secondary sources typically begins at the library's main catalog. This catalog will take the form of actual cards for each book in the library's holdings. These are arranged either by subject or alphabetically by author and by title:

F
106
.J273
1968

U.S. — SOCIAL LIFE AND CUSTOMS — 1866–1918

James, Henry, 1843–1916.
    The American scene.   Introd. and notes by Leon Edel.
Bloomington, Indiana University Press ₍1968₎

    xxiv, 486 p.   21 cm.

    Bibliographical references included in "Notes" (p. ₍466₎–479)

    CONTENTS.—New England: an autumn impression.—New York revisited.—New York and the Hudson: a spring impression.—New York: social notes.—The Bowery and thereabouts.—The sense of Newport.—Boston.—Concord and Salem.—Philadelphia.—Baltimore.—Washington.—Richmond.—Charleston.—Florida.

    1. Atlantic States—Descr. & trav.   2. U.S.—Descr. & trav.—1900–1920.   3. U.S.—Soc. life & cust.—1865–1918.   I. Edel, Leon, 1907– ed.   II. Title.

F106.J273   1968   917.4   68–14605
Library of Congress   ₍3₎

```
              UNITED STATES--SOCIAL LIFE AND
              CUSTOMS--20TH CENTURY.
E
169.02
.C85          Curtis, Charlotte.
1976            The rich and other atrocities / by
              Charlotte Curtis. New York: Harper &
              Row, c1976.
                xiii, 318 p. : ill. ; 24 cm.
                Includes index.




              1. United States--Social life and
              customs--20th century.   2. Upper
              classes--United States.   I. Title


OAkU     022h0132301*            AKRRsc        76-5121
```

In recent years some libraries have dispensed with card catalogs and have put a record of their holdings on computer. If this is the case in your school or city library, your search will prove to be a bit easier: instead of thumbing through card catalogs, you will be able to call up a certain subject, title, or author on the computer and print out the lists:

```
You searched for the SUBJECT: computers
@ 164 SUBJECTS found, with 886 entries; SUBJECTS 1-8 are:

  1 Computers . . . . . . . . . . . . . . 166 entries
  2 Computers Abbreviations . . . . . . .   2 entries
  3 Computers Abstracts . . . . . . . . .   2 entries
  4 Computers Abstracts Periodicals . . .   6 entries
  5 Computers Access Control . . . . . . . 65 entries
  6 Computers Access Control Bibliography .  1 entry
  7 Computers Access Control Case Studies .  1 entry
  8 Computers Access Control Congresses . . 20 entries
```

```
Please type the NUMBER of the item you want to see, OR
F>Go FORWARD                    A>ANOTHER Search by SUBJECT
W>Same search as WORD search  P>PRINT
N>NEW search                    O>OTHER options
Choose one (1-8, F, W, N, A, P, D, T, L, J, U, O) 1
 You searched for the SUBJECT: computers
@ 166 entries found, entries 1-8 are:  @@        CALL #
  @Computers@
@  1 @Advances in computational and
         mathematical techni          @@TP151 .A59
@  2 @Algorithm design for
         computer system design       @@QA76.6 .A34 1984
@  3 @Algorithms and automatic
         computing machines.          @@QA76 .T713
@  4 @All about minicomputers         @@TK7888.3 .D26 197
@  5 @All about small business
         computers                     @@QA76 .D28x
@  6 @Alternative computers           @@QA 76 .A565 1989
@  7 @Analysis of a benchmark suite
         to evaluate mixed n          @@
   8 @@The application of computer
         simulation techniques         @HF5429 .S94



R : simons, g.1. You searched for the AUTHOR: simons g l
@ 8 entries found, entries 1-8 are:  @@        Call #
  @Simons G L Geoffrey Leslie 1939@
@  1 @Are computers alive? :
         evolution and new life for   @@Q 335 .S53 1983
@  2 @Expert systems and micros       @@QA76.76.E95 S56 1
@  3 @Introducing artificial
         intelligence                  @@Q335 .S54 1984
@  4 @Iraq : from Sumer to Saddam     @@DS70.9 .S56 1994
@  5 @Sex and superstition,           @@HQ64 .S44
@  6 @Silicon shock : the menace of
         the computer invasi          @@QA76.9.C66 S55 19
@  7 @Viruses, bugs and star wars :
         the hazards of unsa          @@QA76.76.C68 S456
   8 @@The witchcraft world            @BF1566 .S5 1974
```

```
                                N>NEW Search
B>Go BACKWARD                   A>ANOTHER Search by SUBJECT
R>RETURN to Browsing
     9-16, F, B, R, N, A, P, D, L, J, E, U, O)  1 1
```

```
CALL #       Q 335 .S53 1983.
AUTHOR       Simons, G. L. (Geoffrey Leslie), 1939-
TITLE        Are computers alive? : evolution and new
                 life forms / Geoff Simons.
IMPRINT      Boston, [Mass.] : Birkhauser, [1983]
PHYS DESCR   xi, 212 p. ; 22 cm.
BIBLIOG      Bibliography: p. 196-206.
NOTE         Includes index.
SUBJECT      Artificial intelligence.
             Computers.
             Robotics.
OCLC #       9464443.
ISBN         0817631429.
0
```

Begin your search by looking at the listings for the subject of your paper. The subject will be broken down into topics, which will help you to narrow your search. Continue looking for books you think might be suitable for finding helpful information. Make sure that you have accurate call numbers for those books, so you do not have to make a return trip to the card catalog or computer when your inability to locate the book is the result of incorrect information. While you are searching for your books in the stacks, take time to peruse the books surrounding the ones you are looking for: because most books are arranged together by topic, sometimes you can find additional suitable sources close by.

Periodical Indexes

When researching your question, don't restrict yourself to looking only at books. Another valuable source is the periodical indexes. These are lists of articles from the most popular newspapers, magazines, and journals, and they are compiled either in book form (e.g., *Readers' Guide to Periodical Literature*) or on CD-ROM disk for computers. There are many advantages to looking at periodicals: instead of having to read or familiarize yourself with entire books, you can look at shorter articles. Another advantage is that you have the opportunity to read the most currently written material on your topic. Because you want your research to be as current as possible and to reflect the most recent ideas on your topic, it is best to refer to the periodical indexes.

Most libraries also have a number of indexes that are geared toward specialized disciplines or subjects. Some of the most common and useful indexes, besides *Readers' Guide to Periodical Literature*, are the following:

Applied Science and Technology Index (an index to periodical articles dealing with aeronautics, automation, earth sciences, engineering, physics, telecommunications, and transportation).

Art Index (lists art periodicals, museum bulletins, and other literature related to art).

Biography Index (for biographical information about a person).

Book Review Digest (a compilation of excerpts from book reviews).

Business Periodical Index (for articles on business-related topics, including advertising, marketing, public relations, and management).

Current Biography (an index of articles about people in the news).

Current Index to Journals in Education (a comprehensive index to articles dealing with all aspects of education).

Editorials on File (arranged by subject, a compilation of editorials published in United States and Canadian newspapers).

Education Index (for information about education, especially child development and children's education).

Film Literature Review (covers films and television, categorized by subject and author).

General Science Index (for general science articles in such areas as biology, botany, chemistry, environment, health and medicine, physics, and zoology).

Humanities Index (for subjects related to the humanities, such as archaeology, classics, folklore, history, politics, philosophy, and religion).

MLA International Bibliography of Books and Articles in Modern Language and Literature (an index of scholarly articles on language and literature).

Music Index (lists articles by author, subject, composer, and performer).

Philosophers' Index (an index of scholarly articles in books and periodicals on philosophy).

Psychological Abstracts (an index covering books, articles, reports, and scientific documents on psychology).

Social Sciences Index (for disciplines including anthropology, economics, environmental science, geography, political science, psychology, and sociology).

Because each library has different indexes, consult its list of indexes and restrict your search to the indexes that will provide you with the most useful information.

Newspaper Indexes

Along with periodical indexes that deal with journals and magazines, it is often helpful to consult newspaper indexes. These are devoted exclusively to one particular newspaper. Most libraries subscribe to the major newspaper indexes, which include the *New York Times Index*, the *Wall Street Journal Index*, and the *Christian Science Monitor Index*. The *National Newspaper Index* lists indexes for the *Chicago Tribune*, the *Los Angeles Times*, and the *Washington Post*. Again, consult your library's holdings for its list of periodical indexes.

Databases

Growing numbers of libraries now subscribe to database services. Using databases can save you valuable time that would otherwise be spent searching through print versions of materials that are housed in the library's reference section. Listing sources available to libraries, databases are geared to most specific disciplines you may want to research. Some popular databases include DIALOG (a compilation of over 250 databases), BRS (Biographical Retrieval Service), and RLIN (Research Library Information Network). Ask your librarian for a list of the databases to which your library subscribes.

Other Resources

While the card catalog and indexes will often yield the greatest number of helpful sources for your research, don't ignore other valuable material that the library has to offer. For example, the reference section of the library will provide useful information if you are looking for specific facts. Some of these resources include *Facts on File*, chronological summaries of news items; *Who's Who*, biographical information on important people; *Statistical Abstracts of the United States*, graphs, charts, and tables compiled by the Bureau of Statistics; and *Book Review Digest*, a compilation of book summaries and book reviews.

Of course, you can always consult the many encyclopedias that libraries have in their reference sections. Most libraries have general encyclopedias such as the *Encyclopedia Americana* and the *Encyclopaedia Britannica*. More specialized encyclopedias include the *Encyclopedia of Education*, the *Encyclopedia of Biological Sciences*, the *Encyclopedia of Philosophy*, the *Encyclopedia of Sociology*, and the *International Encyclopedia of the Social Sciences*. To find which encyclopedias are in your library's holdings, call up *encyclopedia* on the computer or look in the card catalog for a complete list.

If you find yourself lost or confused about finding any materials, ask the librarian for assistance. Having a library employee answer a few of your questions can save you hours of time that otherwise could be spent on reading and writing.

TAKING NOTES

Sometimes you are tempted to begin taking notes as soon as you find something even remotely related to your topic. But just as you should wait to begin researching until you have a well-defined research topic, it is often helpful to postpone actual note taking until you have a good, workable research question. I offer this advice for an important reason: summarizing, paraphrasing, or recording direct quotations of everything you read is not only time-consuming but unproductive. The purpose of note taking is to document your ideas and advance your argument, not to transcribe everything you read on your topic.

While it may be tempting to duplicate all of the material you find for later reference, such an enterprise is costly (even at three or five cents a page, it adds up), time-consuming (not only does it take a lot of time to duplicate what you find, you will have to reread it before using it in your paper), and cumbersome (it is much easier to shuffle note cards than copies of articles). Because you will probably find abundant sources, you will not be able to use everything you read, or even want to. Thus, it is best to read with an open mind, to learn, to discover, to find confirming and opposing perspectives to your own thinking before actually deciding what you want to commit to paper.

Although you are most likely familiar with taking notes on three-by-five inch note cards, you might want to try five-by-seven inch note cards, which will provide you with additional space.

When using note cards, use one source per card. This will enable you to shuffle cards as you organize them to use in your paper. Keep two sets of note cards. One set would be content notes:

Salter

A humorous essay that recalls the author's disappointing experiences at Woodstock. (summary) p. 20

The 25th anniversary festivals "only heighten the recollection and deepen the resultant sentimental doo-doo" (20).

The other set would be for recording full bibliographic information for each source:

Salter, Stephanie. "25 Years Later – – Forgetting Woodstock." <u>Akron Beacon Journal</u>. August 11, 1994. A20.

When recording bibliographical information, be sure to include the author's name, the full title of the book or the journal in which it appears, the date of publication, and page reference. Record all of the information carefully so that you do not have to retrace your steps for information you neglected to include.

Include on the note cards the author's name, a brief version of the title of the source, page references, and a reminder to yourself whether you have summarized or paraphrased the information on the card. For direct quotes, use quotation marks and record the author's words *exactly*, including punctuation marks. As with bibliography cards, make sure that you clearly enter all pertinent information.

Because reading and writing often aid in stimulating your own thinking about a topic, it is essential that you distinguish between the ideas you read and those you think of yourself. Keeping a third set of note cards to record your own ideas—as well as how you might use the source in your paper—proves very useful:

Salter

Interesting reaction to Woodstock's 25th year anniversary. Different from other perspectives that praise Woodstock. Can use as a first-person perspective that contradicts the way people and the media romanticize Woodstock.

Of course, if you have access to a notebook or laptop computer, you can use it for taking notes. Establish a new directory for your research paper (e.g., WOODMYTH). Instead of jotting down information on a notecard, create a new file for each of your sources (e.g., SALTER or LOVE). Except for your bibliographical information, which can be recorded on one file, follow the preceding information on using note cards when entering computer notes on your sources. Make sure you periodically save everything you enter on your computer. Also, at the end of every note-taking session, save everything on a floppy disk and put the disk in a safe place. When it comes time to use your notes in your paper, you can print out your files to refer to and/or transfer pertinent information from your files into the actual text of your paper. A few keyboard commands will also enable you to transfer the information you need into the "Works Cited" or "Reference" section of your paper.

Accurate note taking will save you valuable time in not having to return to the library to recheck your information. If you are unsure whether you should record a piece of information on a note card, it's better to err on the side of caution. Having to return to the library because you have forgotten to record the publication date of a book or have neglected to note whether you have summarized or paraphrased a paragraph in an article is not only time-consuming and frustrating; it is risky. Someone might have checked out the book or be reading the article when you return.

Because good note taking involves accurate summarizing, paraphrasing, and direct quoting, the next section shows you how to perform those research skills correctly.

PARAPHRASING, SUMMARIZING, AND QUOTING

When using outside sources in your writing, one rule is cardinal: you *must* give credit to other people's ideas. In researched writing, there are three ways to correctly acknowledge thinking that is not your own: paraphrasing, summarizing, and directly quoting. If you do not correctly credit your sources in the text, you are guilty of plagiarism—even if you do so unintentionally. Each of the three ways in which to properly credit your sources requires different kinds of work on your part.

To keep from confusing summaries, paraphrases, and direct quotations, it is essential that you keep accurate records. The carpenter's adage "measure twice, cut once" can apply to researchers: check twice how you are using the sources (whether it be summarizing, paraphrasing, or quoting) as you are conducting your research so that you can write up the research and not have to retrace your steps later on. One of the more disconcerting and time-consuming experiences in using outside sources is having to return to them later in the writing process to check to see whether you have used them accurately. Just think of the valuable time you will save in not having to return to the library, locate your sources, and check to see if you have summarized, paraphrased, or directly quoted!

Summarizing a source means getting the gist of the ideas down *in your own words*. Summaries are short overviews of a book or article that capture the author's main points *and* your understanding or interpretation of them. It enables your readers to get a condensed overview of the main idea of the book or article. What follows is an example of the original passage, a correct summary, and an incorrect summary.

> ORIGINAL PASSAGE: "I cannot tell you whether I saw Joan Baez, Richie Havens, or what. I could almost swear I didn't see Janis Joplin. I know I didn't see Jimi Hendrix. But I have no idea who I did see on that teeny-tiny little lighted stage so far down the muddy hill . . . . I was so miserable, Jimi and Janis themselves could have strolled up to our car and said, 'Hey, man, what do you wanna hear?' and it wouldn't have made any difference to me. I haven't even mentioned the borderline dysentery I did bring back as a memento."

> CORRECT SUMMARY: In "Forgetting Woodstock," Salter describes her disappointing experiences at the 1969 music festival.

> INCORRECT SUMMARY: Salter could swear she didn't see Joplin or Hendrix at Woodstock, but she was miserable and got sick there.

Notice how the correct summary is short, uses my own words, and reflects my own reading of Salter's paper. Summaries are important because in a brief statement they capture the essence of the article or book to which you are referring.

Paraphrasing is yet another way to acknowledge a source. Unlike summarizing, however, paraphrasing requires you to *retain the exact meaning* of a text, but in your own words. Another way that paraphrases differ from summaries involves the length of the source: whereas in summaries you deal with texts of any size, paraphrases are restricted to relatively short passages. When paraphrasing, it is essential that you remain true not only to the content of the text but to its tone and spirit. Paraphrasing is not as conflated as summarizing; that is, you must retain all the points in the order in which the author made them. Unlike summaries, paraphrases do *not* include your own interpretation, analysis, or reading of the text.

At this point, you might be wondering why you should even bother with paraphrasing when it is easier and simpler to directly quote from the source. The answer to this question is that paraphrasing provides an excellent opportunity to stay close to the text you are discussing without resorting to lengthy and frequent direct quotes in your paper. Paraphrasing can be accomplished by using synonyms for the words the author uses, and varying the length of or condensing the sentences in the text. Remember, though, that paraphrases must be documented: mention the author and/or the source in the paraphrase so that you can give credit to the author if you do not cite the author or source in the parenthetical documentation.

Paraphrasing provides a helpful alternative to one of the problems that can occur when direct quotes are overused. Paraphrases are also a useful change from summaries when you want to provide your readers with more of the flavor of the text but refrain from offering your own understanding or analysis of the source. What follows is an example of the original passage, a correct paraphrase, and an incorrect paraphrase.

ORIGINAL PASSAGE: "If the essence of Woodstock was not sex, drugs and music but a commonality, a willingness to share and care for one another, why are we as much a mess as we were in '69?

CORRECT PARAPHRASE: In "Woodstock Lessons Are Just an Illusion," Steve Love wonders why in 1994 our nation is so troubled if the spirit of Woodstock professed goodwill and democracy.

INCORRECT PARAPHRASE: Because Woodstock wasn't about music, drugs, and sex, how come our nation is in so much trouble these days, especially since people claim to have learned from the previous generation?

Notice how the correct paraphrase captures the essence and flavor of Love's text, using synonyms and not adding any extraneous commentary. The incorrect paraphrase, however, deletes an important idea from Love's text and adds commentary that was not in the original text.

Direct quoting is a third way in which you can use outside sources. Using direct quotations is a way of hearing exactly what the author is stating. It is occasionally fitting to hear the author's precise words to retain the flavor and quality of his or her language. Sometimes, authors will use technical or complicated language. In these cases, direct quotation is the appropriate forum to use.

Several points of caution are in order. First, refrain from overuse, stringing together direct quotation after direct quotation. Some inexperienced writers allow direct quotations to dominate their writing, so much so that the paper reads like a list of glued-together quotes with no indication of the writer's own thinking. It is essential to remember that even when you use direct quotes in your paper, *your ideas* must be present in your writing. The same advice holds for summaries and paraphrases. Remember that *your* ideas should be the star of the paper; outside sources only help to support your thesis, ideas, or claims. They are used in addition to, not in lieu of, your own thinking.

Second, it is best not to begin a paper with a direct quotation, that is, to substitute a direct quote for your own claim or thesis statement. Again, quotations should support your own thinking, not replace it. Finally, you do not want to repeat, summarize, or paraphrase what you just quoted. Discussing the quotation is appropriate; restating it isn't. What follows is an example of the original passage, a correct direct quotation, and an incorrect direct quotation.

ORIGINAL PASSAGE: "In another few months they would have us turning our weapons on our own on a rolling hillside in Kent, a bucolic place of learning where the lesson was bloody and lasting and haunts us still."

CORRECT DIRECT QUOTATION: Love recalls the Kent State University massacre in "a bucolic place of learning where the lesson was bloody and lasting and haunts us still" (1).

INCORRECT DIRECT QUOTATION: Love remembers the time
when Kent State University
would turn on their own
and the lesson was "bloody
and lasting and haunts us
still."

Notice how, in the correct use of a direct quote, I capture Love's exact words and place them within quotation marks. The period is placed inside the quotation mark. (Commas would also be placed inside; however, semicolons and colons are placed outside if you are continuing the sentence with your own words. Quotes within quotes are enclosed in single quotation marks, and if you want to include your own words within a direct quote, place them in brackets). Although I could have paraphrased the essence of Love's thinking, I opt for direct quotes because I want to capture the power and tone of his own language.

The incorrect direct quotation example does not place all of Love's words within the quotation marks. Further, the sentence distorts the meaning of the original text: the National Guard was responsible for the murders, not the students at Kent State.

Exercise

Select an essay from Part 2 of this text and (1) write a summary of it; (2) paraphrase a short passage from the selection; and (3) choose a phrase or sentence that you think deserves to be quoted (as opposed to summarized or paraphrased), quote it as if you were using it in your own paper, and write a brief explanation of why you think it deserves to be quoted instead of paraphrased.

Introducing Summaries, Paraphrases, and Direct Quotations

When summarizing, paraphrasing, and using direct quotations, it is important to introduce in some fashion the material you are citing. Not only do inexperienced writers string together a series of summaries, paraphrases, and/or direct quotations, they sometimes cite outside sources without introducing them. The cited material just appears in the paper, without being securely attached to anything. (It reminds me of inviting some guests to a party and neglecting to introduce them to the other people in the room. They end up wandering around, feeling awkward and out of place.) Neglecting to introduce direct quotations adequately produces a jerky feel to the paper, one that disrupts its flow. The reader is left with the task of providing the needed transition between the cited material and the writer's ideas. But that is the responsibility of the writer.

The attribution of outside sources can occur at the beginning, middle, or end of the sentence. Read the sentence aloud to determine what sounds most natural. It is helpful to introduce a source the first time you refer to it; not only will your readers know what the source is, but when actually writing your paper you will avoid losing track of your sources—who wrote what. The introduction will provide the information.

When introducing outside sources, try to vary the verbs you use. Instead of writing "So and So says/states/writes," choose a verb that more powerfully illustrates your purpose for using the source. For example, does the author disagree, insist, maintain, argue, observe, explain, emphasize, declare, believe, challenge, propose, question, reflect, stress, etc.? Choosing and varying strong verbs *in the present tense* to introduce outside sources adds interest and energy to your writing.

Here are some examples of weak introductions to cited material, using Stephanie Salter's essay and Steve Love's commentary:

> According to Salter, the 24th anniversary of Woodstock
> has been blown out of proportion (20).

> Steve Love states that the goodwill at Woodstock has died
> in recent years (4).

And here are some strong attributions:

> As someone who attended the original Woodstock, Salter
> is bemused by people's nostalgia (20).

> Reflecting on the Woodstock generation, Love concludes
> that "Emotionally, if not geographically, Woodstock seems far
> removed even from its own citizens" (4).

Notice the way the strong attribution for Salter reveals that she attended Woodstock, thus giving her perspective more credibility than
someone who had not attended. The weak attribution for Salter's essay
provides bare-bones information and misses an opportunity to reveal
her puzzlement. Similarly, in the weak attribution for Love's viewpoint,
minimal information is provided. The strong attribution, however, emphasizes the introspective with which Love offers his reflection. The
two examples of strong attributions also offer introductory phrases that
put the credited material in context.

Another point to keep in mind is that you need not always introduce or attribute the cited material. Do so when you want to add increased emphasis and attention to the material, especially when the
author is well-known or has particular experience related to the topic,
and the cited source is famous or especially recent and timely.

Whether you choose to attribute the cited material or not, the outside sources should merge gracefully with your own writing; the two
should form a smooth seam to give the impression that the source and
your own writing were meant to go together. An illustration of the natural weaving of outside sources and the author's own words appears in
the correct direct quotation example (see page 116). Notice the natural flow from the author's own words into the quotation. Incorporating
your own words into those of the source prevents a bumpy, patchwork
effect between outside sources and your own writing.

Exercise

Using the preceding information on introducing outside sources,
write an example of a weak and a strong introduction or attribution
for each of the summaries, paraphrases, and direct quotations from
the exercise you completed on page 117.

PLAGIARISM

Plagiarism is stealing other people's ideas. Whether intentional (e.g.,
stealing someone's paper, purchasing an already-written paper, consciously lifting someone else's ideas and quotes) or unintentional (e.g.,
failure to accurately credit sources when summarizing, paraphrasing,
and quoting, as well as not documenting accurately and adequately),
many people see plagiarism as plagiarism—that is, the plagiarist is
guilty, no matter what his or her intentions. Remember that your

readers do not know what your intentions might have been. The consequences of plagiarism can be severe: a reprimand, a failing grade on the paper, failing the course, a letter placed in your permanent file, or even expulsion from the university.

Careful attention to acknowledging and documenting your sources can prevent you from falling victim to plagiarism. All the more reason to keep very clear and accurate records when you are researching outside sources. This point cannot be overemphasized. The adage "better safe than sorry" applies to this advice. You might want to keep this book close at hand when you are conducting your research so that you can refer to the pertinent sections on citations and documentation, should any questions arise when you are writing your papers.

A final rule of thumb is: when in doubt, document the source. Whereas plagiarism is thievery, overdocumentation is not. If you are unsure of exactly what is required when crediting and documenting the sources in your paper, ask your instructor.

CHECKLIST FOR CITING OUTSIDE SOURCES

- Will your readers understand your reasons for using outside sources? That is, are the sources relevant and specific to your paper or are they there because you wanted to use a summary, paraphrase, or direct quote?
- Do the outside sources sufficiently support your ideas?
- Do you provide a sufficient number of outside sources to support your ideas?
- Do you correctly summarize, paraphrase, and/or use direct quotes? Will your readers be confused about which ideas are yours and which are the source's?
- Is the use of direct quotes warranted or might that material be better summarized or paraphrased? Will your readers recognize your reasons for using direct quotation when you did?
- Are the outside sources varied (e.g., different books and articles), current (the most recently published material on the topic), and reliable (responsible, trustworthy sources)?
- Do you refrain from stringing together summaries, paraphrases, and/or direct quotes?
- Do you introduce the outside sources or attribute to the author(s) the cited material, when appropriate?

- Are your ideas still visible in the paper or are they overwhelmed by outside sources?
- Have you made every effort to avoid intentional or unintentional plagiarism in your paper?

CREDITING AND DOCUMENTING SOURCES

In the preceding section of this chapter, you read about using summaries, paraphrases, and direct quotes from outside sources in your papers. Not only is it necessary to give proper credit to those sources, it is necessary to document them properly. In high school, you may have credited your sources by using footnotes. A more "reader-friendly" type of citation has taken the place of footnoting: in-text citations. As you will see, in-text parenthetical citations allow the reader to know who the source of the idea is without having to find the footnote at the bottom of the page or at the end of the paper.

Another major change in documenting sources is what was once called the bibliography page. Depending on the specific discipline or course for which you are writing the paper, you will probably use either the MLA (Modern Language Association) or the APA (American Psychological Association) form of documentation. If you are unsure which one to use, check with your instructor. The rest of this chapter will discuss parenthetical citations and the documentation that appears at the end of the paper.

Documentation is a twofold process: it involves crediting the source not only within the paper but also at the end of the paper in the "Works Cited" (for MLA) or "References" (for APA) section. Papers that use outside sources, whether it be summaries, paraphrases, or direct quotes, require *both* kinds of documentation.

Not only is accuracy essential when crediting your sources, it is also necessary when documenting your sources because you want to provide correct information should your audience want to read more of the source than you have provided. Think of documentation as a map that will lead your readers to exactly where you found the material you have summarized, paraphrased, or quoted. Documentation is one professional helping another in locating the information you found pertinent to the topic. Just as cartographers must be accurate in making maps, so too must you be accurate in documenting your sources. Correct documentation is *not* busy work. It is a way to foster an intellectual conversation among interested parties.

What follows are examples of the most frequently used citation of sources for both MLA and APA formats, as well as models of both MLA and APA forms that frequently appear on the "Works Cited" page for MLA and "References" page for APA. A complete list and discussion of the MLA form can be found in the MLA *Handbook for Writers of Research Papers*, 4th ed., by Joseph Gibaldi (New York: MLA, 1995). For a complete manual for the APA format, refer to the *Publication Manual of the American Psychological Association*, 4th ed. (Washington, DC: APA, 1994).

MLA Documentation

In-text citations take the form of parenthetical references. Citations include only the author's name and the page number(s) on which the material appears. A full citation is given in the "Works Cited" section at the end of the paper. If you mention the author's name in the sentence, do not repeat the name in the citation; provide just the page reference. When no author is given for the source you are using, provide a brief form of the title, followed by the appropriate page number(s). No comma is needed between the name and the page reference. Here are some examples of correct MLA parenthetical citations using William A. Henry III's article, which appears in Part 2 of this book:

William A. Henry III asserts that the quest to offer students an education, no matter what their skills and interests, has weakened the entire educational system (63–5). [An example of crediting a summary of Henry's argument. No name is needed in the parenthetical citation, since his name is mentioned in the sentence.]

Colleges educate more people for professional fields than are needed to fill positions (Henry 64). [An example of crediting Henry's idea. His name appears because it is not mentioned in the sentence.]

When decrying what has happened to education, Henry claims that "No longer a mark of distinction or proof of achievement, a college education is these days a mere rite of passage, a capstone to adolescent party time" (63). [An example of a direct quote from Henry's article. No name is needed in the parenthetical citation, since his name appears in the sentence.]

Note: If a direct quotation exceeds four typed lines, indent one inch or ten spaces to block the quotation, and double-space.

The MLA format is used widely in the humanities. What follows is a list of the correct format:

- "Works Cited" should be centered an inch from the top of the page.
- Follow the order that appears in nearly all MLA "Works Cited" forms of documentation: Last name of author, first name of author, title of publication, place of publication, publisher, year of publication, and, when applicable, page number(s).
- All entries should appear on the "Works Cited" page in alphabetical order of author's name or title of the work.
- If no author is listed, use the first major word of the title to retain the alphabetical order of the entries.
- Put names of articles in quotation marks.
- Capitalize all major words in the title.
- If an entry exceeds one line, indent one-half inch or five spaces for all succeeding lines.
- All lines on the "Works Cited" page should be double-spaced.

Books

General format for MLA documentation of books:

Author. *Title of Book.* Edition. City of publication: Publisher, Year of publication.

If you can set italics on your computer (as shown above), check with your instructor to see if he or she would prefer italics or the more traditional underlining.

Book with One Author

Schor, Juliet B. *The Overworked American: The Unexpected Decline of Leisure.* New York: Basic, 1992.

For more than one book by the same author, after citing the author's name for the first book, use three hyphens instead of repeating the author's name, and continue the documentation.

Book with Two Authors

Lauer, Janice M., and J. William Asher. *Composition Research: Empirical Designs*. New York: Oxford, 1988.

Book with Three Authors

Young, Richard E., Alton Becker, and Kenneth L. Pike. *Rhetoric: Discovery and Change*. New York: Harcourt, 1970.

For a book with more than three authors, name only the first, then add *et al.* (which stands for "and others"), and follow the rest of the form.

Book Authored by an Organization or Group

Reader's Digest. *Fix-It-Yourself Manual*. Pleasantville, NY: Reader's Digest, 1977.

Translation

Derrida, Jacques. *Of Grammatology*. Trans. Gayatri Chakravorty Spivak. Baltimore: Johns Hopkins UP, 1976.

Edited Book

Rosen, Michael J., ed. *The Company of Dogs: Twenty-One Stories by Contemporary Masters*. New York: Doubleday, 1990.

Work in an Anthology or Collection

Britton, James. "Language and Learning Across the Curriculum." *Fforum: Essays on Theory and Practice in the Teaching of Writing*. Ed. Patricia L. Stock. Upper Montclair, NJ: Boynton/Cook, 1983. 221–24.

Reprinted Book

Herbert, Frank. *Dune*. 1965. New York: Berkley, 1977.

An Unpublished Dissertation

Durant, Raphael E. "The Alcoholic in Treatment: A Study of Anxiety and Self-Actualization." Diss. U of Akron, 1989.

Forewords, Prefaces, Introductions, and Afterwords

Erdrich, Louise. Foreword. *The Broken Cord*. By Michael Dorris. New York: HarperCollins, 1989. iv–xx.

Articles in Journals, Magazines, and Newspapers

General format for MLA documentation of articles:

Author's last name, author's first name. "Title of Article." *Journal or Magazine Title* volume number (date of publication): inclusive pages.

Scholarly Article in a Journal with Continuous Pagination

Perl, Sondra. "Understanding Composing." *College Composition and Communication* 31 (1980): 363–369.

Review

Block, J. H. "Debatable Conclusions about Sex Differences." Rev. of *The Psychology of Sex Differences*, by E. E. Maccoby and C. N. Jacklin. *Contemporary Psychology* Aug. 1976: 517–522.

Magazine Article

Dowie, Mark. "Light Green: Environmentalism Today." *Utne Reader* July-Aug. 1994: 73–78.

For unsigned articles in magazines, begin the citation with the title of the article and continue the documentation.

Newspaper Article

> Hockenberry, John. "Limited Seating on Broadway." *New York Times* 6 Apr. 1992: 2:1+.

[The 1+ indicates that the article began on page 1 and was continued elsewhere in the newspaper.]

Anonymous Article

> "Building a New Midwest." *Akron Beacon Journal* 25 July 1994: B:1+.

Signed Newspaper Editorial

> Feinberg, Richard. "Tenure and the Political Microscope." Editorial. *Akron Beacon Journal* 19 July 1994: 7-A.

Unsigned Newspaper Editorial

> "Rwandan Tragedy." Editorial. *Akron Beacon Journal* 19 July 1994: 6-A.

Letter to the Editor

> Clough, Gene. Letter. *Chronicle of Higher Education* 32 (1994): B3.

Miscellaneous Forms

Published Interview

> Klass, Perri. Interview. *Writing on the Edge.* By Dale Flynn. Davis, CA: U of CA, 1992. 88–97.

Personal Interview

> Buffett, Jimmy. Personal interview. 30 Aug. 1991.

Personal Correspondence

> Rich, Adrienne. Letter to the author. 3 Apr. 1978.

Lecture

> Jamison, Frederic. "Beyond Deconstruction." Michigan State University, East Lansing. 22 Feb. 1980.

Database Source

> Dickerson, Mary Jane. *A Voice of One's Own: Creating Writing Identities.* ERIC, 1988. ED 294 178.

Computer Software

> *Encarta '95.* Computer software. Microsoft, 1994.

Television Program

> "Conceiving the Future." *Medicine at the Crossroads.* Narr. Melvin Konner. PBS. 5 June 1994.

Film

> *Do the Right Thing.* Dir. Spike Lee. Videocassette. Paramount, 1989.

Sample MLA Paper

The following sample paper, which argues for a new view of multiculturalism, uses the MLA documentation system.

Amy Pruneski

English Composition II

Professor Kaufman

October 11, 1994

Multiculturalism on the College Campus

To many people, multiculturalism is a black and white issue, but in reality it is much more than that. Multiculturalism can be seen as an example of "variety being the spice of life." This idea encompasses not only differences in race but those in religion, gender, and sexual preference as well. Because of the flood of diverse students onto college campuses, the debate over multiculturalism has become more prevalent. Forcing multiculturalistic ideas on students is not a solution to any of the problems. As Shelby Steele, author of a book on race relations, states, "I think universities should emphasize commonality as a higher value than diversity and pluralism . . . (120).

In the 1960s, for the first time, racial equality was enforceable by law. Many people were offended by this. Due to students' dislike toward these new policies, riots and protests became fairly common on college campuses. Steele believes some of these uprisings were ". . . born of the rub between racial differences and a settling, the campus itself, devoted to interaction and equality" (106).

In 1972, in an effort to remedy the turmoil of the past decade, the government passed the Equal Employment Opportunity Act. Affirmative action was a part of this act. Seemingly a good idea, affirmative action has caused delays for the acceptance of multiculturalism. Quotas are perhaps the most controversial aspect of affirmative action. Many legal battles have been fought over whether quotas are constitutional. Steele, an African-American, believes that affirmative action leads to a "myth of . . . inferiority" (107) in black students.

When I recently interviewed students at my school, the University of Akron, most of them said that affirmative action has served its purpose and is no longer needed. They further stated that because some degree programs (e.g., business and engineering) are very competitive, students should have to be admitted on their merit, not to fill a quota. These sentiments are evident on other campuses as well: in an interview with Steele, a U.C.L.A. student stated, "They [my classmates] see me as an affirmative action case" (108). These feelings of superiority and inferiority cause further separation of students on college campuses. Affirmative action is a government-enforced policy, and resentful feelings among student have developed on college campuses. The argument over affirmative action is far from being settled. It is not surprising, then, that

a recent CBS news broadcast noted that the Supreme
Court's docket includes four cases that pertain to
affirmative action.

Debaters on both sides of the multiculturalism
battle agree that pushing the issue can sometimes
make matters worse. George Will, a strong opponent of
affirmative action, states that ". . . there is ample
evidence of the Balkanization of American's intellectual life" (270). This type of break-up is possibly caused by the strong opinions many college
students bring with them to the campus. If, for example, a prejudiced student is forced to take an
African-art-appreciation class, that one class is unlikely to change the views he or she has had for
years concerning African-Americans. Will summarizes
his thoughts by saying:

> Some policies instituted in the name of
> "multiculturalism" are not celebrations of
> the pluralism from which American unity is
> woven. Some of these policies are capitula-
> tion: they involve withdrawal from the
> challenge of finding and teaching common
> ground on which Americans can stand togeth-
> er--not the little patches of fenced-off
> turf for irritable groups, but the common
> ground of citizenship in the nation. (273)

Today, multicultural policies are enacted to
show sensitivity to a certain group, but as Will remarks, even sensitivity is good only "up to a point"
(273). Professor Troy Duster of the University of

Pruneski 4

California at Berkeley, a supporter of multiculturalism, interviewed students at his university to assist
him in comprising a list of "don'ts" when it comes to
diversity awareness (254). First on the list was re-
moval of sensitivity sessions. To raise the human
consciousness about gender, racial, or homophobic issues, much more than a three-hour sensitivity session
is needed.

Multiculturalism does have its advantages: "In
the last two decades the Law Center's national reputation has grown significantly. This is exactly the
period in which we have achieved much greater diversity in our faculty, student body, and administration," claims Dean Judith Areen of Georgetown Law
Center (12). This example helps to prove that if multiculturalism is allowed to develop, it can strength-
en a university. Universities such as Georgetown have
gained recognition for their diversity. Other universities may not be as widely known, but their students will recognize what a wonderful opportunity
they have to learn about groups unlike themselves if
multicultural programs are offered.

This fact will become more important in the future as the job market becomes more globalized. Signs
of this are apparent now as companies go to Kuwait
and many other nations to help build businesses. How
are these businesses going to survive without the two
cultures cooperating? With the new diverse group of
college students learning about different cultures,
there is hope.

The <u>Sesame Street</u> and <u>Cosby Show</u> generations have a unique opportunity. These people are the first to have the chance to attend desegregated schools from pre-school through post-secondary school. As Steele remarks, "College students . . . have had more opportunities to know each other than any previous generation in American history" (104). When people are young, their minds are like a blank computer disk just waiting to be filled. It doesn't matter to many young children that they are building a Lego house with someone of a different race or religion. Learning to work together to build the Lego house is the cornerstone for building skyscrapers in the future. Cooperation like this can only help improve the way race and other diversities are perceived. With this new understanding, the generation born in the mid-1970s should have a better chance at helping this newly developing world market to succeed.

Multiculturalism is not something that needs a quick fix. The solution is not a simple one. Students don't have to become part of a diverse culture or even know a culture's history to make the idea of multiculturalism work. They just have to accept that it exists. If universities would focus on this acceptance, some of the burning tensions might be extinguished. <u>Los Angeles Times</u> reporter James O. Freeman supports this idea when he writes,

> Students attending colleges and universities today--white and black, majority and

Pruneski 6

minority--are part of a transitional generation, the members of which are learning
to relate to one another in ways not yet
entirely familiar and comfortable. But they
are doing so with achievement of true
equality than this country has yet known.
(17)

Works Cited

Areen, Judith. "Diversity Fosters Excellence." The Washington Post 26 May 1991, sec.1: 1+.

"CBS Evening News." Harry Smith, news anchor. CBS. 7 October 1994.

Duster, Troy. "Universities Should Strive for a Culturally Diverse Student Body." Education in America. Ed. Charles P. Cozic. San Diego: Greenhaven, 1992.

Freeman, James O. "Positive Race Relations." Los Angeles Times 26 August 1991, sec.1: 1+.

Steele, Shelby. The Content of our Character. New York: St. Martin's, 1990.

Will, George F. "Multiculturalism Harms Higher Education." Education in America Ed. Charles P. Cozic. San Diego: Greenhaven, 1992.

APA Documentation

In-text citations take the form of parenthetical references. Citations include only the author's name and the year of publication, separated by a comma. When the author is named in the sentence, the year of publication should appear after his or her name. Include page number(s) for specific parts of the source and for all direct quotes. Here are some examples of correct APA citations using William A. Henry III's "In Defense of Elitism," which appears in Part 2 of this book.

> William A. Henry III (1994) asserts that the quest to offer students an education no matter what their skills or interests, has weakened the entire education system (63-5). [An example of including the year of publication after the author's name in a summary of his article.]

> Colleges educate more people for professional fields than are needed to fill positions (Henry, 1994). [An example of the author's name followed by a comma and the year of publication.]

> When decrying what has happened to education, Henry claims that "No longer a mark of distinction or proof of achievement, a college education is these days a mere rite of passage, a capstone to adolescent party time" (Henry, 1992, p. 63). [An example of the direct quote being credited to the author, followed by the date of publication, and the specific page on which the quote appeared.]

Note: If a direct quotation exceeds four typed lines, indent ten spaces to block, and double-space.

Used primarily in the social sciences, the APA format shares many features of the MLA format, but it differs in some of the ways in which notations are made. Here is a list of the correct ways to use APA documentation:

- Center "References" at the top of the documentation page.
- The correct APA order is as follows: last name of author, initials of author, date of publication in parentheses, place of publication, and publisher.
- Alphabetize by the author's last name.

- Use initials instead of first names.
- Only the first word of a book title is capitalized.
- Titles of articles are not put in quotation marks.
- If the entry exceeds one line, indent three spaces for all succeeding lines.
- All lines on the "References" page should be double-spaced.
- A period should follow each of the elements in the documentation. One space follows each period, comma, semicolon, and colon.

Books

General APA format for documenting books:

Author. (Year of Publication). Title of book. City of publication: Publisher.

Book with One Author

Schor, J. (1992). *The overworked American: the unexpected decline of leisure*. New York: Basic.

For two or more books by the same author, repeat the author's last name and initial of first name, and continue the documentation.

Book with Two Authors

Lauer, J., & Asher, J. W. (1988). *Composition research: empirical designs*. New York: Oxford.

[Notice that the ampersand (&) is used in lieu of the word "and" in citations and documentation, but never when referring to the authors in the text of the paper.]

Book with Three Authors

Young, R., Becker, A., & Pike, K. L. (1970). *Rhetoric: discovery and change*. New York: Harcourt.

For books with six or more authors or editors, you may use *et al.*

Book Authored by a Group or an Organization

Reader's Digest. (1977). *Fix-it-yourself manual.* Pleasantville, NY: Reader's Digest.

Translation

Derrida, J. (1976). *Of grammatology.* (G. Spivak, Trans.) Baltimore: Johns Hopkins UP.

Edited Book

Rosen, M. (Ed.). (1990). *The company of dogs: twenty-one stories by contemporary masters.* New York: Doubleday.

Work in an Anthology or Collection

Britton, J. (1983). Language and learning across the curriculum. In Stock, P. (Ed.), *Fforum: essays on theory and practice in the teaching of writing.* (pp. 221–224). Upper Montclair, NJ: Boynton/Cook.

Reprint

Herbert, F. (1977). *Dune.* New York: Berkley. (Original work published 1965).

Dissertation

Durant, R. (1989). *The alcoholic in treatment: a study of anxiety and self-actualization.* Unpublished doctoral dissertation, University of Akron, Ohio.

Foreword, Preface, Introduction, and Afterword

Erdrich, L. (1989). Foreword. In M. Dorris, *The broken cord.* New York: HarperCollins.

Articles in Journals, Magazines, and Newspapers

General APA format for documenting articles:

> Author's Last Name, initial of author's first name. (Date of Publication). Title of article. *Journal or magazine, volume number*, inclusive pages.

Scholarly Article

> Perl, S. (1980). Understanding composing. *College composition and communication, 13*, 363–369.

Review

> Block, J. H. (1976). Debatable conclusions about sex differences. [Review of the book *The psychology of sex differences*]. *Contemporary psychology, 39*, 517–522.

Magazine Article

> Dowie, M. (1994, July/August). Light green: environmentalism today. *Utne reader*, 73–78.

Newspaper Article

> Hockenberry, J. (1992, April 6). Limited seating on Broadway. *New York Times*, sec. 2, p. 1, p. 4.

Anonymous Newspaper Article

> Building a new midwest. (1994, July 24). *Akron beacon journal*, p. B1, p. B7.

Signed Newspaper Editorial

> Feinberg, R. (1994, July 19). Tenure and the political microscope [Editorial]. *Akron beacon journal*, p. A7.

Unsigned Newspaper Editorial

Rwandan tragedy (1994, July 19). [Editorial]. *Akron beacon journal*, p. A6.

Letter to the Editor

Clough, G. (1994, June 30). [Letter to the editor]. *Chronicle of higher education*, p. B3.

Miscellaneous Forms

Published Interview

Klass, P. (1992). The biorhythms of a writer [Interview with Perri Klass]. *Writing on the edge*, pp. 88–97.

Personal Interview

Buffett, J. (1991, 30 August). [Personal interview].

[Although included in the in-text citation, not all types of personal communication are required in the "References" in the APA format.]

Personal Correspondence

Rich, A. (personal communication, April 3, 1978).

Lecture

Jamison, F. (1980, February 22). *Beyond deconstruction.* Michigan State University, East Lansing, MI.

Database Source

Dickerson, M. J. (1988, March). *A voice of one's own: creating written identities.* Paper presented at the Conference on College Composition and Communication, St. Louis. [ERIC Document Reproduction Service No. ED 294 178].

Computer Software

Microsoft. (1994). *Encarta '95*. [Computer program].

Television Program

Konner, M. (1994). Conceiving the future. In M. Konner
(Producer), *Medicine at the crossroads*. New York:WNET.

Film

Do the right thing. (1989). Videotape. Directed by Spike Lee.
Hollywood, CA. Paramount, 1989. 120 min.

Sample APA Paper

The following sample paper, which follows the APA citation system,
argues that children fare better when cared for at home rather than in
day care.

Day Care vs. Home Care: Is There Really a Choice?

Nancy Dawson

English Composition II

Ms. Hoffman

December 3, 1994

Abstract

This paper examines the debate concerning whether child care or home care is better for raising children. Research on both sides of the issue is reported before the paper finally argues that home care is preferable.

Day Care vs. Home Care: Is There Really a Choice?

No one would argue that the family is in the midst of continual change. The "Ozzie and Harriet" style family of two parents in the same household, one working, one at home, is no longer in the majority. Today, fewer than 22% of households are made up of the male breadwinner/female homemaker pattern, compared to 80% in 1950. In 1960, 19% of women with children under six years old were working; today that number has risen to 58%, and nearly one-third of these are women with babies under seven months old. This is obviously creating major changes in the upbringing of this young generation.

Studies on the effect of these changes on the family, and specifically the young children, are still in progress and results are just now beginning to be reported. The debate, however, is continually raging. Is this generation being harmed by less direct parental care? Or is the household enhanced by the resulting increased income and potential for better organization? The issue is emotional and complicated, and evidence for both sides can be found.

Most working parents would like to know that their jobs have little or no adverse impact on their children. Government statistics show that 90% of women who work say they "have" to work, not just that they want to. Whether by necessity or by choice, many of these parents feel they can still provide adequate

care for their children, without harm to their development. There has, in fact, been research done supporting their claim. Trends from some present
research show that there is no significant relationship between maternal employment and children's development from infancy through school-entry years.
In fact, these same studies often showed that employed mothers held higher educational attitudes for
their young children and that their households
watched less TV than those with a parent at home
(Gottfried, 1988, p. 51). This would tend to support
the idea that both parents can pursue careers and
small children can still have normal, well-adjusted
lives.

Some parents even go beyond this. They assert
that their children actually benefit from the separation resulting from their employment. Anthropologist
Margaret Mead wrote that it is a mistake to assume
that "all [child-mother] separation even for a few
days, is inevitably damaging" and that "cross-cul-
tural studies suggest that adjustment is most facil-
itated if the child is cared for by many warm,
friendly people" (Berg, 1986, p. 59). Certain sociologists go so far as to say that when both parents
have fulfilling careers, the family benefits more
than if one parent were at home. They contend that
satisfied career-oriented adults make better people,
and therefore, better parents. Toby Parcel and Elizabeth Menaghan, professors of sociology at Ohio State

Day Care 5

University have done a study on the effect of a mother's work on her children's intellectual development.
They say that "if she has a complex, interesting job
with a high degree of autonomy, her children are more
likely to benefit from her returning to work somewhere between the ages of birth to 3 years and may
even show adverse effects if she doesn't" (qtd. in
Little, 1994, p. 18).

This leads us to the day-care portion of the
issue, because ultimately this is where these children are spending the majority of their waking
hours. It is important to see, therefore, what effect this day care is having on them. Today's working parents are constantly calling for improved and
increased day-care choices, because effective, caring environments in day care are vital to the support these parents need. John Bowlby, a psychiatrist
who has done many studies on child development, supports this somewhat by saying that "as long as a
mother substitute behaves in an appropriately mothering way towards a child, the child will respond in
the same way as another child would treat her natural mother" (qtd. in Mullan 1987, p. 45). According
to Bowlby, children in adequate day-care environments thrive exactly like their home-cared counterparts. This is the reason, working parents say, that
the government needs to step in to provide these
types of day-care surroundings. Dr. Sandra Scarr,
chairperson of the Department of Psychology at the

University of Virginia, says that, "Who administers
the care and where it takes place are not nearly so
important as the quality" (Time-Life, 1987, p. 18).

Looking at these results might lead us to believe, therefore, that both parents can be out of the
home for most of the day without adverse effect on
their small children. But is this really the case?
Are we being misled by these results, perhaps toward
an answer that, as a society turning more and more
into two-wage-earner families, is one we want to
find? It is much easier to go ahead with our lives if
we think we can find evidence that supports our decision. But it is necessary to take a closer look at
this "evidence."

First of all, results coming from studies like
the above examples must be looked at critically. When
the subject matter is the psychological aspect of
human life, it is almost impossible to study it sci-
entifically. "We act upon the world, we change our
behavior over time, indeed we are often motivated unconsciously. The best we can hope for are plausible
answers to our own subjective questions; if we claim
anything else we will be in trouble. Investigators,
in the way they go about their research [in child
psychology] and in the manner in which they attempt
to prove their hypotheses, invariably find what they
are looking for--in other words, they will ensure
that their world view is not contaminated by contrary
facts" (Mullan, 1987, p. 56). This is especially true

when the subject is as politically volatile as that
of working mothers.

Secondly, most of the research now being reported follows children through early childhood or,
at most, through adolescence. But the effects of a
major change in family structure go beyond the teen
years. There is little or no research on longer-term
effects, into adulthood, or the impact on society in
general, related to generations now being raised for
the most part by someone other than a parent. It is
important to study more broad, extensive consequences, and because this trend is so recent, there
has not been time to see these effects. There are
also other questions to be explored that could be
secondary impacts of both parents working. One might
be how divorce rates are related to two-earner families. There is certainly no question that there is
added stress put on a household when both parents
work, especially with small children. What effect is
this having on the marriage? This ultimately greatly
effects the children involved.

Even if we decide to rely on research evidence,
we can find equal results showing negative consequences on children. One of the early predictors of
adult violent crimes is a childhood history of maternal deprivation or poor father identification, or
both (Dutile, _et al._, 1982, p. 14). The actual definition of what constitutes "deprivation" is debated.
Other research shows that there is no question that

Day Care 8

parents who work have less time to spend with their
children. Between 1973 and 1985, men and women reported one-third less time available for leisure activities, down from 26 to less than 18 hours per week
(Levitan, et al., 1988, p. 104). As for women "needing" to work, surveys have shown that as many as 8
out of 10 mothers who work would continue to do so
even if all financial conditions were removed.
Whether they need to or not, many women are working
because they want to.

It seems that most mothers report as much anxiety as satisfaction relating to their decisions to
leave the home for careers. Guilt, due to uncertain-
ty, is a problem experienced by many working mothers. Historically, there has been much emphasis
placed on the importance of infant/mother bonding
and it is still not clear how maternal employment is
affecting this bonding. Most mothers sense that they
are taking a chance. One mother stated, "I feel so
guilty because my baby is so little, and I am at
work eight hours a day . . . I'm guilty because I
don't feel like I'm a good mother" (Berg, 1986, p.
58). This guilt can have its own consequences. Many
parents find themselves overcompensating--giving in
when they shouldn't, because of this guilt. Another
mother says, "Because I work, I give in more, over-
compensate with toys," while another states, "I
cover guilt when traveling with presents" (Berg,
1986, p. 83). This only compounds the problems, and

Day Care 9

clearly has an eventual adverse effect on the child.
"Unlike our love or affection, the presents we heap
on our children cannot comfort them or provide any
lasting security; this causes them constantly to
long for more, a longing that is perpetuated by its
very insatiability" (Berg, 1986, p. 83).

One of the largest issues is day care, and like
other aspects of this issue, the results of research
can be misleading. As stated above, studies can show
that children in "adequate" day care environments
show no ill effects. This is where the problem lies:
are most day care centers "adequate"? What does this
really mean? Ross Thompson, in studying the effect of
infant day care maintains:

> Those who conclude that existing research pro-
> vides no basis for concern would be as guilty of
> reaching premature conclusions from this evi-
> dence as those who argue that infant day care is
> a cause for concern. In addition to the research
> reviewed earlier, we are wise to think careful-
> ly and cautiously about the effects of infant
> care because of the limitations experienced by
> many young families in the cost of care they can
> afford, the generally high turnover of child
> care workers, widespread social perceptions that
> caring for young children is essentially "un-
> skilled" labor, and the very limited regulatory
> standards and enforcement processes used to en-
> sure minimal health and safety requirements. In

fact, however, there is also much that we do not know concerning its development consequences. (Berg, 1986, p. 85).

In truth, day care was initiated not as an enhancement to child development, but as a convenience to the parent. Children did not "insist that both parents work in order to amass greater material wealth. This is not a moral argument: the point is that day care was introduced for the adult's benefit; and investigations into whether or not it is helpful or damaging for the child come later. Day care is about adult economics, adult behavior and adult desires" (Mullan, 1987, p. 95).

The one thing that all researchers seem to agree on is that evidence does not clearly show whether day care and the other consequences of both parents working is positive or negative on the child. And, in the end, this is where all the arguments for two parents working breaks down. With all the conflicting results, should we really be taking chances with the upbringing of an entire generation, and generations beyond? Can we really afford to "wait" for conclusive evidence, on the chance that this evidence will fall "for" our children rather than "against"?

One of the most disturbing trends in today's society is the increasing tendency to do what is best for "me" without fully considering the consequences. One mother summed up the attitude many of today's working parents have: "I find myself asking, 'Am I doing the right thing?' I guess in the end, we'll all muddle along with our kids, and thirty years from now we'll see if they're geniuses or ax murderers" (Darling, 1994, p. 126). She may have been exaggerating, but these are lives we are gambling with. Parents who work full-time do so for material gain or personal fulfillment, even though the repercussions on their children are not fully understood. This is dangerous and often unnecessary.

There are situations where one might say that day care is unavoidable, such as in a single-parent household. However, most of these situations also result from a parental choice--divorce. This is an area of great controversy, and another example, no matter what the cause, of the consequences on children not being fully understood. Again, the parent makes the choice for him- or herself, and the child suffers the consequences. The cases where the single parents must work by no choice of their own--death of a spouse-- are rare, especially those with preschool children involved.

We <u>must</u> begin to view the raising of future generations as being of highest importance. This is not an area for taking chances, rather one where we must make sacrifices in order to do it well. And there are plenty of sacrifices to be made, whether it be a lower standard of living, less perceived "challenge" in staying home, or working harder at making a marriage work. Even though it is occasionally the father who chooses to stay home, most studies focus on the mother working, since she has traditionally been

Day Care 12

the one at home, and both parents need to concentrate on the question of the best environment for their children. As Mullan (1987) contends, "The only way we can create the 'good and just' society is through new people. Those new people can only come from women. But in order to make motherhood work . . . it has to be seen quite simply as the most important piece of work anyone can do" (p. 176), not something on which we can ill afford to gamble.

Day Care 13

REFERENCES

Beard, L. (1993, September). Family life in the 90s. Good housekeeping, 150-156.

Berg, B. (1986). The crisis of the working mother. New York: Summit Books.

Darling, L. (1994, March). What's maternally correct? Redbook, 74-77.

Dutile, F., Foust, C., & Webster, D. R. (1992). Early childhood intervention and juvenile delinquency. Lexington: Lexington Books.

Gottfried, A., & Gottfried, A. (Eds.). (1988). Maternal employment and children's development. New York: Plenum.

Lerner, J., & Galambos, N. (1991). Employed mothers and their children. New York: Garland.

Levitan, S., Belous, R., & Gallo, F. (1988). What's happening to the American family? Baltimore: Johns Hopkins.

Little, H. (1994, November 1). The whole family benefits if mom's career is challenging. The Plain Dealer, p. E2.

Mullan, B. (1987). Are mothers really necessary? New York: Weidenfeld & Nicolson.

Schroeder, P. (1989). Champion of the great American family. New York: Random House.

Time-Life, Inc. (1987). When others care for your child. Alexandria: Time-Life Books.

PREPARING THE MANUSCRIPT

No matter what kind of documentation you use (MLA, APA, or any other), type on one side of 8½-by-11-inch white typing paper. Leave 1–1½-inch margins on all sides, and double-space throughout. Number the pages sequentially in the top right-hand corner.

For papers that require MLA documentation, provide a title page if your instructor requires one. The title page should include the title of your paper, your name, the instructor's name, the name of the course, and the date. All of these entries should be double-spaced and centered on the page. Type your name before each page number, so that your instructor will know the paper is yours in case any pages become misplaced. Do not put the title of your paper in quotation marks.

For papers that use APA documentation, no title page is required unless you include an abstract (see model on page 142). An abstract page follows the title page and consists of a brief one-paragraph summary or abstract of your paper. If you do not have a title page, on the first page of your paper, type your name, the course name, the instructor's name, and the date flush left on successive lines. Double space each of these lines, and then type the title of your paper, centered on the page. Do not put the title of your paper in quotation marks. On the top right-hand corner of each page, type a short title of your paper and the page number as a "running head" so that your instructor will know the page is yours in case any pages become misplaced.

If you are unsure of the format your instructor prefers, ask him or her, preferably before you begin your research. Knowing which format to use will save you from having to convert your documentation into another format in the middle or at the end of your project.

PART 2

READINGS FOR DISCUSSION AND ANALYSIS

CHAPTER 6

EDUCATION

How to Make People Smaller Than They Are

Norman Cousins

> Norman Cousins was born in 1915 and died in 1990. He attended Columbia University and served as the editor of the *Saturday Review* for thirty-eight years. Cousins is the author of numerous books, including *Who Speaks for Man?* (1953), *Present Tense* (1967), *The Celebration of Life* (1974), *The Quest for Immortality* (1974), and *Anatomy of an Illness as Perceived by the Patient: Reflections on Healing and Regeneration* (1979). From 1978 until his death, he was on the medical faculty at UCLA. In 1990, Cousins was awarded the Albert Schweitzer Prize for Humanitarianism. In the following selection, which first appeared in the *Saturday Review* in 1978, Cousins reflects on the "increasing vocationalization of our colleges and universities" and discusses his reasons for promoting the idea that schools should pay more attention to the humanities.

1   Three months ago in this space we wrote about the costly retreat from the humanities on all the levels of American education. Since that time, we have had occasion to visit a number of campuses and have been troubled to find that the general situation is even more serious that we had thought. It has become apparent to us that one of the biggest problems confronting American education today is the increasing vocationalization of our colleges and universities. Throughout the country, schools are under pressure to become job-training centers and employment agencies.

2   The pressure comes mainly from two sources. One is the growing determination of many citizens to reduce taxes—understandable and even commendable in itself, but irrational and irresponsible when connected to the reduction or dismantling of vital public services. The second source of pressure comes from parents and students who tend to scorn courses of study that do not teach people how to become attractive to employers in a rapidly tightening job market.

3   It is absurd to believe that the development of skills does not also require the systematic development of the human mind. Education is being measured more by the size of the benefits the individual can extract from society than by the extent to which the individual can come into possession of his or her full powers. The result is that the life-giving juices are in danger of being drained out of education.

4   Emphasis on "practicalities" is being characterized by the subordination of words to numbers. History is seen not as essential experience to be transmitted to new generations, but as abstractions that carry dank odors. Art is regarded as something that calls for indulgence or patronage and that has no place among the practical realities. Political science is viewed more as a specialized subject for people who want to go into politics than as an opportunity for citizens to develop a knowledgeable relationship with the systems by which human societies are governed. Finally, literature and philosophy are assigned the role of add-ons—intellectual adornments that have nothing to do with "genuine" education.

5   Instead of trying to shrink the liberal arts, the American people ought to be putting pressure on colleges and universities to increase the ratio of the humanities to the sciences. Most serious studies of medical-school curricula in recent years have called attention to the stark gaps in the liberal education of medical students. The experts agree that the schools shouldn't leave it up to students to close those gaps.

6   The irony of the emphasis being placed on careers is that nothing is more valuable for anyone who has had a professional or vocational education than to be able to deal with abstractions or complexities, or to feel comfortable with subtleties of thought or language, or to think sequentially. The doctor who knows only disease is at a disadvantage alongside the doctor who knows at least as much about people as he does about pathological organisms. The lawyer who argues in court from a narrow legal base is no match for the lawyer who can connect legal precedents to historical experience and who employs wide-ranging intellectual resources. The business executive whose competence in general management is bolstered by an artistic ability to deal with people is of prime value to his company. For the technologist, the engineering of consent can be just as important as the engineering of moving parts. In all these respects, the liberal arts have much to offer. Just in terms of career preparation, therefore, a student is shortchanging himself by short-cutting the humanities.

7   But even if it could be demonstrated that the humanities contribute nothing directly to a job, they would still be an essential part of the educational equipment of any person who wants to come to terms with life. The humanities would be expendable only if human beings didn't have to make decisions that affect their lives and the lives of others; if the human past

never existed or had nothing to tell us about the present; if thought process-es were irrelevant to the achievement of purpose; if creativity was beyond the human mind and had nothing to do with the joy of living; if human re-lationships were random aspects of life; if human beings never had to cope with panic or pain, or if they never had to anticipate the connection be-tween cause and effect; if all the mysteries of mind and nature were fully plumbed; and if no special demands arose from the accident of being born a human being instead of a hen or a hog.

8   Finally, there would be good reason to eliminate the humanities if a free society were not absolutely dependent on a functioning citizenry. If the main purpose of a university is job training, then the underlying philosophy of our government has little meaning. The debates that went into the mak-ing of American society concerned not just institutions or governing prin-ciples but the capacity of humans to sustain those institutions. Whatever the disagreements were over other issues at the American Constitutional Con-vention, the fundamental question sensed by everyone, a question that lay over the entire assembly, was whether the people themselves would under-stand what it meant to hold the ultimate power of society, and whether they had enough of a sense of history and destiny to know where they had been and where they ought to be going.

9   Jefferson was prouder of having been the founder of the University of Virginia than of having been President of the United States. He knew that the educated and developed mind was the best assurance that a political system could be made to work—a system based on the informed consent of the governed. If this idea fails, then all the saved tax dollars in the world will not be enough to prevent the nation from turning on itself.

Discussion Questions

1. What do you think Cousins means by the title of his viewpoint?

2. For what audience do you think Cousins was aiming his writing: Students? Parents? Teachers? Advisors? Administrators? Scientists? What leads you to your answer?

3. Cousins assumes that values and sensitivity can be acquired through studying liberal arts. To what extent does this assumption or warrant strengthen or weaken his perspective?

4. How convincing is Cousins in his stance that the liberal arts have much to offer those studying other disciplines? Discuss how his support of the main idea contributes to his viewpoint's credibility.

5. How do you imagine those in medicine, law, business, and technology would react to Cousins' stance? How well does Cousins address opposing points of view?

Why It's So Important
that Our Students Learn
More about Science

V. V. Raman

Varadaraja Venkata Raman was born in Calcutta, India. A graduate of St. Xavier's College (India), Raman earned his M.S. degree from the University of Calcutta and his Ph.D. degree in theoretical physics from the University of Paris. Raman has worked at the Saha Institute of Nuclear Physics in India and chaired the Telecommunications Department at Columbia University. He is currently a professor of physics at the Rochester Institute of Technology. In the following viewpoint, which originally appeared in *The Chronicle of Higher Education,* Raman discusses his reasons for believing that students need to know more about science than they currently do, not because of technological and military reasons as much as "because of the value system it fosters, because of its criteria for the acceptance of points of views as valid propositions."

1 Many prestigious groups, including the National Commission on Excellence in Education, have lamented the sorry plight of science education in this country. They warn us that, unless we correct the situation, it will not be long before the Europeans—and what's even more serious, the Soviets—will overtake us in science, if they haven't already.

2 A great deal of impressive data have been amassed to show that we have been neglecting science education for some time. Invariably such data are related to the numbers of science graduates and teachers as well as to the average test scores of science students.

3 We must produce more science graduates and engineers, the argument goes, because unless we train enough people in these fields, there will be disastrous consequences in vital facets of out technology and defense capability. We need scientists and engineers to push forward the frontiers of

technology so that our industry can turn out more competitive products, and more and better military hardware to keep the country safe from foreign aggressors.

4   I am not concerned here with the merits of such goals and concerns; obviously, to keep a technologically sophisticated society functioning properly we need technically well-trained people. But I do question the notion that we need to teach our students good *science* to accomplish the goals or to respond to the concerns. Technical skills and useful information, yes; but not necessarily science.

5   Indeed, our enormous technological progress has resulted not from teaching good science but rather because ingenious people have been able to exploit scientific knowledge and manage the business end of it as well. It is entirely possible for a thriving and militarily strong industrial society to function successfully with a sizable cadre of technically trained people at various levels who may be as unscientific in their extraprofessional lives as anyone else.

6   It is naive to think that the millions who are engaged in the myriad scientific and technical projects in this country are all scientific in any serious sense of the term. Science is not required to handle or solve specific technical problems.

7   That a strict scientific training is not indispensable for contriving useful gadgetry is amply illustrated in the lives of many competent inventors. From Savery and Newcomen to Edison and the originators of air-conditioning and the helicopter, there have been any number of imaginative and ingenious people who have contributed significantly to the advancement of technology. Conversely, there are some illustrious names in the history of science—Copernicus and Huygens, Pauli and Bohr, to name just a few—who were not directly associated with any major engineering device.

8   Science as an intellectual enterprise has had little impact on the way people in general look at things. It is a sad but not surprising spectacle when well-meaning science teachers and others argue in this day and age from medieval and more ancient perspectives. Respectable school systems are urged to teach mythologies in science courses, because many parents and teachers are convinced that ancient views on the origins of life or of the planet have the same validity as any modern scientific theory. At the other extreme, in some societies so-called scientists have argued that everything from the theory of relativity to the quark model are confirmations of Marxist-Leninist theology.

9   These would be merely amusing instances of human folly were it not for the fact that looking to dogma for ultimate and unalterable truths about the world and history has often led to rigid and belligerent ideologies that

have wrought much harm and ill will among peoples. A fanatical conviction that one's chosen way is the only route to celestial Paradise or terrestrial utopia has been at the root of many international conflicts.

10   What has all this to do with the teaching of science? I contend that science should be taught not simply as a body of useful knowledge clothed in technical vocabulary but as a mode of inquiry into the nature of the perceived world, as an intellectual framework to guide us in the adoption of tentative interpretations of what is observed, and as a world view that is not ultimate truth but is applicable and acceptable only in the context of a given set of available facts. If that point of view is also encouraged in situations beyond technical problems, we may see a world where there is less dogmatism and greater mutual understanding.

11   Science should be taught because of the value system it fosters, because of its criteria for the acceptance of points of view as valid propositions—not because of its potential exploitable results, or even for its beautiful and powerful theories. Science taught without reference to the scope and limits of human knowledge, without alluding to the collective nature of the enterprise, is incomplete.

12   Individual scientists are not always reasonable, of course, nor are they always exclusively motivated by the highest ideals in their quest for truth. The irrationality and self-serving strategies of many scientists, from Galileo and Newton to more recent members of the scientific community, have been amply exposed by historians and philosophers of science. Yet as a collective enterprise, science is a model of dispassionate exploration and objective analysis—more so, perhaps, than any other human endeavor.

13   To challenge the teacher or a text, to raise questions and objections until one is fully satisfied, to reject unsubstantiated propositions—even if they come from the highest authorities—these are among the attitudes we need to develop while teaching science.

14   It is our failure to do so that makes possible the appalling paradox of the twentieth century: the indiscriminate acceptance of medieval—and sometimes pernicious—world views by the masses in many societies, including our own. Not one in a million has looked at a constellation, but practically everyone knows his or her astrological sign, and millions take seriously the inane predictions corresponding to their birthdays that are published in magazines and newspapers. To say nothing of numerology or the pseudo-psychologies and pseudo-religions with mantras that dupe the multitude.

15   The reasons for this situation are twofold. On one hand, the scientific world view is not only difficult to comprehend in its details, it is also far less reassuring than more simplistic and homocentric versions of the universe.

On the other hand, formulas and principles, rather than scientific outlook and critical analysis, are generally taught in our science courses.

16   The spiritual and aesthetic components of the scientific quest are usually neglected in favor of the practical. Efforts must be made to convey to students the thrill and excitement associated with new discoveries, the beauty and harmony of physical laws, the mind-boggling vastness and also the minuteness that constitute the universe, the ultimate simplicity and order underlying scientific processes, the frustrations and triumphs of individual scientists in their struggle to unravel a secret of nature.

17   The Copernican revolution kicked man off the center of the universe. Later, even our sun was shown to be an insignificant speck at the edge of a grand galaxy that in turn is but one of billions in the vast expanse of void. There would seem to be no greater deflater of the ego than the revelations of astronomy. A little reflection, however, should reassure us that we are not all that insignificant.

18   As far as we know, no star ever speculates on the birth and death of human beings; no galaxy computes its distance from Earth; no quasar compares its mighty energy with that of our sun; and there is no pulsar or black hole, no nova or galactic center that is concerned with the human condition.

19   Yet the human mind has penetrated the most distant recesses of space and time, and the most subtle palpitations of physical reality. Aside from electromagnetic radiation, only the human mind is capable of bringing together the past and the present, the near and the distant elements of the universe.

20   All this suggests our pre-eminence in the cosmos, fleeting though it may be. It reminds us that our true glory lies not in our physical dimensions or cosmic location but in our intellectual and spiritual capacities—to think and probe, to feel and reflect, to experience joy and sorrow. We have been made aware of such basic truths most effectively by science. It will be unfortunate if that insight is not experienced by our students—all the more so now, when the myopic equate science with nuclear bombs, acid rain, and pollution.

21   Scientific appraisal invariably transcends cultural and nationalistic narrowness, puts parochial claims of religious distinctiveness in their proper perspective, and reveals the absurdity of racial and sexual prejudices. If we can enrich the awareness resulting from such appraisal by encouraging our students to develop respect, compassion, and consideration for other human beings, how fruitful our educational efforts will prove to be.

Discussion Questions

1. Summarize Raman's main idea and discuss how he supports it.

2. Explain why Raman's distinction between "technical skills" and "science" is important to his stance.

3. Whom do you think Raman envisioned as his audience? What in his viewpoint leads you to your answer?

4. Throughout his viewpoint, Raman cites luminaries in the field of science. What effect does this have on his success in convincing you that students should learn more about science than they currently do?

5. How do you think Norman Cousins would respond to Raman's viewpoint? Identify specific points of agreement and disagreement.

In Defense of Elitism

William A. Henry III

Born in 1950, William A. Henry III earned his B.A. degree from Yale University and did postgraduate work at Boston University. He began his career as an editorial writer for the *Boston Globe* in 1971, and then was the *Globe's* arts critic and state house political reporter before becoming *Time* magazine's television editor and columnist in 1977. Before his death in 1994, Henry was the culture critic for *Time* magazine. Henry is the author of *Visions of America: How We Saw the 1984 Election* (1985) and *The Great One: The Life and Legend of Jackie Gleason* (1992). The following selection is excerpted from his highly controversial book, *In Defense of Elitism* (1994), which was published shortly after his death. In it, Henry discusses the ways in which he sees "mediocrities . . . hav[ing] . . . flooded into colleges" and argues for a "forceful program for diverting intellectual also-rans out of the academy and into the vocational one" by reducing the percentage of high school graduates entering college from "nearly 60 percent to a still generous 33 percent."

1   While all the major social changes in postwar America reflect egalitarianism of some sort, no social evolution has been more willingly egalitarian than opening the academy. Half a century ago, a high school diploma was a significant credential, and college was a privilege for the few. Now high school graduation is virtually automatic for adolescents outside the ghettos and barrios, and college has become a normal way station in the average person's growing up. No longer a mark of distinction or proof of achievement, a college education is these days a mere rite of passage, a capstone to adolescent party time.

2   Some 63 percent of all American high school graduates now go on to some form of further education, according to the Department of Commerce's *Statistical Abstract of the United States,* and the bulk of those continuing students attain at least an associate's degree. Nearly 30 percent of high school

graduates ultimately receive a four-year baccalaureate degree. A quarter or so of the population may seem, to egalitarian eyes, a small and hence elitist slice. But by world standards this is inclusiveness at its most extreme—and its most peculiarly American.

3   For all the socialism of British or French public policy and for all the paternalism of the Japanese, those nations restrict university training to a much smaller percentage of their young, typically by 10 percent to 15 percent. Moreover, they and other First World nations tend to carry the élitism over into judgments about precisely which institution one attends. They rank their universities, colleges and technical schools along a prestige hierarchy much more rigidly gradated—and judged by standards much more widely accepted—than we Americans ever impose on our jumble of public and private institutions.

4   In the sharpest divergence from American values, these other countries tend to separate the college-bound from the quotidian masses in early adolescence, with scant hope for a second chance. For them, higher education is logically confined to those who displayed the most aptitude for lower education.

5   The opening of the academy's doors has imposed great economic costs on the American people while delivering dubious benefits to many of the individuals supposedly being helped. The total bill for higher education is about $150 billion per year, with almost two-thirds of that spent by public institutions run with taxpayer funds. Private colleges and universities also spend the public's money. They get grants for research and the like, and they serve as a conduit for subsidized student loans—many of which are never fully repaid. President Clinton refers to this sort of spending as an investment in human capital. If that is so, it seems reasonable to ask whether the investment pays a worthwhile rate of return. At its present size, the American style of mass higher education probably ought to be judged a mistake—and one based on a giant lie.

6   Why do people go to college? Mostly to make money. This reality is acknowledged in the mass media, which are forever running stories and charts showing how much a college degree contributes to lifetime income (with the more sophisticated publications very occasionally noting the counterweight costs of tuition paid and income forgone during the years of full-time study.)

7   But the equation between college and wealth is not so simple. College graduates unquestionably do better on average economically than those who don't go at all. At the extremes, those with five or more years of college earn about triple the income of those with eight or fewer years of total schooling. Taking more typical examples, one finds that those who stop their educations after earning a four-year degree earn about 1½ times as much as those who stop at the end of high school. These outcomes,

however, reflect other things besides the impact of the degree itself. College graduates are winners in part because colleges attract people who are already winners—people with enough brains and drive that they would do well in almost any generation and under almost any circumstances, with or without formal credentialing.

8   The harder and more meaningful question is whether the mediocrities who have also flooded into colleges in the past couple of generations do better than they otherwise would have. And if they do, is it because college actually made them better employees or because it simply gave them the requisite credential to get interviewed and hired? The U.S. Labor Department's Bureau of Labor Statistics reports that about 20 percent of all college graduates toil in fields not requiring a degree, and this total is projected to exceed 30 percent by the year 2005. For the individual, college may well be a credential without being a qualification, required without being requisite.

9   For American society, the big lie underlying higher education is akin to Garrison Keillor's description of the children in Lake Wobegon: they are all above average. In the unexamined American Dream rhetoric promoting mass higher education in the nation of my youth, the implicit vision was that one day everyone, or at least practically everyone, would be a manager or a professional. We would use the most élitist of all means, scholarship, toward the most egalitarian of ends. We would all become chiefs; hardly anyone would be left a mere Indian. On the surface, this New Jerusalem appears to have arrived. Where half a century ago the bulk of jobs were blue collar, now a majority are white or pink collar. They are performed in an office instead of on a factory floor. If they still tend to involve repetition and drudgery, at least they do not require heavy lifting.

10   But the wages for them are going down virtually as often as up. And as a great many disappointed office workers have discovered, being better educated and better dressed at the workplace does not transform one's place in the pecking order. There are still plenty more Indians than chiefs. Lately, indeed, the chiefs are becoming even fewer. The major focus of the "downsizing" of recent years has been eliminating layers of middle management—much of it drawn from the ranks of those lured to college a generation or two ago by the idea that a degree would transform them from the mediocre to magisterial.

11   Yet our colleges blithely go on "educating" many more prospective managers and professionals than we are likely to need. In my own field, there are typically more students majoring in journalism at any given moment than there are journalists employed at all the daily newspapers in the U.S. A few years ago, there were more students enrolled in law school than there were partners in all law firms. As trends shift, there have been periodic

oversupplies of M.B.A.-wielding financial analysts, of grade school and high school teachers, of computer programmers, even of engineers. Inevitably many students of limited talent spend huge amounts of time and money pursuing some brass-ring occupation, only to see their dreams denied. As a society we consider it cruel not to give them every chance at success. It may be more cruel to let them go on fooling themselves.

12 Just when it should be clear that we are already probably doing too much to entice people into college, Bill Clinton is suggesting we do even more. In February 1994, for example, the President asserted that America needs a greater fusion between academic and vocational training in high school— not because too many mediocre people misplaced on the college track are failing to acquire marketable vocational skills, but because too many people on the vocational track are being denied courses that will secure them admission to college. Surely what Americans need is not a fusion of the two tracks but a sharper division between them, coupled with a forceful program for diverting intellectual also-rans out of the academic track and into the vocational one. That is where most of them are heading in life anyway. Why should they wait until they are older and must enroll in high-priced proprietary vocational programs of often dubious efficacy—frequently throwing away not only their own funds but federal loans in the process—because they emerged from high school heading nowhere and knowing nothing that is useful in the marketplace?

13   If the massive numbers of college students reflected a national boom in love of learning and a prevalent yen for self-improvement, America's investment in the classroom might make sense. There are introspective qualities that can enrich any society in ways beyond the material. But one need look no further than the curricular wars to understand that most students are not looking to broaden their spiritual or intellectual horizons. Consider three basic trends, all of them implicit rejections of intellectual adventure. First, students are demanding courses that reflect and affirm their own identities in the most literal way. Rather than read a Greek dramatist of 2,000 years ago and thrill to the discovery that some ideas and emotions are universal, many insist on reading writers of their own gender or ethnicity or sexual preference, ideally writers of the present or the recent past.

14   The second trend, implicit in the first, is that the curriculum has shifted from being what professors desire to teach to being what students desire to learn. Nowadays colleges have to hustle for students by truckling trendily. If the students want media-studies programs so they can all fantasize about becoming TV news anchors, then media studies will abound. There are in any given year some 300,000 students enrolled in undergraduate communications courses.

15   Of even greater significance than the solipsism of students and the pusillanimity of teachers is the third trend, the sheer decline in the amount and quality of work expected in class. In an egalitarian environment the influx of mediocrities relentlessly lowers the general standards at colleges to levels the weak ones can meet. When my mother went to Trinity College in Washington in the early 1940s, at a time when it was regarded more as a finishing school for nice Catholic girls than a temple of discipline, an English major there was expected to be versed in Latin, Anglo-Saxon and medieval French. A course in Shakespeare meant reading the plays, all 37 of them. In today's indulgent climate, a professor friend at a fancy college told me as I was writing this chapter, taking a half semester of Shakespeare compels students to read exactly four plays. "Anything more than one a week," he explained, "is considered too heavy a load."

16   This probably should not be thought surprising in an era when most colleges, even prestigious ones, run some sort of remedial program for freshmen to learn the reading and writing skills they ought to have developed in junior high school— not to mention an era when many students vociferously object to being marked down for spelling or grammar. Indeed, all the media attention paid to curriculum battles at Stanford, Dartmouth and the like obscures the even bleaker reality of American higher education. As Russell Jacoby points out in his book *Dogmatic Wisdom*, most students are enrolled at vastly less demanding institutions, where any substantial reading list would be an improvement.

17   My modest proposal is this: Let us reduce, over perhaps a five-year span, the number of high school graduates who go on to college from nearly 60 percent to a still generous 33 percent. This will mean closing a lot of institutions. Most of them, in my view, should be community colleges, current or former state teachers' colleges and the like. These schools serve the academically marginal and would be better replaced by vocational training in high school and on-the-job training at work. Two standards should apply in judging which schools to shut down. First, what is the general academic level attained by the student body? That might be assessed in a rough-and-ready way by requiring any institution wishing to survive to give a standardized test—say, the Graduate Record Examination—to all its seniors. Those schools whose students perform below the state norm would face cutbacks or closing. Second, what community is being served? A school that serves a high percentage of disadvantaged students (this ought to be measured by family finances rather than just race or ethnicity) can make a better case for receiving tax dollars than one that subsidizes the children of the prosperous, who have private alternatives. Even ardent egalitarians should recognize the injustice of taxing people who wash dishes or mop floors for a living to pay for the below-cost

public higher education of the children of lawyers so that they can go on to become lawyers too.

18   Some readers may find it paradoxical that a book arguing for greater literacy and intellectual discipline should lead to a call for less rather than more education. Even if college students do not learn all they should, the readers' counterargument would go, surely, they learn something, and that is better than learning nothing. Maybe it is. But at what price? One hundred fifty billion dollars is awfully high for deferring the day when the idle or ungifted take individual responsibility and face up to their fate. Ultimately it is the yearning to believe that anyone can be brought up to college level that has brought colleges down to everyone's level.

Discussion Questions

1.   Describe the tone of Henry's argument. Do you think he could have achieved the same effect by using a different tone? Explain your answer.

2.   Which of Henry's examples do you find the most convincing? Which the least? Explain your response.

3.   What kind of proof does Henry use to support his stance? Identify specific examples and evaluate their effectiveness.

4.   Does Henry's argument appeal to reason, emotion, or ethics? Explain why you think his choice of appeals is appropriate for his argument.

5.   Do you think Henry sees his audience as holding the same or opposite views on who should go to college? What in his argument leads you to your response?

Human Time and
the College Student

Page Smith

Born in 1917, Page Smith earned his B.A. degree from
Dartmouth College and his M.A. and Ph.D. degrees
from Harvard University. From 1964 to 1970, Smith was
the Provost at the University of California at Santa Cruz.
He is currently Professor Emeritus of American History
at that university. Smith is the author of some fifteen
books, including *John Adams* (1962), *The Historian
and History* (1964), *Daughters of the Promised Land:
Women in American History* (1970), *Thomas Jefferson:
A Revealing Biography* (1976), *Shaping the Nation*
(1980), *The Nation Comes of Age: A People's History of
the Ante-Bellum Years* (1981), and *Killing the Spirit*
(1990). In the following essay, which was first published in 1957, Smith denounces final exams.

1   The tension in the large room is almost palpable. The air is tainted with the
odor of sweat. The faces of the men and women are drawn and taut. Their
bodies are twisted in postures of agonized thought, of supplication, of despair.
The scene is not that of a torture chamber but of a roomful of students taking a final examination.

2   Surely a professor's most disheartening experience is to patrol the classroom during the final examination for his course. If he has tried to make the
course a vital one, if he has tried to catch the students up in an adventure of
learning that has contained some joy and play as well as high seriousness, he
cannot but feel downhearted as he watches their strained faces, observes
their exhaustion and anxiety. This is certainly a dismal end to an at least
theoretically enlivening experience. Only convention can make it tolerable
to the professor and his students. We are bound to ask ourselves, it seems to
me, how well the aims of a particular course or of education in general are
served by this ordeal. Its avowed purpose is to make sure that the student has
accomplished something measurable in mastering a certain body of material, that he has increased his efficiency or his knowledge. We assure ourselves that the final examination accomplishes this, but we have ample

testimony that it does not. I suspect that most of us have little conviction that six years or six months after the completion of this or that course, its graduates could pass even a vastly simplified examination on its content. What we might call the "retention quotient" is, in most courses, very low indeed. There is much to suggest that because the final examination presents both a frightening hurdle and an obvious terminus, it actually inhibits retention of the course content. Students at least believe so and often speak cynically of final examinations as a kind of intellectual purge by which the mind is evacuated of all the material that has been stored in it during the course.

3   It should be obvious that the typical examination is not the proper means to ensure the student's carrying away from the work of a semester an important residue of information or knowledge. It does give us, however, a conviction that we are discriminating, that we are forcing the student to comply with certain standards, that we have transferred, even if on a temporary basis, certain information to our passive auditors. What is perhaps most important of all, we have provided a means by which the student's advance toward his ultimate goal—a degree—can be measured. Using it we are able to assign a "mark" which presumably measures the student's accomplishment. And this mark is an integral part of our educational process.

4   While the final examination is only the concluding trial of the average course, we might take it as a symbol of much that is wrong with our instructional methods on the college level. The fact is that our colleges are, to a considerable degree, neither subject-oriented nor student-oriented but mark-oriented. They are set up, on the undergraduate level, to facilitate the awarding and the recording of marks. Individual courses of instruction are almost invariably organized with an eye on marking procedures. In large courses where the instructor is assisted by graduate students who read and grade the papers, it is especially important to devise examinations that require essentially factual answers. These answers may be in the form of multiple choices, in which case they are often graded by a machine, or they may be in the form of an essay. The essay-type question is an improvement over the true-false or multiple choice examination since it requires that the student be more or less literate. But in practice this type of examination must still place its emphasis on the factual in order to make possible a uniform system of grading by one or more "readers."

5   However much, in courses of this kind, the professor may affirm his desire to have the students "think for themselves," the students cannot in fact do so. Ideal answers in these mass-administered and mass-graded tests have to be devised and marks awarded on the basis of the number of essential points included in each answer. Such courses, moreover, are usually taught in conjunction with a textbook, and here the student's impulse, not

unnaturally, is to memorize the text at the expense of a thoughtful, critical review of the lecture material. The large lecture courses which use a textbook and in which the grading is done by "readers" or "assistants" are self-defeating. The complex, unfamiliar, and elusive ideas given in lectures cannot compete successfully, in most instances, with the neatly assembled data in the textbook. The student is further discouraged in any speculation by the consciousness that he may have missed or misunderstood the precise point the lecturer was trying to make and may thus render it up in mutilated or unrecognizable form.

6   Let us assume that the student accepts the invitation to "think for himself." In most cases his thoughts will be confused and banal, a mish-mash of rather unformed ideas that he has picked up in high-school civics courses, at home, from random reading, from movies and television. They will not be worth much in terms of a mark. How is the professor, or his surrogate, the reader, to react? Does he give the student an A for effort, thus encouraging him in the idea that he is a thinker of considerable power and originality? Or does he admonish him gently and give him a C, thus confirming the student's suspicions that the professor never meant what he said anyway?

7   Again the mark is the culprit. The fact is that the mark should be used only as an incentive, as a corrective, as a stimulus. A first-rate student often needs to be most severely marked for sloppy thinking, for intellectual short cuts, for the facile use of academic clichés. As a Cambridge tutor expressed it to me, "The teacher should be free, if the character of the student suggests it is the best course, to tear up his paper before him, denounce his work as careless and inaccurate, berate him soundly, and send him off to do the work of which he is capable." Perhaps the student who suffers most under our marking system is the outstanding individual who, in any comparison with his fellows, must be given an A and thus cannot be treated with the rigor that would eventually make the most of his superior capacities.

8   Since all marks are carefully recorded, added up, weighed and assessed, and stand unalterable upon the student's record, they cannot be used with any real freedom or flexibility. Most of us are reluctant to give a mark that will perhaps count against a scholarship, a job, or a cherished academic plum.

9   I suspect that largely as a result of the grading system a majority of the students regard the professor as, in a sense, the enemy. That is to say, the professor represents an unknown quantity that has the potentiality of damaging the student. As professor he is in a position of almost unlimited power. To counter this the student has a kind of cunning which he has acquired as a by-product of the educational process. He is conditioned to play the game according to the rules. He knows that if, like the psychologist's pigeon, he pecks the right button, he will get a kernel of corn. He has, therefore, very little to gain and much to lose by taking liberties with the system. The

prevailing educational conventions combine to make him cagey. He knows that his teachers are at least partly human and that however remote most of them may seem from his real life and interests, they have their crotchets, their small vanities, and their prejudices. At the beginning of a class the student is alert to penetrate these and to discern in what way they can be made to work to his advantage. He knows that despite a pretense of professional objectivity, the instructor has a fairly well-developed set of biases, and the student welcomes evidences of these because they are guideposts to him. Correspondingly, the absence of discernible prejudices is unsettling for the student—it means another anxiety-producing unknown element in the equation that should yield up the desired mark.

10   The only way that the professor can overcome the student's habit of calculation, which is generally fatal to the learning process, is by lessening some of his apprehensions. The student's attitude is indeed ambivalent, and this is the professor's opportunity. In addition to their feelings of anxiety and hostility, many students genuinely wish to be touched and affected by the professor. The student has had, in his learning experience, a few teachers who have done this and he knows that, while it is unlikely, it can happen. But the professor, in his efforts to create this kind of *rapport,* is at a disadvantage. He is inviting a confidence that he cannot honor. The student may in fact be drawn from his shell and inspired to venture some independent judgment, but the assessment of this hesitant enterprise will not be made by the man who has solicited it but, in many instances, by a third party, the reader.

11   Even if it were possible to set up a grading procedure by which efforts at original and independent thinking would be encouraged and rewarded, there would still be little incentive for the bright student to make the effort. Being examination-oriented and acutely mark-conscious he knows that there is always an element of chance in examinations and he has a strong impulse to keep this to a minimum.

12   He realizes that it is often not so much what he knows as how much mileage he can get out of the information that he has committed to memory. The means of testing now used in most colleges and universities often fall short of measuring the excellence or the capacity of the student. For the most part they record his ability to memorize and record a certain rather narrow range of information, and here technique is of great importance. If, by the painstaking accumulation of facts and approved theories and their careful regurgitation, the student can get the desired mark, he is borrowing trouble to attempt something more ambitious.

13   The teacher is, of course, as much the victim of our testing conventions as the student is. Examinations play an important part in his conception of himself as teacher and scholar. Not infrequently he comes to view them

as weapons in a contest between himself and his students. Unexpected and unorthodox questions affirm his "toughness" and give a comforting spread in marks. Even in the most straightforward examination, some conscientious students will have failed to prepare certain questions adequately since all the significant material in a given course can seldom be mastered with complete thoroughness and an element of chance inevitably enters in. Difficult and obscure questions will scatter the field even further, reducing the number of A's and B's and giving the professor the reassuring feeling that he is a stern marker who is upholding "standards."

14   It might be said that the whole matter of "distribution" and grading on the "curve" is one of the most patent fallacies in the marking system. It seems to be based on the assumption that the student population in any particular course should be spread out with a certain percentage of A's, B's, and C's, and so on, but this assumption, which is treated by many professors with the sanctity of a kind of natural law of education, will not bear close scrutiny. It is certainly conceivable that rigorous and demanding courses can be given to large numbers of students in which no "proper" distribution occurs. When this happens, however, the professor involved often feels under compulsion to revamp his testing techniques to produce a result more in accord with accepted practice lest his colleagues suspect that he is "soft" or perhaps trying to win students by relaxed standards—a kind of academic scab who is willing to accept less than the prevailing scale.

15   What I have to say about the inadequacies of the marking system applies most directly to freshman and sophomore "survey" courses taken by large numbers of students who, it is hoped, will thereby get a nodding acquaintance with, say, Western Civilization, or Art in World History, or Patterns of Social Development. My strictures apply with somewhat less force to the more advanced courses, but even here, especially in the larger institutions, readers are in evidence, and the more onerous features of the grading system are only slightly ameliorated.

16   In the first place, by the time they are upperclassmen, the majority of students are thoroughly conditioned to the corruption of marks, and it is correspondingly difficult to break through to the individual, to lure him into any free and uninhibited expression of feeling or opinion. As an advanced student he has found his level—A, B, or C. He knows what kind of effort is required to maintain it in the average course, provided again that the student-intelligence service is functioning effectively.

17   The student accepts the system because it can be figured out, anticipated, and made, in general, to yield the desired token. The professor often values it for its very impersonality, or "objectivity." Every student, if he is known, presents the teacher with a unique problem. Is the middle-aged schoolteacher from Louisiana, seeking a salary increase by the accumulation

of additional course credits, to be judged by the same standards as the brilliant and precocious high school student, or the man with two children who works twenty or thirty hours a week, or the boy who works on a night shift in a railroad yard to help put a younger brother though school, or the housewife who wishes to secure a primary-school teaching credential? Perhaps it can be argued that these are extreme cases, but our existing canons of grading dictate that we treat all individuals the same way.

18   Now this is not quite as bad if we are giving an essentially professional education to a homogeneous student body with a common cultural background, but if this is no longer our basic task, the only alternative is to attempt to assess each student individually. Of course, such a suggestion alarms the bureaucrats since it involves difficult and dangerous decisions on the part of the professor and smacks of the "progressive" ideas that most of us view with suspicion when we observe them in operation on the secondary-school level. But it might be answered that the failure of the secondary schools is not so much caused by trying to meet the needs of the individual student as it is by watering down and destroying the content of the traditional curriculum in the name of "adjustment" or of "practical" education. If the liberals arts curriculum is maintained and strengthened as the heart of higher education, the effort to adopt a more flexible and more personal approach to the student can only be salutary in its effects. Both the mediocre and the outstanding student will profit from such a change in emphasis, and standards, instead of being lowered, will be raised, since the student who is in a one-to-one relationship to his teacher will more often have his best efforts evoked.

19   The answer to such proposals will, of course, be that the present ratio of professors to students is not great enough to permit attention to the needs and capacities of individual students. I believe that there is much that can be done within the existing framework of most college and university curriculums without submerging the professor, but it is probably true that some institutional reforms are needed to reduce the rigidity of the present system. In any event, a necessary first step toward breaking the tyranny of the marking and examination system is the frank admission that these are at best necessary evils that have about them no savor of salvation, but rather, by their own interior logic, work toward the increasing formalization of higher education. Perhaps an uprising against the existing practices should begin with the destruction of the I.B.M. machines and the dispersion of those who tend them, followed by the rout of the academic bureaucrats.

20   Such a revolt would open the way for the establishment of more human and more flexible procedures. One hesitates to say what these procedures should be. Perhaps it is enough, at this stage, to insist that time spans must be created for the student that will relieve him of the continual anxiety of

recurrent tests and examinations. The fragmentation of the student's learning experience seriously inhibits his intellectual growth and his personal
development. Information can be dispensed on a unit basis, but formation
and reformation require unbroken increments of time. In our present curriculum all marks, all assignments, all chapters are of equal significance because, as weighed by a mark, all weigh the same. The trivial takes equal
rank with the important and the student's power of discrimination is soon
lost.

21   A renewed dialogue, the creation of generous time spans, the bold and
unabashed reenactment of the historic drama of the self confronting the
cosmos, these are the directions American higher education must take if it
is not to degenerate into a fact mill or a colossal trade school.

Discussion Questions

1. Smith begins his argument with a vivid description of a class-
    room in which a final exam is being administered. What effect
    does Smith achieve by beginning his argument that way?

2. Explain how deductive logic helps Smith argue his claim. Do
    you think his choice of deductive logic is effective? Why or
    why not?

3. If it weren't for grades and exams, do you think most students
    would be inclined to study as hard as they currently do? Would
    they learn as much if they didn't have exams and weren't being
    graded? Explain your answer and discuss the degree to which
    Smith answers these questions.

4. Given that most students would probably agree with Smith's
    claim, whom do you think Smith envisioned as his audience?
    Explain your answer.

5. Does Smith offer any viable and convincing solutions to the
    problems he poses in argument? What alternatives do you see
    to exams and grading?

Questioning the Great, Unexplained . . . College Major

Jonathan Z. Smith

Jonathan Z. Smith was born in 1938 and earned his B.A. degree from Haverford College. After attending Yale University's Divinity School for postgraduate work, Smith taught at Dartmouth College and the University of California at Santa Barbara. In 1968, he joined the University of Chicago, where he is currently the Robert O. Anderson Distinguished Service Professor in the Humanities. Smith is the author of *Drudgery Divine: On the Comparison of Early Christianities and the Religions of Late Antiquity* (1990). In the following selection, Smith argues that most college majors and departments "lack coherence because they are neither subject matter nor disciplines."

1   The college major is the great, unexamined aspect of undergraduate education. Despite its fairly recent introduction into the curriculum, its purpose and design have come to seem all but self-evident. While there are periodic convulsions in institutions of higher learning over general education and its requirements, there has rarely been discussion of the major, save when a particular major is introduced at a given institution and seeks a license. In principle, general education is everybody's business—hence, it all too often becomes nobody's business, especially after the thrill of constructing a new program subsides. But the major is the daily business of a small, quite particular, and often well-organized group of faculty—hence, no one else's business. To be busy about someone else's major is to be a busybody indeed!

2   Although majors consume more than half of a student's college career, and more than half of a faculty member's teaching effort, the major is held to be largely unaccountable to the wider faculty or institution except in the most ceremonial sense. It remains the privileged responsibility of a small group within the institution as well as, to some degree, the larger profession without. The prime issue confronting the integrity of the baccalaureate degree is faulty governance, and the assumption of corporate responsibility

for the totality of the degree. The failure to assume such responsibility is most evident in the major.

3   The history of the major has been recounted (most recently, in Frederick Rudolph's *History of the Curriculum*), and its chief claim reiterated at educational conferences, in college catalogues, and during department meetings. The major, we are told, was introduced to bring focus and depth to what was perceived as an unfocused (elective) and over-generalizing curriculum. But rarely was the question asked, depth and focus for what? (The answer was assumed to be self-evident: to begin the training of academics such as ourselves).

4   The present four-year liberal arts curriculum is an uneasy compromise growing out of this history. It consists of *general requirements* (core or distribution) to introduce breadth, as determined by the faculty; *major requirements* to introduce depth as determined by a sub-set of the faculty; and *electives*, which may be used to further either breadth or depth of study as determined by the student.

5   In practice, there has been no compromise at all. In the majority of institutions, as Rudolph has noted, "by 1976, the concentration or major was in charge of the curriculum." While the pattern varies, general education requirements are most usually fulfilled through patterns of required distribution with these distribution courses most frequently introductory departmental courses, i.e. courses introductory to the major. (They are, in fact, perceived by many departments as recruitment devices for the major). In many instances, sample distribution patterns are "recommended" by the various major programs. As students are asked to make increasingly early decisions with respect to their major, the major determines both the shape and content of their general education courses. As a result, major courses represent a disproportionately large part of most students' baccalaureate programs, and electives are most frequently taken within the chosen field of the major or in closely allied fields (these latter, often stipulated by the major).

6   If the major has rarely been defended on intellectual grounds, save for vague appeals to "depth," whence cometh its power? The power of the major is preeminently political for the major is coextensive with departments, whether at a university (where some attempt has been made to provide them with a rationale) or in a college (where there appears to be little justification). Because of this, any inquiry into the major begins with the fact that, although there have been a variety of experiments, no convincing alternative to the department as an organizing principle for academic affairs has gained assent.

7   As with the major, so with departments: they have rarely been justified on educational grounds. They are a convenience, like zip-codes, a way of

sorting the mail, a mode of governance, a convenient way of doing business. It is often conceded by even their strongest advocates that departments lack intellectual coherence. But if this is true, we are entitled to ask some questions. What has become of the putative rationale for the major, if departments lack coherence? What could it possibly mean to experience a depth of incoherence? It is one thing to plumb the depths of clear water; it is surely another matter to muck about in a swampy ooze.

8   When we reflect on our daily lives as citizens of the academy, we see the fraudulence of the claim that the department is an adequate mapping of human knowledge and inquiry. Many of us find our most proximate colleagues in other departments, yet, through the hegemony of the major, we deny this to our students. It is as if we were compelled to confine our research and inquiry only to those areas of the library arbitrarily assigned "to us" by the Dewey Decimal or Library of Congress system. Through the major's domination of the curriculum we often confine our students to such an odd set of limitations, those areas of inquiry arbitrarily assigned to a given major by faculty action and academic tradition. The library, at least, pretends no status for its system other than ease in retrieval. Our system confers status. Perhaps most explicitly when we confer a degree (despite all formulae) in the name of a major.

9   In most cases, departments and majors lack coherence because they are neither subject matters nor disciplines. Rather than the principled stipulation of a domain of inquiry (a perfectly legitimate endeavor), they are the result of a series of gentlemen's agreements. Take, as an example, a department or a major in English literature—frequently one of the larger and most politically self-conscious units on campus. Scholars in English employ a host of methods, not one of which is unique to their field of inquiry, most of which are shared with the majority of other departments in the humanities and, increasingly, with the social sciences as well. Nor is there any coherent limit, any modesty, to their domain. Almost anything printed from left to right in Roman type may be taught: from Greek tragedies to world literature; from myth to mysticism; psychoanalytic theory, social anthropology, popular literature, technical texts.

10   But there is a sine qua non about which they are uncommonly clear: the number of slots they are entitled to. The formula is well-known to any academic administrator. The ideal department of English will have twenty-five slots, divided thusly: Literature from the 15th to 20th century, five slots; double that for England and America to total ten slots; and of course, prose and poetry for each of these must be considered, making twenty slots. Add Chaucer, Shakespeare, or drama and creative writing and the department is up to twenty-three places. Be avant-garde and include black literature,

cinema, or some such and you have a staff of twenty-five. What is discipli-
nary about this? What are the principles of coherence? What could depth
possibly mean in such a context?

11   The frequent answer, that such programs are, in fact, interdisciplinary,
will not do. Interdisciplinary work presumes intact, hard-edged disciplines.
The discovery of an area of inquiry, a subject matter, that might fruitfully be
addressed by more than a single discipline is an enterprise (Venn-diagram-
like) always and necessarily narrower than either discipline's full domain.

12   Lacking principled stipulation, most majors are incoherent. This is especially noticeable at the middle range. While the first course is frequently
a well-organized survey, and the last course an individualized research project, what comes in-between is political rather than substantive: a course
with each of the major professors, or the like. Most majors, at their middle
range, are miniaturized distribution requirements, and fall prey to the same
criticism of such requirements at a more general level. It would be difficult
to articulate in most instances in what respects they bring depth study.

13   Depending upon definition, it is possible to test for depth in such courses. If depth be defined in the context of the total curriculum, then depth
must have a relation to the general education courses. That is to say, one
could test a course in the major for its explicit reference to and use of general education courses, and for its capacity to "come at" the same or analo-
gous materials in a more complex, "deeper" fashion. If depth be defined in
terms of a particular subject matter, then one would expect that textbooks
would be rarely used and that the seminar format would prevail. That students would be exposed to primary materials, to genuine areas of uncer-
tainty and debate within the discipline. The majority of syllabi I have
reviewed fail these two, most obvious tests.

14   Finally there is what is not taught because it is not well captured by the
department major. For example, when the intellectual history of this century
is written, it will probably lift up the linguistic turn and the enormous influence thinking about language-as-such has had on most areas of inquiry in
the humanities and social sciences (indeed, the linguistic turn has called
into question many of the traditional borders between the humanities and
the social sciences) as well in the biological and physical sciences. But where
is this turn taught and studied in our colleges? Glimmers of it are found in a
variety of programs, but its liberating and challenging aspects are rarely experienced. Its depth remains unplumbed by our students because it has been
diffused (and defused).

15   One cannot think about a major except in the context of some overall
conception of the baccalaureate degree. In the staggering diversity of colleges, there are a multitude of spatial arrangements—ways in which blocks

of courses are organized—but there is uniformity and harsh limitation of time. Regardless of the academic calendar employed, there are almost always less than one hundred hours of course time in a year-long course, and regardless of what we do, we must do it in the equivalent of four years. It is with this bureaucratic fact that thinking about the curriculum must begin. For, under these conditions, everything cannot be taught, nothing (so long as the baccalaureate degree is properly conceived as a terminal degree and not merely as preparation for post-baccalaureate studies or careers) needs to be taught. Thinking about the components of an undergraduate education is an occasion for institutional choice, for articulate and self-conscious selection.

16   I take as a corollary to this that each thing taught or studied is taught or studied not because it is "there," but because it is an example, an exempli gratia of something fundamental that may serve as a precedent for further interpretation and understanding. By providing an arsenal of skills and paradigms from which to reason, that which may first appear to be strange or novel can become intelligible.

17   Given this: that each thing which is taught is taught by way of an example and that the curriculum is an occasion for institutional choice, then the primary choice is: What shall the things taught exemplify? This ought to be explicit in every academic endeavor, at every level of the curriculum.

18   If this be so, then the curricular choices, the choice of what each component exemplifies, ought to be a conscious faculty decision which may well presume other modes of faculty governance than the present federation of departments. The implication is that these goals are public, that they may be tested by the faculty as a whole, rather than owned by some sub-set. For it will be the goals and choices which generate the components of the curriculum, much as one may design a course by starting with the final examination.

19   To these matters of choice and exemplification no single answer can be given. These must remain institutional choices which fit each institution's peculiar ecology. But we may demand that they be articulated, and tested for, and that the goals be explicitly built into every course of study and not left for accidental discovery by a student. Students ought not to be asked to organize and integrate what the faculty will not. Distribution requirements—whether at the level of general education or the middle-range of a major, violate these two injunctions at will.

20   What has been suggested so far might be seen as the irreducible minimum for a baccalaureate program to argue that it had a curriculum, and indicates the ways in which the hegemony of the major, by its self-evident

character, has deflected attention from such matters. The argument has been in terms of academic processes and governance, but behind such a view stands a set of presuppositions concerning knowledge. I expose these now as an example of the sort of debate that ought to go on among a faculty which takes seriously its responsibility for curriculum, but not as the necessary presuppositions for assuming such responsibilities or for questioning the major.

21   The world is not "given." It is not simply "there." We constitute it by acts of interpretation. (Some of which, in their characteristic modes and strategies, might well be organizing principles for domains of knowledge in the academy.) Above all, we constitute the world by speech, by memory, and by judgment. It is by an act of human will, through projects of language and history, through symbols and memory, that we fabricate the world and ourselves. But there is a double sense to the word "fabrication." It means both "to build" and "to lie." Education comes to life in the moment of tension generated by this duality. For, though we have no other means than language for treating with the world, words and symbols are not the same as that which they seek to name and describe. Though we have no other recourse than to memory and precedent if the world is not to be endlessly novel and, hence, forever unintelligible, the fit is never exact, nothing is ever quite the same. What is required at this point of tension is the trained capacity for judgment, for appreciating and criticizing the relative adequacy and insufficiency of any proposal of language and of memory.

22   This quest for the powers and skills of informed judgment, for the dual capacities of appreciation and criticism might well stand as the explicit goal of every level of college curriculum. The difficult enterprise of making interpretive decisions and facing up to their full consequences ought to inform each and every course, each and every object of study.

23   The fundamentals of a college education, from such a viewpoint, are decisions between interpretations, the skills attendant upon the understanding of particular interpretations, and the ability to translate one interpretation in terms of another. Above all, they are that which leads to the capacity for argumentation, and, therefore, to responsible judgments. *Baccalaureate education is argument about interpretations.*

24   Of course there will be generalities and particulars. Knowledge is always knowledge about something in terms of something else. This is the act of interpretation, this is the generator of argument. But it is these acts rather than the "somethings," which comprise the goal of the curriculum.

25   From such a view, there is even more pressure for articulate faculty argument and choice. For surely we must be able to undertake these

endeavors before we dare to claim that we are teaching choice to our students. But one can dissent from these presuppositions, and yet affirm the consequences.

26   For, as faculty, we are not passive, we do not merely report and transmit what is there (indeed, much of what we teach was not there until we began to teach, to inquire, to interpret it). This implies a willingness, as a faculty, to experience the delicious terror of freedom and the awesome, concomitant exhilaration of decision.

27   Let us have an end to passing off our responsibility to our students and their high schools. It is not the careerism of our students that has disfigured liberal learning, but our own, and that of our colleagues. It is not the deficiencies of secondary education students that has weakened liberal learning, but rather that of graduate schools, dominated, as they are, by departmental concerns, which train our faculty and which we, rather than local school boards, control.

28   The question of the major and the status of the baccalaureate degree is a matter of faculty assuming their chartered responsibility. The convenience and political advantages of domination by the major have obscured this task. If the faculty does not make itself publicly and articulately responsible to itself, it will be made responsible to some other body. That would be a high cost, indeed.

Discussion Questions

1. Not only is Smith critical of the college major, he attacks the department as well. How effectively does he make the transition between the two? Explain your response.

2. Do you think Smith offers a reasonable alternative to the college major? Explain how this strengthens or weakens his argument.

3. Explain how Smith establishes his credibility.

4. Smith uses the English literature major and an English department as examples of the lack of coherence in a discipline in the university. How successfully does Smith argue his point using this one example? Explain your answer.

5. What do you think the proponents of the college major and academic department would say to Smith? Does Smith adequately address opposing points of view? Explain your responses.

ARGUMENT

A Proposal to Abolish Grading

Paul Goodman

Paul Goodman was born in 1911 and died in 1972. A college professor, Goodman wrote *The Empire City* (1959), *Growing Up Absurd: Problems of Youth in the Organized System* (1960), *The Community of Scholars* (1962), *Freedom and Order in the University* (1967), and *People or Personnel* (1968). In the following article, which was originally published in *Compulsory Miseducation* (1964), Goodman argues for grades to be abolished.

1   Let half a dozen of the prestigious Universities—Chicago, Stanford, the Ivy League—abolish grading, and use testing only and entirely for pedagogic purposes as teachers see fit.

2   Anyone who knows the frantic temper of the present schools will understand the transvaluation of values that would be effected by this modest innovation. For most of the students, the competitive grade has come to be the essence. The naive teacher points to the beauty of the subject and the ingenuity of the research; the shrewd student asks if he is responsible for that on the final exam.

3   Let me at once dispose of an objection whose unanimity is quite fascinating. I think that the great majority of professors agree that grading hinders teaching and creates a bad spirit, going as far as cheating and plagiarizing. I have before me the collection of essays, *Examining in Harvard College*, and this is the consensus. It is uniformly asserted, however, that the grading is inevitable; for how else will the graduate schools, the foundations, the corporations *know* whom to accept, reward, hire? How will the talent scouts know whom to tap?

4   By testing the applicants, of course, according to the specific task-requirements of the inducting institution, just as applicants for the Civil Service or for licenses in medicine, law, and architecture are tested. Why should Harvard professors do the testing *for* corporations and graduate schools?

5   The objection is ludicrous. Dean Whitla, of the Harvard Office of Tests, points out that the scholastic-aptitude and achievement tests used for

admission to Harvard are a super-excellent index for all-around Harvard performance, better than high-school grades or particular Harvard course-grades. Presumably, these college-entrance tests are tailored for what Harvard and similar institutions want. By the same logic, would not an employer do far better to apply his own job-aptitude test rather than to rely on the vagaries of Harvard section-men? Indeed, I doubt that many employers bother to look at such grades; they are more likely to be interested merely in the fact of a Harvard diploma, whatever that connotes to them. The grades have most of their weight with the graduate schools—here, as elsewhere, the system runs mainly for its own sake.

6   It is really necessary to remind our academics of the ancient history of Examination. In the medieval university, the whole point of the grueling trial of the candidate was whether or not to accept him as a peer. His disputation and lecture for the Master's was just that, a masterpiece to enter the guild. It was not to make comparative evaluations. It was not to weed out and select for an extramural licensor or employer. It was certainly not to pit one young fellow against another in an ugly competition. My philosophic impression is that the medievals thought they knew what a good job of work was and that we are competitive because we do not know. But the more status is achieved by largely irrelevant competitive evaluation, the less will we ever know.

7   (Of course, our American examinations never did have this purely guild orientation, just as our faculties have rarely had absolute autonomy; the examining was to satisfy Overseers, Elders, distant Regents—and they as paternal superiors have always doted on giving grades, rather than accepting peers. But I submit that this set-up itself makes it impossible for the student to *become* a master, to *have* grown up, and to commence on his own. He will always be making A or B for some overseer. And in the present atmosphere, he will always be climbing on his friend's neck.)

8   Perhaps the chief objectors to abolishing grading would be the students and their parents. The parents should be simply disregarded; their anxiety has done enough damage already. For the students, it seems to me that a primary duty of the university is to deprive them of their props, their dependence on extrinsic valuation and motivation, and to force them to confront the difficult enterprise itself and finally lose themselves in it.

9   A miserable effect of grading is to nullify the various uses of testing. Testing, for both student and teacher, is a means of structuring, and also of finding out what is blank or wrong and what has been assimilated and can be taken for granted. Review—including high-pressure review—is a means of bringing together the fragments, so that there are flashes of synoptic insight.

10   There are several good reasons for testing, and kinds of test. But if the aim is to discover weakness, what is the point of down-grading and punishing it, and thereby inviting the student to conceal his weakness, by faking and bulling, if not cheating? The natural conclusion of synthesis is the insight itself, not a grade for having had it. For the important purpose of placement, if one can establish in the student the belief that one is testing *not* to grade and make invidious comparisons but for his own advantage, the student should normally seek his own level, where he is challenged and yet capable, rather than trying to get by. If the student dares to accept himself as he is, a teacher's grade is a crude instrument compared with a student's self-awareness. But it is rare in our universities that students are encouraged to notice objectively their vast confusion. Unlike Socrates, our teachers rely on power-drives rather than shame and ingenuous idealism.

11   Many students are lazy, so teachers try to goad or threaten them by grading. In the long run this must do more harm than good. Laziness is a character-defense. It may be a way of avoiding learning, in order to protect the conceit that one is already perfect (deeper, the despair that one *never* can be). It may be a way of avoiding just the risk of failing and being downgraded. Sometimes it is a way of politely saying, "I won't." But since it is the authoritarian grown-up demands that have created such attitudes in the first place, why repeat the trauma? There comes a time when we must treat people as adult, laziness and all. It is one thing courageously to fire a do-nothing out of your class; it is quite another thing to evaluate him with a lordly F.

12   Most important of all, it is often obvious that balking in doing the work, especially among bright young people who get to great universities, means exactly what its says: The work does not suit me, not this subject, or not at this time, or not at this school, or not in school altogether. The student might not be bookish; he might be school-tired; perhaps his development ought now to take another direction. Yet unfortunately, if such a student is intelligent and is not sure of himself, he *can* be bullied into passing, and this obscures everything. My hunch is that I am describing a common situation. What a grim waste of young life and teacherly effort! Such a student will retain nothing of what he has "passed" in. Sometimes he must get mononucleosis to tell his story and he believed.

13   And ironically, the converse is also probably commonly true. A student flunks and is mechanically weeded out, who is really ready and eager to learn in a scholastic setting, but he has not quite caught on. A good teacher can recognize the situation, but the computer wreaks its will.

Discussion Questions

1. Goodman seems to assume that the point of grading is to detect students' weaknesses. Explain how this assumption affects the effectiveness of his claim.

2. Goodman addresses the proponents of grading in one brief paragraph. Is his response to his opponents sufficient? Do you detect a logical fallacy in his remarks regarding parents and students? Explain your answers.

3. Goodman seems to overlook the ways in which grades can motivate and be beneficial to students. Do you think this omission weakens his argument? Why or why not?

4. Does Goodman offer a reasonable solution to the problem of grading? Discuss how this strengthens or weakens his argument.

5. Both Page Smith and Paul Goodman oppose grades as a way to measure student performance. Which of their arguments do you find more convincing? Why?

WRITING TOPICS

1. Do you think that school should be a place where skills are taught (pre-job training) or a place where students should learn how to deal with abstractions, complexities, and ideas? Discuss your thinking in a paper that examines the reasons for and consequences of the stance you take. You might also want to investigate what local employers and professors at your school think about this issue as possible sources to include in your inquiry into this topic.

2. What courses do you think should be required of all university-level students? Devise a core curriculum and support your choices. You might want to use your own school's curriculum or look at other schools' requirements to assist you in your planning. Be sure, however, that your paper reflects *your* own thinking and not a rehashing of others'.

3. Given that the goal of colleges is to "educate" students, do you think schools should sponsor athletics programs the way they currently do? To investigate this question, you might want to

solicit the viewpoints of your school's athletes, coaches, and professors. How do you reconcile your own thinking with theirs?

4. Do you think that schools that admit only certain students (e.g., all-male, all-female, or all African-American) are a good idea? What is gained from excluding some students and what is lost? To what extent can the admissions policies of such schools be seen as discriminatory? Write a paper that examines the issues these questions raise.

5. In many states, until students reach the age of sixteen, attendance at school is mandatory. Do you agree with this law? Why or why not? Write a paper in which you take a stand and support it.

6. Discuss the advantages and disadvantages of motivating students by "bribing" them with rewards. Use your own experiences (or those of friends) to support your viewpoint. Be sure to discuss the *issue* that emerges from this form of motivation rather than just relate incidents from your own life.

7. Write a paper that responds to the following question: To what extent do you think that lavishing praise on students is harmful or beneficial? Besides using your own experiences to support your thinking, include the viewpoints of learning theorists and psychologists.

8. Do you think that state proficiency tests should be administered to students throughout their elementary and secondary school education to determine their placement as students and whether they should be allowed to graduate? If your state requires proficiency testing, read newspaper and magazine articles that provide the history of and discussion about them. Ask your teachers and peers what their reactions are to such testing. In a paper, examine what you see as the advantages and disadvantages of such tests.

9. In a paper, examine the issue of standardized testing: In what ways do you think that standardized tests fail to accurately measure students' knowledge or potential for achievement? Given that tests such as SATs and ACTs have been used for a number of years, how do you account for their widespread use? Include the opinions of people who have relied on these tests for a number of years. For example, you might want to

interview admissions officers and professors at your school for their reactions. Do you think that such tests are accurate barometers of what they seek to measure? If so, examine what leads you to that conclusion.

10. What do you think about the growing use of computers and other technologies (e.g., calculators, videos) in the classroom? How are they enhancing and/or harming students' education? Obviously, proponents of these technologies will offer ample support for their products. But play devil's advocate for a moment. Do you see their use in the classroom as detrimental to learning in any way? Examine these questions in a paper that addresses the technological age as it enters the classroom.

CHAPTER 7

WORKING FOR A LIVING

VIEWPOINT

WHAT IS THE POINT OF WORK?

Lance Morrow

Lance Morrow was born in 1939, educated at Harvard University, and began his career as a reporter for the *Washington Star*. Since 1976 he has worked as a contributing editor to *Time* magazine. Morrow is the author of *The Chief: A Memoir of Father and Sons* (1984) and *Fishing in the Tiber* (1988). The 1981 recipient of a National Magazine Award for his *Time* essays, Morrow has distinguished himself as an astute observer of American lifestyles and popular trends. First published in *Time* magazine in 1981, the following essay reviews the history of the American work ethic before offering the viewpoint that "the work ethic is not dead, but it is weaker now."

1 When God foreclosed on Eden, he condemned Adam and Eve to go to work. Work has never recovered from that humiliation. From the beginning, the Lord's word said that work was something bad: a punishment, the great stone of mortality and toil laid upon a human spirit that might otherwise soar in the infinite, weightless playfulness of grace.

2   A perfectly understandable prejudice against work has prevailed ever since. Most work in the life of the world has been hard, but since it was grindingly inevitable, it hardly seemed worth complaining about very much. Work was simply the business of life, as matter-of-fact as sex and breathing. In recent years, however, the ancient discontent has grown elaborately articulate. The worker's usual old bitching has gone to college. Grim tribes of sociologists have reported back from office and factory that most workers find their labor mechanical, boring, imprisoning, stultifying, repetitive, dreary, heartbreaking. In his 1972 book *Working*, Studs Terkel began: "This book, being about work, is, by its very nature, about violence—to the spirit as well as to the body." The historical horrors of industrialization (child labor, Dickensian squalor, the dark satanic mills) translate into the 20th century's robotic busywork on the line, tightening the same damned screw on the Camaro's fire-wall assembly, going nuts to the banging, jangling

Chaplinesque whirr of modern materialism in labor, bringing forth issue, disgorging itself upon the market.

3   The lamentations about how awful work is prompt an answering wail from the management side of the chasm: nobody wants to work anymore. As American productivity, once the exuberant engine of national wealth, has dipped to an embarrassingly uncompetitive low, Americans have shaken their heads: the country's old work ethic is dead. About the only good words for it now emanate from Ronald Reagan and certain beer commercials. Those ads are splendidly mythic playlets, romantic idealizations of men in groups who blast through mountains or pour plumingly molten steel in factories, the work all grit and grin. Then they retire to flip around iced cans of sacramental beer and debrief one another in a warm sundown glow of accomplishment. As for Reagan, in his presidential campaign he enshrined work in his rhetorical "community of values," along with family, neighborhood, peace and freedom. He won by a landslide.

4   Has the American work ethic really expired? Is some old native eagerness to level wilderness and dig and build and invent now collapsing toward a decadence of dope, narcissism, income transfers and aerobic self-actualization?

5   The idea of work—work as an ethic, an abstraction—arrived rather late in the history of toil. Whatever edifying and pietistic things may have been said about work over the centuries (Kahlil Gibran called work "love made visible," and the Benedictines say, "To work is to pray"), humankind has always tried to avoid it whenever possible. The philosophical swells of ancient Greece thought work was degrading; they kept an underclass to see to the laundry and other details of basic social maintenance. That prejudice against work persisted down the centuries in other aristocracies. It is supposed, however, to be inherently un-American. Edward Kennedy likes to tell the story of how, during his first campaign for the Senate, his opponent said scornfully in a debate: "This man has never worked a day in his life!" Kennedy says that the next morning as he was shaking hands at a factory gate, one worker leaned toward him and confided, "You ain't missed a goddamned thing."

6   The Protestant work ethic, which sanctified work and turned it into vocation, arrived only a few centuries ago in the formulations of Martin Luther and John Calvin. In that scheme, the worker collaborates with God to do the work of the universe, the great design. One scholar, Leland Ryken of Illinois' Wheaton College, has pointed out that American politicians and corporate leaders who preach about the work ethic do no understand the Puritans' original, crucial linkage between human labor and God's will.

7   During the 19th century industrialization of America, the idea of work's inherent virtue may have seemed temporarily implausible to generations who labored in the mines and mills and sweatshops. The century's huge machinery of production punished and stunned those who ran it.

8   And yet for generations of immigrants, work *was* ultimately availing; the numb toil of an illiterate grandfather got the father a foothold and a high school education, and the son wound up in college or even law school. A woman who died in the Triangle Shirtwaist Co. fire in lower Manhattan had a niece who made it to the halcyon Bronx, and another generation on, the family went to Westchester County. So for millions of Americans, as they labored through the complexities of generations, work worked, and the immigrant work ethic came at last to merge with the Protestant work ethic.

9   The motive of work was all. To work for mere survival is desperate. To work for a better life for one's children and grandchildren lends the labor a fierce dignity. That dignity, an unconquerably hopeful energy and aspiration—driving, persisting like a life force—is the American quality that many find missing now.

10   The work ethic is not dead, but it is weaker now. The psychology of work is much changed in America. The acute, painful memory of the Great Depression used to enforce a disciplined and occasionally docile approach to work—in much the way that older citizens in the Soviet Union do not complain about scarce food and overpopulated apartments, because they remember how much more horrible everything was during the war. But the generation of the Depression is retiring and dying off, and today's younger workers, though sometimes laid off and kicked around by recessions and inflation, still do not keep in dark storage that residual apocalyptic memory of Hoovervilles and the Dust Bowl and banks capsizing.

11   Today elaborate financial cushions—unemployment insurance, union benefits, welfare payments, food stamps and so on—have made it less catastrophic to be out of a job for a while. Work is still a profoundly respectable thing in America. Most Americans suffer a sense of loss, of diminution, even of worthlessness, if they are thrown out on the street. But the blow seldom carries the life-and-death implications it once had, the sense of personal ruin. Besides, the wild and notorious behavior of the economy takes a certain amount of personal shame out of joblessness; if Ford closes down a plant in New Jersey and throws 3,700 workers into the unemployment lines, the guilt falls less on individuals than on Japanese imports or American car design or an extortionate OPEC.

12   Because today's workers are better educated than those in the past, their expectations are higher. Many younger Americans have rearranged their

ideas about what they want to get out of life. While their fathers and grand-fathers and great-grandfathers concentrated hard upon plow and drill press and pressure gauge and tort, some younger workers now ask previously unimaginable questions about the point of knocking themselves out. For the first time in the history of the world, masses of people in industrially advanced countries no longer have to focus their minds upon work as the central concern of their existence.

13   In the formulation of psychologist Abraham Maslow, work functions in a hierarchy of needs: first, work provides food and shelter, basic human maintenance. After that, it can address the need for security and then for friendship and "belongingness." Next, the demands of the ego arise, the need for respect. Finally, men and women assert a larger desire for "self-actualization." That seems a harmless and even worthy enterprise but sometimes degenerates into self-infatuation, a vaporously selfish discontent that dead-ends in isolation, the empty face that gazes back from the mirror.

14   Of course in patchwork, pluralistic America, different classes and ethnic groups are perched at different stages in the work hierarchy. The immigrants—legal and illegal—who still flock densely to America are fighting for the foothold that the jogging tribes of self-actualizers achieved three generations ago. The zealously ambitious Koreans who run New York City's best vegetable markets, or boat people trying to open a restaurant, or chicanos who struggle to start a small business in the *barrio* are still years away from est [a popular self-improvement program created by Werner Erhard in the 1960s] and the Sierra Club. Working women, to the extent that they are new at it, now form a powerful source of ambition and energy. Feminism—and financial need—have made them, in effect, a sophisticated-immigrant wave upon the economy.

15   Having to work to stay alive, to build a future, gives one's exertions a tough moral simplicity. The point of work in that case is so obvious that it need not be discussed. But apart from the sheer necessity of sustaining life, is there some inherent worth in work? Carlyle believed that "all work, even cotton spinning, is noble; work is alone noble." Was he right?

16   It is seigneurial cant to romanticize work that is truly detestable and destructive to workers. But misery and drudgery are always comparative. Despite the sometimes nostalgic haze around their images, the pre-industrial peasant and the 19th century American farmer did brutish work far harder than the assembly line. The untouchable who sweeps excrement in the streets of Bombay would react with blank incomprehension to the malaise of some $17-an-hour workers on a Chrysler assembly line. The Indian, after all, has passed from "alienation" into a degradation that is almost mystical. In Nicaragua, the average 19-year-old peasant has worked longer and

harder than most Americans of middle age. Americans prone to restlessness about the spiritual disappointment of work should consult unemployed young men and women in their own ghettos: they know with painful clarity the importance of the personal dignity that a job brings.

17   Americans often fall into fallacies of misplaced sympathy. Psychologist Maslow, for example, once wrote that he found it difficult "to conceive of feeling proud of myself, self-loving and self-respecting, if I were working, for example, in some chewing-gum factory . . . " Well, two weeks ago, Warner-Lambert announced that it would close down its gum-manufacturing American Chicle factory in Long Island City, N.Y.; the workers who had spent years there making Dentyne and Chiclets were distraught. "It's a beautiful place to work," one feeder-catcher-packer of chewing gum said sadly. "It's just like home." There is a peculiar elitist arrogance in those who discourse on the brutalizations of work simply because they cannot imagine themselves performing the job. Certainly workers often feel abstracted out, reduced sometimes to dreary robotic functions. But almost everyone commands endlessly subtle systems of adaptation; people can make the work their own and even cherish it against all academic expectations. Such adaptations are often more important than the famous but theoretical alienation from the process and product of labor.

18   Work is still the complicated and crucial core of most lives, the occupation melded inseparably to the identity; Freud said that the successful psyche is one capable of love and of work. Work is the most thorough and profound organizing principle in American life. If mobility has weakened old blood ties, our co-workers often form our new family, our tribe, our social world; we become almost citizens of our companies, living under the protection of salaries, pensions, and health insurance. Sociologist Robert Schrank believes that people like jobs mainly because they need other people; they need to gossip with them, hang out with them, to schmooze. Says Schrank: "The workplace performs the function of community."

19   Unless it is dishonest or destructive—the labor of a pimp or a hit man, say—all work is intrinsically honorable in ways that are rarely understood as they once were. Only the fortunate toil in ways that express them directly. There is a Renaissance splendor in Leonardo's effusion: "The works that the eye orders the hands to make are infinite." But most of us labor closer to the ground. Even there, all work expresses the laborer in a deeper sense: all life must be worked at, protected, planted, replanted, fashioned, cooked for, coaxed, diapered, formed, sustained. Work is the way that we tend the world, the way that people connect. It is the most vigorous, vivid sign of life—in individuals and in civilizations.

Discussion Questions

1. What effect does the brief historical overview of work have in Morrow's viewpoint?

2. When in his viewpoint does Morrow explicitly state his main idea? Do you think it is in an appropriate place? Why or why not?

3. Discuss how well Morrow supports his idea that "The work ethic is not dead, but it is weaker now. The psychology of work is much changed in America." Identify specific passages that support his main point.

4. What purpose do the two questions that Morrow asks in paragraph 4 serve?

5. To what extent does the success of Morrow's viewpoint hinge on his audience accepting his idea of the meaning of work? Explain your response.

Good-bye to the Work Ethic

Barbara Ehrenreich

Barbara Ehrenreich was born in 1941 and was educated at Reed College and Rockefeller University. She has worked as a contributing editor at *Ms.* magazine and currently writes for *Time* magazine. Her essays have appeared in such magazines as *Mother Jones, Nation,* and the *New York Times Magazine.* Ehrenreich is the author of *Fear of Falling: The Inner Life of the Middle Class* (1989), *The Worst Years of Our Lives: Irreverent Notes from a Decade of Greed* (1990), in which the following essay appears, and *Kipper's Game* (1994), her first novel. In "Good-bye to the Work Ethic," Ehrenreich discusses her observations about why work is an "inappropriate subject for an 'ethic.'"

1   The media have just buried the last yuppie, a pathetic creature who had not heard the news that the great pendulum of public consciousness has just swung from Greed to Compassion and from Tex-Mex to meatballs. Folks are already lining up outside the mausoleum bearing the many items he had hoped to take with him, including a quart bottle of raspberry vinegar and the Cliff Notes for *The Wealth of Nations.* I, too, have brought something to throw onto the funeral pyre—the very essence of yupdom, its creed and its meaning. Not the passion for money, not even the lust for tiny vegetables, but the *work ethic.*

2   Yes, I realize how important the work ethic is. I understand that it occupies the position, in the American constellation of values, once held by motherhood and Girl Scout cookies. But yuppies took it too far; they *abused* it.

3   In fact, one of the reasons they only lived for three years (1984–87) was that they *never* rested, never took the time to chew between bites or gaze soulfully past their computer screens. What's worse, the mere rumor that someone—anyone—was not holding up his or her end of the work ethic was enough to send them into tantrums. They blamed lazy workers for the Decline of Productivity. They blamed lazy welfare mothers for the Budget Deficit. Their idea of utopia (as once laid out in that journal of higher yup

thought, the *New Republic*) was the "Work Ethic State": no free lunches, no handouts, and too bad for all the miscreants and losers who refuse to fight their way up to the poverty level by working eighty hours a week at Wendy's.

4   Personally, I have nothing against work, particularly when performed, quietly and unobtrusively, by someone else. I just don't happen to think it's an appropriate subject for an "ethic." As a general rule, when something gets elevated to apple-pie status in the hierarchy of American values, you have to suspect that its actual *monetary* value is skidding toward zero.

5   Take motherhood: nobody ever thought of putting it on a moral pedestal until some brash feminists pointed out, about a century ago, that the pay is lousy and the career ladder nonexistent. Same thing with work: would we be so reverent about the "work ethic" if it wasn't for the fact that the average working stiff's hourly pay is shrinking, year by year, toward the price of a local phone call?

6   In fact, let us set the record straight; the work ethic is not a "traditional value." It is a johnny-come-lately value, along with thin thighs and non-smoking hotel rooms. In ancient times, work was considered a disgrace inflicted on those who had failed to amass a nest egg through imperial conquest or other forms of organized looting. Only serfs, slaves, and women worked. The yuppies of ancient Athens—which we all know was a perfect cornucopia of "traditional values"—passed their time rubbing their bodies with olive oil and discussing the Good, the True, and the Beautiful.

7   The work ethic came along a couple of millennia later, in the form of Puritanism—the idea that the amount of self-denial you endured in this life was a good measure of the amount of fun awaiting you in the next. But the work ethic only got off the ground with the Industrial Revolution and the arrival of the factory system. This was—let us be honest about it—simply a scheme for extending the benefits of the slave system into the age of emancipation.

8   Under the new system (aka capitalism in this part of the world), huge numbers of people had to be convinced to work extra hard, at pitifully low wages, so that the employing class would not have to work at all. Overnight, with the help of a great number of preachers and other well-rested propagandists, work was upgraded from an indignity to an "ethic."

9   But there was a catch: the aptly named *working class* came to resent the resting class. There followed riots, revolutions, graffiti. Quickly, the word went out from the robber barons to the swelling middle class of lawyers, financial consultants, plant managers, and other forerunners of the yuppie: Look busy! Don't go home until the proles have punched out! Make 'em think *we're* doing the work and that they're lucky to be able to hang around and help out!

10   The lawyers, managers, etc., were only too happy to comply, for as the perennially clever John Kenneth Galbraith once pointed out, they themselves comprised a "new leisure class" within industrial society. Of course, they "work," but only under the most pleasant air-conditioned, centrally heated, and fully carpeted conditions, and then only in a sitting position. It was in their own interest to convince the working class that what looks like lounging requires intense but invisible effort.

11   The yuppies, when they came along, had to look more righteously busy than anyone, for the simple reason that they did nothing at all. Workwise, that is. They did not sow, neither did they reap, but rather sat around pushing money through their modems in games known as "corporate takeover" and "international currency speculation." Hence their rage at anyone who actually works—the "unproductive" American worker, or the woman attempting to raise a family on welfare benefits set below the average yuppie's monthly health spa fee.

12   So let us replace their cruel and empty slogan—"Go for it!"—with the cry that lies deep in every true worker's heart: "Gimme a break!" What this nation needs is not the work ethic, but a *job* ethic: If it needs doing—highways repaired, babies changed, fields plowed—let's get it done. Otherwise, take five. Listen to some New Wave music, have a serious conversation with a three-year-old, write a poem, look at the sky. Let the yuppies Rest in Peace; the rest of us deserve a break.

Discussion Questions

1. Describe how Ehrenreich's emotionally charged language adds to or detracts from the credibility of her argument.

2. Which of Ehrenreich's statements that support her thesis do you find the strongest and which the weakest? Why?

3. Ehrenreich states that work is "an inappropriate subject for an 'ethic.'" Discuss how well she makes her case.

4. At the end of her viewpoint, Ehrenreich states that "What this nation needs is not the work ethic, but a *job* ethic." Is the distinction she makes between a work and job ethic plausible to you? Why or why not? How does the distinction affect the strength of her viewpoint?

5. Imagine that you are a yuppie about whom Ehrenreich writes. What would you say in defense of yourself and your peers? What about your life does Ehrenreich seem to ignore? Provide your own perspective.

ARGUMENT

Teenagers and Work

Laurence Steinberg and Ellen Greenberger

Born in 1952, Laurence Steinberg earned a Ph.D. from Cornell University and currently works as a psychology professor at Temple University. Steinberg's publications include *The Life Cycle: Readings in Human Development* (1981) and *Adolescence* (1989). Born in 1935, Ellen Greenberger earned a Ph.D. from Harvard University and is a professor of social ecology at the University of California, Irvine. Greenberger's articles have appeared in such publications as *American Psychologist, Social Forces,* and *Journal of Youth and Adolescence.* Steinberg and Greenberger are coauthors of *When Teenagers Work: The Psychological and Social Costs of Adolescent Employment* (1986). In the following article, which first appeared in the *Washington Post,* Steinberg and Greenberger vehemently argue against teenagers working while attending school and point to all of the negative consequences that ensue when teenagers have paying jobs while they are still students.

1   Recent reports of widespread child-labor law infractions by employers of teenagers are stirring public concern, but the more important question is whether, and how much, our children should be working at all.

2   When teenagers work a great deal—even within the limits imposed by current legislation—they perform worse in school, report higher rates of drug and alcohol use and develop cynical attitudes toward work itself.

3   The idea that work is good for teenagers, no matter how miserable or time-consuming their jobs, is held with a deep moral conviction comparable to that surrounding the joys of motherhood or the benefits of apple pie. This idea has its origins in images of diligent adolescent apprentices working side by side with caring adult mentors.

4   Although the workplace has changed, it is still widely held that paid work is a character-building enterprise for young people—even more so than schooling. Yet studies indicate that the sorts of characters work builds in the current workplace aren't exactly what most of us have in mind.

5   Teens who work long hours in today's routinized adolescent workplace of mostly dead-end jobs are more cynical about the value of hard work and more tolerant of improprieties on the job than their peers who work less or not at all.

6   The more teenagers work, the more likely they are to endorse such attitudes as "People who work harder at their jobs than they have to are a little bit crazy," and "People who break a few laws to make a profit aren't doing anything I wouldn't do in their position." Given that many young people work for employers who wink at child-labor regulations, it isn't surprising that one of the first lessons learned at work is that laws are meant to be violated.

7   According to recent estimates, more than two-thirds of all U.S. high school juniors and seniors, and about half of all sophomores, hold jobs during the school year. Government statistics indicate that a large proportion of employed high school students work more than 20 hours per week. Contrary to popular wisdom, the vast majority of these student workers are not from disadvantaged backgrounds, but are middle class.

8   Ours is the only major industrialized nation that encourages student employment among college-bound teenagers. Whereas Japanese, German and Swedish youngsters spend their afternoons and evenings studying, ours are flipping burgers and staffing checkout counters.

9   We often hear about our loss of competitiveness, our high rate of consumption relative to saving and the declining competence of our workers. Yet we continue to encourage adolescents to place the short-term goal of earning and spending money above the goal of investing in educational activities.

10   Today, high school is all too often something that American adolescents fit into their work schedules. And, contrary to public opinion, the majority of student workers do not save the bulk of their earnings for college, but spend most of their wages on cars, fashions, stereo equipment, drugs and alcohol.

11   There is now broad consensus among educators and scholars that teenagers who work more than 15 or 20 hours per week, especially those in high-stress jobs, are at risk for problems in school and heightened drug and alcohol use.

12   While the argument to limit students' work hours has been well-received among educators, it has generated controversy, anger and incredulity outside the educational community.

13   The good news is that many school districts and several states are reexamining their practices and policies concerning student employment. Unfortunately, most current statutes permit students to work much more than is probably in their best interest.

14   And as if this weren't troublesome enough, the major employers of teenagers constantly lobby Washington to relax existing restrictions on the hours children are permitted to work. They would rather our 14-year-olds work longer hours, and for lower wages to boot.

15   By permitting our adolescents to compromise their schooling and health in the pursuit of self-indulgent consumerism, we continue to violate the spirit of adolescence.

Discussion Questions

1.   Explain how accurate you find Steinberg and Greenberger's characterization of the typical American teenage worker. How does this strengthen or weaken their argument?

2.   What assumptions do you think Steinberg and Greenberger are making about teenagers who do *not* work after school and on weekends? How do those assumptions affect their argument about teenagers who *do* work?

3.   Do you agree with Steinberg and Greenberger when they claim that "we continue to encourage adolescents to place the short-term goal of making and spending money above the goal of investing in educational activities"? Why or why not?

4.   What kind of proof do Steinberg and Greenberger offer to support their claim? Is it sufficient? Why or why not?

5.   How well do you think Steinberg and Greenberger address the opposing side of the argument: it is acceptable for teenagers to have paying jobs while still in school? Explain your response.

ARGUMENT

THE IMPORTANCE OF WORK

Gloria Steinem

Gloria Steinem was born in 1934 in Toledo, Ohio. After graduating from Smith College, she studied in India at universities in Delhi and Calcutta. In 1960, Steinem worked at *Help!,* a political satire magazine in New York City. Soon after that, her articles began appearing in such magazines as *Vogue, Glamour,* and *Cosmopolitan.* In 1968, Steinem wrote a weekly column for *New York* magazine and became involved in feminism and the women's movement. In 1971, she helped found the National Women's Caucus with Betty Friedan, Bella Abzug, and Shirley Chisholm. In the same year, she and Pat Carbine cofounded and edited *Ms.* magazine. She is the author of *Outrageous Acts and Everyday Rebellions* (1983), in which the following essay appears; *Marilyn* (1986), a biography of Marilyn Monroe; *Revolution from Within: A Book of Self-Esteem* (1992); and *Moving Beyond Words* (1994). In the following selection, Steinem argues why women's reasons for work far exceed "womenworkbecausewehaveto."

1 Toward the end of the 1970s, *The Wall Street Journal* devoted an eight-part, front-page series to "the working woman"—that is, the influx of women into the paid-labor force—as the greatest change in American life since the Industrial Revolution.

2   Many women readers greeted both the news and the definition with cynicism. After all, women have always worked. If all the productive work of human maintenance that women do in the home were valued at is replacement cost, the gross national product of the United States would go up by 26 percent. It's just that we are now more likely than ever before to leave our poorly rewarded, low-security, high-risk job of homemaking (though we're still trying to explain that it's a perfectly good one and that the problem is male society's refusal both to do it and to give it an economic value) for more secure, independent, and better-paid jobs outside the home.

3   Obviously, the real work revolution won't come until all productive work is rewarded—including child rearing and other jobs done in the home—and men are integrated into so-called women's work as well as vice versa. But the radical change being touted by the *Journal* and other media is one part of that long integration process: the unprecedented flood of women into salaried jobs, that is, into the labor force as it has been male-defined and previously occupied by men. We are already more than 41 percent of it—the highest proportion in history. Given the fact that women also make up a whopping 69 percent of the "discouraged labor force" (that is, people who need jobs but don't get counted in the unemployment statistics because they've given up looking), plus an official female unemployment rate that is substantially higher than men's, it's clear that we could expand to become fully half of the national work force by 1990.

4   Faced with this determination of women to find a little independence and to be paid and honored for our work, experts have rushed to ask: "Why?" It's a question rarely directed at male workers. Their basic motivations of survival and personal satisfaction are taken for granted. Indeed, men are regarded as "odd" and therefore subjects for sociological study and journalistic reports only when they *don't* have work, even if they are rich and don't need jobs or are poor and can't find them. Nonetheless, pollsters and sociologists have gone to great expense to prove that women work outside the home because of dire financial need, or if we persist despite the presence of a wage-earning male, out of some desire to buy "little extras" for our families, or even out of good old-fashioned penis envy.

5   Job interviewers and even our own families may still ask salaried women the big "Why?" If we have small children at home or are in some job regarded as "men's work," the incidence of such questions increases. Condescending or accusatory versions of "What's a nice girl like you doing in a place like this?" have not disappeared from the workplace.

6   How do we answer these assumptions that we are "working" out of some pressing or peculiar need? Do we feel okay about arguing that it's as natural for us to have salaried jobs as for our husbands—whether or not we have young children at home? Can we enjoy strong career ambitions without worrying about being thought "unfeminine"? When we confront men's growing resentment of women competing in the work force (often in the form of such guilt-producing accusations as "You're taking men's jobs away" or "You're damaging your children"), do we simply state that a decent job is a basic human right for everybody?

7   I'm afraid the answer is often no. As individuals and as a movement, we tend to retreat into some version of a tactically questionable defense: "Womenworkbecausewehaveto." The phrase has become one word, one key on the typewriter—an economic form of the socially "feminine" stance

of passivity and self-sacrifice. Under attack, we still tend to present our-selves as creatures of economic necessity and familial devotion. "Women-workbecausewehaveto" has become the easiest thing to say.

8   Like most truisms, this one is easy to prove with statistics. Economic need *is* the most consistent work motive—for women as well as men. In 1976, for instance, 43 percent of all women in the paid-labor force were single, widowed, separated, or divorced, and working to support themselves and their dependents. An additional 21 percent were married to men who had earned less than ten thousand dollars in the previous year, the minimum then required to support a family of four. In fact, if you take men's pensions, stocks, real estate, and various forms of accumulated wealth into account, a good statistical case can be made that there are more women who "have" to work (that is, who have neither the accumulated wealth, nor husbands whose work or wealth can support them for the rest of their lives) than there are men with the same need. If we were going to ask one group "Do you really need this job?" we should ask men.

9   But the first weakness of the whole "have to work" defense is its decep-tiveness. Anyone who has ever experienced dehumanized life on welfare or any other confidence-shaking dependency knows that a paid job may be preferable to the dole, even when the handout is coming from a family member. Yet the will and self-confidence to work on one's own can dimin-ish as dependency and fear increase. That may explain why—contrary to the "have to" rationale—wives of men who earn less than three thousand dol-lars a year are actually *less* likely to be employed than wives whose hus-bands make ten thousand dollars a year or more.

10   Furthermore, the greatest proportion of employed wives is found among families with a total household income of twenty-five to fifty thousand dol-lars a year. This is the statistical underpinning used by some sociologists to prove that women's work is mainly important for boosting families into the middle or upper middle class. Thus, women's incomes are largely used for buying "luxuries" and "little extras": a neat double-whammy that renders us secondary within our families, and makes our jobs expendable in hard times. We may even go along with this interpretation (at least, up to the point of getting fired so a male can have our job). It preserves a husbandly ego-need to be seen as the primary breadwinner, and still allows us a safe "feminine" excuse for working.

11   But there are often rewards that we're not confessing. As noted in *The Two-Career Couple*, by Francine and Douglas Hall: "Women who hold jobs by choice, even blue-collar routine jobs, are more satisfied with their lives than are the full-time housewives."

12   In addition to personal satisfaction, there is also society's need for all its members' talents. Suppose that jobs were given out on only a "have to

work" basis to both women and men—one job per household. It would be unthinkable to lose the unique abilities of, for instance, Eleanor Holmes Norton, the distinguished chair of the Equal Employment Opportunity Commission. But would we then be forced to question the important work of her husband, Edward Norton, who is also a distinguished lawyer? Since men earn more than twice as much as women on the average, the wife in most households would be more likely to give up her job. Does that mean the nation could do as well without millions of its nurses, teachers, and secretaries? Or that the rare man who earns less than his wife should give up his job?

13   It was this kind of waste of human talents on a society-wide scale that traumatized millions of unemployed or underemployed Americans during the Depression. Then, a one-job-per-household rule seemed somewhat justified, yet the concept was used to displace women workers only, create intolerable dependencies, and waste female talent that the country needed. That Depression experience, plus the energy and example of women who were finally allowed to work during the manpower shortage created by World War II, led Congress to reinterpret the meaning of the country's full-employment goal in its Economic Act of 1946. Full employment was officially defined as "the employment of those who want to work, without regard to whether their employment is, by some definition, necessary. This goal applies equally to men and to women." Since bad economic times are again creating a resentment of employed women—as well as creating more need for women to be employed—we need such a goal more than ever. Women are again being caught in a tragic double bind: We are required to be strong and then punished for our strength.

14   Clearly, anything less than government and popular commitment to this 1946 definition of full employment will leave the less powerful groups, whoever they may be, in danger. Almost as important as the financial penalty paid by the powerless is the suffering that comes from being shut out of paid and recognized work. Without it, we lose much of our self-respect and our ability to prove that we are alive by making some difference in the world. That's just as true for the suburban woman as it is for the unemployed steel worker.

15   But it won't be easy to give up the passive defense of "weworkbecausewehaveto."

16   When a woman who is struggling to support her children and grandchildren on welfare sees her neighbor working as a waitress, even though that neighbor's husband has a job, she may feel resentful; and the waitress (of course, not the waitress's husband) may feel guilty. Yet unless we establish the obligation to provide a job for everyone who is willing and able to work, that welfare woman may herself be penalized by policies that give

out only one public-service job per household. She and her daughter will have to make a painful and divisive decision about which of them gets that precious job, and the whole household will have to survive on only one salary.

17   A job as a human right is a principle that applies to men as well as women. But women have more cause to fight for it. The phenomenon of the "working woman" has been held responsible for everything from an increase in male impotence (which turned out, incidentally, to be attributable to medication for high blood pressure) to the rising cost of steak (which was due to high energy costs and beef import restrictions, not women's refusal to prepare the cheaper, slower-cooking cuts). Unless we see a job as part of every citizen's right to autonomy and personal fulfillment, we will continue to be vulnerable to someone else's idea of what "need" is, and whose "need" counts the most.

18   In many ways, women who do not have to work for simple survival, but who choose to do so nonetheless, are on the frontier of asserting this right for all women. Those with well-to-do husbands are dangerously easy for us to resent and put down. It's easier still to resent women from families of inherited wealth, even though men generally control and benefit from that wealth. (There is no Rockefeller Sisters Fund, no J. P. Morgan & Daughters, and sons-in-law may be the ones who really sleep their way to power.) But to prevent a woman whose husband or father is wealthy from earning her own living, and from gaining the self-confidence that comes with that ability, is to keep her needful of that unearned power and less willing to disperse it. Moreover, it is to lose forever her unique talents.

19   Perhaps modern feminists have been guilty of a kind of reverse snobbism that keeps us from reaching out to the wives and daughters of wealthy men; yet it was exactly such women who refused the restrictions of class and financed the first wave of feminist revolution.

20   For most of us, however, "womenworkbecausewehaveto" is just true enough to be seductive as a personal defense.

21   If we use it without also staking out the larger human right to a job, however, we will never achieve that right. And we will always be subject to the false argument that independence for women is a luxury affordable only in good economic times. Alternatives to layoffs will not be explored, acceptable unemployment will always be used to frighten those with jobs into accepting low wages, and we will never remedy the real cost, both to families and to the country, of dependent women and a massive loss of talent.

22   Worst of all, we may never learn to find productive, honored work as a natural part of ourselves and as one of life's basic pleasures.

Discussion Questions

1. "The Importance of Work" was written over twenty years ago. Explain what relevance you think it has for workers today.

2. What do you think is Steinem's most compelling reason for her impatience with the term "womenworkbecausewehaveto"? Which is her least? Explain your answers.

3. What reactions do you think Steinem's opponents would raise to her argument? Discuss how well you think Steinem addresses their concerns.

4. Whom do you think Steinem envisioned as her audience? What in her argument leads you to your answer?

5. How do you think Lance Morrow would respond to the points Steinem raises in her essay? Explain your response.

Incentives Can Be

Bad for Business

Alfie Kohn

Alfie Kohn received his education at Brown University and the University of Chicago. The author of *No Contest: The Case Against Competition* (1986), *The Brighter Side of Human Nature: Altruism & Empathy in Everyday Life* (1990), and *Punished by Rewards: The Trouble with Gold Stars* (1993), his articles have appeared in such publications as *Psychology Today, The Nation, Atlantic Monthly, Harvard Business Review,* the *Journal of Education, Ladies' Home Journal, The Humanist, Change, The Los Angeles Times,* the *New York Times,* and *Inc.* magazine, from which the following article is taken. Kohn lectures widely and has appeared on over two hundred radio and television programs, including "Donahue" and the "Today" show. Kohn is a fervent critic of competition, and "Incentives Can Be Bad for Business" examines the problems that competition creates in the workplace.

1   Whether they know it or not, most executives are Skinnerians. It was Harvard psychologist B. F. Skinner who popularized the theory of reinforcement, which holds that presenting a reward after a desired behavior will make that behavior more likely to occur in the future. To our pets we say, "Good dog!" and offer a biscuit. To our employees we say, "Good job!" and offer a performance bonus.

2   It seems to make sense. But research has been accumulating that shows tangible rewards as well as praise can actually lower the level of performance, particularly in jobs requiring creativity. Study after study has shown that intrinsic interest in a task—the sense that something is worth doing for its own sake—typically declines when someone is given an external reason for doing it.

3   Author and sociologist Philip Slater put it starkly in his book *Wealth Addiction*: "Getting people to chase money . . . produces nothing except people

chasing money. Using money as a motivator leads to a progressive degradation in the quality of everything produced."

4   The problem is not with money per se, which most of us find desirable. Rather, it is the fact that waving dollar bills in front of people leads them to think of themselves as doing work *only* for the reward. Performance tends to suffer as a result.

5   In one study, Teresa M. Amabile, associate professor of psychology at Brandeis University, asked seventy-two creative writers to write some poetry. She gave one group of subjects a list of extrinsic reasons for writing, such as impressing teachers and making money, and asked them to think about their own writing with respect to those reasons. She showed others a list of intrinsic reasons: the enjoyment of playing with words, for example, and satisfaction from self-expression. A third group was not given any list. All were then asked to do more writing.

6   The results were clear. Those given the extrinsic reasons not only wrote less creatively than the others, as judged by twelve independent poets, but the quality of their work dropped significantly after this brief exposure to the extrinsic reasons.

7   This effect, according to other studies, is by no means limited to poets. When young tutors were promised free movie tickets for teaching well, they took longer to communicate ideas, got frustrated more easily, and did a poorer job in the end that those who got nothing. In another study, a group of subjects who contracted in advance for a reward made less creative collages and told less inventive stories. Students who were offered a reward for participating in still another experiment not only did more poorly at a creative task, but also failed to memorize as well as the subjects who received no reward.

8   What's going on here? The experts offer three explanations for such findings, and all of them have important implications for managers.

9   First, rewards encourage people to focus narrowly on a task, to do it as quickly as possible, and to take few risks. "If they feel, 'This is something I have to get through to get the prize,' they're going to be less creative," says Amabile. The more emphasis placed on the reward, the more inclined someone will be to do the minimum necessary to get it. And that means lower-quality work.

10   The very fact of turning a task into a means for attaining something else changes the way that task is perceived, as a clever series of experiments by Mark R. Lepper, a professor of psychology at Stanford University, demonstrated. He told a group of children that they could not engage in one activity they liked until they took part in another. Although they had enjoyed both activities equally, the children came to dislike the task that was a prerequisite for the other.

11   Second, extrinsic rewards can erode intrinsic interest. People who come
to see themselves as working for money or approval find their tasks less
pleasurable and therefore do not do them as well. "Money may work to 'buy
off' one's intrinsic motivation for an activity," says Edward L. Deci, a professor of psychology at the University of Rochester and a leading authority
on the subject.

12   What's true of money is also true of competition, which, contrary to
myth, is nearly always counterproductive (see "No Contest," *Managing People*, November 1987). Deci put eighty subjects to work on a spatial-rela-
tions puzzle, and he asked some to solve it more quickly than those sitting
next to them. Then each of the subjects sat alone—but secretly observed—
in a room that contained a similar puzzle. It turned out that those who had
been competing spent less time working on the task voluntarily—and later
told Deci they found it less interesting—compared with those who didn't
have to compete. The external prod of winning a contest, like that of a
bonus, makes a task seem less enjoyable in its own right. Not surprisingly,
what's seen as less enjoyable is usually done less well.

13   But there is a third reason that the use of external motivators can backfire. People come to see themselves as being controlled by a reward. They feel
less autonomous, and this often interferes with performance.

14   There's no shortage of data showing that a feeling of freedom translates
into happier and more productive employees. In 1983–84, Amabile and
Stan Gryskiewicz, of the Center for Creative Leadership, in Greensboro,
N.C., interviewed 120 research-and-development scientists, asking each to
describe one event from their work experience that exemplified high creativity and one that reflected low creativity. The factor they mentioned
most often, by far, was freedom or its absence. Receiving a clear overall direction on a project is useful, the scientists said, but they worked best when
they could decide for themselves how to accomplish those goals.

15   Rewards are often offered in a controlling way, and to that extent, says
Deci's colleague Richard Ryan, they stifle productivity. He emphasizes the
enormous difference between saying, "I'm giving you this reward because I
recognize the value of your work," and "You're getting this reward because
you've lived up to my standards." Likewise for verbal feedback: the question
isn't whether you give enough of it, or even how positive it is. What matters
is how controlling the person perceives it to be.

16   This point was made in a study conducted by Deci, Ryan, and James
Connell. From questionnaires completed by several hundred workers in a
corporation that manufactured business machines, they found that those
who worked for controlling managers were less satisfied with their jobs and
more concerned with pay and benefits. The attitude seemed to be, "If you're
going to control me, I'm going to be alienated, and what I'm going to focus

on is money." In a related laboratory study, Ryan found that when subjects were praised, told in effect, "Good, you're doing as you should," instead of simply letting them know how well they had done, motivation was low.

17   Does all this mean that employees should be paid less or ignored when they do good work? Definitely not. Is it an argument for scrapping incentive plans? Probably not. What the research indicates is that all incentive systems—along with verbal feedback—should be guided by two clear principles. Higher-quality work, particularly on jobs requiring creative thinking, is more likely to occur when a person focuses on the challenge of the task itself, rather than on some external motivator, and feels a sense of self-determination, as opposed to feeling controlled by means of praise or reward.

18   Practically speaking, this means that incentives announced in advance are more likely to undermine performance than are unexpected bonuses that recognize an outstanding job after the fact. Particularly deadly are incentive programs run as contests in which some teams (or individuals) will not receive bonuses no matter how well they perform. Managers need to consider the impact of any incentive payment on the workers who *don't* receive it—another hidden cost of rewards.

19   Provided these conditions are met—and everyone feels the system for awarding bonuses is fair—incentives may not be harmful. But a supportive workplace, one in which workers are allowed autonomy and are not only informed about company goals but help determine them, may not even need incentive systems.

20   The larger point is that innovation cannot be forced but only allowed to happen. You can help create the conditions that allow it by playing down the significance of rewards and playing up what employees find appealing about the task itself. Effective supervisors take care of their subordinates' financial needs but don't make a big deal about money and its relationship to performance. Instead, they concentrate on the most powerful motivator that exists: the intrinsic interest people have in solving problems. People are most interested when their curiosity is aroused—when discrepancies exist between what they thought was true and what they've just encountered—and when they are challenged by a task that's neither so difficult as to be overwhelming nor so simple as to be boring.

21   What's more, employees should be matched with the kind of work that they find interesting. "In hiring we almost never look at intrinsic motivation," Amabile observes of most organizations. Yet having someone work on the sort of problem to which he or she is naturally attracted is likely to produce better results than using some artificial means to boost performance.

22   Of course, some tasks are universally regarded as dull. In these cases, the idea is to get people to internalize the importance of doing them—to

transform external reasons into internal incentive. Deci and his colleagues have recently turned their attention to this problem. Their findings suggest that a manager should acknowledge that the task is boring, explain why it needs to be done, and try to maximize a feeling of autonomy.

23   In another experiment, Deci and graduate student Haleh Eghrari had ninety subjects press a computer-keyboard space bar every time a dot of light appeared on the screen, a task most found uninteresting. The researchers admitted to one group that the activity wasn't much fun, but they explained that it could be useful for learning about concentration. These individuals were praised for their performance afterward. A second group was told that they "should attend to [the task] very carefully . . . since it will be for your own good." Later they were informed that they had done well "as [they] should." The third group was given only instructions without explanation.

24   As with the competition study, each subject was then left alone in a room and given the option of continuing to play with the computer once the experiment was over. Those in the first group chose to do this more often and also did a better job at the task. "People need to experience a sense of initiation," Deci explains, "so the less you're controlling and demanding, the more they have a chance to feel that initiation themselves."

25   Self-determination, then, proves decisive with boring tasks as well as with interesting ones. And it isn't only an autocratic environment that wipes out feelings of autonomy. Even well-meaning managers can be controlling in the way they praise or reward. Likewise, financial incentives can come to seem so important that they reduce the attraction of the task itself. Lest managers squelch the very innovation they hope to create, rewards should be used with caution.

Discussion Questions

1. Kohn cites a number of studies as a way to prove his point. How effective do you think these studies are in making his argument convincing?

2. Whom do you think Kohn envisioned as his audience? What leads you to your answer?

3. Kohn presents three explanations that prove the findings concerning extrinsic versus intrinsic value in work. How convincing do you find these explanations? What do they add to his argument?

4. If rewards and praise don't produce happy workers, what do you think does? How satisfactorily does Kohn address this question?

5. To what extent do you think Lance Morrow would agree with Kohn's argument? Explain your response.

ARGUMENT

Overworked Americans

Robert J. Samuelson

Robert J. Samuelson was born in 1945 and earned a B.A. degree from Harvard University. Beginning in 1969, he worked for the *Washington Post* for four years, after which he freelanced for four years. He has also written for the *National Journal*. Since 1984, he has been a columnist for *Newsweek,* magazine where the following selection first appeared. In it, Samuelson disputes the ideas Juliet Schor makes in her much-publicized *The Overworked American* as he argues that people, despite their claims to the contrary, are not working harder these days.

1   As I write, I am feeling severely overworked. The deadline for this column looms, and it looks as if I won't make it, although I know I will because I always have. But my writing isn't getting any faster, something I can't seem to change. I have fallen so far behind on so many things that my office—normally an organized clutter—is now so strewn with piles of papers and books that it's virtually inaccessible.

2   When I get home, matters won't improve. I anticipate a long struggle with my two-year-old son to undress him for bed. John is a chunky kid with a strong allergy to authority. He refuses to undress. We fight over every inch of every stitch of clothing. He kicks, grabs my glasses and screams, "NO DADDEE." The undressing usually takes twenty minutes and leaves me exhausted.

3   Just about everyone (it seems) feels stressed and strained. Count me in. But feelings aren't facts, and we shouldn't confuse the two. Are we really losing leisure? Yes, says Harvard economist Juliet Schor in a widely publicized new book *The Overworked American*. Compared with the late 1960s, the average worker now puts in about a month's more time on the job (163 hours to be exact) every year, she contends. I simply don't believe her.

4   Hers is mostly a case of mistaken identity. What's causing the sense of time squeeze—and a lot of other turmoil as well—is the huge influx of women into the work force. In 1950, 34 percent of women had jobs; today, it's 57 percent. Life has become more complicated. Families do feel torn by

different demands. Men and women are sliding into unaccustomed roles. But this upheaval is distinct from what Schor claims has happened: that workers are being forced to spend more time at their jobs and, in the process, sacrificing precious leisure time.

5   Superficially, this seems plausible. Schor's argument is that companies have reacted to growing competitive pressures by demanding more time from their workers. People put in more overtime (it's often cheaper for firms to pay overtime than hire new workers with expensive fringe benefits). Vacations and paid holidays have been cut. Sounds sensible.

6   But the supporting evidence isn't there. Virtually all of the increase in work time—even by Schor's calculations, which subtly modify the basic statistics—occurs among women. This has little to do with the pressure from employers (if it did, similar increases would occur among men) and everything to do with women's assimilation into the labor market on terms increasingly comparable with men's. Women have gone into more occupations, are moving up career ladders and spend more time on the job.

7   Just about everyone feels oppressed by work at times. Some companies (or bosses) routinely demand long hours—often unreasonably so. In the 1980s, pressures may have increased. But Schor requires us to believe that matters have dramatically worsened. Not so.

8   In 1969, the average work week for men was 42.5 hours, reports the Bureau of Labor Statistics. In 1991, it was 42 hours. Nor does there seem to have been any major drop in paid time off (mainly vacations and holidays). Among firms with more than one hundred workers, vacation time has risen slightly since 1980 for workers with up to fifteen years of service and decreased slightly for those with twenty years or more. The number of paid holidays has slipped a bit, from 10.1 days in 1980 to 9.2 days in 1989.

9   Leisure for all Americans has risen, because people retire earlier and live longer. In 1950, 87 percent of men between fifty-five and sixty-four worked; that dropped to 83 percent in 1970 and 67 percent in 1991. No one, including Schor, denies this rise in leisure. The main dispute involves two-earner couples with children. What's happened to their leisure? Frankly, it's hard to tell. Some time-use surveys contradict Schor's conclusions. These studies ask people in great detail about their activities in a single day.

10   **More leisure?** A study by Thomas Juster and Frank Stafford at the University of Michigan suggests that everyone's leisure has risen. Between the mid-1960s and the early 1980s, they find that women's average weekly housework decreased (from forty-two to thirty-one hours) while their time at jobs increased (from nineteen to twenty-four hours). The gain in weekly leisure was about six hours. Men's housework increased (from twelve to fourteen hours), while their time at jobs dropped (from fifty-one to forty-four

hours). The gain is five hours. Unfortunately, this survey might be misleading because it includes retirees and the unemployed. Schor (who has tried to correct the data for these shortcomings) contends that workers have lost about three hours a week of leisure. But another time-use study by John Robinson of the University of Maryland, comparing 1985 and 1965, finds that leisure has risen.

11   I'm not sure the debate over statistics matters much. With children, what counts is not only how much time you've got but also when you've got it. Two-earner couples with children are obviously squeezed, because they're supposed to be in too many places at the same time. But the conflicts are not only conflicts of time but also of careers and values. Companies and families are trying to come to terms with the tensions. An extra half an hour a day would be glorious. However, it would not relieve the underlying stress of trying to serve so many masters simultaneously.

12   Schor admires Europe's more relaxed lifestyles, where long vacations are often mandated (five weeks in Sweden, four weeks in Belgium). She thinks we should be more addicted to leisure and less to consumption. Maybe she's right, but her preferences are—for better of worse—fundamentally un-American. Ours has always been a hurried society, brimming (perhaps excessively) with ambition. We crowd more things into already-crowded schedules. We are uneasy with ease. The constant quest for achievement and self-fulfillment can be exhausting and frustrating.

13   It may be a curse, but it's our culture. The resulting discontents haven't changed much since Alexis de Tocqueville first noted them in the 1830s. Americans (he wrote) "are forever brooding over advantages they do not possess. It is strange to see with what feverish ardor [they] pursue their own welfare, and to watch the vague dread that constantly torments them lest they should not have chosen the shortest path which may lead to it."

Discussion Questions

1.   Analyze how Samuelson tries to convince you that his perspective is correct and Juliet Schor's is misleading. Is he successful? Explain your response.

2.   Samuelson begins his argument with a personal story. Do you find this an effective way for him to begin? Why or why not?

3.   Samuelson uses Schor's ideas as a springboard to present his argument about Americans purportedly being overworking and returns to her findings as a way to advance his own

perspective. Do you find this an effective technique? Why or why not?

4. Do Samuelson's concessions to Schor's points strengthen or weaken his argument? Explain your answer.

5. Samuelson concludes his argument with an observation made by Alexis de Tocqueville. Although it was written over 150 years ago, do you think it still characterizes Americans? Why or why not? Discuss the effectiveness of Samuelson ending his argument with this quote.

WRITING TOPICS

1. In a paper, discuss what you see as the meaning of work (besides the obvious: money). Do not restrict your paper to personal experiences; rather, include what sociologists, psychologists, journalists, and business people have written about what meaning people derive from work to add support to your own thinking.

2. Much attention has been given to the work ethic in America. While some critics say that it has declined in the past decades, others maintain that is has never been stronger. Where do *you* stand on the issue? Write a paper in which you explain and defend your stand. Include research that helps to support your claim.

3. In "Teenagers and Work," Steinberg and Greenberger suggest that teenagers should not attempt to have paying jobs while going to school. If you disagree with their stand, write a paper that argues your own perspective.

4. "The Importance of Work" by Gloria Steinem was written some twenty-five years ago. Write a paper in which you argue that her perspective is still timely or is outdated.

5. Americans seem to enjoy complaining about how overworked they are. But are they, really? Write a paper in which you examine the topic of overworked (or underworked) Americans.

6. Employers try to motivate workers by offering them incentives: praise, cash bonuses, shares in company stock, perks, turkeys or hams at Christmas, and so on. Interview workers from a range of occupations to see what motivates them to work harder. Research what industrial psychologists have to contribute to the

issue. What do *you* think is the best way to motivate workers? Write a paper that incorporates your own perspective and that of the workers and critics you research.

7. Along with complaining about being overworked, Americans claim to be stressed and suffering from burnout. Do you see these complaints as recent phenomena or have workers always been troubled by them? You might find it interesting, if not revealing, to trace the history of such terms as *burnout* and *workaholic* to see when they first appeared in the English language. Write a paper that supports your stance on burnout.

8. As much as discrimination is a part of life, it is also a part of work: No one seems to be immune to it. Whether the discrimination is because of race, ethnicity, gender, sexual orientation, age, or appearance, discrimination exists. Write a paper in which you examine the following questions: Do you think that discrimination will disappear in your lifetime? Why or why not? How do other critics answer these questions?

9. Some professions are renowned for paying their workers huge salaries (for example, actors, athletes, and CEOs). Should some workers who make important contributions to society (such as teachers, social workers, nurses) earn salaries equal to those of athletes and movie stars? Support your claim.

10. In recent years, the workplace has undergone some dramatic changes: New to the workplace and workforce are flex-time schedules, job sharing, daycare on the premises, home offices, and such. Describe how you envision the workplace in the beginning of the twenty-first century and whether you see the changes improving working conditions.

CHAPTER **8**

SPORTS AND LEISURE

VIEWPOINT

Football Red and

Baseball Green

Murray Ross

Born in 1942, Murray Ross directs the theater program
at the University of Colorado in Colorado Springs. He is
also the artistic director of Theatreworks, the resident
theater group. "Football Red and Baseball Green" originally appeared in the *Chicago Review* in 1971. In the
following revised and updated version, Ross compares
and contrasts two popular American sports and discusses what makes them so appealing to Americans.

1   The Super Bowl, the final game of the professional football season, draws a
larger television audience than any of the moon walks or Tiny Tim's wedding. This revelation is one way of indicating just how popular spectator
sports are in this country. Americans, or American men anyway, seem to
care about the games they watch as much as the Elizabethans cared about
their plays, and I suspect for some of the same reasons. There is, in sport,
some of the rudimentary drama found in popular theater: familiar plots,
type characters, heroic and comic action spiced with new and unpredictable
variations. And common to watching both activities is the sense of participation in a shared tradition and in shared fantasies. If sport exploits these
fantasies, without significantly transcending them, it seems no less satisfying
for all that.

2   It is my guess that sport spectating involves something more than the
vicarious pleasures of identifying with athletic prowess. I suspect that each
sport contains a fundamental myth which it elaborates for its fans, and that
our pleasure in watching such games derives in part from belonging briefly
to the mythical world which the game and its players bring to life. I am especially interested in baseball and football because they are so popular and
so uniquely *American;* they began here and unlike basketball they have not
been widely exported. Thus whatever can be said, mythically, about these
games would seem to apply to our culture.

3   Baseball's myth may be the easier to identify since we have a greater
historical perspective on the game. It was an instant success during the

Industrialization, and most probably it was a reaction to the squalor, the faster pace and the dreariness of the new conditions. Baseball was old-fashioned right from the start; it seems conceived in nostalgia, in the resuscitation of the Jeffersonian dream. It established an artificial rural environment, one removed from the toil of an urban life, which spectators could be admitted to and temporarily breathe in. Baseball is a *pastoral* sport, and I think the game can be best understood as this kind of art. For baseball does what all good pastoral does—it creates an atmosphere in which everything exists in harmony.

4   Consider, for instance, the spatial organization of the game. A kind of controlled openness is created by having everything fan out from home plate, and the crowd sees the game through an arranged perspective that is rarely violated. Visually this means that the game is always seen as a constant, rather calm whole, and that the players and the playing field are viewed in relationship to each other. Each player has a certain position, a special area to tend, and the game often seems to be as much a dialogue between the fielders and the field as it is a contest between players themselves; will that ball get through the hole? Can that outfielder run under that fly? As a moral genre, pastoral asserts the virtue of communion with nature. As a competitive game, baseball asserts that the team which best relates to the playing field (by hitting the ball in the right places) will win.

5   I suspect baseball's space has a subliminal function too, for topographically it is a sentimental mirror of older America. Most of the game is played between the pitcher and the hitter in the extreme corner of the playing area. This is the busiest, most sophisticated part of the ball park, where something is always happening, and from which all subsequent action originates. From this urban corner we move to a supporting infield, active but a little less crowded, and from there we come to the vast stretches of the outfield. As is traditional in American lore, danger increases with distance, and the outfield action is often the most spectacular in the game. The long throw, the double off the wall, the leaping catch—these plays take place in remote territory, and they belong, like most legendary feats, to the frontier.

6   Having established its landscape, pastoral art operates to eliminate any reference to that bigger, more disturbing, more real world it has left behind. All games are to some extent insulated from the outside by having their own rules, but baseball has a circular structure as well which furthers its comfortable feeling of self-sufficiency. By this I mean that every motion of extension is also one of return—a ball hit outside is a *home* run, a full circle. Home—familiar, peaceful, secure—it is the beginning and end. You must go out and come back; only the completed movement is registered.

7   Time is a serious threat to any form of pastoral. The genre poses a timeless world of perpetual spring, and it does its best to silence the ticking of

clocks which remind us that in time the green world fades into winter. One's sense of time is directly related to what happens in it, and baseball is so structured as to stretch out and ritualize whatever action it contains. Dramatic moments are few, and they are almost always isolated by the routine texture of normal play. It is certainly a game of climax and drama, but it is perhaps more a game of repeated and predictable action: the foul balls, the walks, the pitcher fussing around on the mound, the lazy fly ball to centerfield. This is, I think, as it should be, for baseball exists as an alternative to a world of too much action, struggle and change. It is a merciful release from a more grinding and insistent tempo, and its time, as William Carlos Williams suggests, makes a virtue out of idleness simply by providing it:

> The crowd at the ball game
> is moved uniformly
> by a spirit of uselessness
> Which delights them . . .

8   Within this expanded and idle time the baseball fan is at liberty to become a ceremonial participant and a lover of style. Because the action is normalized, how something is done becomes as important as the action itself. Thus baseball's most delicate and detailed aspects are often, to the spectator, the most interesting. The pitcher's windup, the anticipatory crouch of the infielders, the quick waggle of the bat as it poises for the pitch—these subtle miniature movements are as meaningful as the home runs and the strikeouts. It somehow matters in baseball that all the tiny rituals are observed: the shortstop must kick the dirt and the umpire must brush the plate with his pocket broom. In a sense baseball is largely a continuous series of small gestures, and I think it characteristic that the game's most treasured moment came when Babe Ruth pointed to where he subsequently hit a home run.

9   Baseball is a game where the little things mean a lot, and this, together with its clean serenity, its open space, and its ritualized action is enough to place it in a world of yesterday. Baseball evokes for us a past which may never have been ours, but which we believe was, and certainly that is enough. In the Second World War, supposedly, we fought for "Baseball, Mom and Apple Pie," and considering what baseball means that phrase is a good one. We fought then for the right to believe in a green world of tranquillity and uninterrupted contentment, where the little things would count. But now the possibilities of such a world are more remote, and it seems that while the entertainment of such a dream has an enduring appeal, it is no longer sufficient for our fantasies. I think this may be why

baseball is no longer our preeminent national pastime, and why its myth is being replaced by another more appropriate to the new realities (and fantasies) of our time.

10   Football, especially professional football, is the embodiment of a newer myth, one which in many respects is opposed to baseball's. The fundamental difference is that football is not a pastoral game; it is a heroic one. One way of seeing the difference between the two is by the juxtaposition of Babe Ruth and Jim Brown, both legendary players in their separate genres. Ruth, baseball's most powerful hitter, was a hero maternalized (his name), an epic figure destined for a second immortality as a candy bar. His image was impressive but comfortable and altogether human: round, dressed in a baggy uniform, with a schoolboy's cap and a bat which looked tiny next to him. His spindly legs supported a Santa-sized torso, and this comic disproportion would increase when he was in motion. He ran delicately, with quick, very short steps, since he felt that stretching your stride slowed you down. This sort of superstition is typical of baseball players, and typical too is the way in which a personal quirk or mannerism mitigates their awesome skill and makes them poignant and vulnerable.

11   There was nothing funny about Jim Brown. His muscular and almost perfect physique was emphasized further by the uniform which armored him. Babe Ruth had a rough face, but boyish and innocent; Brown was an expressionless mask under the helmet. In action he seemed invincible, the embodiment of speed and power in an inflated human shape. One can describe Brown accurately only with superlatives, for as a player he was a kind of Superman, undisguised.

12   Brown and Ruth are caricatures, yet they represent their games. Baseball is part of a comic tradition which insists that its participants be humans, while football, in the heroic mode, asks that its players be more than that. Football converts men into gods, and suggests that magnificence and glory are as desirable as happiness. Football is designed, therefore, to impress its audience rather differently than baseball.

13   As a pastoral game, baseball attempts to close the gap between the players and the crowd. It creates the illusion, for instance, that with a lot of hard work, a little luck, and possibly some extra talent, the average spectator might well be playing; not watching. For most of us can do a few of the things the ball players do: catch a pop-up, field a ground ball, and maybe get a hit once in a while. Chance is allotted a good deal of play in the game. There is no guarantee, for instance, that a good pitch will not be looped over the infield, or that a solidly batted ball will not turn into a double play. In addition to all of this, almost every fan feels he can make the manager's decision for him, and not entirely without reason. Baseball's statistics are

easily calculated and rather meaningful; and the game itself, though a subtle one, is relatively lucid and comprehensible.

14   As a heroic game football is not concerned with a shared community of near-equals. It seeks almost the opposite relationship between its spectators and players, one which stresses the distance between them. We are not allowed to identify directly with Jim Brown any more than we are with Zeus, because to do so would undercut his stature as something more than human. The players do much of the distancing themselves by their own excesses of speed, size and strength. When Bob Brown, the giant all-pro tackle says that he could "block King Kong all day," we look at him and believe. But the game itself contributes to the players' heroic isolation. As George Plimpton has graphically illustrated in *Paper Lion,* it is almost impossible to imagine yourself in a professional football game without also considering your imminent humiliation and possible injury. There is scarcely a single play that the average spectator could hope to perform adequately, and there is even a difficulty in really understanding what is going on. In baseball what happens is what meets the eye, but in football each action is the result of eleven men acting simultaneously against eleven other men, and clearly this is too much for the eye to totally comprehend. Football has become a game of staggering complexity, and coaches are now wired in to several "spotters" during the games so they can find out what is happening.

15   If football is distanced from its fans by its intricacy and its "superhuman" play, it nonetheless remains an intense spectacle. Baseball, as I have implied, dissolves time and urgency in a green expanse, thereby creating a luxurious and peaceful sense of leisure. As is appropriate to a heroic enterprise, football reverses this procedure and converts space into time. The game is ideally played in an oval stadium, not in a "park," and the difference is the elimination of perspective. This makes football a perfect television game because even at first hand it offers a flat, perpetually moving foreground (wherever the ball is). The eye in baseball viewing opens up; in football it zeroes in. There is no democratic vista in football, and spectators are not asked to relax, but to concentrate. You are encouraged to watch the drama, not a medley of ubiquitous gestures, and you are constantly reminded that this event is taking place in time. The third element in baseball is the field; in football this element is the clock. Traditionally heroes do reckon with time, and football players are no exceptions. Time in football is wound up inexorably until it reaches the breaking point in the last minutes of a close game. More often than not it is the clock which emerges as the real enemy, and it is the sense of time running out that regularly produces a pitch of tension uncommon in baseball.

16   A further reason for football's intensity is that the game is played like a war. The idea is to win by going through, around or over the opposing team and the battle lines, quite literally, are drawn on every play. Violence is somewhere at the heart of the game, and the combat quality is reflected in football's army language ("blitz," "trap," "zone," "bomb," "trenches," etc.). Coaches often sound like generals when they discuss their strategy. Woody Hayes of Ohio State, for instance, explains his quarterback option play as if it had been conceived in the Pentagon: "You know," he says, "the most effective kind of warfare is siege. You have to attack on broad fronts. And that's all the option is—attacking on a broad front. You know General Sherman ran an option through the south."

17   Football like war is an arena for action, and like war football leaves little room for personal style. It seems to be a game which projects "character" more than personality, and for the most part football heroes, publicly, are a rather similar lot. They tend to become personifications rather than individuals, and, with certain exceptions, they are easily read emblematically as embodiments of heroic qualities such as "strength," "confidence," "perfection," etc.—clichés really, but forceful enough when represented by the play of a Dick Butkus, a Johnny Unitas or a Bart Starr. Perhaps this simplification of personality results in part from the heroes' total identification with their mission, to the extent that they become more characterized by their work than by what they intrinsically "are." At any rate football does not make allowances for the idiosyncrasies that baseball actually seems to encourage, and as a result there have been few football players as uniquely crazy or human as, say, Casey Stengel or Dizzy Dean.

18   A further reason for the underdeveloped qualities of football personalities, and one which gets us to the heart of the game's modernity, is that football is very much a game of modern technology. Football's action is largely interaction, and the game's complexity requires that its players mold themselves into a perfectly coordinated unit. Jerry Kramer, the veteran guard and author of *Instant Replay*, writes how Lombardi would work to develop such integration:

> He makes us execute the same plays over and over, a hundred times, two hundred times, until we do every little thing automatically. He works to make the kickoff-team perfect, the punt-return team perfect, the field-goal team perfect. He ignores nothing. Technique, technique, technique, over and over and over, until we feel like we're going crazy. But we win.

Mike Garrett, the halfback, gives the player's version:

> After a while you train your mind like a computer—put the ideas in, and the body acts accordingly.

19 As the quotations imply, pro football is insatiably preoccupied with the smoothness and precision of play execution, and most coaches believe that the team which makes the fewest mistakes will be the team that wins. Individual identity thus comes to be associated with the team or unit that one plays for to a much greater extent than in baseball. To use a reductive analogy, it is the difference between *Bonanza* and *Mission Impossible*. Ted Williams is mostly Ted Williams, but Bart Starr is mostly the Green Bay Packers. The latter metaphor is a precise one, since football heroes stand out not because of purely individual acts, but because they epitomize the action and style of the groups they are connected to. Kramer cites the obvious if somewhat self-glorifying historical precedent: "Perhaps," he writes, "we're living in Camelot." Ideally a football team should be what Camelot was supposed to have been, a group of men who function as equal parts of a larger whole, dependent on each other for total meaning.

20 The humanized machine as hero is something very new in sport, for in baseball anything approaching a machine has always been suspect. The famous Yankee teams of the fifties were almost flawlessly perfect and never very popular. Their admirers took pains to romanticize their precision into something more natural than plain mechanics—Joe DiMaggio, for instance, was the "Yankee Clipper," Even so, most people hoped fervently the Brooklyn Dodgers (the "bums") would thrash them in every World Series. To take a more recent example, the victory of the Mets in 1969 was so compelling largely because it was at the expense of a superbly homogenized team, the Baltimore Orioles, and it was accomplished by a somewhat random collection of inspired leftovers. In baseball, machinery seems tantamount to villainy, whereas in football this smooth perfection is part of the expected integration a championship team must attain.

21 It is not surprising, really, that we should have a game which asserts the heroic function of a mechanized group, since we have become a country where collective identity is a reality. Football as a game of groups is appealing to us as a people of groups, and for this reason football is very much an "establishment" game—since it is in the corporate business and governmental structures that group America is most developed. The game comments on the culture, and vice versa:

> President Nixon, an ardent football fan, got a football team picture as an inaugural anniversary present from his cabinet . . . .
> Superimposed on the faces of real gridiron players were the faces of cabinet members.(A.P.)

This is not to say that football appeals only to a certain class, for group America is visible everywhere. A sign held high in the San Francisco

Peace Moratorium . . . read: "49er Fans against War, Poverty and the Baltimore Colts."

22   Football's collective pattern is only one aspect of the way in which it seems to echo our contemporary environment. The game, like our society, can be thought of as a cluster of people living under great tension in a state of perpetual flux. The potential for sudden disaster or triumph is as great in football as it is in our own age, and although there is something ludicrous in equating interceptions with assassinations and long passes with moonshots, there is also something valid and appealing in the analogies. It seems to me that football does successfully reflect those salient and common conditions which affect us all, and it does so with the end of making us feel better about them and our lot. For one thing, it makes us feel that something can be released and connected in all this chaos; out of the accumulated pile of bodies something can emerge—a runner breaks into the clear or a pass finds its way to a receiver. To the spectator plays such as these are human and dazzling. They suggest to the audience what it has hoped for (and been told) all along, that technology is still a tool and not a master. Fans get living proof of this every time a long pass is completed; they see at once that it is the result of careful planning, perfect integration and an effective "pattern," but they see too that it is human and that what counts as well is man, his desire, his natural skill and his "grace under pressure." Football metaphysically yokes heroic action and technology by violence to suggest that they are mutually supportive. It's a doubtful proposition, but given how we live it has its attractions.

23   Football, like the space program, is a game in the grand manner, yet it is a rather sober sport and often seems to lack that positive, comic vision of which baseball's pastoral mannerisms are a part. It is a winter game, as those fans who saw the Minnesota Vikings play the Detroit Lions one Thanksgiving were graphically reminded. The two teams played in a blinding snowstorm, and except for the small flags in the corners of the end zones, and a patch of mud wherever the ball was downed, the field was totally obscured. Even through the magnified television lenses the players were difficult to identify; you saw only huge shapes come out of the gloom, thump against each other and fall in a heap. The movement was repeated endlessly and silently in a muffled stadium, interrupted once or twice by a shot of a barelegged girl who fluttered her pompons in the cold. The spectacle was by turns pathetic, compelling and absurd; a kind of theater of oblivion.

24   Games such as this are by no means unusual, and it is not difficult to see why for many football is a gladiatorial sport of pointless bludgeoning played by armored monsters. However accurate this description may be, I still believe that even in the worst of circumstances football can be a liberating

activity. In the game I have just described, for instance, there was one play, the turning point of the game, which more than compensated for the sluggishness of most of the action. Jim Marshall, the huge defensive end (who hunts on dogsleds during the off season), intercepted a pass deep in his own territory and rumbled upfield like a dinosaur through the mud, the snow, and the opposing team, lateraling at the last minute to another lineman who took the ball in for a touchdown. It was a supreme moment because Marshall's principal occupation is falling on quarterbacks, not catching the ball and running with it. His triumphant jaunt, something that went unequaled during the rest of that dark afternoon, was a hearty burlesque of the entire sport, an occasion for epic laughter in bars everywhere (though especially in Minnesota),and it was more than enough to rescue the game from the snowbound limbo it was in.

25   In the end I suppose both football and baseball could be seen as varieties of decadence. In its preoccupation with mechanization, and in its open display of violence, football is the more obvious target for social moralists, but I wonder if this is finally more "corrupt" than the seductive picture of sanctuary and tranquillity that baseball has so artfully drawn for us. Almost all sport is vulnerable to such criticism because it is not strictly ethical in intent, and for this reason there will always be room for puritans like the Elizabethan John Stubbes who howled at the "wanton fruits which these cursed pastimes bring forth." As a long-time dedicated fan of almost anything athletic, I confess myself out of sympathy with most of this; which is to say, I guess, that I am vulnerable to those fantasies which these games support, and that I find happiness in the company of people who feel as I do.

26   A final note. It is interesting that the heroic and pastoral conventions which underlie our most popular sports are almost classically opposed. The contrasts are familiar: city versus country, aspirations versus contentment, activity versus peace and so on. Judging from the rise of professional football we seem to be slowly relinquishing that unfettered rural vision of ourselves that baseball so beautifully mirrors, and we have come to cast ourselves in a genre more reflective of a nation confronted by constant and unavoidable challenges. Right now, like the Elizabethans, we seem to share both heroic and pastoral yearnings, and we reach out to both. Perhaps these divided needs account in part for the enormous attention we as a nation now give to spectator sports. For sport provides one place where we can have our football and our baseball too.

Discussion Questions

1. In the opening paragraph, Ross posits the idea that sports share some of the characteristics of popular theater. He later likens football to war and to the space program. How convincing do you find these analogies and what do they contribute to his viewpoint? Explain your responses.

2. Do you find Ross's analysis of baseball or of football more plausible? Why?

3. Do you think Ross was directing his viewpoint to fans of baseball and football or to people unfamiliar with and not particularly interested in the sports? To which group do you think his viewpoint would be more convincing? Explain your response.

4. Analyze the organization of Ross's viewpoint. Do you think it is an effective way for Ross to present his ideas? Why or why not?

5. What purpose is served by Ross quoting William Carlos Williams, Jerry Kramer, and Mike Garrett?

How Pro Football Was Ruined

Roland Merullo

> Roland Merullo is a novelist who works at Bennington College. He is the author of *Loving Losapas* (1987) and *A Russian Requiem* (1992). The following viewpoint appeared in a 1984 "My Turn" column of *Newsweek* magazine. In it, Merullo comments on how television networks' instant replay has ruined his watching of pro football.

1 In the old days—about fifteen years ago—I could sit down in front of my television on a Sunday afternoon in the fall and spend a few relaxing hours watching a professional football game. But those days are gone.

2   The pros still play on Sundays and their games continue to be televised: that part is reassuringly the same. What has changed is that watching football is no longer relaxing. I make all the same preparations I used to make: something to drink and invitations perhaps to a friend or two with whom to share the pleasure. But then the game begins and, instead of relaxing, I feel only a subtle dulling of the senses, a kind of electronic Novocain that numbs the brain.

3   I watched a close game recently, the kind of seesaw battle that, fifteen years ago, would have had me clutching the arms of my chair until the final seconds. But I could barely sit through it. Every play, no matter how mundane, was shown two or three times, accompanied by volumes of analysis. By the start of the fourth quarter I felt as if I had watched three games and been through two years of coaching school.

4   **Fourth Down:** Now I have nothing against the instant replay. Besides ensuring us that we will never miss a big play, it has helped reduce domestic violence. Arguments over a referee's call can now be settled the second time the play is shown—or the third or the fourth. The instant replay is a good thing. But too much of anything good becomes bad. There is only a handful of crucial plays in even the most important games; replaying three out of every four downs only dilutes the action and renders this fan impassive.

5   To make matters worse, we are continually being tuned in—for four or five seconds—to other games all over the country. More big plays, more analysis, more chatter and more confusion.

6   Years ago one announcer and one game sufficed. The video presentation was not as polished: occasionally an ad would run beyond the allotted time and we'd miss part of a play. Still I felt like I was watching a *football game* and not a colorful antic concocted in a TV studio. My train of thought wasn't constantly interrupted by people screaming at me or removing half their clothes to try to get me to buy something. What expert commentary I had came from a friend in the next chair who had played three years of high-school ball. Things may have been slow at times, but that fit the mood of a Sunday and made me appreciate and remember, for years in some cases, the really great plays.

7   It would be bad enough if only the regular-season games were being spoiled this way. But Super Sunday has also gone to the dogs. I am told to tune in at 1 o'clock, which I do. But the game doesn't start at 1; it starts at 4. Meanwhile I am treated to the expert prognostications of everyone from former stars to the local bookmaker. By game time my mind is saturated: the real action seems like an afterthought.

8   I make my living as a carpenter and sometimes, after a weekend of trying to watch football, I imagine what it would be like if my work were televised and the same standard of broadcasting overkill applied. The action goes like this:

9   "Merullo's about to put that two-by-six in place now, Vic. It's a tricky one."

10   "It's in, Ric."

11   "I'm not sure."

12   "Yes, the referee on the far side of the house just gave the signal. It's in."

13   "Right, let's see that one again."

14   "OK, Ric. At six feet, 165 pounds, Merullo is one of the smallest framers in the league, but he gets that nail out of the apron as fast as anyone. Still holds the record at Iowa State, I believe."

15   "We can watch that now on STOP-AC-INSTA-DIAGRAM. This line marks Merullo's left index finger. Notice how he slips his hand into the apron here, at X, grasps the head of the nail—looks like a tenpenny common nail."

16   "It is, Ric."

17   "Then he'll put it in place here—at Y, and drive it home. You'll notice that his right wrist is heavily taped. The trainers were working on that last night. He's playing in pain today."

18   "One of the toughest old boys in the league, Ric."

19   "Right, Vic. Now let's go to Burnt Michalson who'll give us some of the action in Missoula."

20   "Thank you, Ric. This is Burnt Michalson. It's 25 above zero today in Missoula, Mont., and at lunchtime the roof the Berdard brothers are

working on is two-thirds complete. Here's some of the action from earlier in the day when Jason Berdard slipped and nearly fell from the staging. You can see the expression of alarm on his brother's face. Again, at lunchtime in Missoula, it's the Berdard brothers' roof two-thirds complete."

21   Carpentry, it's fair to say, is not much of a spectator sport—no contact, no cheerleaders, no high salaries. Football, on the other hand, is something millions of people enjoy watching. Unfortunately, what we are shown these days is not football, but a collage of bits of football-like action each surrounded by several more bits of information. The old simple beauty is gone and Sunday afternoons will never be the same.

Discussion Questions

1.   Merullo writes his viewpoint largely in the first person. Discuss how this contributes to the believability of the writing as opposed to if he had written it in the third person.

2.   Where does Merullo explicitly state the main point of his viewpoint? Is the placement of his main idea well placed? Explain your response.

3.   Do you find Merullo's comparing football to carpentry a convincing analogy that strengthens his viewpoint or a tenuous comparison that weakens it? Explain your answer.

4.   What do you think people opposing Merullo's viewpoint would say in their own defense?

5.   Does Merullo offer any alternatives to the instant replay? If so, are they credible? If not, would they strengthen his viewpoint? Explain your answer.

So Much of the Joy Is Gone

Dick Schaap

Dick Schaap was born in 1934. A sports commentator for ABC News and an Emmy Award winner, Schaap is the author of numerous books, including *An Illustrated History of the Olympics* (1963), *Turned On* (1967), *Massacre at Winged Foot: The U. S. Open Minute-by-Minute* (1974), *Sport/Dick Schaap* (1975), *Steinbrenner* (1982), and *Bo Knows Bo* (1991), written in collaboration with Bo Jackson. In the following selection, which first appeared in *Forbes* magazine in 1992, Schaap argues that money has had a detrimental impact on sports.

1 Athletes are better than ever. They are taller, heavier, faster, stronger, smarter. In every sport in which achievement can be measured objectively, their progress is stunning.

2 A girl barely into her teens swims more swiftly than Johnny Weismuller swam in the Olympics, or in his loincloth.

3 A high school boy jumps farther and sprints faster than Jesse Owens jumped and sprinted in front of Adolf Hitler.

4 A thirty-year-old married woman surpasses Jim Thorpe's best marks in a variety of track and field events.

5 Even a man over forty runs a mile faster than Paavo Nurmi ran in his prime.

6 The performances are so much better.

7 But so much of the joy is gone.

8 Sports has too often been called a microcosm of society, yet its present state certainly reflects the uneasy prosperity of the times, the suspicion that, despite encouraging facts and heartening figures, something is fundamentally wrong. The cheers may be louder than ever, but they ring a little hollow.

9 It is almost impossible to overstate the pervasiveness of sports in American society, the breadth and strength of its special appeal, to bricklayers and novelists, accountants and comedians. "Have you met Mr. Nixon yet?" the future President's press secretary once asked me. "You'll like him. He reads the sports pages first."

10   Then when I did meet Richard Nixon, he phrased his political thoughts in sports terms, spoke of hitting home runs and getting to first base and striking out. Sports is a language and a diversion and sometimes an obsession, and more than ever, it is a business.

11   The stakes are so high now. The *average* major league baseball player earns more than a million dollars a year. Losing pitchers and feeble hitters, men with stunningly modest statistics, demand much more. Steve Greenberg, the deputy commissioner of baseball, used to be an agent, negotiating players' contracts. He once told his father, Hank Greenberg, the Hall of Famer, who was the first ballplayer to earn $100,000 in a season, that he was representing a certain player. "What should I ask for?" Steve said. "He hit .238."

12   "Ask for a uniform," Hank said.

13   Steve shook his head. "Dad," he said, "you just don't understand baseball any more."

14   Nobody understands baseball any more. No one relates to the salaries. Not even the players themselves. They earn so much more than they ever dreamed of.

15   They also throw pitches Cy Young never dreamed of. (Ever see Cy Young's glove? Small. Very small. Now they have big hands, hands that can wrap around a ball and deliver a palm ball.) They swing bats with muscles Babe Ruth never dreamed of. They sprint from home to first, or first to third, with incredible speed. That's the biggest difference, the way they run these days. They fly.

16   But they don't know how to bunt. They don't know how to hit and run. They don't know which base to throw to. They didn't spend childhoods in cornfields playing baseball ten or twelve hours a day, absorbing the nuances of the game. They may have developed terrific hand-eye coordination playing video games, but that didn't teach them how to hit the cutoff man.

17   Baseball players earn up to $7 million a season. So do basketball players. Football players are embarrassed. Their ceiling is a few million dollars lower. Golfers and tennis players only go up to a million or two a year in prize money, but they can quadruple their income by wearing the right clothes, wielding the right clubs, advertising the right corporate logos on their visors and their sleeves.

18   Even athletes who are officially amateurs, runners and skaters and skiers, earn hundreds of thousands of dollars a year. How can anyone afford to have fun?

19   Once there was a camaraderie among athletes. They competed on the field, but afterward they were friends, sharing a common experience, a common attitude, bonded by their love for their game. Tennis players, for instance,

traveled together, roomed together, partied together, exchanged advice and rackets. Now each has a coach, and an agent, and a father or brother, and a fistful of sponsors, walling them off, separating them. Then can face each other across the net for years and never get to know each other.

20   Even in team sports, team spirit is, for the most part, gone, rekindled only occasionally by victory. "We are family," in sports terms, means: "We won." It doesn't mean we worry about each other, bolster each other, counsel each other.

21   How can fans relate to these athletes? How can they embrace heroes who have so much money and so little loyalty? Players change teams now as casually as they change jockstraps. Once you could fall in love with a lineup, commit it to your heart and your memory, and not have to learn more than one or two new names a year.

22   "The names, just to say the names, you could sing them," the playwright Herb Gardner once wrote, lamenting the Dodgers' move to Los Angeles. "Sandy Amoros, Jim Gilliam, Hodges, Newcombe, Campanella, Erskine, Furillo, Podres, gone, gone . . . even the sound is gone. What's left? A cap, I got a cap, Dodgers, '55, and sometimes on the wind I hear a gull, and Red Barber's voice . . . ."

23   Now the Dodger lineup changes every day, millionaires come and go, succumbing to minor injuries, whining about imagined slights, and even the manager, Tom Lasorda, who loves the team so much he says he bleeds Dodger blue, can't call all his players by name.

24   Once Dodgers were Dodgers for decades, and Cardinals Cardinals, and Red Sox Red Sox, but now they're L.A. Kings for a day, or maybe a month or a season, and if an athlete puts in a full career with one team, in one city, he isn't a hero, he's a monument.

25   It's easy to fault the players for earning so much money, for displaying so little loyalty, but it isn't fair. They didn't invent greed, or ingratitude. They learned from their mentors, the owners. The baseball players of the 1950s, the football players of the 1960s, had little idea of how underpaid they were. Soon after the salaries started to soar, a baseball player named Ken Singleton told me, "The owners screwed the players for one hundred years. We've been screwing them for five. We've got ninety-five more years coming."

26   The owners came up with the idea of moving for the money, too. The Braves went from Boston to Milwaukee to Atlanta, strip-mining stadia along the way. The Dodgers and the Giants traveled west hand in hand, with the other hands, of course, thrust out. They left shattered fans behind.

27   "They went, and the city went with them," Herb Gardner wrote. "The heart went with them, and the city started to die. Look what you got now, look what you got without no heart. What's to root for? Duke Snider! He

went away! How many years in the stands hollering? A lifetime in the afternoon hollering, 'I'm witcha, Duke, I'm witcha,' never dreaming for a moment that he wasn't with *me!*"

28   Teams, and owners, and athletes, have disappointed us in so many ways. The disappointment goes beyond the greed, beyond the selfishness. How can you put athletes up on a pedestal who flaunt fast cars at illegal speeds, who succumb to the lures of social drugs and performance-enhancing drugs, who maltreat women as spoils, who lose gambling fortunes that would change most people's lives? How can you pick a hero any more and count on him?

29   Sports has let us down.

30   Half a century ago, when Jackie Robinson became a Brooklyn Dodger and Joe Louis was the greatest fighter in the world, sports held out so much hope, so much promise. Equality, that elusive gift bestowed on all Americans by the Declaration of Independence, was going to be won and secured, finally, on the playing fields.

31   Of course. On the playing fields, every competitor was equal. The scoreboard knew no race, no religion, no nationality. Sports offered the ultimate democracy, where a man or a woman's success derived purely from his or her ability.

32   But, as brave as Jackie Robinson was, as good as Jimmy Brown was, and Henry Aaron and Bob Gibson and O. J. Simpson and Ernie Davis and Wilt Chamberlain and Bill Russell and Althea Gibson and Arthur Ashe and Rod Carew and Bill White and Julius Erving and Muhammad Ali and Sugar Ray Leonard and Magic Johnson and Oscar Robertson and Willie Davis and Lawrence Taylor and Alan Page and Jerry Rice and Walter Payton and so many more, the brotherhood of man has flourished no more on the playing fields than in the streets.

33   Thanks to sports, there are many more black millionaires now than there were a few decades ago, but there is not equality, not the kind of equality that not so long ago seemed possible, or even likely. Black players still tend to sit with black players on team buses and at training tables, and white players cluster together, and so do the black wives of black players.

34   For every Bill Bradley or Jack Kemp, who learned from the sports experience, who gained some insight into the dreams and fears of teammates of different color, who has sought to translate those into political action, dozens of athletes slip back into prejudice as soon as black teammates are out of sight, or out of hearing. They use privately the same cruel words that Jackie Robinson heard publicly.

35   Corporate America is no better, only more polite. Michael Jordan and David Robinson and O. J. Simpson and Bo Jackson, men so much larger

than life, have been able to transcend color and earn millions for endorse-
ments, but below the superstar level, white athletes have an unmistakable
edge, have first call on commercials and appearances and exposure.

36   It is ludicrous, the infinitesimally low percentage of black managers and
coaches and executives in professional and collegiate sports. They don't
have "the necessities," Alex Campanis, a Los Angeles Dodgers executive,
once blurted out on network television, clumsily sharing "a truth," as he, and
many other management people in sports, perceived it. What necessities?
Yogi Berra's IQ? Whitey Herzog's charm? They both managed first-place
teams in both big leagues; so much for necessities. There are plenty of black
Berras and black Whiteys, and smarter and more charming blacks—I
thought Willie Davis, the former Green Bay Packer, a Hall of Fame defensive end, an enormously successful businessman and civic leader, a warm
and thoughtful man, would have been a perfect commissioner of the National Football League; he got only token consideration—but they are so
often overlooked, and more often snubbed.

37   I share the guilt. When I was editor of a sports magazine, I was frequently
scolded by my employer for putting too many black athletes on the cover. I
was told that white athletes sell more magazines, and I cycled and recycled
Joe Namath and Tom Seaver and Dave DeBusschere and Pete Rose. ("I've
been on the cover of *Sport* three times," Rose once cracked at a luncheon I
hosted. "That's not bad for a white guy.") I've collaborated on books with
many athletes—Namath, Seaver, DeBusschere, Bill Freehan, Frank Beard,
Jerry Kramer and Bo Jackson—and only one was black. I accepted the publishing belief, nourished by an Ali autobiography that was a commercial
disaster, that blacks did not buy books. When the Bo Jackson book became
the best selling sports autobiography ever, far outgrossing all my other works,
that belief was sternly tested. Still, when I write and narrate feature stories
for television, I realize, with a twinge, that I lean heavily upon white athletes
as subjects and as interviewees. They certainly take up a larger portion of the
screen than they do of the playing field.

38   Fans can be as harsh as they ever were. Once, I was on a plane to Birmingham, Ala. to visit Bo Jackson's home, and a passenger across the aisle,
watching me flip through Jackson clippings, leaned over and said, "You
know why they call him 'Bo?'" Before I could answer, he said, "'Cause they
didn't know how to spell 'Bob.'"

39   I don't know why I was stunned.

40   Sports could be forgiven its flaws, at least some of them, if it had compensating strengths, if it taught the heroic lessons that Homer once sang of,
if it emphasized positive values, if it truly rewarded perseverance and teamwork and similar virtues.

41   But these days sports preaches greed above all else. Bad enough that the status of all professional athletes is determined, to a considerable extent, by their income; in golf, pretense is stripped away and the players are ranked, officially, by their earnings. Worse, the sports world also glamorizes hypocrisy and deception and corruption.

42   Big-time college athletic programs are a disgrace. In almost all of the major schools, the question isn't: Do the athletic departments cheat? It's: How baldly do they cheat? Even the squeaky clean programs, the Dukes and the Stanfords and the Notre Dames, the schools that offer prestige and power and tradition instead of cash and cars (low monthly payments? would you believe zero?), do not treat the so-called student athletes the way they treat student nonathletes. And the Ivy League, which preaches purity, does not always practice it. Any good Ivy League football player, and there are more than a few every year, who does not have a summer job on Wall Street paying an inflated salary is either remarkably passive or independently wealthy.

43   Colleges with winning big time football and basketball programs are making millions of dollars a year, and their coaches, with their camps and their clinics and their TV shows, are earning hundreds of thousands of dollars—all of that money dependent on the skills and moods of agile and powerful teenagers. To keep all those dollars coming in, virtually all colleges and coaches to some extent are willing to lie or distort or bribe or glorify, to stretch rules and ignore academic deficiencies, to pamper the more gifted athletes beyond belief. (Paul Hornung, after whom the Golden Dome at Notre Dame, his alma mater, may have been named, once said his own epitaph should be: "He went through life on scholarship.")

44   Too many college football and basketball players are treated, to use the title of a book one of them wrote, like "meat on the hoof," but surely black athletes are the most abused, fed visions of professional sports careers that will never materialize, steered away from academic courses that might challenge or inspire them, presented with scholarships to nowhere, free room, free board, free tuition, but not free thought. A few years ago I visited a very talented college football player, a likable young man, whose dormitory room was outfitted with the latest in stereo equipment and Nike posters. There wasn't a book in his student-athlete room, not one. He was lucky. He made it to the National Football League. He was one of the rare ones.

45   In all this gloom there are glimmers of hope. In high schools and colleges and even in international competition, not all sports corrupt and demean. A pure amateur may be as rare as a whooping crane, but in such college sports as lacrosse (Princeton, of all schools, upset Syracuse for the national

championship a few months ago) and field hockey (a dominion dominated by Old Dominion), to name two, sports which hold out little promise of fame or financial reward, men and women still can have fun, still can build character and self-confidence. In the Olympics, I love to wander among the winter biathletes, who couple such contradictory disciplines as shooting and skiing, and the summer pentathletes, who blend riding, shooting, fencing, swimming and running, the pursuits of an ancient courier. Their names are unknown outside the smallest circles, and their per diems are minimal, but their interests often seem to be as varied as their skills. "Our worlds are not confined by ski wax," as a biathlete once told me.

46   I still find individual athletes who lift my spirits: Bonny Warner, America's best female luger in the 1980s, a graduate of Stanford, a reformed sportscaster, now a United Airlines pilot; Jim Abbott, one of the few baseball players ever to leap straight from college to the major leagues, a man who expects neither sympathy nor attention for the fact that he was born with only one hand, yet a man who quietly offers time and hope and encouragement to children with physical differences; Mike Reid, first an All-American football player, then an All-Pro tackle, from Altoona, Pa., a town in which it is easy to play football but takes courage to play piano, now a Grammy Award-winning songwriter and singer of sensitive ballads.

47   In all sports, I find stars with the ultimate saving grace, the ability to laugh at themselves; stars who rose to great wealth from the meanest streets without forgetting their roots; stars whose intellect contradicts athletic stereotypes; stars whose values are the decent traditional ones that start with family and loyalty. "When I was growing up," Bo Jackson recalled, "my mom cleaned people's houses during the day and cleaned a motel at night. She also raised ten children by herself. And people try to tell me that playing two sports is hard." Bo Jackson's wife is a counseling psychologist; their three children are his most prized trophies.

48   Some athletes are better than ever.

49   Even off the field.

50   When I was a graduate student at Columbia, the school had a very good basketball team.

51   The best player on the team became a degenerate gambler, a convicted criminal.

52   The second best player became president of the Ford Foundation.

53   I still see both of them, on infrequent occasion, and they remind me of the potential of sports, and the peril. Sports can inspire greatness, but, too often these days, it inspires only greed.

Discussion Questions

1. Schaap states that "Sports is a language and a diversion and sometimes an obsession, and more than ever, it is a business." How well do you think he supports this argument?

2. How well do you think Schaap makes the transition from discussing professional sports to discussing collegiate sports? Explain your response.

3. Does Schaap's argument appeal to reason, emotion, or ethics? Cite specific passages that support your answer.

4. Schaap does not blame the players for "earning so much money, for displaying so little loyalty" but condemns the owners. What do you think they would say in their defense?

5. Schaap writes that "sports could be forgiven its flaws, at least some of them, if it had compensating strengths, if it taught the heroic lessons that Homer once sang of, if it emphasized positive values, if it truly rewarded perseverance and teamwork and similar values." In what ways do you think this statement strengthens or weakens Schaap's argument? Explain your answer.

Sports Heroes Wanted

Felicia E. Halpert

Felicia E. Halpert's article first appeared in a 1988 issue of *Ms.* magazine. In it, she examines the need for the media to cover the performance of female athletes as a way to encourage young girls to participate in sports.

1   This summer the Olympic games will spotlight the U.S. women's volleyball team as it attempts to replicate the medal-winning performance of 1984. Much about this year's squad is different from the powerhouse group put together for the Los Angeles Games. There are new players, a different coach. One person's absence from the team, however, will be especially poignant.

2   Flo Hyman, the 31-year-old star of the 1984 team, suddenly collapsed and died in the midst of a televised volleyball match in Japan two years ago. At the time of her death she was arguably the finest female player in the world. In leading the American team to its first-ever Olympic medal, Hyman generated excitement with her great power, strong defense, and blistering spikes.

3   Her death was a major loss for the women's sports world. Yet reporting on the tragedy by the sports media was scarce. Most television commentators chose to run clips of college basketball games rather than the footage of Hyman's collapse.

4   The lack of media attention makes sense, sadly, considering the sporadic coverage Flo Hyman received while alive. She was one of the best athletes this country has produced. Even so, few sports fans had heard of her. She was the subject of occasional newspaper and magazine pieces, especially during the Olympics. But she never got the frequent media coverage needed to create and sustain national recognition.

5   In a 1984 survey of five hundred 15- to 17-year-old girls and boys asked to name the athlete they most admired, the boys picked ten male athletes in four sports, with Julius Erving, at 10 percent, topping the list. Fifteen percent of the boys said they had no sports heroes. The girls, on the other hand, chose Mary Lou Retton as their hero by an overwhelming 24 percent. The three other athletes who garnered enough votes to be tabulated at all were

all males. Thirty-two percent of the girls said there was no athlete they particularly admired.

6   What this seems to show is not that girls have little interest in sports, but rather how few role models they recognize or identify with. The reason is that the major media continue to cover only male teams on a daily basis. Sports with women participants remain occasional special-interest stories.

7   Rarely, except for perhaps golf and tennis, do we see or hear consistently about athletes who are female. Yet, as the poll results illuminate, those people who receive day-in and day-out attention become our children's heroes. When provided with a heroic figure, as they were with Retton during the 1984 Olympics, girls admire that person as surely as boys do. And then they try to emulate her. The number of girls participating in gymnastics programs expanded after the Olympic Games. Media attention on the exploits of Joan Benoit, Grete Waitz, and Mary Decker has helped to spur tremendous growth in running among girls and women. Increased coverage of women's tennis and stars, such as Billie Jean King, Chris Evert, and Martina Navratilova, has helped to boost the numbers of young female competitors in that field.

8   Now it's time to broaden mainstream media coverage to include women's team sports as well. Team sports, after all, are the primary athletic activities we emphasize in our schools. With them, we teach the balancing of selflessness and pride, cooperation and competitiveness, and emotional and physical exhilaration. Yet when the media focus on a female star, she's usually in a nonteam sport, the kind where body consciousness, poise, and above all self-control are most visible. If we want to spur the increase in ability levels among the rapidly growing number of girls playing on teams— as well as broadening attitudes about what things girls can and cannot do— it will be by providing, on a frequent basis, role models who run, sweat, grimace, leap for joy in victory, and are pained but not dishonored by defeat. Women need to be seen not only in sports that emphasize holding one's body precisely, but in those where diving for a line drive or controlling a ball is crucial.

9   Sports fans know that putting together a list of recognizable female athletes isn't easy. But naming the standouts in team sports is nearly impossible.

10   Even former basketball star Cheryl Miller, until recently the most widely known (and some might say only known) female team player in the United States, was hardly ever a household name. And of those who have heard of the 1986 USC graduate, how many ever saw her play? Compare her collegiate career to that of Patrick Ewing. Four years of steady press attention and eighteen nationally televised Georgetown games effectively secured his

future. Miller, on the other hand, had the option upon graduation of either playing pro ball in Europe or finding a different line of work in America. (She opted for TV sportscasting.)

11   Professional women's leagues in basketball, softball, and volleyball have risen and perished in the United States. The pattern will continue if there is no media coverage, the essential ingredient in generating audiences and revenue.

12   Since the passage in 1972 of Title IX of the Education Amendments Act, female participation in sports programs in high school and college has grown phenomenally. There are six times as many girls competing in high school athletics as there were before Title IX. Participation by women in intercollegiate sports has also jumped dramatically, surging from 16,000 in 1972 to about 150,000 in 1985. Prior to the existence of Title IX, athletic scholarships for college women were scarce. Currently, more than 10,000 are being offered in a variety of sports.

13   The result has been the development of a far greater pool of athletic talent than existed even ten years ago.

14   Yet the future remains unclear. Although a structure now exists to encourage athletic skills, the women who are the products of it find themselves with nowhere to go once the Olympics are over, or graduation has arrived. The reality remains that for them there is no future in sports. At least not in this country.

15   Over the past decade, there has been noticeably more media attention to women's sports. The payoff in terms of our kids has been significant. Basketball and volleyball are increasingly popular with school-age girls, no doubt assisted by such things as additional Olympics coverage and the Harlem Globetrotters' decision to hire Lynette Woodard. (Although Woodard has moved on, she's been replaced by double her value: Sandra Hodge and Joyce Walker.) As skills improve, it's important to continue building this reporting so that eventually the names of groups of players become familiar. It will help move women's events out from under the stigma of being considered second-rate substitutes for men's games.

16   At a time when television is looking for ways to increase sports revenues, appealing to female fans may be the answer.

17   When presented with a potential hero of their own, girls and women are quick to identify with her, much as they have with Sally Ride or Corazon Aquino.

18   As more and more girls and women join teams and become interested in athletics, what remains sorely lacking are the female sports heroes they can look up to, cheer passionately for, and then try to emulate. When I was growing up, I wanted to be Bud Harrelson, Tom Seaver, and Willie Mays. If

I had known about a Flo Hyman and a Cheryl Miller, I would have wanted to be them, too.

Discussion Questions

1. Halpert begins her essay with a specific example and delays stating the main point of her argument until later. Discuss the effectiveness of this organization.

2. How convincing are Halpert's examples in proving her main idea? Explain your response.

3. Which of Halpert's points do you find most convincing? How does she support them?

4. Halpert's article was published in Ms. magazine, the majority of whose subscribers are women. What, if any, changes do you think she would have made if her article was published in, say, Sports Illustrated, whose readership is largely men? Explain your answer.

5. Halpert concludes her argument with a personal reference. Discuss the effectiveness of such an ending.

Navratilova Is Ace of All Female Athletes

Tom Weir

Born in 1952, Tom Weir attended the University of California at Berkeley before earning his bachelor's degree in journalism from San Francisco State University. Weir began his career by writing for the *Oakland Tribune* and the *Santa Rosa Press Democrat*. For the past twelve years, he has been the general sports columnist for *USA TODAY,* where his columns appear thrice weekly. The following selection first appeared in a June 1994 issue of *USA TODAY* as the 1994 Wimbledon tournament got underway with opening-round matches. Martina Navratilova went on to the finals at Wimbledon that year where she lost to Conchita Martinez. In November of the same year, Navratilova announced her retirement from tennis. In the following selection, Weir argues that Navratilova is the best female athlete of the twentieth century by dismissing other potential candidates.

1   Much has been made of Martina Navratilova's nostalgic farewell to Wimbledon, yet the truth of the moment has been overlooked. This really is a send-off for the best female athlete of this century.

2   Quibble with that assessment if you wish, but it is Navratilova who set her gender's athletic standards for quantity, quality, consistency and impact.

3   For those who want to argue against Navratilova, let's start with the old-timers, and the woman who in an Associated Press poll was voted the best female athlete of the first half of the century.

4   Babe Didrikson won two Olympic gold medals and a silver in track and field in 1932, but look closer at her competitions. Those were restrictive times, when female athletes were viewed with skepticism.

5   As evidence of that era's limited talent pool, the fourth-place finisher in Didrikson's 80-meter hurdles race had taken up the event only three months

before. The woman who beat Didrikson in the high jump later lost her amateur eligibility because she had—gasp!—worked as a swim instructor.

6   And by the end of 1932 even Didrikson herself was banned from further Olympic participation because her picture had appeared in an automobile ad.

7   Yes, Didrikson was the best of her era, but what flawed times they were.

8   Didrikson did go on to an unparalleled career in women's golf, once winning fourteen consecutive tournaments. But that's the walking game of golf. Jack Nicklaus' nerves of steel have given him a singular place in the world of sports, but it isn't alongside Michael Jordan or Joe Montana.

9   Today, Navratilova's most obvious challenger is Jackie Joyner-Kersee. With two Olympic gold medals and a silver in track and field's heptathlon, some have granted Joyner-Kersee the title of world's greatest female athlete.

10   Make no mistake, Joyner-Kersee owns an incredible resume, which also includes Olympic gold in the long jump.

11   But her seven-event challenge has existed at the Olympics only since 1984. Even the five-event pentathlon that preceded it wasn't included in the Games until 1964.

12   Similarly, any nominee from women's basketball comes from a sport that's just beginning to blossom. The Olympics didn't let women play hoops until 1976, and the scattered pro leagues are at about the level of the Continental Basketball Association.

13   Truth is, the person who eventually will be recognized as the world's greatest female basketball player probably is in grammar school right now. Or maybe even diapers.

14   So, back to Navratilova, who's still alive for a tenth Wimbledon title after a second-round victory Thursday.

15   She owns virtually every career record in tennis, which was the first big-money sport for women, and where three of the grand slam events date back to the 1800s.

16   Instead of winning her titles once every four years at the Olympics, she did it just about every weekend. Her seventy-four-match winning streak ought to rank right alongside Joe DiMaggio's fifty-six-game hitting streak.

17   In 1982, her singles and doubles record was a combined 160-7. Add up the regular-season victory totals of that year's champions from the World Series, Super Bowl and NBA Finals and they barely beat Navratilova, 162-160.

18   Take any other female athlete—Peggy Fleming, Dorothy Hamill, Mary Lou Retton, Wilma Rudolph, Florence Griffith Joyner, Janet Evans, whoever—none had Navratilova's staying power. Nor did any face the ordeal of defecting.

19   Along the way, she also revolutionized notions of how women should train, and in terms of being a sports pioneer for her gender, she probably ranks behind only Billie Jean King.

20   Now, at thirty-seven, she's clearly somewhat over the hill. But it's a climb that went higher than any other woman's.

Discussion Questions

1.   Whom do you think Weir envisioned as his audience? Explain your answer.

2.   Explain how Weir addresses opposing perspectives in his argument. What effect does this have on the strength of his argument?

3.   Weir bases his argument largely on facts and figures. Are they enough to make his argument convincing or should he have included reasons other than statistics? Explain your response.

4.   Analyze the method by which Weir presents his argument. Is it the most effective choice? Explain your answer.

5.   Are there any points Weir raises in his argument that you think need additional attention? What are they and why?

ARGUMENT

CHILDREN AND SPORTS

Lyle J. Micheli

Lyle J. Micheli was born in 1940 and graduated from
Harvard College with an A.B. degree and Harvard
Medical School with an M.D. degree. Currently, Micheli is the Director of Sports Medicine at Boston Children's Hospital and Associate Clinical Professor of
Orthopedic Surgery at Children's Hospital. Since 1977,
he has also served as the attending physician for the
Boston Ballet. Micheli has written over one hundred
scientific articles and reviews and is the author of
Sports for Life (1979) and *Sportwise: An Essential
Guide for Young Athletes, Parents, and Coaches*
(1990), a book that addresses ways to prevent children's sports injuries. Micheli is also one of the editors
of the *Oxford Textbook of Sports Medicine* (1994). In
the following selection, Micheli argues that changes
are needed in youth sports to prevent the occurrence
of sports-related injuries.

1 When I cofounded the country's first pediatric sports-medicine clinic at
Boston Children's Hospital in 1974, many people scoffed at my ambition to
not only treat sports injuries but also prevent them. "Mix kids and sports and
you'll always get injuries," they said. Some injuries are an inevitable byproduct of sports, and I should know. In the '50s, I boxed and played football,
lacrosse and rugby for Harvard and took my share of knocks. Most of the injuries my teammates and I suffered—sprains, strains, the occasional broken
bone—were known hazards of the sports we played. But the last quarter
century has seen an explosion in the different *types* of injuries suffered by
young athletes, often in the so-called "safe" sports such as swimming, distance running and dance. The fact that most of these injuries are pre-
ventable raises troubling questions about children and organized sports.

2   Let me make one thing clear: I'm a passionate advocate of organized
sports. Every day I see happy, healthy, confident youngsters with a glint in
their eye that tells me they're hooked on sports for life. But I'm not so gung-
ho that I can't recognize the profound changes taking place in children's

sports and the problems some of these changes are creating, injuries in particular. The U.S. Consumer Product Safety Commission reports that four million children seek emergency-room treatment for sports injuries every year, and estimates that another eight million are treated for such injuries by family physicians.

3   Many of the sports injuries I'm now seeing were unknown in previous generations. Talk of stress fractures, tendinitis and bursitis was confined to the pro athletes' locker room; now it can be heard in high-school corridors. "Little League elbow," "swimmer's shoulder" and "gymnast's back" have become buzzwords in the youth-sports lexicon. Consider the fact that knee injuries such as patellar pain syndrome were unheard of in kids until recently. Now it's the No. 1 diagnosis in my clinic!

4   What happened? The whole complexion of children's sports has changed. Organized sports have replaced free play and the sandlot. An astonishing twenty million of this country's boys and girls participate in nonschool recreational and competitive sports. And now organized sports have brought on "overuse" injuries caused by repetitive microtrauma to the body's tissues: constant overarm throwing in baseball; pounding of the feet against the ground in dancing and distance running, and the flexion and extension of the back in gymnastics and dance.

5   Overuse injuries were unknown in free play and sandlot sports. Hurt or sore athletes generally went home and didn't return to play until they felt better. But children in organized sports often overtrain and play when hurt. Kids may conceal sore elbows or aching knees because they don't want to look like sissies. A child with swimmer's shoulder told me recently that he kept quiet because he didn't want to seem like a "wimp" in front of his teammates. His shoulder required surgery.

6   Sports injuries in children are serious. Growing children are predisposed to overuse injuries because of the softness of their growing bones, and the relative tightness of their ligaments, tendons and muscles during growth spurts. And because overuse injuries develop slowly and insidiously, unlike sprains or fractures, which happen all of a sudden, they often go undetected. The damage to a growing child's hard and soft tissues caused by an unreported or undetected overuse injury can be permanent. Evidence suggests that overuse injuries sustained in childhood may continue to cause problems in later life—arthritis, for instance.

7   **Safe training:** We desperately need to overhaul our youth sports. America simply hasn't responded adequately to the enormous changes needed when moving from free play and sandlot sports to organized sports. I am especially concerned about the quality of our volunteer coaches, who form the backbone of nonschool organized sports. Think about it: we allow coaches to make our kids run laps, lift weights, perform strenuous athletic

maneuvers and engage in other potentially injurious activities. Rarely do we require them to have background in safe training and playing techniques, basic first aid or injury prevention. Only a small fraction of volunteer coaches have any formal training.

8   Although America's volunteer coaches are well meaning and committed, most are unaware of the child athlete's vulnerability to injury, especially overuse injury. Training errors by coaches are one of the most common causes of overuse injury. Little League elbow is usually seen in young baseball players who are taught incorrect throwing technique or are simply told to throw too much. In a poorly coached track program, runners are susceptible to knee injuries caused by excessive increases in their training regimen.

9   Parents must ensure that their children are enrolled in an organized sports program with a certified coach at the helm. As part of his training a coach trained in one of the three major certification organizations will know how to condition athletes. The coach will include warm-up and cool-down exercises in practice sessions, discourage unsafe playing tactics, ensure proper equipment is used and quickly recognize injuries. Parents should withhold children from programs where certification is not required.

10   When certification becomes widely mandatory—as it will, I'm convinced, by the year 2000—it will be a win, win, win situation. Coaches will win: they'll be better trained and more knowledgeable in fitness principles and injury prevention. Parents will win: they'll know their children are being instructed by qualified personnel. But the biggest winners will be our kids: they'll be better trained and less likely to be injured, and thus prepare for a lifetime of healthy living through sports.

Discussion Questions

1. Micheli begins his argument with a personal reference. Would his argument have been just as persuasive had he not included it? Explain your answer.

2. How well does Micheli convince you that organized sports are to blame for the increasing number of children's sports injuries? Can you identify other reasons that he fails to address? Explain your answer.

3. What do you think volunteer coaches would say in their own defense? How well does Micheli address counterarguments to his perspective? Explain your response.

4. Does Micheli base his argument on the appeal of *logos*, *ethos*, *pathos*, or a combination of the three? Cite specific examples of the way he argues his case.

5. Whom do you think Micheli envisioned as his audience: Parents? Coaches? Children? Explain your answer.

WRITING TOPICS

1. Baseball is considered American's national pastime. Research how and when it acquired that title, and write a paper in which you discuss whether such a reputation is still warranted. Pay attention to what about baseball makes it uniquely American and worthy (or unworthy) of the title "national pastime."

2. In "How Pro Football Was Ruined," Roland Merullo criticizes instant replay in football. Think about a recent innovation in another sport, and write a paper that shows why the innovation has improved or harmed the sport.

3. Some athletes earn phenomenally high salaries. Do you think such salaries are deserved? Research the earnings of the highest paid athletes in three sports and make a case for your stance.

4. When asked who their heroes are, many children cite athletes. Select an athlete (or athletes) you think is (are) a good role model for children and discuss the reasons for your selection.

5. Competition in children's sports has become quite fierce, and overly zealous parents have been blamed. Do you think that parents are the culprit or are other factors responsible for the competition? Discuss your answer to this question in a short paper.

6. Technology has changed the nature of sports: once made of wood, tennis racquets are now fiberglass and oversized; wooden sailboats are now fiberglass with mylar and kevlar sails; and so on. Some critics have claimed that such changes have been detrimental to these sports, putting the emphasis more on the equipment than on the participant. Where do you stand on this controversy? Examine your perspective in a paper.

7. Some sports have always been associated with violence (such as boxing). In recent years, however, other sports have become violent for players and fans alike (for example, soccer and

hockey). Write a paper in which you discuss the purported problem of violence in sports: do you see it as a growing social problem or one that should be an expected byproduct of the sport?

8. Some people view sports as a microcosm of society, reflecting human values and human nature. Research the views of sociologists and sports psychologists regarding this perspective. Write a paper in which you support or refute such a claim.

9. Some sports are perennial favorites among American fans (baseball, football, basketball). Why do you think this is the case? Why don't other sports (such as tennis, soccer, and swimming) warrant American viewers' and fans' attention? Write a paper in which you explain this topic.

10. Originally, Olympic athletes were required to be amateurs. Recently, however, the issue of whether professional athletes should be allowed to participate in the Olympics has been raised. Indeed, several sports now allow professional athletes in the Olympics. Do you think this is a good idea? Research this controversy and write a paper that supports your position.

CHAPTER

POPULAR
CULTURE

Hate Radio

Patricia J. Williams

Patricia J. Williams was born in 1951 and educated at Harvard Law School. Currently, Williams teaches at Columbia Law School. She is the author of *The Alchemy of Race and Rights* (1991). Most of Williams's publications deal with issues involving legal ethics and civil rights. In the following viewpoint, which originally appeared in a 1994 issue of *Ms.* magazine, Williams reflects on the popularity of talk radio shows, in particular those that spawn hatred.

1   Three years ago I stood at my sink, washing the dishes and listening to the radio. I was tuned to rock and roll so I could avoid thinking about the big news from the day before—George Bush had just nominated Clarence Thomas to replace Thurgood Marshall on the Supreme Court. I was squeezing a dot of lemon Joy into each of the wineglasses when I realized that two smoothly radio-cultured voices, a man's and a woman's, had replaced the music.

2   "I think it's a stroke of genius on the president's part," said the female voice.

3   "Yeah," said the male voice. "Then those blacks, those African Americans, those Negroes—hey 'Negro' is good enough for Thurgood Marshall—whatever, they can't make up their minds [what] they want to be called. I'm gonna call them Blafricans. Black Africans. Yeah, I like it. Blafricans. Then they can get all upset because now the president appointed a Blafrican."

4   "Yeah, well, that's the way those liberals think. It's just crazy."

5   "And then after they turn down his nomination the president can say he tried to please 'em, and then he can appoint someone with some intelligence."

6   Back then, this conversation seemed so horrendously unusual, so singularly hateful, that I picked up a pencil and wrote it down. I was certain that a firestorm of protest was going to engulf the station and purge those foul radio mouths with the good clean soap of social outrage.

7   I am so naive. When I finally turned on the radio and rolled my dial to where everyone else had been tuned while I was busy watching Cosby reruns, it took me a while to understand that there's a firestorm all right, but not of protest. In the two and a half years since Thomas has assumed his post on the Supreme Court, the underlying assumptions of the conversation I heard as uniquely outrageous have become commonplace, popularly expressed, and louder in volume. I hear the style of that snide polemicism everywhere, among acquaintances, on the street, on television in toned-down versions. It is a crude demagoguery that makes me heartsick. I feel more and more surrounded by that point of view, the assumptions of being without intelligence, the coded epithets, the "Blafrican"-like stand-ins for "nigger," the mocking angry glee, the endless tirades filled with nonspecific, nonempirically based slurs against "these people" or "those minorities" or "feminazis" or "liberals" or "scumbags" or "pansies" or "jerks" or "sleazeballs" or "loonies" or "animals" or "foreigners."

8   At the same time I am not so naive as to suppose that this is something new. In clearheaded moments I realize I am not listening to the radio anymore, I am listening to a large segment of white America think aloud in ever louder resurgent thoughts that have generations of historical precedent. It's as though the radio has split open like an egg, Morton Downey, Jr.'s clones and Joe McCarthy's ghost spilling out, broken yolks, a great collective of sometimes clever, sometimes small, but uniformly threatened brains— they have all come gushing out. Just as they were about to pass into oblivion, Jack Benny and his humble black sidekick Rochester get resurrected in the ungainly bodies of Howard Stern and his faithful black henchwoman, Robin Quivers. The culture of Amos and Andy has been revived and reassembled in Bob Grant's radio minstrelsy and radio newcomer Daryl Gates's sanctimonious imprecations on behalf of decent white people. And in striking imitation of Jesse Helms's nearly forgotten days as a radio host, the far Right has found its undisputed king in the personage of Rush Limbaugh—a polished demagogue with a weekly radio audience of at least twenty million, a television show that vies for ratings with the likes of Jay Leno, a newsletter with a circulation of 380,000, and two best-selling books whose combined sales are closing in on six million copies.

9   From Churchill to Hitler to the old Soviet Union, it's clear that radio and television have the power to change the course of history, to proselytize, and to coalesce not merely the good and the noble, but the very worst in human nature as well. Likewise, when Orson Welles made his famous radio broadcast "witnessing" the landing of a spaceship full of hostile Martians, the United States ought to have learned a lesson about the power of radio to appeal to mass instincts and incite mass hysteria. Radio remains a peculiarly

powerful medium even today, its visual emptiness in a world of six trillion flashing images allowing one of the few remaining playgrounds for the aural subconscious. Perhaps its power is attributable to our need for an oral tradition after all, some conveying of stories, feelings, myths of ancestors, epics of alienation, and the need to rejoin ancestral roots, even ignorant bigoted roots. Perhaps the visual quiescence of radio is related to the popularity of E-mail or electronic networking. Only the voice is made manifest, unmasking worlds that cannot—or dare not?—be seen. Just yet. Nostalgia crystallizing into a dangerous future. The preconscious voice erupting into the expressed, the prime time.

10   What comes out of the modern radio mouth could be the *Iliad*, the *Rubaiyat*, the griot's song of our times. If indeed radio is a vessel for the American "Song of Songs," then what does it mean that a manic, adolescent Howard Stern is so popular among radio listeners, that Rush Limbaugh's wittily smooth sadism has gone the way of prime-time television, and that both vie for the number one slot on all the best-selling book lists? What to make of the stories being told by our modern radio evangelists and their tragic unloved chorus of callers? Is it really just a collapsing economy that spawns this drama of grown people sitting around scaring themselves to death with fantasies of black feminist Mexican able-bodied gay soldiers earning $100,000 a year on welfare who are so criminally depraved that Hillary Clinton or the antichrist-of-the-moment had no choice but to invite them onto the government payroll so they can run the country? The panicky exaggeration reminds me of a child's fear . . . . *And then, and then, a huge lion jumped out of the shadows and was about to gobble me up, and I can't ever sleep again for a whole week.*

11   As I spin the dial on my radio, I can't help thinking that this stuff must be related to that most poignant of fiber-optic phenomena, phone sex. Aural Sex. Radio Racism with a touch of S & M. High-priest hosts with the power and run-amok ego to discipline listeners, to smack with the verbal back of the hand, to smash the button that shuts you up once and for all. "Idiot!" shouts New York City radio demagogue Bob Grant and then the sound of droning telephone emptiness, the voice of dissent dumped out some trap-door in aural space.

12   As I listened to a range of such programs what struck me as the most unifying theme was not merely the specific intolerance on such hot topics as race and gender, but a much more general contempt for the world, a verbal stoning of anything different. It is like some unusually violent game of "Simon Says," this mockery and shouting down of callers, this roar of incantations, the insistence on agreement.

13   But, ah, if you *will* but only agree, what sweet and safe reward, what soft enfolding by a stern and angry radio god. And as an added bonus, the

invisible shield of an AM community, a family of fans who are Exactly Like You, to whom you can express, in anonymity, all the filthy stuff you imagine "them" doing to you. The comfort and relief of being able to ejaculate, to those who understand, about the dark imagined excess overtaking, robbing, needing to be held down and taught a good lesson, needing to put it in its place before the ravenous demon enervates all that is true and good and pure in this life.

14   The audience for this genre of radio flagellation is mostly young, white, and male. Two thirds of Rush Limbaugh's audience is male. According to *Time* magazine, 75 percent of Howard Stern's listeners are white men. Most of the callers have spent their lives walling themselves off from any real experience with blacks, feminists, lesbians, or gays. In this regard, it is probably true, as former Secretary of Education William Bennett says, that Rush Limbaugh "tells his audience that what you believe inside, you can talk about in the marketplace." Unfortunately, what's "inside" is then mistaken for what's "outside," treated as empirical and political reality. The *National Review* extols Limbaugh's conservative leadership as no less than that of Ronald Reagan, and the Republican party provides Limbaugh with books to discuss, stories, angles, and public support. "People were afraid of censure by gay activists, feminists, environmentalists—now they are not because Rush takes them on," says Bennett.

15   U.S. history has been marked by cycles in which brands of this or that hatred come into fashion and go out, are unleashed and then restrained. If racism, homophobia, jingoism, and woman-hating have been features of national life in pretty much all of modern history, it rather begs the question to spend a lot of time wondering if right-wing radio is a symptom or a cause. For at least four hundred years, prevailing attitudes in the West have considered African Americans less intelligent. Recent statistics show that 53 percent of people in the U.S. agree that blacks and Latinos are less intelligent than whites, and a majority believe that blacks are lazy, violent, welfare-dependent, and unpatriotic.

16   I think that what has made life more or less tolerable for "out" groups have been those moments in history when those "inside" feelings were relatively restrained. In fact, if I could believe that right-wing radio were only about idiosyncratic, singular, rough-hewn individuals thinking those inside thoughts, I'd be much more inclined to agree with Columbia University media expert Everette Dennis, who says that Stern's and Limbaugh's popularity represents the "triumph of the individual" or with *Time* magazine's bottom line that "the fact that either is seriously considered a threat . . . is more worrisome than Stern or Limbaugh will ever be." If what I were hearing had even a tad more to do with real oppressions, with real white *and* black levels of joblessness and homelessness, or with the real problems of real

white men, then I wouldn't have bothered to slog my way through hours of Howard Stern's miserable obsessions.

17   Yet at the heart of my anxiety is the worry that Stern, Limbaugh, Grant, et al. represent the very antithesis of individualism's triumph. As the *National Review* said of Limbaugh's ascent, "It was a feat not only of the loudest voice but also of a keen political brain to round up, as Rush did, the media herd and drive them into the conservative corral." When asked about his political aspirations, Bob Grant gloated to the Washington *Post*, "I think I would make rather a good dictator."

18   The polemics of right-wing radio are putting nothing less than hate onto the airwaves, into the marketplace, electing it to office, teaching it in schools, and exalting it as freedom. What worries me is the increasing-to-constant commerce of retribution, control, and lashing out, fed not by fact but fantasy. What worries me is the reemergence, more powerfully than at any time since the institution of Jim Crow, of a socio-centered self that excludes "the likes of," well, me for example, from the civic circle, and that would rob me of my worth and claim and identity as a citizen. As the *Economist* rightly observes, "Mr. Limbaugh takes a mass market—white, mainly male, middle-class, ordinary America—and talks to it as an endangered minority."

19   I worry about this identity whose external reference is a set of beliefs, ethics, and practices that excludes, restricts, and acts in the world on me, or mine, as the perceived if not real enemy. I am acutely aware of losing *my* mythic individualism to the surface shapes of my mythic group fearsomeness as black, as female, as left wing. "I" merge not fluidly but irretrievably into a category of "them." I become a suspect self, a moving target of loathsome properties, not merely different but dangerous. And that worries me a lot.

20   What happens in my life with all this translated license, this permission to be uncivil? What happens to the social space that was supposedly at the sweet mountaintop of the civil rights movement's trail? Can I get a seat on the bus without having to be reminded that I *should* be standing? Did the civil rights movement guarantee us nothing more than to use public accommodations while surrounded by raving lunatic bigots? "They didn't beat this idiot [Rodney King] enough," says Howard Stern.

21   Not long ago I had the misfortune to hail a taxicab in which the driver was listening to Howard Stern undress some woman. After some blocks, I had to get out. I was, frankly, afraid to ask the driver to turn it off—not because I was afraid of "censoring" him, which seems to be the only thing people will talk about anymore, but because the driver was stripping me too, as he leered through the rearview mirror. "Something the matter?" he demanded, as I asked him to pull over and let me out well short of my destination. (I'll spare you the full story of what happened from there—trying

to get another cab, as the cabbies stopped for all the white businessmen who so much as scratched their heads near the curb; a nice young white man, seeing my plight, giving me his cab, having to thank him, he hero, me saved-but-humiliated, cabdriver pissed and surly. I fight my way to my destination, finally arriving in bad mood, militant black woman, cranky feminazi.)

22   When Yeltsin blared rock music at his opponents holed up in the parliament building in Moscow, in imitation of the U.S. Marines trying to torture Manual Noriega in Panama, all I could think of was that it must be like being trapped in a crowded subway car when all the portable stereos are tuned to Bob Grant or Howard Stern. With Howard Stern's voice a tinny, screeching backdrop, with all the faces growing dreamily mean as though some soporifically evil hallucinogen were gushing into their bloodstreams, I'd start begging to surrender.

23   Surrender to what? Surrender to the laissez-faire resegregation that is the metaphoric significance of the hundreds of "Rush rooms" that have cropped up in restaurants around the country; rooms broadcasting Limbaugh's words, rooms for your listening pleasure, rooms where bigots can capture the purity of a Rush-only lunch counter, rooms where all those unpleasant others just "choose" not to eat? Surrender to the naughty luxury of a room in which a Ku Klux Klan meeting could take place in orderly, First Amendment fashion? Everyone's "free" to come in (and a few of you outsiders do), but mostly the undesirable nonconformists are gently repulsed away. It's a high-tech world of enhanced choice. Whites choose mostly to sit in the Rush room. Feminists, blacks, lesbians, and gays "choose" to sit elsewhere. No need to buy black votes, you just pay them not to vote; no need to insist on white-only schools, you just sell the desirability of black-only schools. Just sit back and watch it work, like those invisible shock shields that keep dogs cowering in their own backyards.

24   How real is the driving perception behind all the Sturm und Drang of this genre of radio-harangue—the perception that white men are an oppressed minority, with no power and no opportunity in the land that they made great? While it is true that power and opportunity are shrinking for all but the very wealthy in this country (and would that Limbaugh would take that issue on), the fact remains that white men are still this country's most privileged citizens and market actors. To give just a small example, according to the *Wall Street Journal*, blacks were the only racial group to suffer a net job loss during the 1990–91 economic downturn at the companies reporting to the Equal Employment Opportunity Commission. Whites, Latinos, and Asians, meanwhile, gained thousands of jobs. While whites gained 71,144 jobs at these companies, Latinos gained 60,040, Asians gained 55,104, and blacks lost 59,479. If every black were hired in the United States tomorrow,

the numbers would not be sufficient to account for white men's expanding balloon of fear that they have been specifically dispossessed by African Americans.

25   Given deep patterns of social segregation and general ignorance of history, particularly racial history, media remain the principal source of most Americans' knowledge of each other. Media can provoke violence or induce passivity. In San Francisco, for example, a radio show on KMEL called "Street Soldiers" has taken this power as a responsibility with great consequence: "Unquestionably," writes Ken Auletta in the *New Yorker*, "the show has helped avert violence. When a Samoan teenager was slain, apparently by Filipino gang members, in a drive-by shooting, the phones lit up with calls from Samoans wanting to tell [the hosts] they would not rest until they had exacted revenge. Threats filled the air for a couple of weeks. Then the dead Samoan's father called in, and, in a poignant exchange, the father said he couldn't tolerate the thought of more young men senselessly slaughtered. There would be no retaliation, he vowed. And there was none." In contrast, we must wonder at the phenomenon of the very powerful leadership of the Republican party, from Ronald Reagan to Robert Dole to William Bennett, giving advice, counsel, and friendship to Rush Limbaugh's passionate divisiveness.

26   The outright denial of the material crisis at every level of U.S. society, most urgently in black inner-city neighborhoods but facing us all, is a kind of political circus, dissembling as it feeds the frustrations of the moment. We as a nation can no longer afford to deal with such crises by *imagining* an excess of bodies, of babies, of job-stealers, of welfare mothers, of overreaching immigrants, of too-powerful (Jewish, in whispers) liberal Hollywood, of lesbians and gays, of gang members ("gangsters" remain white, and no matter what the atrocity, less vilified than "gang members," who are black), of Arab terrorists, and uppity women. The reality of our social poverty far exceeds these scapegoats. This right-wing backlash resembles, in form if not substance, phenomena like anti-Semitism in Poland: there aren't but a handful of Jews left in that whole country, but the giant balloon of heated anti-Semitism flourishes apace, Jews blamed for the world's evils.

27   The overwhelming response to right-wing excesses in the United States has been to seek an odd sort of comfort in the fact that the First Amendment is working so well that you can't suppress this sort of thing. Look what's happened in Eastern Europe. Granted. So let's not talk about censorship or the First Amendment for the next ten minutes. But in Western Europe, where fascism is rising at an appalling rate, suppression is hardly the problem. In Eastern and Western Europe as well as the United States, we must begin to think just a little bit about the fiercely coalescing power of media to spark mistrust, to fan it into forest fires of fear and revenge. We

must begin to think about the levels of national and social complacence in the face of such resolute ignorance. We must ask ourselves what the expected result is, not of censorship or suppression, but of so much encouragement, so much support, so much investment in the fashionability of hate. What future is it that we are designing with the devotion of such tremendous resources to the disgraceful propaganda of bigotry?

Discussion Questions

1. Williams begins with and intersperses personal narrative in her viewpoint. Discuss the effectiveness of this technique.

2. What do you see as the purpose of the many questions Williams asks in her viewpoint? Evaluate the effectiveness of this technique.

3. Does Williams appeal to logic, emotions, or ethics? Cite specific examples that lead you to your response.

4. How do you think radio personalities such has Rush Limbaugh and Howard Stern would respond to Williams's viewpoint? Assume the role of the people about whom Williams writes and offer your reactions to her observations.

5. Williams ends her viewpoint with a question. Do you think this is an effective ending? Why or why not?

The Comfort of Being Sad

Sarah Ferguson

Born in 1964, Sarah Ferguson studied at Rutgers University and Oxford University. Her articles have appeared in such magazines as *The Nation, Mother Jones,* and *Esquire.* From 1988 to 1993, she was also a regular contributor to *The Village Voice.* Ferguson is currently the senior editor of *High Times* magazine. In the following article, which originally appeared in a 1994 issue of the *Utne Reader,* Ferguson examines the appeal that the grunge culture has for American youth.

1   I came face to face with the essence of grunge culture last summer, when I was out in Seattle interviewing street punks. I was hanging out with a runaway vegan anarchist named Jackie and his street friend Anthony when we decided to go party with their friends from the band Suffocated. We took a shortcut to their house on the outskirts of the U district, tramping through the woods and under the bridge where the "trolls" (street kids) slept when they didn't have a squat to crash, then circling around the back of Safeway to scavenge for moldy sandwiches in the Dumpster.

2   Suffocated's lead guitarist received us nonchalantly, nodding at the 40-ounces we'd picked up with Jackie and Anthony's panhandled change. Anthony said he wanted to try out his new piercing needle and disappeared into the bathroom upstairs. He said he wanted to pierce his scrotum, said he liked the experience of pain.

3   So Jackie and I sat there in the living room, watching the band members scarf down lines of speed and bong hits amid a blistering blur of crustcore and metal. At the end of the tape, the guitarist dug out a new one. "Mind if we listen to Nirvana?" he asked, almost apologetically, like he was 'fessing to being a Bon Jovi fan. "Sure," Jackie shrugged, but I just smiled. These were Kurt Cobain's people, the forgotten white trash he celebrated. If I'd asked them up front, they would have said they hated Nirvana for the same sellout reasons that Cobain hated himself. Yet even among this jaded crowd, Cobain's anguished wail offered a refuge of authentic despair.

4   Courtney Love said, "Every kid in America who's been abused loves Kurt Cobain's music." In fact, Nirvana made abuse his generation's defining

metaphor. The hit "Smells Like Teen Spirit" was an anthem of powerless rage and betrayal. It was a resounding fuck you to the boomers and all the false expectations they saddled us with about rock 'n' roll revolution. And it made psychological damage—with all its concurrent themes of child abuse, drug addiction, suicide, and neglect—a basis for social identity.

5   Like Pearl Jam's "Jeremy," which tells the story of an alienated kid who blows his head off in school, Nirvana's "Teen Spirit," and indeed all of grunge culture, is rooted in the feeling of damage. Coming out of the get-ahead '80s, it's easy to understand the appeal. Being damaged is a hedge against the illusory promises of consumer culture. For grunge's primary audience, white male teens, damage offers a defense against the claims of gangsta rappers and punk rock feminists. It's a great equalizer at a time when multiculturalism seems to have devolved into competing schools of victimization. Grunge appeals to white kids because it tells them that they're not responsible for the evils of racism and injustices, that they are victims too.

6   The empowered feeling you get from listening to these songs lies in unearthing that essential nugget of shame. It's like going to a twelve-step meeting. You stand up, announce the wrongs done to you as a child, your response (drugs, suicide attempts). Simply identifying and acknowledging your damage is empowering, because society seems to deny you the right to feel damaged.

7   What's frustrating is how the politics of the music remains so acutely personal. When the Sex Pistols screamed "No Future," they were condemning a society that gave young people no hope, no prospects for change. Yet underlying that nihilistic message was a vital rage at all the politicians and people in power who, they felt, had restricted their prospects. In other words, punk knew who the enemy was.

8   By contrast, grunge music seems more muddled. It's as if kids don't know who to blame: their parents, the media, the schools—or themselves. Even Cobain doubted the privilege of his despair. "I'm a product of a spoiled America," he once said. "Think of how much worse my family life could be if I grew up in a depression or something. There are so many worse things than a divorce. I've just been brooding and bellyaching about something I couldn't have, which is a family, a solid family unit, for too long."

9   In fact, the dissolution of the American family has exerted a tremendous torque on the members of Cobain's generation. And while they may not be growing up in the midst of the Great Depression, with the official unemployment rate for young people hovering at 13.2 percent, kids have reason to complain. The dwindling timber economy of Cobain's hometown, Aberdeen, Washington, was certainly no picnic. Yet Cobain and his fellow grunge balladeers never really aspire to protest, preferring to remain mired in their own sense of inadequacy. The inverted pose of the music mirrors the

incoherence of the left and the replacement of class politics with self-help politics. In the absence of a viable counterculture, it's no wonder young people don't know who to blame.

10   Indeed, grunge expresses this generation's almost willful refusal to reach for larger truths. Instead, it engages in a kind of mournful nostalgia for a childhood without violation. Grunge sees the lie of consumer culture but still yearns for the manufactured suburban bliss of *Leave It to Beaver* and *Mayberry R.F.D.* (two of Cobain's favorite shows). It's an odd yet poignant stance, given rock's traditional aversion to the constraints of the nuclear family. "Daddy didn't give attention / To the fact that mommy didn't care," Eddie Vedder anguishes. Grunge is music for kids who grew up too fast. They keep reaching back for a childhood denied.

11   The contrast between Cobain's self-deprecation and his fans' adulation was jarring when I saw Nirvana play New York's Coliseum during their last concert tour. As the roadies wheeled out the hermaphroditic figurines and fiberglass trees for the *In Utero* stage set, I was struck by the band's unwillingness to indulge the audience's yearning for spectacle. Despite the corporate veneer of a big band setup, these hulking plastic dummies with their exposed innards had a kind of malevolent camp, like a twisted take on the witch's forest on *H. R. Pufnstuff*.

12   The crowd let out a dull roar as Dave Grohl's rapid-fire drumroll launched the band into the opening chords of "Breed." But Cobain steadfastly refused to play the role of a revered rock star, insulting his fans with sloppy chords and (apparently) drug-addled stupor. The overwhelmingly white, overwhelmingly male, overwhelmingly suburban crowd didn't seem to care. They sang along blithely to "Polly," a song about a girl being molested, and pogoed to "Rape Me," Cobain's angst-filled response to commercial fame.

13   The saddest moment came when the band played "Dumb": "I think I'm dumb, or maybe just happy. Think I'm just happy . . ." Cobain droned, underscoring the terribleness of not knowing the difference. The crowd stilled, grew listless, then restless, but Cobain kept intoning, "I think I'm dumb, I think I'm dumb." And for the first time it wasn't his audience's stupidity that he was railing at but his own, the horror of finding out that this was all his art could attract—people who stare back sheepishly, or worse, reverently, at your rage. He'd succeeded beyond his wildest dreams of combining punk and pop and created a Frankenstein that by its success seems to invalidate the thrust of its rebellion. You could hear him wanting to scoop it down the garbage disposal, nuke it in the microwave, except he couldn't. It just kept mutating into some yet more profitable venture.

14   What Cobain's suicide in April and the whole trajectory of his band's success prove is the inability of youth to own their own rebellion. The loop taken by a new musical style from the underground to the mainstream is now so compressed that there's no moment of freedom and chaos when a counterculture can take root. Even anti-corporatism can be rerouted into a marketing ploy. MTV makes fun of itself in order to ingratiate itself with its audience, but it's still one big extended commercial.

15   "There is no youth culture. It's like we've been robbed of culture," a street punk named Bones told me last summer as we were hopping freight trains through the South. A skinny nineteen-year-old with droopy brown eyes, he had covered his body with a lattice-work of tattoos tracing the different stages of his youth: skinhead, heroin addict, born-again Christian, skatepunk, acidhead, sous-chef. His latest "tat" was an almost photographic image of an Iraqi woman weeping over a skull.

16   Yet what struck me most was the battered *Sesame Street* Ernie doll that he'd sewn on the top of his backpack. It was meant to be goofy. But a flea-ridden high school dropout on food stamps tramping through train yards with this remnant of his childhood was a little like thrusting a stuffed animal into a propeller blade.

17   Nirvana's formula of Beatle-esque pop juxtaposed with bursts of harsh heavy metal captures the same dissonance. It recapitulates the violation of childhood innocence, the ultimate betrayal kids see in commercial culture, which promised *Brady Bunch* lives and gave them single-parent homes. The fact that this generation bought the *Brady Bunch* myth in the first place is testament to the totalitarian nature of commodity culture. Their dreams and desires have been manufactured and controlled at such an early age, they lack a clear sense of authentic experience. Perhaps that's why the theme of child abuse is so engaging. It's a visceral pain that adults produce but don't control.

18   And it's an accusation. In kids' eyes, it's the adults of America who are truly damaged. Their children are just collateral damage.

Discussion Questions

1.   Ferguson cites Pearl Jam and Nirvana as examples of the grunge culture's music. Are these examples sufficient to support her observations about the grunge culture? Why or why not?

2. How convincing is Ferguson's analogy that the "empowering feeling" derived from the music of the grunge culture is "like going to a twelve-step meeting"? How does this analogy strengthen or weaken Ferguson's viewpoint?

3. Throughout her viewpoint, Ferguson makes a number of claims about the grunge culture. Which strike you as the most perceptive and which the least? Explain your answers.

4. Does Ferguson appeal to logic, emotion, or ethics in her viewpoint? Identify specific examples to support your answer.

5. How do you think members of the grunge culture would respond to Ferguson's viewpoint? Explain your response.

T V's Anti-Families:
Married . . . with Malaise

Josh Ozersky

Born in 1967, Josh Ozersky received his B.A. from Rutgers University and studied at the New York University School of Journalism. He is currently pursuing a doctoral degree in cultural history at Notre Dame University. His articles have appeared in such publications as *Seventeen, Tikkun, The Washington Times,* and *Chronicles.* Ozersky specializes in studying American culture of the past forty years, an interest evident in the following article about two popular television shows.

1   It's an odd thing when a cartoon series is praised as one of the most trenchant and "realistic" programs on TV, but there you are. Never mind the Cosby-size ratings: If merchandising says anything about American culture, and it does, then America was utterly infatuated with*The Simpsons* in 1990. "Utterly," because unlike other big winners in the industry such as the Teenage Mutant Ninja Turtles and the New Kids on the Block, the Simpsons graced not only T-shirts for the clamoring young, but T-shirts (and sweatshirts and posters and mugs) that went out in droves to parents, who rivaled kids for viewer loyalty.

2   The animated series chronicles the life of the Simpson family: father Homer, who works in a nuclear power plant and reads bowling-ball catalogs; mother Marge, with her blue beehive hairdo and raspy voice; misunderstood-Bohemian daughter Lisa; baby Maggie; and bratty son Bart, the anti-everything star of the series. Bart appeals to kids, who see a flattering image of themselves, and to their parents, who, even as they identify with Bart against his lumpkin parents, enjoy Bart's caricature of their own children, with his incomprehensible sloganeering ("Don't have a cow, man!") and bad manners. Nor, tellingly, has the popularity of the show stopped with the white mainstream: a black Bart soon began to turn up in unlicensed street paraphernalia.

3   In the first of the unauthorized shirts, Bart was himself, only darkened. The novelty soon wore off, however, and in successive generations Bart found himself ethnicized further: "Air Bart" had him flying toward a

basketball hoop exclaiming "In your face, home boy." Another shirt had Bart leering at zaftig black women, loutishly yelling "Big Ole Butt!" at their retreating figures. And in later versions, Bart has a gold tooth, a razor cut, and an angry snarl—the slogan "I got the power!" juts overhead in an oversized balloon.

4   The "I got the power!" Bart is barely recognizable, disfigured by rancor. But even more jarring than his appearance is his vitriol, so out of keeping with the real Bart's laid-back, ironic demeanor—an endemic condition among TV characters. The naked discontent on that shirt is jarring, disturbing. It lacks the light touch. TV does not—but then the playful suppression of unhappiness has always been one of TV's great strengths; and in its latest, ugliest form, it subtly discourages alarm at the decline of the family, its own complicity in that decline, and the resulting effects on a disintegrating society.

5   The success in the last few seasons of new, "antifamily" sitcoms, such as Fox's *Married . . . with Children* and *The Simpsons* and ABC's *Roseanne*, began a trend that has made waves in television. "Whether it's the influence of Bart Simpson and those cheeky sitcoms from Fox," wrote *TV Guide* in September [1990] "or ABC's artsy anti-soap *Twin Peaks*, unconventionality is in; slick and safe are out." The "cheeky sitcoms" began that trend. *Roseanne*, about an obese and abrasive proletarian mom, and *Married . . . with Children*, a half hour of pure viciousness, represented along with *The Simpsons* a new development of the situation comedy, TV's definitive genre. Each program (as well as its inevitable imitators) focuses on a family marked by visual styles and characterization as bleak and miserable as those of former TV families had been handsome or cheerful.

6   The innovation received a lot of attention in the mass media, most of it favorable. Richard Zoglin in *Time* hailed the "real-world grit these shows provide," produced psychological authorities, and quoted Barbara Ehrenreich's wide-eyed "Zeitgeist Goddess" piece in the *New Republic*. The *New York Times's* Caryl Rivers wrote approvingly of the new realism, although she noted perfunctorily that gays, minorities, and women were less visible than they should have been. What all sides had in common, however, was a willingness to point out the improvement over other forms of TV. "The antifamily shows aren't against the family, exactly, just scornful of the romantic picture TV has often painted of it," Zoglin pointed out. "We're like a mutant Ozzie and Harriet," *Simpsons* creator Matt Groening boasted in *Newsweek*, which went on to point out that the show was "hardly the stuff of Saturday-morning children's programming." "Thankfully, we are past the days of perfect Mom and all-wise Dad and their twin beds," wrote the *New York Times's* Rivers, speaking for reviewers and feature writers everywhere. And this was

prior to the advent of the "unconventional" mystery serial *Twin Peaks*, which still has feature writers striving for superlatives to describe its "innovations" and "departures."

7   This unanimous juxtaposition of the "antifamilies" to the stern TV households of yesteryear is a specious comparison designed to amuse and flatter. Not as the result of any conspiracy—writers in the commercial mass media generally write to please, and what they say is true enough if you have as your entire frame of reference the past and present of TV. But far from the "authenticity" it pretends to, the "grit" for the new shows is merely an improved artifice, a challenge only to the verisimilitude of art directors and casting companies. By pretending to realism, TV only extends its own hegemony, in which every standard of comparison points back to another sham. "Gosh," gushed *TV Guide* of Bart, "can you imagine Bud Anderson being so . . . *disrespectful* to Dad?" As if the lead of *Father Knows Best* had only recently become a figure of fun.

8   It is through this sort of pseudo self-deprecation that TV tries to ingratiate itself with Americans, who in an age marked by pervasive irony want to run with the hare and hunt with the hound—to feel superior to TV and yet keep watching it. TV offers this target audience an abundance of self-images that will permit them this trick. The target viewers may be enlightened, making the "choice of a new generation" by seeing through *My Little Margie*, or avant-garde, on the cutting edge, for watching *Twin Peaks*, which, like *Hill Street Blues* before it, supposedly "breaks all the rules." They are in utter harmony with the very mechanics of TV production, which has no secrets from us, as we know from David Letterman's insider gags, such as the "Late Night Danger Cam."

9   As for discrediting paternalistic authority figures, Mark Crispin Miller has pointed out that the imperious Dads of fifties TV, now such a rich source of burlesque, were overturned by a maturing medium very early on. The "grim old abstinence" of the Puritan patriarch stood in the way of the "grim new self-indulgence" of consumer culture and was hence banished. Dads turned into "pleasant nullities," like Dick York in *Bewitched* and Timothy Busfield in *thirtysomething*, or unenlightened butts of knowing and self-flattering jokes, like Archie Bunker and Homer Simpson.

10   The downfall of Dad, however, saw no concomitant rise of Mom or the kids. Rather, it was advertisers and corporations that benefited from the free-spending self-indulgence of all parties, liberated from patriarchal discipline. And the networks, of course, cashed in and sold advertisers airtime. In the world beyond the screen, the family has disintegrated into epidemic divorces and deteriorating marriages, latchkey children, and working parents reduced to spending "quality time" with their children, as though they were hospital visitors or the lovelorn spouses of soldiers on leave. Meanwhile,

the TV world—not only in sitcoms but in endless "special reports" and talk shows and (particularly) commercials—insists again and again that we are hipper, more "open," more enlightened, and facing changing "relationships" in a new and better way. Mom, often divorced and underpaid, has her new "independence," a standard theme of programming, and Dad and the kids, faced with other losses and hardships, are offered the bold new "grittiness" of prime-time entertainment. TV has absorbed the American family's increasing sense of defeat and estrangement and presented it as an ironic in-joke.

11   This dynamic is seldom noted, although the mere *fact* of watching is noted by critics and commentators everywhere, and nowhere more visibly than on TV itself. The opening credits of *The Simpsons* end with the family, assembled at the end of the day, jumping mutely into fixed position on the sofa and clicking on the TV set. This absorption of criticism is and has been, except for sheer distraction, TV's greatest weapon against criticism. The transformation of the hearth into an engine of negation, after all, should have caused *some* stir. And so it would have, if TV were no more than the yammering salesman it has caricatured itself as in satirical moments. But, as Miller demonstrates, TV has never shown us TV; rather, it shows itself to us as a laughable, absurd, and harmless entity, much like the characters on its shows.

12   When not played for background noise—whooping Indians in older shows, unctuous game-show hosts or newsmen in newer ones—depictions of the TV set on TV itself render it invisible and omnipresent. TV itself, its conventions and production, may be the crucial point of reference for the sophisticated appeal it enjoys today, but the set as household centerpiece is seldom seen, and then only as a joke, as on *The Simpsons*. Instead, the set most often poses as a portal to the outer world: hence its constant stream of images that tease us with alluring beaches, blue waters, busy city streets. Even in its living rooms, where we know its presence to be inescapable, the TV is often missing. This effect is accomplished by a simple trick of photography when the family watches TV in *All in the Family*, in *Good Times*, in *Married . . . with Children*, etc., the scene is shot from behind the TV set. As the family sits facing us, with the screen nowhere in sight, the illusion exists for a moment that the TV really is, if not a portal, then a mirror or reflection of us. A close look at these families, and at our own, soon banishes this impression. We are not like these TV families at all; and the TV set is obtrusive, ideological, and tendentious.

13 When speaking of the "anti-family" sitcoms, most of the commentators seem to have in mind *Married . . . with Children*. No other show so luridly plays up the sheer negativity of the current "authenticity" trend, nor does

any other show do so with such predictable regularity. The series portrays the Bundys, a lower-middle-class family with two children and a dog. Father Al (Ed O'Neill) only has "knotted bowels" to show for his life supporting the family. Peg (Katey Sagal) is Al's castrating wife. There is also the inevitable sharp-tongued teenage son, who singles out for special heckling his brainless and sleazy sister. The relentlessly ironic quality of a happy family turned thoroughly upside-down flatters the audience for their enlightenment (no *Donna Reed*, this) even as it invites them to enjoy the ongoing frenzy of spite in which the show indulges. And frenzy is indeed the word. Every member of the family despises everyone else, and any given program consists of little more than continuous insults, interspersed with snide loathing or occasional expressions of despair.

> FATHER (to son): Did I ever tell you not to get married?
> SON: Yeah, Dad.
> FATHER: Did I ever tell you not to become a shoe salesman?
> SON: Yeah, Dad.
> FATHER: Well, then I've told you everything I know.

14   This sort of resigned and paralytic discontent dominates the tone of *Married . . . with Children*; it lacks even the dim rays of hope that occasionally lifted Ralph Kramden's or Riley's gloomy existence. Every show is devoted to a new kind of humiliation: to earn extra money, Al becomes a burger-flipper; when son Bud falls victim to a practical joke perpetrated by an old flame his slutty sister Kelly comes to his defense by crucifying the girl against a locker; wife Peg belittles Al's manhood in front of strangers. Again and again, the unrelenting negativity of the show finds new ways to expand, purifying itself of any nonironic, positive content. Lovebird neighbors intended for contrast in the first season soon divorce, adding to the show's already vast reserve of bitterness. Christina Applegate, the young actress who plays Kelly, filled out during the first two years, adding a missing element of nasty prurience to the show.

15   The result of this hermetic exclusion of all warmth, say a number of apologists for the show, is positive: "With these new programs," says Barbara Cadow, a psychologist at USC, "we see we're doing all right by comparison." Yet at the same time, it is the very "realism" of these shows that won them praise again and again. This "realism" appeals to a cynical element in us—no one would ever admit to resembling Roseanne Barr or her family, but they are eminently "realistic" portraits of the losers next door. Roseanne Barr is shrewish and miserable to the point of self-parody, and this is seen as the great strength of her series. "Mom" (who Roseanne, it is assumed, represents) "is no longer interested in being a human sacrifice on the altar of 'pro-family' values," says Barbara Ehrenreich in the *New Republic*.

16   The praise of the same style of TV both for its realism and for its horrific exaggeration, while apparently contradictory, is based on a common assumption. In each case, the pervasive unhappiness and derision on TV sitcoms is assumed to be a reflection, albeit a negative one, of the unhappiness of real families. Cadow assumes that it is caricature, and Ehrenreich that it is a manifesto, but neither woman doubts that both shows offer some kind of corrective to real life for their viewers, and that this explains their popularity. This congratulatory view of hit TV shows contains a fundamental error: the old network executive's rationale that TV "gives people what they want," in response to their Nielsen-measured "choice."

17   The concentration of mass media into a few corporate hands invalidates that idea even more today than in the past. Given TV's entirely corporate nature, it is unreasonable to assume that the channels are referenda, since almost every channel, at least until recently, offered almost identical options. What succeeds with the public makes it, yes. But that "success" is determined by TV's agenda—which now, as always, is more than selling dog biscuits. Consumption must be encouraged psychologically; sectors and tendencies in American society have to be identified and exploited. "Since the major broadcasters are no longer winning the big numbers," observes *TV Guide*, "they're now fighting for the youthful demographics that bring in the highest revenues. That's why everyone is hyping bold, hip shows."

18   Of course, the success of a culture based on mass consumption depends on the creation of boundless needs; boundless needs presuppose boundless discontent. Boundless discontent must begin with the family, where social patterns are first internalized. If, latchkey in hand, TV can flatter a kinless and dispossessed child into adulthood and at the same time kid his or her parents about it, perfect consumers are thereby made. The family becomes a breeding ground for easygoing and independent citizens of the marketplace, transported beyond the inner struggle and deep feeling of family life, and bound in their place by the laws of supply and demand, consumer "choices," and a continual negation of their truest selves.

19 By presenting unhappy families to viewers, TV achieves many gains. First, as Cadow rightly points out, mocking the traditional family does flatter the distorted family of our times. However, this does not necessarily lift spirits. On the contrary, it lowers expectations: it stupefies discontent instead of healing it. *Married . . . with Children* is the prototype of this strategy. The petty or profound resentments of real families do not rival those of the Bundys, but then neither does their ability to punish and humiliate each other. By making our problems "seem all right by comparison," the series

trivializes them rather than taking them seriously. It in fact worsens them by its counsel of despair.

20   Secondly, the dysfunctional TV family aids advertisers in their perennial quest for credibility by creating a supersaturated atmosphere of irony, which atrophies our ability to believe in anything. Commercials themselves work on a principle of pseudorebelliousness. Burger King—now officially touted by the Simpsons—proudly sports the "radical" motto, "Sometimes you've gotta break the rules." Swallowing these giant absurdities relies not on credulity, but on an ironic, self-assured disbelief. *Roseanne*, with its trademark sarcasm, and *Twin Peaks*, with its tongue-in-cheek grotesqueries, are good examples.

21   Third, and most insidious, is the stability of TV's dysfunctional families, and their passive acceptance of their fate. A successful cast is the source of "ensemble acting," which has been the formula for success for some time now on TV. Since TV characters now move in herds, they do not get divorced, move out, have devastating affairs, or anything else that would disrupt the fabric of the show's format. Implicitly, these shows assure us that family life is largely a nightmare, but one that is self-perpetuating and only requires handling with a deft, protective irony. This irony, the antithesis of deep feeling, is the essential assault on the family and on all human relationships, reducing them to problems of managerial acumen. Thus, while remaining intact in their own impoverished world, sitcom families undermine the stability of real families, discrediting the embarrassingly earnest, often abject bonds of kin while hermetically sealing themselves off from the possibility of familial collapse. And this while they consume the increasingly rare time in which American families are actually together.

22   *The Simpsons*, the most popular of the group and certainly the least ironic and "antifamily," is TV's most effective reinforcer. This paradox begins with the fact that the show is a cartoon: With their yellow skin, bulging eyes, and comical motions, the Simpsons are funny just to look at, and hence relieve the audience of the need to continually jeer at them. The Bundy family of *Married . . . with Children*, like all sitcom characters, aspire to the televisual purity of cartoon characters, but are stuck in rubbery bags of protoplasm with nothing but one-liners and a laugh track to hide behind. The Simpsons, oddly, are freer than other TV families to act human.

23   And so they do. There is an element of family loyalty and principle to be found in the Simpsons, often combined with witty and valid social criticism. Brother Bart and sister Lisa petulantly demand of baby Maggie to "come to the one you love most," to which the infant responds by crawling lovingly to the TV. Or again, when father Homer's sinister boss inquires disbelievingly, "You'd give up a job and a raise for your principles?" Homer

responds (with almost none of the usual sitcom character's irony), "When you put it that way, it does sound farfetched—but that's the lunk you're lookin' at!" "Hmm," the boss replies. "You're not as dumb as you look. Or sound. Or as our best testing indicates."

24   With pointed jokes such as these, *The Simpsons* might prompt us to conclude the same about its vast audience. The harmlessness of these jokes can be taken for granted; no one who watches TV is going to stop because they see TV criticized. We criticize it ourselves as a matter of course. On the contrary, we feel flattered, and less inclined to stop watching.

25   And we are that much less inclined to object to the continuing presence of unsafe workplaces, vast corporations, the therapy racket, and all the other deserving targets of the Simpsons' harmless barbs. The genial knowingness of shows like *The Simpsons* subverts criticism through an innocuous pseudocriticism, just as the familial discontents of TV shows subvert alarm at graver discontents in real life. Criticism is further weakened by the show's irony, which although less than some other programs is still pervasive and fundamental to its humor. No one in an ironic show can get too far out of line. For example, in one episode, misunderstood Lisa meets that well-worn figure of Caucasian lore, the wise and virtuous old colored bluesman, ever ready to act as mentor to young white people in their search for self-knowledge. *The Simpsons* is far too hip to hand us such a hackneyed cliché. The Virtuous Old Blues Man is as empty a conceit as the Perfect Family—so on the show, he is named "Bleeding Gums Murphy" (Why? "I haven't brushed my teeth in thirty years, that's why.") In place of the usual soulful laments, he sings the "I Don't Have an Italian Suit Blues."

26   Such undercutting is typical of TV as a whole; attempts to transcend the flattened-out emotional landscape of TV are almost invariably punished by some droll comeuppance. But since as bizarre cartoons there is little need to belittle them, the Simpsons get a little more than most, and are occasionally allowed moments of earnestness unmitigated by the selfishness of *thirtysomething*, the weirdness of *Twin Peaks*, or the inevitable "comic relief"— the stock entrances of deadpan tots and witty oldsters, etc.—used to terminate the maudlin embraces of nonanimated sitcomites. None of this is to be had on *The Simpsons*, but the picture it presents is still fundamentally hopeless. The Simpsons are basically boobs, and their occasional bursts of tenderness or insight are buried under biting irony and superior, if affectionate, mockery. More than any of the other "antifamily" shows, *The Simpsons* seems to come close to our lives; more than any of the other shows, as a result, it commits us to a shared vision of pessimism and self-deprecation.

27   Because the TV screen is neither a mirror, reflecting ourselves paralyzed in chairs in front of it, nor a window, through which we observe the antics

of distant players, it is an implicit invitation to participate in a vision of "society" largely designed to flatter us in sinister ways, manipulate our attention, and commit us to the status quo. In discrediting "yesterday's" family values in its various "breakthrough" shows (ostensibly defining A *Different World* for us, as the title of one series has it), TV seeks only to impose its own values—which is to say, the values of the marketplace. Bart Simpson, master sneerer, is the prototype of the modern series character who—by the social scripts of TV—reflects us. Small, ridiculous, and at the same time admirable for his sarcasm and enlightened self-interest, Bart is the child of the culture of TV, his parents mere intermediaries.

28   Paradoxically, that is why the most powerless sector of American society has adopted him, fitting him with their own wishful slogan—"I got the power!" Though black Bart's anger may be incongruous with TV, his proclamation is not, since TV is so successful an invitation to impotent posturing. At the moment, the rage of the underclass cannot be appropriated by TV, yet in black Bart, in the fatal joining of ironic hipness and earnest wrath, we see perhaps a glimpse of the future (and in fact there are already a spate of new black shows—e.g., *Fresh Prince of Bel Air*, *In Living Color*). "I got the power!" says black Bart. But in the world of the TV family, no one has power. Empty fantasies of might, like cynical, knowing giggles, are terminal symptoms of our capitulation to TV's vision.

29   Life outside of that vision *is* ugly and is becoming uglier as ties, familial and societal, dissolve and decay. But the only power we do have is the power of our own real selves to reject the defensive posture of materialist or ironist or cynic, and the soullessness of TV's "hip, bold," antilife world. Bart and his aspirants exist in that world, and their example serves only to impoverish us.

Discussion Questions

1.   When in his essay does Ozersky actually make his claim? What method of argumentation does he then use to support it?

2.   Explain how Ozersky's inclusion of Barbara Cadow's ideas helps to strengthen his argument.

3.   Ozersky discusses three benefits of television airing shows that feature unhappy families. Do you agree with his reasoning? Has he omitted any important ideas? Explain your answers.

4.   To what extent does Ozersky successfully refute the arguments that his opposition might have to his thesis? Explain your response.

5.   How do you think Ozersky would respond to this question:
     What is television's responsibility in its depication of not only
     families but people such as women, African-Americans, His-
     panics, Asian-Americans, gays, and so on? What would be *your*
     answer?

Mythogyny

Claudia Boatright

Born in 1943, Claudia Boatright earned her B.A. degree from the College of Wooster and her M.A. degree from Claremont Graduate School. Her articles have appeared in *Highlights* and *Shaker* magazine. For the past eighteen years, she has been chair of the history department at the Laurel School, a prep school in Cleveland, Ohio. In the following article, which was first published in a 1993 issue of *Northern Ohio Live,* Boatright analyzes the ways in which advertisements have denigrated women.

1   Image #1: In the foreground a blonde, beautiful and voluptuous woman dressed in a body-clinging, bosom-revealing red dress; in the darkened background the silhouetted figure of a man lurks, sinister and predatory.

2   Image #2: A virile young man with the currently fashionable two-day stubble of beard, bare chested, belt loosened, presses his body against that of a girl whose back is to the camera, clad only in jeans.

3   Image #3: A frontal view of bare arms hugging crossed knees which obscure a naked torso, head cut off at the top of the page.

4   Previews for R-rated films coming soon to our local cinema? Lurid covers for trade paperbacks? Porno photos? Answer to the first two questions: no. Answer to the third question: could be.

5   Naomi Wolf, in her best-selling book *The Beauty Myth,* calls such ads "beauty pornography." In fact, these are ads for perfume, designer jeans and athletic socks which appeared in some of the popular fashion and teenage-culture magazines Laurel School seniors analyzed one day last spring during an examination of the images of women in advertising. Although the images just described appeared in copies of *Cosmopolitan, Glamour, Elle, Seventeen* and *Rolling Stone,* they could as easily have been found in the Sunday *New York Times Magazine* or other less gender-specific publications. The girls admitted that they had seen these, and ads like them, hundreds of times, and that they sometimes decorated their bedroom walls and school lockers with ads featuring their favorite models.

6   On this day, however, they looked at these ads for the first time in a new light. Sensitized by reading excerpts from Susan Faludi's *Backlash: The Undeclared War Against American Women* and Naomi Wolf's *The Beauty Myth: How Images of Beauty Are Used Against Women*, the girls began to perceive the underlying themes of sexual violence, dehumanization and sadomasochism that are staples in ads for products ranging from lipstick and lingerie to alcohol and automobiles. What standards of feminine beauty did these ads convey? How did such standards of beauty evolve historically? And what signals did they send about women themselves?

7   We discussed the cyclical nature of female images from Victorian times to the present, noting that in eras when society's expectations for women have been primarily those of wife, mother and homemaker (the late nineteenth century and the postwar 1950s, for example), a full bust and wide hips were portrayed as the ideal female figure.

8   Recall the hourglass shape of Sarah Bernhardt and the voluptuous sensuality of Marilyn Monroe. (It is interesting to note, by the way, that my students today invariably characterize Marilyn as "so fat!") The irony of ads emphasizing thinness, flat-chestedness and a boyish figure in the same eras in which women were moving out of a domestic realm into more public lives was not lost on the students. The flapper of the 1920s, with her short skirt, flaming lipstick and cigarette-holder, was billed as "the New Woman," but she had the bobbed hair and flat-chested look of a young boy. In more recent times, the London model Twiggy took the fashion world by storm at the same time that women were beginning to savor the new freedom conferred by birth control pills. Observing that some of their favorite models—Cindy Crawford, Naomi Campbell and Niki Taylor—are thin and narrow-hipped while being full-busted, the students pondered the implications of such standards for their own era.

9   Indeed, were we to have the same conversation this spring, the students would surely note the cyclical historical phenomenon in the fashion world's announcement that "The mature, big-haired and big-breasted look is out, and the short, waiflike and wafer-like look is in . . ." (Natalie Angier, *The New York Times*, April 11, 1993). My students expect to complete college and graduate programs and to pursue careers throughout most of their adult lives, yet the image now held before them in the fashion spreads is that of Kate Moss, the "gamine girl" who looks like she just left a concentration camp. *Plain Dealer* fashion editor Janet McCue quotes the designer Valentino as stating, "I love these young, new girls, so frail and insecure."

10   Frail? Insecure? That is precisely the point. For the same girls who expect to become engineers, doctors, marketing analysts and environmental lawyers are heard to complain, "Look at my skin—all full of zits!"

11 "I'm so fat! Look at these thighs! They're full of cellulose! I should have liposuction!"

12 It is with mixed emotions—impatience, frustration, sometimes cynicism, and often sadness—that I overhear such complaints. We know that a common theme in early female adolescence is obsession with physical development, fixation on one's own appearance and often idolization of a female celebrity, athlete, media personality, or maybe even an older woman who is part of the young girl's world and whose beauty she seeks to emulate. Yet these girls are sixteen, seventeen and eighteen years old. Why are they fixated on idealized, unattainable standards of beauty? Clearly powerful forces are at work shaping the self-image of adolescent women. Not the least of them is what Naomi Wolf calls "the culture of hunger."

13 My guess is that if statistics at Laurel reflect national norms, then more than fifty percent of my students would probably characterize themselves as being "too fat." Wolf cites surveys that reveal seventy-eight percent of their respondents are dissatisfied with their weight. In fact, "Forty-five percent of women who were actually underweight believed that they were too fat." Whence do such obsessions derive and where do they lead?

14 The answer to the latter question is becoming all too apparent: five to ten percent of American women and girls suffer from anorexia or bulimia, an increase of 400 percent during the twenty years statistics have been recorded. Some estimates place the number of anorexics on college campuses at one woman student in five. Moreover, "if anorexia is defined as a compulsive fear of fixation upon food," as Naomi Wolf suggests, then "perhaps most Western women can be called, twenty years into the backlash, mental anorexics."

15 We know, of course, that anorexia is a complex illness, and it is by no means my purpose here to suggest a direct or exclusive connection between eating disorders and the images of ideal feminine beauty portrayed in advertising, although the number of models who *are* anorexic is high. Noting that most models she knows starve themselves, highly paid model Caprice Beneditti, featured in a recent *New York Times* article, admits the fashion business is deceptive. "It's false advertising," she says. "It's total fantasy. How can a five-foot-five woman with a pear-shaped body put on a pair of leather pants and a tight shirt and look 5-10, 120 pounds and not pear-shaped? It's a shame. We give women false expectations and we make them feel worse about themselves. I know I'm putting something on that most people can't wear. I know this is just a game." Caprice knows it's a game, but does the sixteen-year-old girl, who is constantly on a diet, recognize that *she* is the pawn?

16 Beyond the question of whether deceptive advertising is or is not linked to women's eating disorders, however, I have another concern about what

such images do to female adolescents' perceptions of themselves. That is the element of menace and sexual danger that pervades so many fashion ads—the male shadow hovering over the model advertising body lotion, for example, or the potential for violence implicit in an ad in which a young woman is surrounded by a leather-jacketed gang of men.

17   In trying to analyze why such advertising works, my students admitted that they sometimes find these images titillating. Yet what do ads which cut off a woman's head or hide her face behind a screen of hair say about the female as person, as human being? Says Jill Kilbourne in her 1987 film *Still Killing Us Softly: Advertising's Image of Women*, "The body is turned into a thing, a package . . . [it] is dismembered, hacked apart." One student wondered aloud if there might be any connection between such advertising and the dramatic increase in violent crimes against women—"She asked for it" being a common defense in rape trials ranging from that of boxer Mike Tyson to Kennedy scion Willie Smith. Jill Kilbourne suggests that the answer to this query may well be yes, pointing out that "turning a human being into a thing is often the first step towards acts of physical violence."

18   Judging from the conversation that took place in my class last spring, my sense is that by the time they are juniors and seniors, most of my students are capable of recognizing—on an intellectual level—the source of their insecurity and the extent to which the media manipulates their self-images. The problem, as I see it, lies not with perceptions on the intellectual level but rather with the emotional response to subliminal message ads for Obsession perfume, Calvin Klein jeans and Jockey briefs (to name but a few of the offenders) which characterize female beauty as mindless and vulnerable and present models of "perfection" who weigh seventeen percent below the national average for the female population.

19   Out class discussion last spring was powerful and exhilarating, but what impact, long-term, may it have had on the girls and their own self-images?

20   Much as I might like to end this reflection with a bold plan of action— to report, for example, that the students decided to boycott all products that were promoted in deceptive, offensive or exploitative ads, or that they decided to cancel their subscriptions to the magazines which carried such advertising—no such conclusion would be truthful. I do believe, however, that the discussion was a valuable lesson in consciousness-raising and critical thinking. That these students will, at the very least, become more discriminating readers and more discriminating purchasers may be the most realistic goal to be achieved in the short run. The ability to recognize that the images on the pages of *Vogue* and *Cosmopolitan* are empty and artificial ought to lead to a greater sense of acceptance and self-confidence.

21   Earlier this year one of my advisees told me with great admiration that one of her classmates had, with neither smugness nor vanity, announced to

the other girls in their homeroom during a discussion about beauty that she was quite satisfied with her appearance. She was not on a diet. She had no desire to alter her nose or change her hairstyle. She thought her complexion was, if not perfect, well, okay. She wished neither to be taller nor shorter. She thought the color of her eyes was just fine. "I am who I am," she had quietly proclaimed. How commendable. And how rare.

Discussion Questions

1. Boatright begins her argument with specific examples of advertisements. Discuss how effective you find this opening.

2. Do you think that Boatright provides a sufficient number of examples to support her thesis? Why or why not?

3. Boatright cites the "emotional response to subliminal message ads" her students have to some advertisements. What kind of appeal does Boatright use to argue *her* position?

4. Whom do you think Boatright envisioned as her audience? What specifically leads you to your answer?

5. At the end of her article, Boatright claims that she is not calling for a "bold plan of action." Do you think one is implicit in her ending? Explain your response.

ARGUMENT

In Hollywood, Class Doesn't Put Up Much of a Struggle

Benjamin DeMott

Born in 1924, Benjamin DeMott is the Mellon Professor of Humanities at Amherst College. A prolific writer, his articles have appeared in such publications as *The Atlantic, Harper's,* and *The American Scholar.* He is the author of two novels, *The Body's Cage* (1965) and *A Married Man* (1968). His books of cultural criticism include *Hells & Benefits: A Report on American Minds* (1962), *You Don't Say: Studies of Modern American Inhibitions* (1966), *Supergrow: Essays and Reports on Imagination in America* (1969), *Surviving the Seventies* (1971), *The Imperial Middle: Why Americans Can't Think Straight* (1990), and *Created Equal* (1995). The following article, which originally appeared in the *New York Times* in 1991, argues that contemporary movies fail to responsibly depict the different social classes in the United States.

1   Increasingly in recent years movies have been dealing with power issues and class relationships—interactions between masters and servants, executives and underlings, yuppies and waitresses, millionaires and hookers, rich aristocrats and social-nobody lawyers. Think of "Reversal of Fortune" and "The Bonfire of the Vanities." Think of "White Palace" and "Pretty Woman." Think of Michael Corleone's struggle for social acceptance in "The Godfather Part III." Think of "Working Girl," or "Driving Miss Daisy," or "Dirty Dancing." Script after script links up clout and cloutlessness, often to stunning box-office effect.

2   Not every movie version of the power theme speaks specifically about class relationships, and some versions are only loosely linked to social reality. The two worlds of "Edward Scissorhands," for example—hilltop mansion and tract house; solitary helpless artist versus artist-baiting mob—are derived less from everyday experience than from fairy tales, allegory and satire.

3   Usually, though, conventional realism is the chosen mode, and class skir-
mishes are sketched. The camera in "White Palace," a popular film released
a few months ago, studies St. Louis's fancier suburbs and its rundown Dog
Town; class conflict erupts at the movie's crisis point. Nora, the waitress-
heroine (Susan Sarandon), listens smolderingly to her yuppie lover's upper-
middle friends and relations uttering their hypocritical socio-political pieties,
and explodes. Storming her way out, she cries: "*I'm working class!*"

4   At first glance the angry explicitness of her outcry and the movie's declaration of difference look promising. They could signify that Hollywood is
reaching toward maturity, trying to teach itself and the nation how to think
straight about social hierarchy—the realities of class and class power. The
need for such instruction is patent. This country has an ignoble tradition of
evading social facts—pretending that individual episodes of upward mobility obviate grappling with the hardening socio-economic differences in our
midst. Movies that deal responsibly with class relationships could, in theory, moderate the national evasiveness.

5   But, regrettably, contemporary "class moves" don't deal responsibly with
class. The tone of their treatment of rich and poor is new; it is harsher and
meaner than that of Frank Capra's "little guy" sagas or George Cukor's social
comedies or John Ford's populism that were pleasing to our parents and
grandparents in the 30's, 40's and 50's.

6   The harsher tone, however, doesn't bespeak fundamental change. At
their best, Hollywood's new-style "class movies" nod at realities of social
difference—and then go on to obfuscate them. At their worst, these films
are driven by near-total dedication to a scam—the maddening, dangerous
deceit that there are no classes in America.

7   One favorite story line stresses discovery: people who think firm class
lines exist come to discover, by the end of the tale, that they're mistaken;
everybody's really the same.

8   In the 1988 blockbuster "Working Girl," Tess McGill (Melanie Griffith), initially a bottom-dog secretary-gofer, is positive she can make it to the
top. But her peers in the word-processing pool regard her aspirations as foolish. They tell her, flat out, that the real world has lines and distinctions
and that her daydreams of glory and business power are foolish. "I sing and
dance in my underwear," says one pal, "but I'm not Madonna." The implicit message: Get real, Tess. Accept the reality of levels.

9   But Tess, of course, accepts no such thing. She reads W, takes classes to
improve her accent, seizes her boss's office when the latter breaks her leg skiing—and winds up not only doing deals but ordering the boss (Sigourney
Weaver) to get her bony bottom out of sight. What does it take to get to the
top? Desire, period. Tess's desire flies her straight up to a managerial perch,
allowing her to become, almost effortlessly, all she can be: no problem, few

barriers, class dismissed. In the final frame the doubters in the secretarial pool acknowledge their error; they rise to applaud the heroine who proved them wrong.

10   A second familiar story line involves upendings: characters theoretically on the social bottom shake the cages of characters who try to use their position to humiliate those below. The top dogs are so stupid they don't realize that socioeconomic power only lasts for a second and that they can be overcome by any intrepid underling.

11   Consider "Pretty Woman," the 1990 film that became one of the highest-grossing movies ever and is now near the top of video best-seller and rental charts. The would-be humiliators in this movie are snobbish salespeople on chic Rodeo Drive. Vivian (Julia Roberts), a hooker, runs afoul of them when she is sent on a shopping spree by the corporate raider (Richard Gere) who has hired her for a week. The raider wants elegance and the hooker aims to oblige . . . but on her first pass at the drive she's suited up in hooker garb, and the salespeople are offended. "I don't think we have anything for you. *Please leave.*"

12   Quickly the snobs are undone. The corporate raider flashes plastic and tells a shop manager that they'll be spending big and need appropriate cosseting. In minutes—through instruction in fork-tine-counting, for instance—the raider effects the few alterations of manners required to transform Vivian the street hooker into grandeur.

13   Regally togged, her arms filled with sleek clothes boxes, Vivian returns to the salespeople who were mean to her and sticks it to them in economic not moral terms. If they had been nice to her, they would have made a killing. ("You work on commission, don't you?")

14   Power is temporary and snobs are dopes—so goes the message. Ostracize a hooker in midmorning and she'll ruin you before tea. *Class dismissed.*

15   Comparable dismissals occur in movies drawing huge audiences of high school students. They usually have plot lines showing bottom dogs gliding smoothly and painlessly to the top. In "Dirty Dancing" (1987), Patrick Swayze, playing a talented working-class dancer (he has a card in the "housepainters and plasterers union"), competes for esteem with a Yale medical school student—and wins in a breeze.

16   In John Hughes's "Some Kind of Wonderful" (1987) and "Pretty in Pink" (1986), working-class heroes or heroines become romantically interested in classmates who rank above them, in terms of money and status, in the school society. As the attachments develop, the poor students commence to display gifts and talents that prove them equal to or intrinsically superior to the arrogant, insecure characters in whom they've become interested.

17   Once the nonclass, merit-based order or hierarchy has been established, and superficial, class-based gradations have been eliminated, the poor boy or

girl chooses whether to continue the relationship with the pseudo-superior as an equal or to end it. Either way, the experience bolsters the belief that, in school and out, social strata are evanescent and meaningless.

18   It's hardly surprising that the myth of America as a classless society emerges at its most schematic in movies aimed at relatively youthful, unsophisticated audiences. But the same impulse to paper over social differences surfaces in many more ambitious films purporting to raise subjects considered controversial by Hollywood standards (social injustice, war, the treatment of minorities).

19   And not infrequently that impulse drives film makers—such as Francis Ford Coppola in "The Godfather Part III" and Barry Levinson in "Avalon"— to overplay ethnic influence and underplay class influence on character.

20   But what is truly striking is the array of ploys and devices by which movie makers bring off escapes from significant confrontation with class realities. The Vietnam War film "Platoon" (1986), for example, lets on at the beginning that it will show us an upper-middle white soldier learning about differences between himself and the sons of the working class who compose the majority of his comrades in arms.

21   But in place of the experience of learning, we're offered liberal platitudes and star turns. The hero writes his grandmother that his fellow soldiers are the salt of the earth (little corroboration supplied); the soldiers themselves—particularly the blacks among them—are brought on for a succession of amusing monologues, following which they disappear, shipped out dead or alive; at no point is the gritty stuff of class difference even momentarily engaged.

22   In the much-acclaimed "Driving Miss Daisy" (1989), the early intimation is that the focus will be on relations between white employers and black servants. But almost immediately the outlines of that social difference are blurred. The white employer is Jewish and her synagogue is bombed; poor black and rich white become one, joint victims of discriminatory violence. ("You're my best friend, Hoke.") Class dismissed once more.

23   The story is nearly the same even in those unusual movies that focus solely on minority communities. Social difference is glanced at, defined in a few snippets of dialogue—and then trashed, often by means of a joke. In "House Party," Reginald Hudlin's 1990 film about teen-age life, the joke is about sex. Through establishing shots and talk, two girlfriends are placed at a social distance from each other. One lives in "the projects," the other in an expensively middle-class suburban home.

24   The film offers a single moment of reflection on the social difference in question; a young man points out that there is plenty of space for making out in the rich girl's house, none where the projects girl lives. Yet once more, class dismissed.

25   The reason all this matters is simple. Treating class differences as totally inconsequential strengthens the national delusion that class power and position are insignificant. It encourages the middle-class—those with the clearest shot at upward mobility—to assume, wrongly, that all citizens enjoy the same freedom of movement that they enjoy. And it makes it easier for political leaders to speak as though class power had nothing to do with the inequities of life in America. ("Class is for European democracies or something else," says George Bush. "It isn't for the United States of America. We are not going to be divided by class.")

26   Movies that deal responsibly with class relationships might help to embolden leaders to begin talking candidly about real as opposed to phony issues of "fairness." But movies obviously can't do this as long as their makers are in terror of allowing class permanently out of the closet.

27   It's true that occasional moments occur when movie audiences can grasp the substantive dimensions of social difference. A person reached toward from above or below is seen to possess inner, mysterious resources (or limits) about which someone differently placed on the social scale can have no inkling, and can't conceivably lay claim.

28   There is one such moment in "Working Girl." Following orders, Tess, as secretarial underling, books her boss, Katharine Parker (Ms. Weaver), into a chalet for a ski weekend. She is helping Katharine fasten her new ski boots in the office when she is asked where in the chalet the room is located. Tess doesn't know, Katharine dials the resort and at once a flood of flawless German fills the room.

29   The camera angle shows us Tess's awe; we gaze up with her (from the glossy white boots that she, as footman, is buckling) to this animated, magical, Ivy-educated mistress of the world, self-transformed into Europe, performing in another language. Katharine is demonstrating quite casually that bottom dogs have no exact knowledge of what lies between them and their ideal, that top dogs possess secret skills nobody learns overnight, as in charm class, or by changing hairstyles—skills traceable to uncounted indulgent hours of tutoring, study and travel.

30   The bottom dog's eyes widen, a frightening truth dawns. If a talent so mesmerizing—this poured-forth foreign sell—can be invisible until now, must there not be others equally well concealed? Maybe this dream to be her *is* foolish. What unimaginable barriers stand between me and my desire?

31   In the movie culture the answer to such questions is, of course: no real barriers, none. "Be all you can be" means at the bottom as at the top, "Be whatever you wish," fear no obstacle, see no obstacle, there are no obstacles. "Working Girl" is, finally, a story about how ambitious working girls just can't lose—one more movie that obliterates class.

32   "White Palace," for all its initial explicitness about the reality of social differences, is, finally, a story asserting that such differences simply don't matter, pure passion erases them every time.

33   The other week Senator Daniel Patrick Moynihan told a *Wall Street Journal* reporter that the fundamental issue in this country is "class, not race." It's essential, he said, "to at least start thinking about it, start talking about it. Let's be honest. We're not doing that."

34   One reason we're not is that movies remain firmly resolved against letting us.

Discussion Questions

1.   Throughout his argument, DeMott cites specific movies to illustrate his points. Do you think he provides a sufficient number of movies? Has he overlooked others that realistically portray social classes? Explain your answers.

2.   The movies that DeMott discusses were, for the most part, very successful. What effect do you think this has on his argument? Would his argument have been equally convincing had he discussed flops?

3.   To what extent does the success of DeMott's argument depend on whether his readers have seen the movies about which he writes? Explain your response.

4.   How is DeMott's argument a good example of inductive reasoning? Explain your answer.

5.   To what extent do you think the movie industry reflects popular images of social classes? Do you think that the movie industry's representation of classes differs from other industries (for example, television, advertisements, or commercials)? Based on what he has written in his article, how do you think DeMott would answer these questions? Explain your responses.

ARGUMENT

Let's Keep Christmas

Commercial

Grace April Oursler Armstrong

Grace April Oursler Armstrong wrote the following article for *The Saturday Evening Post*. It appeared in a 1965 issue of the *Post* one week before Christmas. In it, Armstrong refutes the more popular stance when she claims that overall there is nothing wrong with the commercialization of Christmas.

1 Every year right after Halloween, the world becomes Christmas-conscious—and people begin deploring. If only we could have a *real* Christmas, they say. The good old kind. Quiet, inexpensive, simple, devout. If only we could retrieve the holy day from the hands of vulgar moneygrubbers, they say. They say, with earnest horror, that the price tag has become the liturgical symbol of the season.

2   As a Christian, I do find facets of the Christmas season ridiculous, offensive or disturbing, but I believe most complaints about the commercialization of Christmas are unconsciously hypocritical nonsense. I'm afraid that often the complainers are kidding themselves, striking spiritual poses. I'm not ashamed to admit that if I had to spend Christmas somewhere far from the crowd and the vulgar trappings, I'd hate it. I love the lights, the exquisite ones in *boutiques,* the joyful ones in village centers, even the awkward ones strung on drugstores and filling stations. I love the Santa Clauses, including those on street corners, the intricately animated windows, the hot bewilderment of the bargain basement, the sequins of the dime store. Cut off from the whole wild confusion, I'd not be holier. I'd be forlorn. So, I suspect, would most of us.

3   What's supposed to be wrong with a commercialized Christmas?

4   For one thing, it's usually said that Christmas has become the time of parties where people drink and eat too much. ("Turning Yuletide into fooltide"—that exact phrase was used to describe the holiday in Merrie Olde England, so those who yearn for the "good old Christmas" should carefully define their terms.) Oddly enough, it seems to me that often the people who most loudly criticize this holiday partying are those folks who acquire Christmas hangovers and indigestion. And they deplore it as if no

one ever had to avoid hangovers, indigestion or exhaustion at any other time of the year.

5   They say that commercialization has made the buying of Christmas presents a rat race. God knows, most of the gifts we peddle to each other have nothing to do with the infant of Bethlehem. For my part, I enjoy gawking in the catalogues at the new luxuries for people who have everything. My imagination romps over items for my private Ostentatious Wastefulness list: silver-plated golf clubs, hundred-dollar dresses for little girls to spill ice cream on. Dime and department stores are crammed with gifts no wise man would bring anyone. Things like stuffed dinosaurs twelve feet high and replicas of the *Pietà* that glow in the dark.

6   With rare exceptions it is foolishly pompous to get scandalized and accuse manufacturers, advertisers and vendors of desecrating Christmas by trying to sell what you or I may think is silly junk. Obviously some people like it and buy it, and that's their business. It's said to be the fault of the commercializers that parents buy overpriced, unnecessary toys for children. And that's a fancy alibi. It you don't like what's being hawked this Christmas, you don't have to buy it. And if you're a sucker, your problem isn't seasonal.

7   Christians began giving presents to each other to celebrate Jesus' birthday in imitation of the Wise Men who came to Bethlehem. The basic idea was and is to bring joy, to honor God in others, and to give in His name with love for all. But in our social structure, with or without the blessings of the Internal Revenue Service, Christmas presents serve many purposes. Gift givers are, in practice, often diplomats, almoners, egoists, or investors. A shiny box with gold ribbon may be a guilt assuager, a bribe, a bid for attention, or merely payment for services past or future. And what is in the box must look rightly lavish, conveying subliminal impact while not costing too much. That kind of petty ugliness we all know about. And we know that often, too, gift givers play Santa Claus against their will, badgered by cozy reminders in the parking lot about how the boys wish you Season's Greetings, or by collections taken up in offices, clubs, Sunday schools, Scouts and third grades.

8   But are extortion, begging, status seeking and advantage taking so unusual among us that they occur only once a year? Isn't it more realistic to admit that whatever is sleazy about Christmas isn't seasonal?

9   After all, the instinct and art of commercialization are neither good nor bad. People normally, naturally, make a living from every kind of want, aspiration and occasion. We exploit births, weddings, deaths, first communions, bar mitzvahs, the wish to smell nice, the craving for amusement, and the basic desires for housing, clothes, love and food. Is anything more commercialized than food? But no one complains when millions cash in on our need to eat.

10   Do we assume that eating is so earthy and undignified that commercialization upgrades it, while celebrating Christmas should be so totally ethereal a process that it shouldn't be treated in a human way? If so, we are both pretentious and mistaken. We are creatures who both eat and worship, and God doesn't want us as split personalities. When Christ once raised a little girl from death, the next thing He did was to tell her mother to feed her.

11   Simony is a sin, the sin of trying to buy or sell what is sacred. But this is not simony or sin, this peddling of manger sets, this pitchman heralding the season. No one can buy or sell Christmas. No one can steal it from us, or ruin it for us, except ourselves. If we become self-seeking, materialistic, harried and ill-willed in this Christmas melee, that's our problem, not the fault of the world in which we live.

12   Some people are dismayed today in a different way, because they honestly fear Christmas is being de-Christianized, made nonsectarian. They are upset when someone who does not share their faith sets up a tree and exchanges gifts and wishes them "Season's Greetings" instead of naming the holy day. They resent the spelling "Xmas." Others fret over the way Santa Claus and snowmen crowd out the shepherds. Put Christ back into Christmas, these offended people cry.

13   As far as I know, Christ never left it. He could never be cut out of Christmas, except in the privacy of individual hearts. I don't care if some people designate Xmas as the Time for Eggnog, or Toys. Let them call it the Time to Buy New Appliances, the Time to Use the Phone, or the Time for New Loans. The antics of the rest of the world can't change Christmas. Why on earth should we expect everyone to share our special joy our way?

14   Actually, what bothers most people who decry the vulgar American Christmas is a matter of taste, not of morals or of religious commitment. Taste is a very personal matter, relative, changing and worldly; we're all a rather tacky lot anyway, religious or not. Some Christians like those new stark liturgical Christmas cards, and some dote on luminous plastic crèches, and I hate both, and the Lord doesn't care a bit. Maybe you can't stand Rudolf, are bored with the same old carols, and cringe at Santa in a helicopter. But don't blame your discomfort on commercialization and become righteous and indignant. After all, if your taste is better than that of most other people, you're probably proud of it, and you should be willing to suffer the consequences in kindly forbearance.

15   I believe the root of complaints about commercialized Christmas is that we're falling into the dangerous habit of thinking that religion is somehow coarsened by contact with real people. I suspect that unconsciously we're embarrassed at the prospect of trying to live with God here

and now. At times we modern Christians seem to have a neurotic refusal to embrace reality in the name of the Lord who was the supreme realist, and maker of the real.

16   It's always easier, if you're not doing very well religiously, to insist that the secularizing world prevents you from devotion. Christmas is meant to be lived in the noisy arena of the shopping day countdown, amid aluminum trees, neckties and counterfeit French perfume. If all the meditation I get around to is listening to Scrooge and Tiny Tim, or begging heaven for patience to applaud a school pageant, I'm a fool to blame anyone but myself. Census time in Bethlehem was distracting too.

17   I know a man who confides that he learns more about patience and love of his neighbor in post-office lines than anywhere else. More than one mother has learned that Christmas shopping on a tight budget can be a lesson in mortification, humility, willpower and joy. There's grist for meditation in the reflection of tree lights in a sloshy puddle. Families have their own customs, their private windows on glory. And families that are honest and relaxed find that the commercially generated atmosphere of goodwill hinders them not at all in their celebration. God works in wondrous ways still, even among assemble-it-yourself toys.

18   Christmas is a parable of the whole Christian venture. The Christian's attitude toward it, his willingness to make it relevant repeatedly in his own time and space, is a symptom of his whole encounter with God. The first Christmas happened, so Christians believe, because God lovingly plunged Himself into human nature to transform it. He is not honored by men and women who want to disown other people's human nature in His name.

19   Let's not make the mealy-mouthed error of complaining that paganism threatens Christmas today. Christmas has already absorbed and recharged the vestiges of Druid feasts, Norse gods and sun worship. Christmas took the world as it was and built on it, and it's still doing just that.

20   To those who fear that Christmas is prostituted by the almighty dollar, I suggest that it's remarkable and beautiful that Christmas is publicly touted at all. Nor do I make that suggestion, as some might suspect, in a tone of meek appeasement to groups that object to Christmas celebrations in public schools, or crèches in town squares. Realistically, I know that in our society what is important to people and concerns them deeply, whether it's cancer or get-rich-quick schemes, patriotism or religion, is talked about and exploited.

21   If Christmas becomes for some people primarily a subject for commercials, at least God is getting equal time with toothpaste. If people didn't care about Him, He wouldn't even get that.

22   In good taste or bad, by your standards or mine, the fact of Christ, the good news of the meeting of heaven and earth, the tidings of love and peace

for human nature, are announced everywhere. It is still true that he who has ears to hear will hear.

Discussion Questions

1. Which of Armstrong's reasons that support her argument do you find the most persuasive? Which the least? Explain your response.

2. What kind of appeal would you say Armstrong principally uses to argue her position: *logos*, *ethos*, or *pathos*? How effective is her choice?

3. Whom do you think Armstrong envisions as her audience: Christians or non-Christians? What changes would she have had to make in her argument if she perceived a different audience? Explain your answer.

4. Identify any logical fallacies that Armstrong makes in her argument. What effect do they have on her argument?

5. Armstrong seems to speak for God in some of her statements (e.g., "God doesn't want us as split personalities"). Does this add to or detract from her argument's credibility" Explain your response.

WRITING TOPICS

1. In "Hate Radio," Patricia J. Williams offers her reasons why people listen to such programs as Rush Limbaugh and Howard Stern. If you disagree with Williams's position, write a paper defending your position. Ask people you know who listen to such shows for their input; do the same for people who refuse to listen to them. Use their reactions to help support your stance, but remember your paper should reflect your own beliefs.

2. Sarah Ferguson, in "The Comfort of Being Sad," examines the appeal of the grunge culture. Sadness and depression among teenagers, however, is nothing new to the current generation. Some critics believe that such feelings are a natural, albeit painful, part of growing up. In a paper, examine what you think makes the grunge culture so conducive or appealing to

the current generation. If you know of any teens who are a part of the culture, interview them for their reactions. Research what sociologists and psychologists have written about the grunge culture. All of these sources should provide interesting perspectives to advance your perspective.

3. Each generation has been given a label (the me generation, the hippie generation, and so on). The label given to the current generation is *Generation* X or *XGen*. What do you think of that title? Does it accurately and adequately portray you and your peers? Interview your peers as well as members of your parents' and (if possible) grandparents' generations to get their reactions. Research the origins of the term and write a paper that argues whether you think the label *Generation* X is fitting.

4. Select a television show that you think best (or at least accurately) presents a specific group of people based on their race or ethnicity, gender, sexual orientation, age, and so on. In a paper, discuss your reasons for choosing that particular show and examine its appeal to all sectors of society. Draw on critics' reviews of the show as a way to support your stance.

5. Television news shows have been attacked for being more concerned with entertaining and glitz than with reporting the hard news. In a paper, explore your perspective of this issue. Analyze some news shows as a way to argue your point of view. You might want to interview local television news anchors and/or print journalists to get their reactions.

6. Explain what you see as the appeal that soap operas have on people. Pay particular attention to high school and college students. Ask your contemporaries if they watch the soaps. Why or why not? Discuss whether you see soap operas' appeal as a healthy or a dangerous sign.

7. Choose an advertising campaign and analyze the ways in which it demeans or dignifies a certain group of people. How does its portrayal of this group reflect or influence popular opinion?

8. On the whole, do you think that advertisements and commercials *reflect* popular opinion or do they *influence* popular opinion? Be sure to cite specific advertisements and commercials, and discuss your reasoning in a paper.

9. If you had to choose one movie or television show that you think everyone should see, what would it be? Given that there

are literally thousands of movies and television shows, your goal is to write a plausible and convincing paper. Research what critics have written about the show or movie as a way to help support your stance.

10. Movies are given ratings before they are released. Do you think that CDs and computer videos should also be rated and their sales regulated? Research the opposing viewpoints on this controversy and write a paper in which you take and support a stand.

CHAPTER 10

THE AMERICAN FAMILY

What Happened to the Family?

Jerrold Footlick

A senior editor at *Newsweek* magazine, Jerrold Footlick writes on legal matters, education, and families. The editor of *Newsweek on Campus,* he is also the author of *Education: A New Era* (1966) and *The College Scene Now* (1967). The following piece, cowritten with Elizabeth Leonard, was featured in *Newsweek's* special issue, *The Twenty-First Century Family,* in 1990. In it, Footlick offers his observations on the ways in which the American family has changed.

1   The American family does not exist. Rather, we are creating many American families of diverse styles and shapes. In unprecedented numbers, our families are unalike: We have fathers working while mothers keep house; fathers and mothers both working away from home; single parents; second marriages bringing children together from unrelated backgrounds; childless couples; unmarried couples, with and without children; gay and lesbian parents. We are living through a period of historic change in American family life.

2   The upheaval is evident everywhere in our culture. Babies have babies, kids refuse to grow up and leave home, affluent Yuppies prize their BMWs more than children, rich and poor children alike blot their minds with drugs, people casually move in with each other and out again. The divorce rate has doubled since 1965, and demographers project that half of all first marriages made today will end in divorce. Six out of 10 second marriages will probably collapse. One third of all children born in the past decade will probably live in a stepfamily before they are 18. One out of every four children today is being raised by a single parent. About 22 percent of children today were born out of wedlock; of those, about a third were born to a teenage mother. One out of every five children lives in poverty; the rate is twice as high among blacks and Hispanics.

3   Most of us are still reeling from the shock of such turmoil. Americans—in their living rooms, in their boardrooms and in the halls of Congress—are struggling to understand what has gone wrong. We find family life worse than it was a decade ago, according to a *Newsweek* Poll, and we are not

sanguine about the next decade. For instance, two thirds of those polled think a family should be prepared to make "financial sacrifices so that one parent can stay home to raise the children." But that isn't likely to happen. An astonishing two thirds of all mothers are in the labor force, roughly double the rate in 1955, and more than half of all mothers of infants are in the work force.

4   Parents feel torn between work and family obligations. Marriage is a fragile institution—not something anyone can count on. Children seem to be paying the price for their elders' confusion. "There is an increasing understanding of the emotional cost of having children," says Larry L. Bumpass, a University of Wisconsin demographer. "People once thought parenting ended when their children were 18. Now they know it stretches into the 20s and beyond." Divorce has left a devastated generation in its wake, and for many youngsters, the pain is compounded by poverty and neglect. While politicians and psychologists debate cause and solution, everyone suffers. Even the most traditional of families feel an uneasy sense of emotional dislocation. Three decades ago the mother who kept the house spotless and cooked dinner for her husband and children each evening could be confident and secure in her role. Today, although her numbers are still strong— a third of mothers whose children are under 18 stay home—the woman who opts out of a paycheck may well feel defensive, undervalued, as though she were too incompetent to get "a real job." And yet the traditional family retains a profound hold on the American imagination.

5   The historical irony here is that the traditional family is something of an anomaly. From Colonial days to the mid-19th century, most fathers and mothers worked side by side, in or near their homes, farming or plying trades. Each contributed to family income, and—within carefully delineated roles— they shared the responsibility of child rearing. Only with the advent of the Industrial Revolution did men go off to work in a distant place like a factory or an office. Men alone began producing the family income; by being away from home much of the time, however, they also surrendered much of their influence on their children. Mothers, who by social custom weren't supposed to work for pay outside the home, minded the hearth, nurtured the children and placed their economic well-being totally in the hands of their husbands.

6   Most scholars now consider the "bread-winner-homemaker" model unusual, applicable in limited circumstances for a limited time. It was a distinctly white middle-class phenomenon, for example; it never applied widely among blacks or new immigrants, who could rarely afford to have only a single earner in the family. This model thrived roughly from 1860 to 1920, peaking, as far as demographers can measure, about 1890. Demographers and historians see no dramatic turning point just then, but rather a

confluence of social and economic circumstances. Husbands' absolute control of family finances and their independent lives away from home shook the family structure. A long recession beginning in 1893 strained family finances. At the same time, new attention was being paid to women's education. Around this period, the Census Bureau captured a slow, steady, parallel climb in the rates of working women and divorce—a climb that has shown few signs of slowing down throughout this century.

7   The years immediately after World War II, however, seemed to mark a reaffirmation of the traditional family. The return of the soldiers led directly to high fertility rates and the famous baby boom. The median age of first marriage, which had been climbing for decades, fell in 1956 to a historic low, 22.5 years for men and 20.1 for women. The divorce rate slumped slightly. Women, suddenly more likely to be married and to have children, were also satisfied to give up the paid jobs they had held in record numbers during the war. A general prosperity made it possible for men alone to support their families. Then, by the early '60s, all those developments, caused by aberrational postwar conditions, reverted to the patterns they had followed throughout the century. The fertility rate went down, and the age of first marriage went back up. Prosperity cycled to recession, and the divorce rate again rose and women plunged back heartily into the job market. In 1960, 19 percent of mothers with children under 6 were in the work force, along with 39 percent of those with children between 6 and 17. Thus, while the Cleaver family and Ozzie and Harriet were still planting the idealized family deeper into the national subconscious, it was struggling.

8   Now the tradition survives, in a way, precisely because of Ozzie and Harriet. The television programs of the '50s and '60s validated a family style during a period in which today's leaders—congressmen, corporate executives, university professors, magazine editors—were growing up or beginning to establish their own families. (The impact of the idealized family was further magnified by the very size of the postwar generation.) "The traditional model reaches back as far as personal memory goes for most of those who [currently] teach and write and philosophize," says Yale University historian John Demos. "And in a time when parents seem to feel a great deal of change in family experience, that image is comfortingly solid and secure, a counterpoint to what we think is threatening for the future."

9   We *do* feel uneasy about the future. We have just begun to admit that exchanging old-fashioned family values for independence and self-expression may exact a price. "This is an incendiary issue," says Arlie Hochschild, a sociologist at the University of California, Berkeley, and author of the controversial book "The Second Shift." "Husbands, wives, children are not getting enough family life. Nobody is. People are hurting." A mother may go to work because her family needs the money, or to afford luxuries, or because

she is educated for a career or because she wants to; she will be more independent but she will probably see less of her children. And her husband, if she has a husband, is not likely to make up the difference with the children. We want it both ways. We're glad we live in a society that is more comfortable living with gay couples, working women, divorced men, and stepparents and single mothers—people who are reaching in some fashion for self-fulfillment. But we also understand the value of a family life that will provide a stable and nurturing environment in which to raise children—in other words, an environment in which personal goals have to be sacrificed. How do we reconcile the two?

10   The answer lies in some hard thinking about what a family is for. What do we talk about when we talk about family? Many of us have an emotional reaction to that question. Thinking about family reminds us of the way we were, and the way we dreamed we might be. We remember trips in the car, eager to find out whose side of the road would have more cows and horses to count. We remember raking leaves and the sound of a marching band at the high-school football game. We remember doing homework and wondering what college might be like. It was not all fun and games, of course. There were angry words spoken, and parents and grandparents who somehow were no longer around, and for some of us not enough to eat or clothes not warm enough or nice enough. Then we grow up and marvel at what we can accomplish, and the human beings we can produce, and we sometimes doubt our ability to do the things we want to do—have to do—for our children. And live our own lives besides.

11   Practical considerations require us to pin down what the family is all about. Tax bills, welfare and insurance payments, adoption rights and other real-life events can turn on what constitutes a family. Our expectations of what a family ought to be will also shape the kinds of social policies we want. Webster's offers twenty-two definitions. The Census Bureau has settled on "two or more persons related by birth, marriage or adoption who reside in the same household." New York state's highest court stretched the definition last summer: it held that the survivor of a gay couple retained the legal rights to an apartment they had long shared, just as a surviving husband or wife could. Looking to the "totality of the relationship," the court set four standards for a family: (1) the "exclusivity and longevity of a relationship"; (2) the "level of emotional and financial commitment"; (3) how the couple "conducted their everyday lives and held themselves out to society"; (4) the "reliance placed upon one another for daily services." That approach incenses social critic Midge Decter. "You can call homosexual households 'families,' and you can define 'family' any way you want to, but you can't fool Mother Nature," says Decter. "A family is a mommy and a daddy and their children."

12   A State of California task force on the future of the family came up with still another conclusion. It decided a family could be measured by the things it should do for its members, which it called "functions": maintain the physical health and safety of its members; help shape a belief system of goals and values; teach social skills, and create a place for recuperation from external stresses. In a recent "family values" survey conducted for the Massachusetts Mutual Insurance Co., respondents were given several choices of family definitions; three quarters of them chose "a group who love and care for each other." Ultimately, to appropriate U.S. Supreme Court Justice Potter Stewart's memorable dictum, we may not be able to define a family, but we know one when we see it.

13   We enter the 21st century with a heightened sensitivity to family issues. Helping parents and children is a bottom-line concern, no longer a matter of debate. Economists say the smaller labor force of the future means that every skilled employee will be an increasingly valuable asset; we won't be able to afford to waste human resources. Even now companies cannot ignore the needs of working parents. Support systems like day care are becoming a necessity. High rates of child poverty and child abuse are everybody's problem, as is declining school performance and anything else that threatens our global competitiveness. "By the end of the century," says Columbia University sociologist Sheila B. Kamerman, "it will be conventional wisdom to invest in our children."

14   Those are the familiar demographic forces. But there are other potential tremors just below the surface. By 2020, one in three children will come from a minority group—Hispanic-Americans, African-Americans, Asian-Americans and others. Their parents will command unprecedented political clout. Minorities and women together will make up the majority of new entrants into the work force. Minority children are usually the neediest among us, and they will want government support, especially in the schools. At about the same time, many baby boomers will be retired, and they will want help from Washington as well. Billions of dollars are at stake, and the country's priorities in handing out those dollars are not yet clear. After all, children and the elderly are both part of our families. How should the government spend taxpayers' dollars—on long-term nursing care or better day care?

15   So far, the political debate on family issues has split largely along predictable ideological lines. Conservatives want to preserve the family of the '50s; they say there has been too much governmental intrusion already, with disastrous results. Their evidence: the underclass, a veritable caste of untouchables in the inner cities where the cycle of welfare dependency and teenage pregnancy thwarts attempts at reform. Liberals say government can and should help. We can measure which programs work, they

say; we just don't put our money and support in the right places. Enrichment programs like Head Start, better prenatal care, quality day care—no one questions the effectiveness of these efforts. And liberals see even more to be done. "We have a rare opportunity to make changes now that could be meaningful into the next century," says Marian Wright Edelman, president of the Children's Defense Fund. But many elements that liberals would like to see on a children's agenda are certain to generate bitter political controversy. Among some of the things that could be included in a national family policy:

- Child and family allowances with payments scaled to the number of children in each family;
- Guarantees to mothers of full job protection, seniority and benefits upon their return to work after maternity leave;
- Pay equity for working women;
- Cash payments to mothers for wages lost during maternity leave;
- Full health-care programs for all children;
- National standards for day-care.

16   Our legacy to the future must be a program of action that transcends ideology. And there are indications that we are watching the birth of a liberal/conservative coalition on family issues. "Family issues ring true for people across the political spectrum," says David Blankenhorn, president of the Institute for American Values, a New York think tank on family policy issues. "The well-being of families is both politically and culturally resonant; it is something that touches people's everyday lives." The government is already responding to the challenge in some ways. For example, President George Bush agreed at the recent Education Summit to support increased funding for Head Start, which is by common consent the most successful program for preschoolers, yet now reaches only 18 percent of the eligible children.

17   These issues will occupy us on a national level well into the next century. Yet in our everyday lives, we have begun to find solutions. Some mothers, torn between a desire to stay home with their children and to move ahead in their careers, are adopting a style known as sequencing. After establishing themselves in their career or earning an advanced degree, they step off the career ladder for a few years to focus on children and home. When children reach school age, they return to full-time jobs. Others take a less drastic approach, temporarily switching to part-time work or lower-pressure jobs to carve out more time with their young children. But renewing careers that have been on hiatus is not easy, and women will always

suffer vocationally if it is they who must take off to nurture children. There is, obviously, another way: fathers can accept more home and family responsibilities, even to the point of interrupting their own careers. "I expect a significant change by 2020," says sociologist Hochschild. "A majority of men married to working wives will share equally in the responsibilities of home." Perhaps tradition will keep us from ever truly equalizing either child rearing or ironing—in fact, surveys on chore sharing don't hold much promise for the harried working mother. But we have moved a long way since the 1950s. And just because we haven't tried family equality yet doesn't mean we won't ever try it.

18   That's the magic for American families in the 21st century: we can try many things. As certainly as anything can be estimated, women are not going to turn their backs on education and careers, are not going to leave the work force for adult lives as full-time homemakers and mothers. And the nation's businesses will encourage their efforts, if only because they will need the skilled labor. Yet Americans will not turn their backs completely on the idealized family we remember fondly. Thus, we must create accommodations that are new, but reflect our heritage. Our families will continue to be different in the 21st century except in one way. They will give us sustenance and love as they always have.

Discussion Questions

1.   Although Footlick begins his viewpoint by stating, "The American family does not exist," his viewpoint continues with a discussion of "American families of diverse styles and shapes." How effective is the opening of his viewpoint? Explain your answer.

2.   Explain how Footlick backs up his viewpoints about the American family. Which of his evidence seems the most convincing and which the least? Why?

3.   What do you think Footlick's brief history of the American family adds to the strength of his viewpoint? Explain your answer.

4.   Footlick states that "Americans will not turn their backs on the idealized family we remember fondly." What in his viewpoint contributes to this statement's believability?

5. At the end of his viewpoint, Footlick observes, "Our families
    will continue to be different in the 21st century except in one
    way. They will give us sustenance and love as they always
    have." Has Footlick provided any evidence to support this
    statement or is none needed?

Oh, Those Family Values

Barbara Ehrenreich

> Barbara Ehrenreich was born in 1941 and was educated at Reed College and Rockefeller University. She has worked as a contributing editor at *Ms.* magazine and also writes for *Time* magazine. Her essays have appeared in such magazines as *Mother Jones, Nation,* and the *New York Times Magazine.* Ehrenreich is the author of *Fear of Falling: The Inner Life of the Middle Class* (1989), *The Worst Years of Our Lives: Irreverent Notes from a Decade of Greed* (1990), and *Kipper's Game* (1994), her first novel. In the following selection, which first appeared in *Time* magazine in 1994, Ehrenreich examines the idea that "the family may not be the ideal and perfect living arrangement after all."

1   A disturbing subtext runs through our recent media fixations. Parents abuse sons—allegedly at least, in the Menendez case—who in turn rise up and kill them. A husband torments a wife, who retaliates with a kitchen knife. Love turns into obsession, between the Simpsons anyway, and then perhaps into murderous rage: the family, in other words, becomes personal hell.

2   This accounts for at least part of our fascination with the Bobbitts and the Simpsons and the rest of them. We live in a culture that fetishizes the family as the ideal unit of human community, the perfect container for our lusts and loves. Politicians of both parties are aggressively "pro-family," even abortion-rights bumper stickers proudly link "pro-family" and "pro-choice." Only with the occasional celebrity crime do we allow ourselves to think the nearly unthinkable: that the family may not be the ideal and perfect living arrangement after all—that it can be a nest of pathology and a cradle of gruesome violence.

3   It's a scary thought, because the family is at the same time our "haven in a heartless world." Theoretically, and sometimes actually, the family nurtures warm, loving feelings, uncontaminated by greed or power hunger. Within the family, and often only within the family, individuals are loved "for themselves," whether or not they are infirm, incontinent, infantile or eccentric.

The strong (adults and especially males) lie down peaceably with the small and weak.

4 But consider the matter of wife battery. We managed to dodge it in the Bobbitt case and downplay it as a force in Tonya Harding's life. Thanks to O.J., though, we're caught up now in a mass consciousness-raising session, grimly absorbing the fact that in some areas domestic violence sends as many women to emergency rooms as any other form of illness, injury or assault.

5 Still, we shrink from the obvious inference: for a woman, home is, statistically speaking, the most dangerous place to be. Her worst enemies and potential killers are not strangers but lovers, husbands and those who claimed to love her once. Similarly, for every child like Polly Klaas who is killed by a deranged criminal on parole, dozens are abused and murdered by their own relatives. Home is all too often where the small and weak fear to lie down and shut their eyes.

6 At some deep, queasy, Freudian level, we all know this. Even in the ostensibly "functional," nonviolent family, where no one is killed or maimed, feelings are routinely bruised and often twisted out of shape. There is the slap or put-down that violates a child's shaky sense of self, the cold, distracted stare that drives a spouse to tears, the little digs and rivalries. At best, the family teaches the finest things human beings can learn from one another— generosity and love. But it is also, all too often, where we learn nasty things like hate and rage and shame.

7 Americans act out their ambivalence about the family without ever owning up to it. Millions adhere to creeds that are militantly "pro-family." But at the same time millions flock to therapy groups that offer to heal the "inner child" from damage inflicted by family life. Legions of women band together to revive the self-esteem they lost in supposedly loving relationships and to learn to love a little less. We are all, it is often said, "in recovery." And from what? Our families, in most cases.

8 There is a long and honorable tradition of "anti-family" thought. The French philosopher Charles Fourier taught that the family was a barrier to human progress; early feminists saw a degrading parallel between marriage and prostitution. More recently, the renowned British anthropologist Edmund Leach stated that "far from being the basis of the good society, the family, with its narrow privacy and tawdry secrets, is the course of all discontents."

9 Communes proved harder to sustain than plain old couples, and the conservatism of the '80s crushed the last vestiges of life-style experimentation. Today even gays and lesbians are eager to get married and take up family life. Feminists have learned to couch their concerns as "family

issues," and public figures would sooner advocate free cocaine on demand than criticize the family. Hence our unseemly interest in O.J. and Erik, Lyle and Lorena: they allow us, however gingerly, to break the silence on the hellish side of family life.

10   But the discussion needs to become a lot more open and forthright. We may be stuck with the family—at least until someone invents a sustainable alternative—but the family, with its deep, impacted tensions and longings, can hardly be expected to be the moral foundation of everything else. In fact, many families could use a lot more outside interference in the form of counseling and policing, and some are so dangerously dysfunctional that they ought to be encouraged to disband right away. Even healthy families need outside sources of moral guidance to keep the internal tensions from imploding—and this means, at the very least, a public philosophy of gender equality and concern for child welfare. When, instead, the larger culture aggrandizes wife beaters, degrades women or nods approvingly at child slappers, the family gets a little more dangerous for everyone, and so, inevitably, does the larger world.

Discussion Questions

1. Summarize Ehrenreich's viewpoint.

2. Ehrenreich seems to base her viewpoint on high-profile families who have recently been front-page news items: Erik and Lyle Menendez, O.J. Simpson, the Bobbitts, Tonya Harding, and Polly Klass. How convincing are the ideas she offers when they focus on the seeming exceptions to the rule? Explain your response.

3. If the family is supposed to be a safe haven from the world, why do you think it is in such trouble these days? Does Ehrenreich reconcile this seeming contradiction to your satisfaction? Why or why not?

4. Describe the tone of Ehrenreich's viewpoint and identify specific examples that contribute to it.

5. What do you think people opposing Ehrenreich's viewpoint would find as the major flaw in her thinking? Explain your answer.

Evan's Two Moms

Anna Quindlen

Born in 1952, Anna Quindlen is a graduate of Barnard College. From 1977 to 1985, she worked at *The New York Times,* first as a general assignment and City Hall reporter, then as the author of the "About New York" column, and finally as deputy metropolitan editor. From 1986 to 1988, she wrote her syndicated "Life in the 30's" column for the *Times.* Quindlen stepped down at the end of 1994 as a columnist for the *New York Times* to become a full-time novelist. The author of *Living Out Loud* (1988) and *Thinking Out Loud* (1992), both collections of her *Times* columns, Quindlen has also written two novels, *Object Lessons* (1991) and *One True Thing* (1994). In the following selection, Quindlen makes a case for gay marriages.

1   Evan has two moms. This is no big thing. Evan has always had two moms—in his school file, on his emergency forms, with his friends. "Ooooh, Evan, you're lucky," they sometimes say. "You have two moms." It sounds like a sitcom, but until last week it was emotional truth without legal bulwark. That was when a judge in New York approved the adoption of a 6-year-old boy by his biological mother's lesbian partner. Evan. Evan's mom. Evan's other mom. A kid, a psychologist, a pediatrician. A family.

2   The matter of Evan's two moms is one in a series of events over the last year that lead to certain conclusions. A Minnesota appeals court granted guardianship of a woman left a quadriplegic in a car accident to her lesbian lover, the culmination of a seven-year battle in which the injured woman's parents did everything possible to negate the partnership between the two. A lawyer in Georgia had her job offer withdrawn after the state Attorney General found out she and her lesbian lover were planning a marriage ceremony; she's brought suit. The computer company Lotus announced that the gay partners of employees would be eligible for the same benefits as spouses.

3   Add to these public events the private struggles, the couples who go from lawyer to lawyer to approximate legal protections their straight counterparts

take for granted, the AIDS survivors who find themselves shut out of their partners' dying days by biological family members and shut out of their apartments by leases with a single name on the dotted line, and one solution is obvious.

4   Gay marriage is a radical notion for straight people and a conservative notion for gay ones. After years of being sledgehammered by society, some gay men and lesbian women are deeply suspicious of participating in an institution that seems to have "straight world" written all over it.

5   But the rads of twenty years ago, straight and gay alike, have other things on their minds today. Family is one, and the linchpin of family has commonly been a loving commitment between two adults. When same-sex couples set out to make that commitment, they discover that they are at a disadvantage.

6   No joint tax returns. No health insurance coverage for an uninsured partner. No survivor's benefits from Social Security. None of the automatic rights, privileges and responsibilities society attaches to a marriage contract. In Madison, Wis., a couple who applied at the Y with their kids for a family membership were turned down because both were women. It's one of those small things that can make you feel small.

7   Some took marriage statutes that refer to "two persons" at their word and applied for a license. The results were court decisions that quoted the Bible and embraced circular argument: marriage is by definition the union of a man and a woman because that is how we've defined it.

8   No religion should be forced to marry anyone in violation of its tenets, although ironically it is now only in religious ceremonies that gay people can marry, performed by clergy who find the blessing of two people who love one another no sin. But there is no secular reason that we should take a patchwork approach of corporate, governmental and legal steps to guarantee what can be done simply, economically, conclusively and inclusively with the words "I do."

9   "Fran and I chose to get married for the same reasons that any two people do," said the lawyer who was fired in Georgia. "We fell in love; we wanted to spend our lives together." Pretty simple.

10   Consider the case of Loving v. Virginia, aptly named. At the time, sixteen states had laws that barred interracial marriage, relying on natural law, that amorphous grab bag for justifying prejudice. Sounding a little like God throwing Adam and Eve out of paradise, the trial judge suspended the one-year sentence of Richard Loving, who was white, and his wife, Mildred, who was black, provided they got out of the state of Virginia.

11   In 1967 the Supreme Court found such laws to be unconstitutional. Only twenty-five years ago and it was a crime for a black woman to marry a white man. Perhaps twenty-five years from now we will find it just as incredible

that two people of the same sex were not entitled to legally commit themselves to one another. Love and commitment are rare enough; it seems absurd to thwart them in any guise.

Discussion Questions

1. What kind of reasoning does Quindlen employ in her commentary? How does her choice strengthen her argument?

2. Explain how Quindlen addresses opposing perspectives in her paper. Do you think she does so successfully? Why or why not?

3. Does Quindlen appeal to her audience with logic, emotion, or ethics? Cite examples to support your answer.

4. Whom do you think Quindlen had in mind when writing this viewpoint? What leads you to your answer?

5. At the end of her argument, Quindlen muses that while interracial marriages are now legal (although they weren't twenty-five years ago), perhaps gay marriages will be legal in twenty-five years (although they aren't today). How effective do you find this analogy? Explain your answer.

Sneer Not at "Ozzie and Harriet"

John Leo

John Leo was born in 1935 and is a graduate of the University of Toronto. He is the weekly "On Society" columnist for *U.S. News and World Report*. Before joining the magazine in 1988, Leo covered the social sciences and intellectual trends for *Time* magazine and the *New York Times*. Leo has also worked as an associate editor of *Commonwealth* magazine, a book editor of Society, the "Press Clips" columnist for the *Village Voice*, and the deputy administrator of New York City's Environmental Protection Administration. He is the author of a book of humor entitled *How the Russians Invented Baseball and Other Essays of Enlightenment* (1989) and *Two Steps Ahead of the Thought Police* (1994). In the following paper, Leo argues that the values portrayed by Ozzie and Harriet in the popular 1950s television show of the same name are not as old-fashioned as some people might think.

1   "Family values" are not an invention by Dan Quayle, not code words for racism, not a complaint that women should quit the work force, not an unsophisticated yearning for the family of the 1950s. It is simply the current term for resistance to the long assault on the nuclear family that began in the 1960s.

2   The liberation movements of the '60s asserted the rights of individuals against the power of institutions, and the institution hit hardest was the family. Feminism, of necessity, arose as a reaction to the traditional family, and the other movements fed into its early antifamily mood: the New Left, sexual liberation and the me-first pop therapies that preached personal fulfillment over social obligation. On all sides, the family was loudly denounced as a nest of oppression and pathology. Flak was not aimed just at the rigid, father-as-dictator family but at the idea of family itself. A psychiatrist named David Cooper called the family "a secret suicide pact . . . an ideological conditioning device in any exploitative society."

3   This assault from the left bred its own reaction, which plugged into the wider trend toward social conservatism. By the time of Jimmy Carter's disastrous White House Conference on the American Family in 1980, both the pro-family and pro-rights "liberationist" positions were set in stone. Liberationists got the meeting's title changed to the White House Conference on Families (plural), which in effect downgraded the intact family to one family form among many. One attendee said this verbal change was necessary to reflect "the impressive diversity" of the American family, an early use of the word "diversity" to mean "anything goes."

4   **Bad is good?** Two sociologists, Brigitte Berger and Peter Berger, zeroed in on the enormous significance of the insistence on "families" over "family": What appeared to be—in plain English—the growing disintegration of the American family was to be relabeled as something healthy and positive. In their book, "The War Over the Family," the Bergers wrote that "The *empirical fact* of diversity is here quietly translated into a *norm* of diversity . . . demography is translated into a new morality." The allegedly innocent semantic shift, they wrote, "gave governmental recognition to precisely the kind of moral relativism that has infuriated and mobilized large numbers of Americans."

5   The entire war over the family is implied in that word change. The war has been about the conditions under which children are raised and the conflict between self-fulfillment and sacrifice. One side says what everybody thought was obvious until the 1960s: that stably married parents are best, especially if those parents are willing to put children's interests ahead of their own personal fulfillment.

6   The other side, shaped by social movements born in hostility to the family, has emphasized freedom from family obligations and the alleged resilience of children in the face of instability at home. It has been chiefly interested in the family for pathologies it can address (wife-beating, incest) and for rights that can be asserted against it (a residue of the '60s view of family as inherently oppressive, and an increasingly narrow rights-based version of morality). Its honorable insistence that single mothers be treated with respect has been used as a wedge to normalize the no-father home. This justified the short-changing of the young. (If the father who runs out on his kids is merely creating another acceptable family form, how is he any better or worse than the father who stays committed to his "double-parent family"?)

7   Data on the devastation of families have begun to turn the debate around. So has the soaring rate of births to unwed mothers: 27 percent in 1989, 19 percent for whites and 66 percent for blacks. The Rockefeller commission last year emphatically called attention to the need for two-parent families, a breakthrough after so much propaganda on "alternative family

forms." Black intellectuals have begun to relegitimize discussion of the connection between family form and social ills—forbidden by the left since the Moynihan Report of 1965. For instance, columnist William Raspberry says, "My guess is that the greatest increase in child poverty in America is a direct result of the increase in the proportion of mothers-only households." Some prominent feminists now talk about the subject without bristling hostility, emphasizing family over the old agenda of sexual politics. Polls have started to show shifts from stark individualism to concern for the family, responsibility and community. In short, a call for bolstering the family is beginning.

8   Yet in the media the old howitzers boom as if it were still the 1960s. The almost daily fusillade of "Ozzie and Harriet" jeering derides the goal of the intact family as a form of nostalgia. An op-ed piece said that the nuclear family is "fast becoming a relic of the Eisenhower era." The *New York Times* recently referred to the intact family as "the Republican ideal." (Do all Democrats idealize nonintact families?) A week later, it reported that the current "family values" campaign is based on "the warm appeal of the idealized 1950s family as embodied in 'Father Knows Best.'" This sort of tiresome sniping serves no function. It is the work of people who do not realize that the '60s are over, the family is in crisis and the discussion has moved on.

Discussion Questions

1.   In the opening paragraph, Leo defines "family values." How much does the believability of his argument hinge on his audience agreeing with his definition? Explain your answer.

2.   How do the sources Leo quotes strengthen his argument? Could his argument have been just as convincing without them? Explain your response.

3.   What do you think Leo's opponents would find as the main flaw in his argument? Does Leo adequately address the opposing perspective? Explain your answer.

4.   Describe the tone or voice Leo uses in his argument. How does it add to or detract from his argument?

5.   How do you think Barbara Ehrenreich would respond to Leo's argument?

We Have No
"Right to Happiness"

C. S. Lewis

C. S. Lewis was born in 1898 and died in 1963. A prolific writer of fantasy, science fiction, and books on Christian theology, Lewis is read widely by children and adults in England and the United States. His books include *The Allegory of Love* (1938), *The Case for Christianity* (1944), *The Abolition of Man* (1947), and *Surprised by Joy: The Shape of My Early Life* (1959). He is probably best known for "The Narnia Chronicles," a series of children's books, which began with *The Lion, The Witch, and The Wardrobe* (1950). In the following selection, Lewis sets up a scenario in which he examines the changing attitudes toward marriage and divorce.

1   "After all," said Clare, "they had a right to happiness."

2   We were discussing something that once happened in our own neighborhood. Mr. A. had deserted Mrs. A. and got his divorce in order to marry Mrs. B., who had likewise got her divorce in order to marry Mr. A. And there was certainly no doubt that Mr. A. and Mrs. B. were very much in love with one another. If they continued to be in love, and if nothing went wrong with their health or their income, they might reasonably expect to be happy.

3   It was equally clear that they were not happy with their old partners. Mrs. B. had adored her husband at the outset. But then he got smashed up in the war. It was thought he had lost his virility, and it was known that he had lost his job. Life with him was no longer what Mrs. B. had bargained for. Poor Mrs. A., too. She had lost her looks—and all her liveliness. It might be true, as some said, that she consumed herself by bearing his children and nursing him through the long illness that overshadowed their earlier married life.

4   You mustn't, by the way, imagine that A. was the sort of man who nonchalantly threw a wife away like the peel of an orange he'd sucked dry. Her

suicide was a terrible shock to him. We all knew this, for he told us so himself. "But what could I do?" he said. "A man has a right to happiness. I had to take my one chance when it came."

5   I went away thinking about the concept of a "right to happiness."

6   At first this sounds to me as odd as a right to good luck. For I believe—whatever one school of moralists may say—that we depend for a very great deal of our happiness or misery on circumstances outside all human control. A right to happiness doesn't, for me, make much more sense than a right to be six feet tall, or to have a millionaire for your father, or to get good weather whenever you want to have a picnic.

7   I can understand a right to freedom guaranteed me by the laws of the society I live in. Thus, I have a right to travel along the public roads because society gives me that freedom; that's what we mean by calling the roads "public." I can also understand a right as a claim guaranteed me by the laws, and correlative to an obligation on someone else's part. If I have a right to receive £100 from you, this is another way of saying that you have a duty to pay me £100. If the laws allow Mr. A. to desert his wife and seduce his neighbor's wife, then, by definition, Mr. A. has a legal right to do so, and we need bring in no talk about "happiness."

8   But of course that was not what Clare meant. She meant that he had not only a legal but a moral right to act as he did. In other words, Clare is—or would be if she thought it out—a classical moralist after the style of Thomas Aquinas, Grotius, Hooker and Locke. She believes that behind the laws of the state there is a Natural Law.

9   I agree with her. I hold this conception to be basic to all civilization. Without it, the actual laws of the state become an absolute, as in Hegel. They cannot be criticized because there is no norm against which they should be judged.

10   The ancestry of Clare's maxim, "They have a right to happiness," is august. In words that are cherished by all civilized men, but especially by Americans, it has been laid down that one of the rights of man is a right to "the pursuit of happiness." And now we get to the real point.

11   What did the writers of that august declaration mean?

12   It is quite certain what they did not mean. They did not mean that man was entitled to pursue happiness by any and every means—including, say, murder, rape, robbery, treason and fraud. No society could be built on such a basis.

13   They meant "to pursue happiness by all lawful means"; that is, by all means which the Law of Nature eternally sanctions and which the laws of the nation shall sanction.

14   Admittedly this seems at first to reduce their maxim to the tautology that men (in pursuit of happiness) have a right to do whatever they have a

right to do. But tautologies, seen against their proper historical context, are not always barren tautologies. The declaration is primarily a denial of the political principles which long governed Europe: a challenge flung down to the Austrian and Russian empires, to England before the Reform Bills, to Bourbon France. It demands that whatever means of pursuing happiness are lawful for any should be lawful for all; that "man," not men of some particular caste, class, status, or religion, should be free to use them. In a century when this is being unsaid by nation after nation and party after party, let us not call it a barren tautology.

15   But the question as to what means are "lawful"—what methods of pursuing happiness are either morally permissible by the Law of Nature or should be declared legally permissible by the legislature of a particular nation—remains exactly where it did. And on that question I disagree with Clare. I don't think it is obvious that people have the unlimited "right to happiness" which she suggests.

16   For one thing, I believe that Clare, when she says "happiness," means simply and solely "sexual happiness." Partly because women like Clare never use the word "happiness" in any other sense. But also because I never heard Clare talk about the "right" to any other kind. She was rather leftist in her politics, and would have been scandalized if anyone had defended the actions of a ruthless man-eating tycoon on the ground that his happiness consisted in making money and he was pursuing his happiness. She was also a rabid teetotaller; I never heard her excuse an alcoholic because he was happy when he was drunk.

17   A good many of Clare's friends, and especially her female friends, often felt—I've heard them say so—that their own happiness would be perceptibly increased by boxing her ears. I very much doubt if this would have brought her theory of a right to happiness into play.

18   Clare, in fact, is doing what the whole western world seems to me to have been doing for the last forty-odd years. When I was a youngster, all the progressive people were saying, "Why all this prudery? Let us treat sex just as we treat all other impulses." I was simple-minded enough to believe they meant what they said. I have since discovered that they meant exactly the opposite. They meant that sex was to be treated as no other impulse in our nature has ever been treated by civilized people. All the others, we admit, have to be bridled. Absolute obedience to your instinct for self-preservation is what we call cowardice; to your acquisitive impulse, avarice. Even sleep must be resisted if you're a sentry. But every unkindness and breach of faith seems to be condoned provided that the object aimed at is "four bare legs in a bed."

19   It is like having a morality in which stealing fruit is considered wrong—unless you steal nectarines.

20   And if you protest against this view you are usually met with chatter about the legitimacy and beauty and sanctity of "sex" and accused of harbouring some Puritan prejudice against it as something disreputable or shameful. I deny the charge. Foam-born Venus . . . golden Aphrodite . . . Our Lady of Cyprus . . . I never breathed a word against you. If I object to boys who steal my nectarines, must I be supposed to disapprove of nectarines in general? Or even of boys in general? It might, you know, be stealing that I disapprove of.

21   The real situation is skillfully concealed by saying that the question of Mr. A.'s "right" to desert his wife is one of "sexual morality." Robbing an orchard is not an offense against some special morality called "fruit morality." It is an offense against honesty. Mr. A.'s action is an offense against good faith (to solemn promises), against gratitude (toward one to whom he was deeply indebted) and against common humanity.

22   Our sexual impulses are thus being put in a position of preposterous privilege. The sexual motive is taken to condone all sorts of behavior which, if it had any other end in view, would be condemned as merciless, treacherous and unjust.

23   Now though I see no good reason for giving sex this privilege, I think I see a strong cause. It is this.

24   It is part of the nature of a strong erotic passion—as distinct from a transient fit of appetite—that it makes more towering promises than any other emotion. No doubt all our desires make promises, but not so impressively. To be in love involves the almost irresistible conviction that one will go on being in love until one dies, and that possession of the beloved will confer, not merely frequent ecstasies, but settled, fruitful, deep-rooted, lifelong happiness. Hence *all* seems to be at stake. If we miss this chance we shall have lived in vain. At the very thought of such a doom we sink into fathomless depths of self-pity.

25   Unfortunately these promises are found to be quite untrue. Every experienced adult knows this to be so as regards all erotic passions (except the one he himself is feeling at the moment). We discount the world-without-end pretensions of our friends' amours easily enough. We know that such things sometimes last—and sometimes don't. And when they do last, this is not because they promised at the outset to do so. When two people achieve lasting happiness, this is not solely because they are great lovers but because they are also—I must put it crudely—good people; controlled, loyal, fair-minded, mutually adaptable people.

26   If we establish a "right to (sexual) happiness" which supersedes all the ordinary rules of behaviour, we do so not because of what our passion shows itself to be in experience but because of what it professes to be while we are in

the grip of it. Hence, while the bad behavior is real and works miseries and degradations, the happiness which was the object of the behaviour turns out again and again to be illusory. Everyone (except Mr. A. and Mrs. B.) knows that Mr. A. in a year or so may have the same reason for deserting his new wife as for deserting his old. He will feel again that all is at stake. He will see himself again as the great lover, and his pity for himself will exclude all pity for the woman.

27   Two further points remain.

28   One is this. A society in which *conjugal* infidelity is tolerated must always be in the long run a society adverse to women. Women, whatever a few male songs and satires may say to the contrary, are more naturally *monogamous* than men; it is a biological necessity. Where *promiscuity* prevails, they will therefore always be more often the victims than the culprits. Also, domestic happiness is more necessary to them than to us. And the quality by which they most easily hold a man, their beauty, decreases every year after they have come to maturity, but this does not happen to those qualities of personality—women don't really care twopence about our *looks*—by which we hold women. Thus in the ruthless war of promiscuity women are at a double disadvantage. They play for higher stakes and are also more likely to lose. I have no sympathy with moralists who frown at the increasing crudity of female provocativeness. These signs of desperate competition fill me with pity.

29   Secondly, though the "right to happiness" is chiefly claimed for the sexual impulse, it seems to me impossible that the matter should stay there. The fatal principle, once allowed in that department, must sooner or later seep through our whole lives. We thus advance toward a state of society in which not only each man but every impulse in each man claims *carte blanche*. And then, though our technological skill may help us survive a little longer, our civilization will have died at heart, and will—one dare not even add "unfortunately"—be swept away.

Discussion Questions

1. Evaluate the effectiveness of Lewis basing his argument on the hypothetical case of Clare, Mr. A., Mrs. A., Mr. B., and Mrs. B. How does this scenario engage you as a reader?

2. Describe the method by which Lewis argues his point.

3. Does Lewis address opposing viewpoints satisfactorily? Why or why not?

4. Lewis distinguishes between a "legal" and a "moral" right. Do you concur with his explanation of the difference? Why is this distinction central to his argument? Explain your responses.

5. To what extent do you agree with Lewis when he claims that societies that tolerate conjugal infidelity will always be "adverse" to women, and the victims of promiscuity will always be women? Why is this important to his argument? Explain your responses.

MOTHERHOOD: WHO NEEDS IT?

Betty Rollin

Betty Rollin was born in 1936. A journalist, television reporter, and nonfiction writer, Rollin has worked as a writer for *Vogue* and *Look* magazines and as a correspondent for NBC. She is the author of *First, You Cry* (1976), *Am I Getting Paid for This?: A Romance about Work* (1982), and *Last Wish* (1985). In the following article, which originally appeared in *Look* in 1970, Rollin argues that women do not need to be mothers, despite the "Motherhood Myth" which encourages them to think otherwise.

1   Motherhood is in trouble, and it ought to be. A rude question is long overdue: Who needs it? The answer used to be (1) society and (2) women. But now, with the impending horrors of overpopulation, society desperately *doesn't* need it. And women don't need it either. Thanks to the Motherhood Myth—the idea that having babies is something that all normal women instinctively want and need and will enjoy doing—they just *think* they do.

2   The notion that the maternal wish and the activity of mothering are instinctive or biologically predestined is baloney. Try asking most sociologists, psychologists, psychoanalysts, biologists—many of whom are mothers—about motherhood being instinctive: it's like asking department store presidents if their Santa Clauses are real. "Motherhood—instinctive?" shouts distinguished sociologist/author Dr. Jessie Bernard. "Biological destiny? Forget biology! If it were biological, people would die from not doing it."

3   "Women don't need to be mothers any more than they need spaghetti," says Dr. Richard Rabkin, a New York psychiatrist. "But if you're in a world where everyone is eating spaghetti, thinking they need it and want it, you will think so too. Romance has really contaminated science. So-called instincts have to do with stimulation. They are not things that well up inside of you."

4   "When a women says with feeling that she craved her baby from within, she is putting into biological language what is psychological," says University of Michigan psychoanalyst and motherhood-researcher Dr. Frederick

Wyatt. "There are no instincts," says Dr. William Goode, president-elect of the American Sociological Association. "There are reflexes, like eye-blinking, and drives, like sex. There is no innate drive for children. Otherwise, the enormous cultural pressures that there are to reproduce wouldn't exist. There are no cultural pressures to sell you on getting your hand out of the fire."

5   There are, to be sure, biologists and others who go on about biological destiny, that is, the innate or instinctive goal of motherhood. (At the turn of the century, even good old capitalism was explained by a theorist as "the *instinct* of acquisitiveness.") And many psychoanalysts will hold the Freudian view that women feel so rotten about not having a penis that they are necessarily propelled into the child-wish to replace the missing organ. Psychoanalysts also make much of the psychological need to repeat what one's parent of the same sex has done. Since every woman has a mother, it is considered normal to wish to imitate one's mother by being a mother.

6   There is, surely, a wish to pass on love if one has received it, but to insist women must pass it on in the same way is like insisting that every man whose father is a gardener has to be a gardener. One dissenting psychoanalyst says, simply, "There is a wish to comply with one's biology, yes, but we needn't and sometimes we shouldn't." (Interestingly, the woman who has been the greatest contributor to child therapy and who has probably given more to children than anyone alive is Dr. Anna Freud, Freud's magnificent daughter, who is not a mother.)

7   Anyway, what an expert cast of hundreds is telling us is, simply, that biological *possibility* and desire are not the same as biological *need*. Women have childbearing equipment. To choose not to use the equipment is no more blocking what is instinctive than it is for a man who, muscles or no, chooses not to be a weight lifter.

8   So much for the wish. What about the "instinctive" *activity* of mothering? One animal study shows that when a young member of a species is put in a cage, say, with an older member of the same species, the latter will act in a protective, "maternal" way. But that goes for both males and females who have been "mothered" themselves. And studies indicate that a human baby will also respond to whoever is around playing mother—even if it's father. Margaret Mead and many others frequently point out that mothering can be a fine occupation, if you want it, for either sex. Another experiment with monkeys who were brought up without mothers found them lacking in maternal behavior toward their own offspring. A similar study showed that monkeys brought up without other monkeys of the opposite sex had no interest in mating—all of which suggests that both mothering and mating behavior are learned, not instinctual. And, to turn the cart (or the baby carriage) around, baby ducks who lovingly follow their

mothers seemed, in the mother's absence, to just as lovingly follow wooden ducks or even vacuum cleaners.

9   If motherhood isn't instinctive, when and why, then, was the Motherhood Myth born? Until recently, the entire question of maternal motivation was academic. Sex, like it or not, meant babies. Not that there haven't always been a lot of interesting contraceptive tries. But until the creation of the diaphragm in the 1880s, the birth of babies was largely unavoidable. And, generally speaking, nobody really seemed to mind. For one thing, people tend to be sort of good sports about what seems to be inevitable. For another, in the past, the population needing beefing up. Mortality rates were high, and agricultural cultures, particularly, have always needed children to help out. So because it "just happened" and because it was needed, motherhood was assumed to be innate.

10   Originally, it was the word of God that got the ball rolling with "Be fruitful and multiply," a practical suggestion, since the only people around then were Adam and Eve. But in no time, supermoralists like St. Augustine changed the tone of the message: "Intercourse, even with one's legitimate wife, is unlawful and wicked where the conception of the offspring is prevented," he, we assume, thundered. And the Roman Catholic position was thus cemented. So then and now, procreation took on a curious value among people who viewed (and view) the pleasures of sex as sinful. One could partake in the sinful pleasure, but feel vindicated by the ensuing birth. Motherhood cleaned up sex. Also, it cleaned up women, who have always been considered somewhat evil, because of Eve's transgression (". . . but the woman was deceived and became a transgressor. Yet woman will be saved through bearing children . . .," I Timothy, 2:14–15), and somewhat dirty because of menstruation.

11   And so, based on need, inevitability, and pragmatic fantasy—the Myth *worked*, from society's point of view—the Myth grew like corn in Kansas. And society reinforced it with both laws and propaganda—laws that made woman a chattel, denied her education and personal mobility, and madonna propaganda that she was beautiful and wonderful doing it and it was all beautiful and wonderful to do. (One rarely sees a madonna washing dishes.)

12   In fact, the Myth persisted—breaking some kind of record for long-lasting fallacies—until something like yesterday. For as the truth about the Myth trickled in—as women's rights increased, as women gradually got the message that it was certainly possible for them to do most things that men did, that they live longer, that their brains were not tinier— then, finally, when the really big news rolled in, that they could *choose* whether or not to be mothers—what happened? The Motherhood Myth soared higher than ever. As Betty Friedan made oh-so-clear in *The Feminine Mystique*, the '40s and '50s produced a group of ladies who not only

had babies as if they were going out of style (maybe they were) but, as never before, they turned motherhood into a cult. First, they walled in the aesthetics of it all—natural childbirth and nursing became maternal musts. Like heavy-bellied ostriches, they grounded their heads in the sands of motherhood, only coming up for air to say how utterly happy and ful-filled they were. But, as Mrs. Friedan says only too plainly, they weren't. The Myth galloped on, moreover, long after making babies had turned from practical asset to liability for both individual parents *and* society. With the average cost of a middle-class child figured conservatively at $30,000 (not including college), any parent knows that the only people who benefit economically from children are manufacturers of consumer goods. Hence all those gooey motherhood commercials. And the Myth gathered momentum long after sheer numbers, while not yet extinguish-ing us, have made us intensely uncomfortable. Almost all of our social problems, from minor discomforts like traffic to major ones like hunger, the population people keep reminding us, have to do with there being too many people. And who suffers most? The kids who have been so mind-lessly brought into the world, that's who. They are the ones who have to cope with all of the difficult and dehumanizing conditions brought on by overpopulation. They are the ones who have to cope with the psycholog-ical nausea of feeling unneeded by society. That's not the only reason for drugs, but, surely, it's a leading contender.

13   Unfortunately, the population curbers are tripped up by a romantic, stub-born ideological hurdle. How can birth-control programs really be effective as long as the concept of glorious motherhood remains unchanged? (Even poor old Planned Parenthood has to euphemize—why not Planned Unpar-enthood?) Particularly among the poor, motherhood is one of the few in-herently positive institutions that are accessible. As Berkeley demographer Judith Blake points out, "Poverty-oriented birth control programs do not make sense as a welfare measure . . . as long as existing pronatalist policies . . . encourage mating, pregnancy, and the care, support, and rearing of chil-dren." Or, she might have added, as long as the less-than-idyllic child-rear-ing part of motherhood remains "in small print."

14   Sure, motherhood gets dumped on sometimes: Philip Wylie's Momism[1] got going in the '40s and Philip Roth's *Portnoy's Complaint* did its best to turn rancid the chicken-soup concept of Jewish motherhood. But these are viewed as the sour cries of a black humorist here, a malcontent there.

---

[1]Philip Wylie's A *Generation of Vipers* (1942) blamed many of the ills of American society on dominating mothers.

Everyone shudders, laughs, but it's like the mouse and the elephant joke. Still the Myth persists. Last April, a Brooklyn woman was indicted on charges of manslaughter and negligent homicide—eleven children died in a fire in a building she owned and criminally neglected—"But," sputtered her lawyer, "my client, Mrs. Breslow, is a mother, a grandmother, and a great-grandmother!"

15   Most remarkably, the Motherhood Myth persists in the face of the most overwhelming maternal unhappiness and incompetence. If reproduction were merely superfluous and expensive, if the experience were as rich and rewarding as the cliché would have us believe, if it were a predominantly joyous trip for everyone riding—mother, father, child—then the going everybody-should-have-two-children plan would suffice. Certainly, there are a lot of joyous mothers, and their children and (sometimes, not necessarily) their husbands reflect their joy. But a lot of evidence suggests that for more women than anyone wants to admit, motherhood can be miserable. ("If it weren't," says one psychiatrist wryly, "the world wouldn't be in the mess it's in.")

16   There is a remarkable statistical finding from a recent study of Dr. Bernard's, comparing the mental illness and unhappiness of married mothers and single women. The latter group, it turned out, was both markedly less sick and overtly more happy. Of course, it's not easy to measure slippery attitudes like happiness. "Many women have achieved a kind of reconciliation—a conformity," says Dr. Bernard,

> that they interpret as happiness. Since feminine happiness is supposed to lie in devoting one's life to one's husband and children, they do that; so *ipso facto*, they assume they are happy. And for many women, untrained for independence and "processed" for motherhood, they find their state far preferable to the alternatives, which really don't exist.

Also, unhappy mothers are often loath to admit it. For one thing, if in society's view not to be a mother is to be a freak, not to be a *blissful* mother is to be a witch. Besides, unlike a disappointing marriage, disappointing motherhood cannot be terminated by divorce. Of course, none of that stops a woman from expressing her dissatisfaction in a variety of ways. Again, it is not only she who suffers but her husband and children as well. Enter the harridan housewife, the carping shrew. The realities of motherhood can turn women into terrible people. And, judging from the 50,000 cases of child abuse in the U.S. each year, some are worse than terrible.

17   In some cases, the unpleasing realities of motherhood begin even before the beginning. In *Her Infinite Variety*, Morton Hunt describes young married women pregnant for the first time as "very likely to be frightened or

depressed, masking these feelings in order not to be considered contemptible. The arrival of pregnancy interrupts a pleasant dream of motherhood and awakens them to the realization that they have too little, money, or not enough space, or unresolved marital problems . . . ."

18   The following are random quotes from interviews with some mothers in Ann Arbor, Mich., who describe themselves as reasonably happy. They all had positive things to say about their children, although when asked about the best moment of their day, the *all* confessed it was when the children were in bed. Here is the rest:

> Suddenly I had to devote myself to the child totally. I was under the illusion that the baby was going to fit into my life, and I found that I had to switch my life and my schedule to fit *him*. You think, "I'm in love, I'll get married, and we'll have a baby." First there's two, then three, it's simple and romantic. You don't even think about the work. . . .

> You never get away from the responsibility. Even when you leave the children with a sitter, you are not out from under the pressure of the responsibility. . . .

> I hate ironing their pants and doing their underwear, and they never put their clothes in the laundry basket. . . . As they get older, they make less demands on our time because they're in school, but the demands are greater in forming their values. . . . Best moment of the day is when all the children are in bed. . . . The worst time of the day is 4 p.m. when you have to get dinner started, the kids are tired, hungry and crabby—everybody wants to talk to you about *their* day . . . your day is only half over.

> Once a mother, the responsibility and concern for my children became so encompassing. . . . It took a great deal of will to keep up other parts of my personality. . . . To me, motherhood gets harder as they get older because you have less control. . . . In an abstract sense, I'd have several . . . In the non-abstract, I would not have any. . . .

> I had anticipated that the baby would sleep and eat, sleep and eat. Instead, the experience was overwhelming. I really had not thought particularly about what motherhood would mean in a realistic sense. I want to do *other* things, like to become involved in things that are worthwhile—I don't mean women's clubs—but I don't have the physical energy to go out in the evenings. I feel like I'm missing something . . . the experience of being somewhere with people and having them talking about something—something that's going on in the world.

19   Every grownup person expects to pay a price for his pleasures, but seldom is the price as vast as the one endured "however happily" by most mothers. We have mentioned the literal cost factor. But what does that mean? For middle-class American women, it means a life style with severe and usually unimagined limitations; i.e., life in the suburbs, because who can afford three bedrooms in the city? And what do suburbs mean? For women, suburbs mean other women and children and left-over peanut-butter sandwiches and car pools and seldom-seen husbands. Even the Feminine Mystiqueniks—the housewives who finally admitted that their lives behind brooms (OK, electric brooms) were driving them crazy—were loath to trace their predicament to their children. But it is simply a fact that a childless married woman has no child-work and little housework. She can live in a city, or, if she still chooses the suburbs or the country, she can leave on the commuter train with her husband if she wants to. Even the most ardent job-seeking mother will find little in the way of great opportunities in Scarsdale. Besides, by the time she wakes up, she usually lacks both the preparation for the outside world and the self-confidence to get it. You will say there are plenty of city-dwelling working mothers. But most of those women do additional-funds-for-the-family kind of work, not the interesting career kind that takes plugging during childbearing years.

20   Nor is it a bed of petunias for the mother who does make it professionally. Says writer critic Marya Mannes:

> If the creative woman has children, she must pay for this indulgence with a long burden of guilt, for her life will be split three ways between them and her husband and her work. . . . No woman with any heart can compose a paragraph when her child is in trouble. . . . The creative woman has no wife to protect her from intrusion. A man at his desk in a room with closed door is a man at work. A woman at a desk in any room is available.

21   Speaking of jobs, do remember that mothering, salary or not, is a job. Even those who can afford nurses to handle the nitty-gritty still need to put out emotionally. "Well-cared-for" neurotic rich kids are not exactly unknown in our society. One of the more absurd aspects of the Myth is the underlying assumption that, since most women are biologically equipped to bear children, they are psychologically, mentally, emotionally, and technically equipped (or interested) to rear them. Never mind happiness. To assume that such an exacting, consuming, and important task is something almost all women are equipped to do is far more dangerous and ridiculous than assuming that everyone with vocal chords should seek a career in the opera.

22   A major expectation of the Myth is that children make a not-so-hot marriage hotter, or a hot marriage, hotter still. Yet almost every available study indicates that childless marriages are far happier. One of the biggest, of 850 couples, was conducted by Dr. Harold Feldman of Cornell University, who states his finding in no uncertain terms. "Those couples with children had a significantly lower level of marital satisfaction than did those without children." Some of the reasons are obvious. Even the most adorable children make for additional demands, complications, and hardships in the lives of even the most loving parents. If a woman feels disappointed and trapped in her mother role, it is bound to affect her marriage in any number of ways: she may take out her frustrations directly on her husband, or she may count on him too heavily for what she feels she is missing in her daily life.

23   ". . . You begin to grow away from your husband," says one of the Michigan ladies. "He's working on his career and you're working on your family. But you both must gear your lives to the children. You do things the children enjoy, more than things you might enjoy." More subtle and possibly more serious is what motherhood may do to a woman's sexuality. Often when the stork flies in, sexuality flies out. Both in the emotional minds of some women *and* in the minds of their husbands, when a woman becomes a mother, she stops being a woman. It's not only that motherhood may destroy her physical attractiveness, but its madonna concept may destroy her *feelings* of sexuality.

24   And what of the payoff? Usually, even the most self-sacrificing of maternal self-sacrificers expects a little something back. Gratified parents are not unknown to the Western world, but there are probably at least just as many who feel, to put it crudely, shortchanged. The experiment mentioned earlier—where the baby ducks followed vacuum cleaners instead of their mothers—indicates that what passes for love from baby to mother is merely a rudimentary kind of object attachment. Without necessarily feeling like a Hoover, a lot of women become disheartened because babies and children are not only not interesting to talk to (not everyone thrills at the wonders of da-da-ma-ma talk) but they are generally not empathetic, considerate people. Even the nicest children are not capable of empathy, surely a major ingredient of love, until they are much older. Sometimes they're never capable of it. Dr. Wyatt says that often, in later years particularly, when most of the "returns" are in, it is the "good mother" who suffers most of all. It is then she must face a reality: The child—the appendage with her genes—is not an appendage, but a separate person. What's more, he or she may be a separate person who doesn't even like her—or whom she doesn't really like.

25   So if the music is lousy, how come everyone's dancing? Because the motherhood minuet is taught freely from birth, and whether or not she has rhythm or likes the music, every woman is expected to do it. Indeed, she

wants to do it. Little girls start learning what to want—and what to be—when they are still in their cribs. Dr. Miriam Keiffer, a young social psychologist at Bensalem, the Experimental College of Fordham University, points to studies showing that

> at six months of age, mothers are already treating their baby girls and boys quite differently. For instance, mothers have been found to touch, comfort, and talk to their females more. If these differences can be found at such an early stage, it's not surprising that the end product is as different as it is. What is surprising is that men and women are, in so many ways, similar.

Some people point to the way little girls play with dolls as proof of their innate motherliness. But remember, little girls are *given* dolls. When Margaret Mead presented some dolls to New Guinea children, it was the boys, not the girls, who wanted to play with them, which they did by crooning lullabies and rocking them in the most maternal fashion.

26   By the time they reach adolescence, most girls, unconsciously or not, have learned enough about role definition to qualify for a master's degree. In general, the lesson has been that no matter what kind of career thoughts one may entertain, one must, first and foremost, be a wife and mother. A girl's mother is usually her first teacher. As Dr. Goode says, "A woman is not only taught by society to have a child; she is taught to have a child who will have a child." A woman who has hung her life on the Motherhood Myth will almost always reinforce her young married daughter's early training by pushing for grandchildren. Prospective grandmothers are not the only ones. Husbands, too, can be effective sellers. After all, they have the Fatherhood Myth to cope with. A married man is *supposed* to have children. Often, particularly among Latins, children are a sign of potency. They help him assure the world—and himself—that he is the big man he is supposed to be. Plus, children give him both immortality (whatever that means) and possibly the chance to become more in his lifetime through the accomplishments of his children, particularly his son. (Sometimes it's important, however, for the son to do better, but not *too* much better.)

27   Friends, too, can be counted on as myth-pushers. Naturally one wants to do what one's friends do. One study, by the way, found a correlation between a woman's fertility and that of her three closest friends. The negative sell comes into play here, too. We have seen what the concept of non-mother means (cold, selfish, unwomanly, abnormal). In practice, particularly in the suburbs, it can mean, simply, exclusion—both from child-centered activities (that is, most activities) and child-centered conversations (that is, most conversations). It can also mean being the butt of a lot

of unfunny jokes. ("Whaddya waiting for? An immaculate conception? Ha ha.") Worst of all, it can mean being an object of pity.

28   In case she's escaped all those pressures (that is, if she was brought up in a cave), a young married woman often wants a baby just so that she'll (1) have something to do (motherhood is better than clerk/typist, which is often the only kind of job she can get, since little more has been expected of her and, besides, her boss also expects her to leave and be a mother); (2) have something to hug and possess, to be needed by and have power over; and (3) have something to be—e.g., a baby's mother. Motherhood affords an instant identity. First, through wifehood, you are somebody's wife; then you are somebody's mother. Both give not only identity and activity, but status and stardom of a kind. During pregnancy, a woman can look forward to the kind of attention and pampering she may not have ever gotten or may never otherwise get. Some women consider birth the biggest accomplishment of their lives, which may be interpreted as saying not much for the rest of their lives. As Dr. Goode says, "It's like the gambler who may know the roulette wheel is crooked, but it's the only game in town." Also, with motherhood, the feeling of accomplishment is immediate. It is really much faster and easier to make a baby than paint a painting, or write a book, or get to the point of accomplishment in a job. It is also easier in a way to shift focus from self-development to child development—particularly since, for women, self-development is considered selfish. Even unwed mothers may achieve a feeling of this kind. (As we have seen, little thought is given to the after-math.) And, again, since so many women are underdeveloped as people, they feel that, besides children, they have little else to give—to themselves, their husbands, to their world.

29   You may ask why then, when the realities do start pouring in, does a woman want to have a second, third, even fourth child? OK, (1) just because reality is pouring in doesn't mean that she wants to face it. A new baby can help bring back some of the old illusions. Says psychoanalyst Dr. Natalie Shainess, "She may view each successive child as a knight in armor that will rescue her from being a 'bad unhappy mother.'" (2) Next on the horror list of having no children, is having one. It suffices to say that only children are not only OK, they even have a high rate of exceptionality. (3) Both parents usually want at least one child of each sex. The husband, for reasons discussed earlier, probably wants a son. (4) The more children one has, the more of an excuse one has not to develop in any other way.

30   What's the point? A world without children? Of course not. Nothing could be worse or more unlikely. No matter what anyone says in *Look* or anywhere else, motherhood isn't about to go out like a blown bulb, and who says it should? Only the Myth must go out, and now it seems to be dimming.

31   The younger-generation females who have been reared on the Myth have not rejected it totally, but at least they recognize it can be more loving to children not to have them. And at least they speak of adopting children instead of bearing them. Moreover, since the new nonbreeders are "less hung-up" on ownership, they seem to recognize that if you dig loving children, you don't necessarily have to own one. The end of the Motherhood Myth might make available more loving women (and men!) for those children who already exist.

32   When motherhood is no longer culturally compulsory, there will, certainly, be less of it. Women are now beginning to think and do more about development of self, of their individual resources. Far from being selfish, such development is probably our only hope. That means more alternatives for women. And more alternatives mean more selective, better, happier, motherhood—and childhood and husbandhood (or manhood) and peoplehood. It is not a question of whether or not children are sweet and marvelous to have and rear; the question is, even if that's so, whether or not one wants to pay the price for it. It doesn't make any sense any more to pretend that women need babies, when what they really need is themselves. If God were still speaking to us in a voice we could hear, even He would probably say, "Be fruitful. Don't multiply."

Discussion Questions

1. Summarize Rollin's argument and the support she offers to back up her claim.

2. Rollin's article was published over twenty-five years ago. Do you think it is still relevant? Why or why not?

3. Which of Rollin's reasons for opposing compulsory motherhood best supports her stance? Which are the least? Why?

4. Do you think Rollin imagined men or women as her audience? Why?

5. How effectively does Rollin refute the opposing perspective? Explain your answer.

WRITING TOPICS

1. Much has been written about the health of the American family. Using your own observations and the perspectives of

sociologists, psychologists, and so on to back up your ideas, write an essay that addresses your answer to the following question: Is the American family still as healthy as it was in previous generations, or is it ailing?

2. Choose a few popular television shows or movies and discuss the ways in which families are represented. Are the media's representations accurate? If so, why? If not, why not? Is it even the responsibility of the media to portray families accurately?

3. In the past few decades, the growth of single-parent and blended families has escalated dramatically. Compared to the once traditional nuclear family, do you think these new types of families are just as healthy and viable? Read what sociologists and psychologists have to say about the new types of family structures. Write a paper in which you discuss your stance and those of others.

4. Many people believe that both parents working outside of the home has contributed to the downfall of the American family. Others believe that families can be strengthened by this situation. Examine your views in a paper that also brings in sociologists', psychologists', and journalists' perspectives.

5. With both parents working, many "latchkey" children return home after school to empty houses. Write a paper in which you examine the extent to which this is detrimental to children. What benefits can arise from this situation (for example, teaching children how to be independent, participate in hobbies, and so on)? Research what critics have written about this issue as a way to discuss this timely topic.

6. Are you optimistic about the future of the American family? How about your peers? In a paper, discuss where you stand on this issue and your reasons for believing the way you do.

7. In "Evan's Two Moms," Anna Quindlen lists the disadvantages gay couples have when they are not allowed to marry. If you disagree with the stance Quindlen takes, address your reasons for thinking that gay couples should not be allowed the entitlements given to straight couples.

8. Do you think that the roles of mother and father that we find in contemporary American society are outdated? Answer this question in a paper in which you examine and support your perspective.

9. Should married women take their husbands' surnames? Write a paper that supports your stance. If your answer is no, discuss your reasons for thinking so. If your answer is yes, consider the following question: Why shouldn't husbands take their wives' surnames? Regardless of your position on this issue, research when and where the tradition of women changing their names originated. Is the practice still warranted as we approach the twenty-first century?

10. Some of the misconceptions regarding the size of families are that children who grow up without siblings are self-centered and spoiled, a "middle" child is a "problem" child, and so on. Choose what you think is a misconception regarding the make-up of the American family. Using your own thinking and research to support your claim, write a paper that rebuts the myth.

CHAPTER 11

VALUES AND HUMAN NATURE

Putting in a Good Word for Guilt

Ellen Goodman

Born in 1941, Ellen Goodman graduated from Radcliffe College. She worked as a researcher and reporter at *Newsweek* magazine before becoming a feature writer at the *Detroit Free Press*. She is currently the "At Large" columnist for the *Boston Globe* and is a Pulitzer Prize winner. Goodman's columns have been published in *Turning Points* (1979), *At Large* (1983), *Keeping in Touch* (1985), and *Making Sense* (1989). In the following viewpoint, Goodman praises an often-maligned feeling: guilt.

1 Feeling guilty is nothing to feel guilty about. Yes, guilt can be the excess baggage that keeps us paralyzed unless we dump it. But it can also be the engine that fuels us. Yes, it can be a self-punishing activity, but it can also be the conscience that keeps us civilized.

2   Not too long ago I wrote a story about that amusing couple Guilt and the Working Mother. I'll tell you more about that later. Through the mail someone sent me a gift coffee mug carrying the message "I gave up guilt for Lent."

3   My first reaction was to giggle. But then it occurred to me that this particular Lent has been too lengthy. For the past decade or more, the pop psychologists who use book jackets rather than couches all were busy telling us that I am okay, you are okay and whatever we do is okay.

4   In most of their books, guilt was given a bad name—or rather, an assortment of bad names. It was a (1) Puritan (2) Jewish (3) Catholic hangover from our (1) parents (2) culture (3) religion. To be truly liberated was to be free of guilt about being rich, powerful, number one, bad to your mother, thoughtless, late, a smoker or about cheating on your spouse.

5   There was a popular notion, in fact, that self-love began by slaying one's guilt. People all around us spent a great portion of the last decade trying to tune out guilt instead of decoding its message and learning what it was trying to tell us.

6   With that sort of success, guilt was ripe for revival. Somewhere along the I'm-okay-you're-okay way, many of us realized that, in fact, I am not

always okay and neither are you. Furthermore, we did not want to join the legions who conquered their guilt en route to new depths of narcissistic rottenness.

7   At the deepest, most devastating level, guilt is the criminal in us that longs to be caught. It is the horrible, pit-of-the-stomach sense of having done wrong. It is, as Lady Macbeth obsessively knew, the spot that no one else may see . . . and we can't see around.

8   To be without guilt is to be without a conscience. Guilt-free people don't feel bad when they cause pain to others, and so they go on guilt-freely causing more pain. The last thing we need more of is less conscience.

9   Freud once said, "As regards conscience, God has done an uneven and careless piece of work, for a large majority of men have brought along with them only a modest amount of it, or scarcely enough to be worth mentioning."

10   Now, I am not suggesting that we all sign up for a new guilt trip. But there has to be some line between the accusation that we all should feel guilty for, say, poverty or racism and the assertion that the oppressed have "chosen" their lot in life.

11   There has to be something between puritanism and hedonism. There has to be something between the parents who guilt-trip their children across every stage of life and those who offer no guidance, no—gulp—moral or ethical point of view.

12   At quite regular intervals, for example, my daughter looks up at me in the midst of a discussion (she would call it a lecture) and says: "You're making me feel guilty." For a long time this made me, in turn, feel guilty. But now I realize that I am doing precisely what I am supposed to be doing: instilling in her a sense of right and wrong so that she will feel uncomfortable if she behaves in hurtful ways.

13   This is, of course, a very tricky business. Guilt is ultimately the way we judge ourselves. It is the part of us that says, "I deserve to be punished." But we all know people who feel guilty just for being alive. We know people who are paralyzed by irrational guilt. And we certainly don't want to be among them, or to shepherd our children into their flock.

14   But it seems to me that the trick isn't to become flaccidly nonjudgmental, but to figure out whether we are being fair judges of ourselves. Karl Menninger once wrote that one aim of psychiatric treatment isn't to get rid of guilt but "to get people's guilt feelings attached to the 'right' things."

15   In his book *Feelings*, Willard Gaylin quotes a Reverend Tillotson's definition of guilt as "nothing else but trouble arising in our mind from our consciousness of having done contrary to what we are verily perswaded [sic] was our Duty."

16   We may, however, have wildly different senses of duty. I had lunch with two friends a month ago when they both started talking about feeling guilty for neglecting their mothers. One, it turned out, worried that she didn't call "home" every day; the other hadn't even chatted with her mother since Christmas.

17   We are also particularly vulnerable to feelings of duty in a time of change. Today an older and ingrained sense of what we should do may conflict with a new one. In the gaps that open between what we once were taught and what we now believe grows a rich crop of guilt.

18   Mothers now often tell me that they feel guilty if they are working and guilty if they aren't. One set of older expectations, to be a perfect milk-and-cookies supermom, conflicts with another, to be an independent woman or an economic helpmate.

19   But duty has its uses. It sets us down at the typewriter, hustles us to the job on a morning when everything has gone wrong, pushes us toward the crying baby at 3 A.M.

20   If guilt is a struggle between our acceptance of shoulds and should nots, it is a powerful and intensely human one. Gaylin writes, "Guilt represents the noblest and most painful of struggles. It is between us and ourselves." It is better to struggle with ourselves than give up on ourselves.

21   This worst emotion, in a sense, helps bring out the best in us. The desire to avoid feeling guilty makes us avoid the worst sort of behavior. The early guilt of a child who has hurt a younger sister or brother, even when no one else knows, is a message. The adult who has inflicted pain on an innocent, who has cheated, lied, stolen, to get ahead of another—each of us has a list—wakes up in the middle of the night and remembers it.

22   In that sense guilt is the great civilizer, the internal commandment that helps us choose to be kind to each other rather than to join in a stampede of me-firsts. "If guilt is coming back," said Harvard Professor David Riesman, who wrote *The Lonely Crowd*, "one reason is that a tremendous surge of young people overpowered the adults in the sixties. You might say the barbarians took Rome. Now there are more adults around who are trying to restore some stability."

23   Guilt is the adult in each of us, the parent, the one who upholds the standards. It is the internal guide against which we argue in vain that "everybody else is doing it."

24   We even wrestle with ethical dilemmas and conflicts of conscience so that we can live with ourselves more comfortably. I know two people who were faced with a crisis about their infidelities. One woman resolved the triangle she was in by ending her marriage. The other ended her affair. In both cases, it was the pain that had motivated them to change.

25   It is not easy to attach our guilt to the right things. It is never easy to separate right from wrong, rational guilt from neurotic guilt. We may resolve
one by changing our view of it and another by changing our behavior.

26   In my own life as a working mother, I have done both half a dozen times.
When my daughter was small and I was working, I worried that I was not following the pattern of the good mother, my mother. Only through time and
perspective and reality did I change that view; I realized that my daughter
clearly did not feel neglected and I clearly was not uncaring. Good child
care, love, luck and support helped me to resolve my early guilt feelings.

27   Then again, last winter I found myself out of town more than I was comfortable with. This time I changed my schedule instead of my mind.

28   For all of us, in the dozens of daily decisions we make, guilt is one of the
many proper motivations. I am not saying our lives are ruled by guilt. Hardly. But guilt is inherent in the underlying question: "If I do that, can I live
with myself?"

29   People who don't ask themselves that question, people who never get
no for an answer, may seem lucky. They can, we think, be self-centered
without self-punishment, hedonistic without qualms. They can worry about
me-first and forget about the others.

30   It is easy to be jealous of those who go through life without a moment of
wrenching guilt. But envying the guiltless is like envying a house pet. Striving to follow their lead is like accepting a catatonic as your role model. They
are not the free but the antisocial. In a world in which guilt is one of the few
emotions experienced only by human beings, they are, even, unhuman.

31   Guilt is one of the most human of dilemmas. It is the claim of others on
the self, the recognition both of our flaws and of our desire to be the people
we want to be.

Discussion Questions

1.   Goodman writes her viewpoint largely in the first person.
Would it have been just as effective had she used the third person? Explain your response.

2.   Which of Goodman's observations seems the most plausible
and help to make her viewpoint believable? Which the least?
Why?

3.   Can you identify examples when guilt *does* serve a useful purpose? Describe a few. Does Goodman address this issue in her
viewpoint? Explain.

4. Throughout her viewpoint, Goodman introduces quotes by psychiatrists, clergy, and sociologists. How effective are these sources in helping to advance her ideas? Explain your response.

5. To whom do you think Goodman was writing? Explain your answer.

In or Out: To Tell
or Not to Tell

Sarah Pettit

Sarah Pettit was born in 1966 in the Netherlands and lived in France, Germany, and England before settling in the United States. A graduate of Yale University, Pettit worked as an assistant editor at St. Martin's Press and as the arts editor for *Outweek* magazine. As a freelancer, she guest edited *The Nation's* historic first gay and lesbian issue in June of 1993. Pettit and Michael Goff founded *Out* magazine, where she has worked as the executive editor for the past several years. In the following viewpoint, Pettit addresses a controversial and timely topic: whether gays and lesbians should come out of the closet.

1   Years ago, while I was an undergraduate at a liberal Eastern college, a friend stopped me as we left the apartment she and her girlfriend shared and from the clear blue asked, "You aren't a lesbian, are you, Sarah?" I paused and, re-solving to remain honest about my sexuality, answered, "Yes, I am a les-bian. And so are you." At that time I sensed only instinctively what she was driving at, that she wanted my complicity in a kind of personal Don't ask, don't tell, don't pursue this way of questioning. I have over the years come to recognize more readily the feeling of banging up against someone's closet door, of coming face to face with the issue that lesbians and gay men have often found so difficult about ourselves.

2   Even then I understood my friend's question to be less an inquiry than a challenge. Would I pretend along with her, would I say it wasn't so even though we both knew otherwise? I wasn't so much scared or disappointed in her inability to come clean about herself as I was puzzled. It was the early '80s—the struggle for equal rights was in full bloom with battles like the Supreme Court's decision to uphold antiquated sodomy laws. The terror of AIDS was bringing people to their feet and out of the closet in unprece-dented numbers. We were supposed to be part of a young, brave generation of lesbians and gay men; we didn't have to lie and hide the way the last generation had.

3   I now understand that we all follow different roads as adults. Some of us choose to be out to tell the truth about that essential adult identity, our sexuality, while others do not. My friend, who has gone on to professional success and financial security, has never once, except in the company of trusted friends, opened that closet door any wider. I, by contrast, now identify and struggle with people's anguish about their sexual identity for a living. I'm an editor at the nation's largest lesbian and gay magazine, and the closet is, quite literally, my job.

4   But I don't consider that she took the wrong road and I the right one; that I'm better, or healthier, or more well adjusted than she. In fact, one of the hardest lessons my job has taught me is that my friend is not only not alone, but that the great majority of American lesbians and gay men are probably still in the closet and, for the moment, feel more comfortable there. (Among our magazine's readers, for example, 60 percent ask to receive their issues in a plain brown wrapper.) Some are immobile with fear, terrified they'll lose everything they have: family, friends, job. Some have known only the caricatures of lesbians and gay men fed to them by most of the media. They worry they, too, will become like those images: one-dimensional, often menacing and frequently inhuman. Some are greedy for more of what the world offers you if you play by the heterosexual rules of the game.

5   I say this without judgment, but as a frank observation about the choices lesbians and gay men have made and continue to make every day about the level of candor they will allow in their lives. Every day I receive mail from people in the midst of this battle with and for themselves; at least once a week I deal with public figures and their publicists who refuse to appear in the pages of our magazine, whether it be the teen TV darling who is "just being strategic," the righteous African-American activist who fears losing one embattled community by adopting another, or the entertainment figure whose work tackles AIDS but not his homosexuality.

6   Yet the more time I spend wrestling with the closet, the more I understand that it is less an awesome monolith than a slow series of turns, of decisions, of orientations toward honestly. ("Do I have a boyfriend? Uh, no. I'm single.") It's not really about what is black or white, but rather a shifting series of contradictions. The line between being in or out is not always so hard and fast. The reality of many lesbian and gay lives is less one of discernible extremes, of purity and lies, than the actuality of shades, of gradations of outness.

7   The gray areas can be confusing and frustrating, especially to a group of people who have suffered incredible attacks, civil and uncivil, moral and amoral, scientific and medical, at the hands of the Christian Right and even from our allies like Bill Clinton. There are days we wish we could speed up

the clock, cut through the ambivalence and lies. Some have offered up the solution of outing, the term coined for the practice of publicly revealing the lesbian or gay identity of famous public figures against their will. Still others have proposed that we march on Washington in business suits and dresses, so that America will see how normal we really are.

8   But our struggle doesn't need a silver bullet. We will never achieve a greater sense of openness about issues of sexual orientation by forcing people into the public eye. Yes, the revelation of some people's gayness is arresting, but a browbeaten spokesperson is rarely an eloquent one. Nor do we need a face-lift. Wardrobe changes will not convince a leery American public. k.d. lang, Elton John, Clinton appointees Roberta Achtenberg and Bruce Lehman, Martina Navratilova, and RuPaul came as they were—it was their frankness that won people over, not their fashion.

9   More of that frankness supported by a broadening of the American mind and the reinforcement of the basic rights of lesbians and gay men before the law (only seven states protect us from discrimination in housing and employment, and sodomy laws in twenty-one states effectively make criminals of any sexually active adult homosexual) is what will win the day in the end. I'm reconciled to the maddeningly slow struggle ahead, as are many others.

10   Last Christmas, my college friend made a donation to a lesbian and gay legal-defense fund in my name—no, she hasn't come out of her closet yet, but at least she now knows it's there. Everyone needs to make an individual choice to ask and tell when he or she can. But I, like the 40 percent of our magazine's readers who do receive their issues unveiled, also believe that we continually need to show our faces so that Americans know who we are.

Discussion Questions

1.   Discuss the effectiveness of Pettit beginning her viewpoint with a personal story and ending her viewpoint with the conclusion of the story.

2.   Summarize the ideas Pettit expresses in her viewpoint.

3.   Do you think that Pettit sufficiently discusses reasons for coming out of *and* staying in the closet? Explain your answer.

4.   To whom do you think Pettit was addressing her remarks: To straights? To closeted gays? To the media? Explain your answer.

5.   Describe the tone and voice of Pettit's viewpoint. How does it contribute to the overall effect of her piece?

WHAT ARE OUR REAL VALUES?

Nicols Fox

Nicols Fox was born in 1942 and received her education at Mary Baldwin College. Her articles have appeared in such publications as *The American Journalism Review*, *The Economist*, and the *New York Times*. She is currently an independent journalist and a television commentator for *Media Watch*. In the following selection, Fox examines the idea that "real American values are expressed not by what we say we wish for, but what we really do."

1   The recent presidential election, according to the chorus of political pundits on both sides, was a referendum on American values. The candidate who most clearly represented our collective vision of ourself as a people, who promised most convincingly to nurture and protect that vision, was elected. But what are American values? They would appear to be the same fantasies we use to sell soft drinks, phone services and color film—and they have proved equally adaptable to selling presidents.

2   We value, so we like to think, families and fireplaces and front porches with swings; a picture-perfect landscape in which people sit down to eat together and worship together; a place where old folks live at home and young folks don't talk back. We value friendships. We value thrift. We value history and tradition, culture and continuity. We value childhood— a wonderful and mysterious period free from care and full of optimism. We value baseball games on hot summer nights and high-school reunions and holidays.

3   It is a healthy and a happy vision. But like most of the fantasies conjured up by the advertising world, it doesn't really exist. Not really—not in America in the 1980s. And maybe it never existed. What we have come to love is an image of ourselves created by artists like Winslow Homer and Norman Rockwell. And the nostalgia for this America is so strong that for those who have no genuine memory of it, we have created one. Through advertising, even the young can participate in the dream they cannot recall— a pretelevision era where lemonade came from lemons and pizza was an exotic dish, where Grandmother hadn't had a face-lift and Dad didn't have

a girlfriend and 7-year-olds had no idea what a condom was. And the greater the gulf between reality and fantasy, the more we seem drawn to the dream.

4   The trouble is, real American values are expressed not by what we say we wish for, but by what we really do. We love our families but we can't count many friends with intact ones anymore. We love our old people but not for more than an hour or two at a time. And they don't care much for us, either. They seem to prefer their child-free retirement communities to life in extended families. We are a people full of compassion but it extends more freely to three trapped whales than to the homeless huddled over heat grates on the streets of our richest cities. We love our children, but how many children come home to empty houses during the day? We believe in families, but how many families sit down to eat together anymore? Although more of us today say we believe in God, how many of us attend church regularly? We believe in fiscal responsibility but our own balance sheets look pretty much like the federal government's.

5   What are the real American values?

6   Look who our heroes are. They aren't the people who volunteer in the soup kitchens; they aren't struggling writers and artists; they aren't the librarians or the nurses or the social workers. Mainly they are the rich and the famous and the successful and the beautiful, the film and sports stars, the Wall Street barons, even the articulate convicts who charm us on talk shows once they've done their time. Perhaps the best indicator of what we really are is what we spend our money on or what we watch on television. Look at what we read. Look at what we choose to do with our spare time. That's what we value.

7   We complain about the invasion of drugs but our culture tells us that no discomfort can be tolerated and that every desire deserves to be satisfied. We complain about crime but our system demonstrates that good guys finish last—that crime pays. We complain about the moral decadence of our young and the high incidence of teen pregnancies but our young have been carefully taught, by example, that responsibility is old-fashioned. We'd like to do something about pornography and violence but we buy it and we tolerate it and that makes our protests pretty empty.

8   The problem is, changing things is a problem. It's not a question of hoeing at the weeds on the surface of society, but of a real root job. Who makes the rules these days that determine how our society is going to work—the code of ethics behind the laws that determines our values and decides how we are going to live together in community?

9   **Judgment Day:** It isn't the churches. It's not so much that their moral leadership is being ignored as that, to a great extent, they've abdicated the role. Collectively they seem to exude the same relativism and insecurity about right and wrong as the rest of us. The fact is, we all have a pretty

good idea of what is right and what is wrong, but deprived—as the 20th century is—of the ever-handy threat of Judgment Day, we just can't seem to find a good enough explanation for why we should do one thing and not do another. Simply saying "Because God says so" doesn't work very well anymore.

10   And so we are left yearning for the old order. And yearning seems all we're capable of. In spite of what President Bush says, we do seem to have lost our wills. What we'd really like is for someone else to do something about the homeless and the violence and the drugs and the sick and the old. And we'd like for it to be done without a tax increase because we don't want to pay for it. "I share your values," the new president said time and time again during the campaign, but I suspect what he was really saying was "I share your dreams, I share your nostalgia, I share your fantasies and your wishful thinking." But government in a free and democratic society, as Senate Majority Leader George Mitchell has said, is not the enemy of the people. It is ours to do with as we will, to shape and form with our collective resources in order to create a real American Dream—not a hazy, romantic vision from the past to which we pay read-my-lips service.

11   It's time that we started looking at ourselves as we really are because a healthy future will be based on reality, not on ad copy.

Discussion Questions

1. Fox uses the first person plural (*we*) throughout her viewpoint. Would it have been just as effective had she used the third person plural, *people*? Explain your response.

2. Summarize Fox's argument and cite the reasons she offers to support it.

3. Which of Fox's ideas seems the most convincing to you? Which the least? Explain your answer.

4. Describe the organization of Fox's viewpoint. Why, for example, does she ask again in the fifth paragraph, "What are the real American values?"

5. What purpose do the many questions serve in Fox's argument?

The Missing Element:
Moral Courage

Barbara Tuchman

Barbara Tuchman was born in 1912 and died in 1989. After graduating from Radcliffe College, she worked as a research assistant at the Institute of Pacific Relations. In the 1930s, Tuchman wrote on politics for the *Nation*. Later, she was a journalist, based in London, while she covered the Spanish Civil War. A historian and writer, Tuchman's publications include *The Guns of August* (1961) and *Stillwell and the American Experience in China, 1911–1945* (1971), both winners of the Pulitzer Prize. She is also the author of *The Proud Tower* (1966), *A Distant Mirror: The Calamitous 14th Century* (1978), *Practicing History* (1981), *The March of Folly: From Troy to Vietnam* (1984), and *The First Salute: A View of the American Revolution* (1988). Tuchman was awarded the American Academy of Arts and Sciences gold medal for history in 1978. In the following selection, Tuchman discusses the many ways in which people refuse to take moral stands on issues in their lives.

1   What I want to say is concerned less with leadership than with its absence, that is, with the evasion of leadership. Not in the physical sense, for we have, if anything, a superabundance of leaders—hundreds of Pied Pipers, or would-be Pied Pipers, running about, ready and anxious to lead the population. They are scurrying around, collecting consensus, gathering as wide an acceptance as possible. But what they are *not* doing, very notably, is standing still and saying, "*This is* what I believe. This I will do and that I will not do. This is my code of behavior and that is outside it. This is excellent and that is trash." There is an abdication of moral leadership in the sense of a general unwillingness to state standards.

2   Of all the ills that our poor criticized, analyzed, sociologized society is heir to, the focal one, it seems to me, from which so much of our uneasiness and confusion derive is the absence of standards. We are too unsure of ourselves to assert them, to stick by them, or if necessary, in the case of persons

who occupy positions of authority, to impose them. We seem to be afflicted by a widespread and eroding reluctance to take any stand on any values, moral, behavioral, or aesthetic.

3   Everyone is afraid to call anything wrong, or vulgar, or fraudulent, or just bad taste or bad manners. Congress, for example, pussyfooted for months (following years of apathy) before taking action on a member convicted by the courts of illegalities; and when they finally got around to unseating him, one suspects they did it for the wrong motives. In 1922, in England, a man called Horatio Bottomley, a rather flamboyant character and popular demagogue—very similar in type, by the way, to Adam Clayton Powell, with similarly elastic financial ethics—who founded a paper called *John Bull* and got himself elected to Parliament, was found guilty of misappropriating the funds which his readers subscribed to victory bonds and other causes promoted by his paper. The day after the verdict, he was expelled from the House of Commons, with no fuss and very little debate, except for a few friendly farewells, as he was rather an engaging fellow. But no member thought the House had any other course to consider: Out he went. I do not suggest that this represents a difference between British and American morality; the difference is in the *times*.

4   Our time is one of disillusion in our species and a resulting lack of self-confidence—for good historical reasons. Man's recent record has not been reassuring. After engaging in the Great War with all its mud and blood and ravaged ground, its disease, destruction, and death, we allowed ourselves a bare twenty years before going at it all over again. And the second time was accompanied by an episode of man's inhumanity to man of such enormity that its implications for all of us have not yet, I think, been fully measured. A historian has recently stated that for such a phenomenon as the planned and nearly accomplished extermination of a people to take place, one of three preconditions necessary was public indifference.

5   Since then the human species has been busy overbreeding, polluting the air, destroying the balance of nature, and bungling in a variety of directions so that it is no wonder we have begun to doubt man's capacity for good judgment. It is hardly surprising that the self-confidence of the nineteenth century and its belief in human progress has been dissipated. "Every great civilization," said Secretary Gardner last year, "has been characterized by confidence in itself." At mid-twentieth century, the supply is low. As a result, we tend to shy away from all judgments. We hesitate to label anything wrong, and therefore hesitate to require the individual to bear moral responsibility for his acts.

6   We have become afraid to fix blame. Murderers and rapists and muggers and persons who beat up old men and engage in other forms of assault are not guilty; society is guilty; society has wronged them; society beats its breast

and says *mea culpa*—it is our fault, not the wrongdoer's. The wrongdoer, poor fellow, could not help himself.

7   I find this very puzzling because I always ask myself, in these cases, what about the many neighbors of the wrongdoer, equally poor, equally disadvantaged, equally sufferers from society's neglect, who nevertheless maintain certain standards of social behavior, who do *not* commit crimes, who do not murder for money or rape for kicks. How does it happen that they know the difference between right and wrong, and how long will they abide by the difference if the leaders and opinion-makers and pacesetters continue to shy away from bringing home responsibility to the delinquent?

8   Admittedly, the reluctance to condemn stems partly from a worthy instinct—*tout comprendre, c'est tout pardonner*—and from a rejection of what was often the hypocrisy of Victorian moral standards. True, there was a large component of hypocrisy in nineteenth-century morality. Since the advent of Freud, we know more, we understand more about human behavior, we are more reluctant to cast the first stone—to condemn—which is a good thing; but the pendulum has swung to the point where we are now afraid to place moral responsibility at all. Society, that large amorphous, nonspecific scapegoat, must carry the burden for each of us, relieving us of guilt. We have become so indoctrinated by the terrors lurking in the dark corridors of the guilt complex that guilt has acquired a very bad name. Yet a little guilt is not a dangerous thing; it has a certain society utility.

9   When it comes to guilt, a respected writer—respected in some circles—has told us, as her considered verdict on the Nazi program, that evil is banal—a word that means something so ordinary that you are not bothered by it; the dictionary definition is "commonplace and hackneyed." Somehow that conclusion does not seem adequate or even apt. *Of course*, evil is commonplace; *of course* we all partake of it. Does that mean that we must withhold disapproval, and that when evil appears in dangerous degree or vicious form we must not condemn but only understand? That may be very Christian in intent, but in reality it is an escape from the necessity of exercising judgment—which exercise, I believe, is a prime function of leadership.

10   What it requires is courage—just a little, not very much—the courage to be independent and stand up for the standard values one believes in. That kind of courage is the quality most conspicuously missing, I think, in current life. I don't mean the courage to protest and walk around with picket signs or boo Secretary McNamara which, though it may stem from the right instinct, is a group thing that does not require any very stout spirit. I did it myself for Sacco and Vanzetti when I was about twelve and picketed in some now forgotten labor dispute when I was a freshman and even got arrested. There is nothing to that; if you don't do that sort of thing when you are eighteen, then there is something wrong with you. I mean, rather, a kind of

lonely moral courage, the quality that attracted me to that odd character, Czar Reed, and to Lord Salisbury, neither of whom cared a rap for the opinion of the public or would have altered his conduct a hair to adapt to it. It is the quality someone said of Lord Palmerston was his "you-be-damnedness." That is the mood we need a little more of.

11   Standards of taste, as well as morality, need continued reaffirmation to stay alive, as liberty needs eternal vigilance. To recognize and to proclaim the difference between the good and the shoddy, the true and the fake, as well as between right and wrong, or what we believe at a given time to be right and wrong, is the obligation, I think, of persons who presume to lead, or are thrust into leadership, or hold positions of authority. That includes— whether they asked for it or not—all educators and even, I regret to say, writers.

12   For educators it has become increasingly the habit in the difficult circumstances of college administration today to find out what the students want in the matter of curriculum and deportment and then give it to them. This seems to me another form of abdication, another example of the prevailing reluctance to state a standard and expect, not to say require, performance in accord with it. The permissiveness, the yielding of decision to the student, does not—from what I can tell—promote responsibility in the young so much as uneasiness and a kind of anger at *not* being told what is expected of them, a resentment of their elders' unwillingness to take a position. Recently a student psychiatric patient of the Harvard Health Services was quoted by the director, Dr. Dana Farnsworth, as complaining, "My parents never tell me what to do. They never stop me from doing anything." That is the unheard wail, I think, extended beyond parents to the general absence of a guiding, reassuring pattern, which is behind much of society's current uneasiness.

13   It is human nature to want patterns and standards and a structure of behavior. A pattern to conform to is a kind of shelter. You see it in kindergarten and primary school, at least in those schools where the children when leaving the classroom are required to fall into line. When the teacher gives the signal, they fall in with alacrity; they know where they belong and they instinctively like to *be* where they belong. They like the feeling of being in line.

14   Most people need a structure, not only to fall into but to fall out of. The rebel with a cause is better off than the one without. At least he knows what he is "agin." He is not lost. He does not suffer from an identity crisis. It occurs to me that much of the student protest now may be a testing of authority, a search for that line to fall out of, and when it isn't there students become angrier because they feel more lost, more abandoned than ever. In the late turmoil at Berkeley, at least as regards the

filthy speech demonstration, there was a missed opportunity, I think (however great my respect for Clark Kerr) for a hearty, emphatic, and unmistakable "No!" backed up by sanctions. Why? Because the act, even if intended as a demonstration of principle, was in this case, like any indecent exposure, simply offensive, and what is offensive to the greater part of society is antisocial, and what is antisocial, so long as we live in social groups and not each of us on his own island, must be curtailed, like Peeping Toms or obscene telephone calls, as a public nuisance. The issue is really not complicated or difficult but, if we would only look at it with more self-confidence, quite simple.

15   So, it seems to me, is the problem of the CIA. You will say that in this case people have taken a stand, opinion-makers have worked themselves into a moral frenzy. Indeed they have, but over a false issue. The CIA is not, after all, the Viet Cong or the Schutzstaffel in black shirts. Its initials do not stand for Criminal Indiscretions of America. It is an arm of the American government, our elected, representative government (whatever may be one's feelings toward that body at the moment). Virtually every government in the world subsidizes youth groups, especially in the international relations, not to mention in athletic competitions. (I do not know if the CIA is subsidizing our Equestrian Team, but I know personally a number of people who would be only too delighted if it were.) The difficulty here is simply that the support was clandestine in the first place and not the proper job of the CIA in the second. An intelligence agency should be restricted to the gathering of intelligence and not extend itself into operations. In armies the two functions are distinct: intelligence is G2 and operations is G3. If our government could manage its functions with a little more precision and perform openly those functions that are perfectly respectable, there would be no issue. The recent excitement only shows how easily we succumb when reliable patterns or codes of conduct are absent, to a confusion of values.

16   A similar confusion exists, I think, with regard to the omnipresent pornography that surrounds us like smog. A year ago the organization of my own profession, the Authors League, filed a brief *amicus curiae* in the appeal of Ralph Ginzburg, the publisher of a periodical called *Eros* and other items, who had been convicted of disseminating obscenity through the mails. The League's action was taken on the issue of censorship to which all good liberals automatically respond like Pavlov's dogs. Since at this stage in our culture pornography has so far gotten the upper hand that to do battle in its behalf against the dragon Censorship is rather like doing battle today against the bustle in behalf of short skirts, and since I believe that the proliferation of pornography in its sadistic forms is a greater social danger at the moment than censorship, and since Mr. Ginzburg was not an author anyway but a commercial promoter, I raised an objection, as a member of the

Council, to the Authors League's spending its funds in the Ginzburg case. I was, of course, outvoted; in fact, there was no vote. Everyone around the table just sat and looked at me in cold disapproval. Later, after my objection was printed in the *Bulletin*, at my request, two distinguished authors wrote privately to me to express their agreement but did not go so far as to say so publicly.

17   Thereafter, when the Supreme Court upheld Mr. Ginzburg's conviction, everyone in the intellectual community raised a hullaballoo about censorship advancing upon us like some sort of Frankenstein's monster. This seems to me another case of getting excited about the wrong thing. The cause of pornography is *not* the same as the cause of free speech. There *is* a difference. Ralph Ginzburg is *not* Theodore Dreiser and this is not the 1920s. If one looks around at the movies, especially the movie advertisements, and the novels and the pulp magazines glorifying perversion, and the paperbacks that make de Sade available to schoolchildren, one does not get the impression that in the 1960s we are being stifled in the Puritan grip of Anthony Comstock. Here again, leaders—in this case authors and critics—seem too unsure of values or too afraid of being unpopular to stand up and assert the perfectly obvious difference between smut and free speech, or to say "Such and such is offensive and can be harmful." Happily, there are signs of awakening. In a *Times* review of a book called *On Iniquity* by Pamela Hansford Johnson, which related pornography to the Moors murders in England, the reviewer concluded that "this may be the opening of a discussion that must come, the opening shot."

18   In the realm of art, no less important than morals, the abdication of judgment is almost a disease. Last fall when the Lincoln Center opened its glittering new opera house with a glittering new opera on the tragedy of Antony and Cleopatra, the curtain rose on a gaudy crowd engaged in energetic revels around a gold box in the shape of a pyramid, up whose sides (conveniently fitted with toe-holds, I suppose) several sinuous and reasonably nude slave girls were chased by lecherous guards left over from "Aida." When these preliminaries quieted down, the front of the gold box suddenly dropped open, and guess who was inside? No, it was not Cleopatra; it was Antony, looking, I thought, rather bewildered. What was he doing inside the box was never made clear. Thereafter everything happened—and in crescendos of gold and spangles and sequins, silks and gauzes, feathers, fans, jewels, brocades, and such a quantity of glitter that one began to laugh, thinking that the spectacle was intended as a parody of the old Shubert revue. But no, this was the Metropolitan Opera in the vaunted splendor of its most publicized opening since the Hippodrome. I gather it was Mr. Bing's idea of giving the first-night customers a fine splash. What he achieved was simply vulgarity, as at least some reviewers had the courage to say next day.

Now, I cannot believe that Mr. Bing and his colleagues do not know the difference between honest artistry in stage design and pretentious ostentation. If they know better, why do they allow themselves to do worse? As leaders in their field of endeavor, they should have been setting standards of beauty and creative design, not debasing them.

19   One finds the same peculiarities in the visual arts. Non-art, as its practitioners describe it—the blob school, the all-black canvasses, the paper cutouts and Campbell soup tins and plastic hamburgers and pieces of old carpet—is treated as art, not only by dealers whose motive is understandable (they have discovered that shock value sells); not only by a gullible pseudocultural section of the public who are not interested in art but in being "in" and wouldn't, to quote an old joke, know a Renoir from a Jaguar; but also, which I find mystifying, by the museums and the critics. I am sure they know the difference between the genuine and the hoax. But not trusting their own judgment, they seem afraid to say no to anything, for fear, I suppose, of making a mistake and turning down what may be next decade's Matisse.

20   For the museums to exhibit the plastic hamburgers and twists of scrap iron is one thing, but for them to *buy* them for their permanent collection puts an imprimatur on what is fraudulent. Museum curators, too, are leaders who have an obligation to distinguish—I will not say the good from the bad in art because that is an elusive and subjective matter dependent on the eye of the time—but at least honest expression from phony. Most of what fills the galleries on Madison Avenue is simply stuff designed to take advantage of current fads and does not come from an artist's vision or an honest creative impulse. The dealers know it; the critics know it; the purveyors themselves know it; the public suspects it; but no one dares say it because that would be committing oneself to a standard of values and even, heaven forbid, exposing oneself to being called square.

21   In the fairy story, it required a child to cry out that the Emperor was naked. Let us not leave that task to the children. It should be the task of leaders to recognize and state the truth as they see it. It is their task not to be afraid of absolutes.

22   If the educated man is not willing to express standards, if he cannot show that he has them and applies them, what then is education for? Its purpose, I take it, is to form the civilized man, whom I would define as the person capable of the informed exercise of judgment, taste and values. If at maturity he is not willing to express judgment on matters of policy or taste or morals, if at fifty he does not believe that he has acquired more wisdom and informed experience than is possessed by the student at twenty, then he is saying in effect that education has been a failure.

Discussion Questions

1. Tuchman defines "moral courage" by offering a number of examples from history. How important is this historical comparison in proving her claim that we no longer have moral courage? Explain your response.

2. What is the principal kind of appeal Tuchman uses to advance her argument: logic, emotion, or ethics? Identify some examples to support your answer.

3. Whom does Tuchman blame for the lack of moral courage? Do you agree with her? Why or why not?

4. Tuchman wrote this argument some thirty years ago. In what ways do you think it is still as valid now as it was then?

5. On what points do you think Nicols Fox and Tuchman would agree? Cite specific passages from both arguments that support your answer.

What Makes Superman So Darned American

Gary Engle

Born in 1947, Gary Engle earned his B.A. degree from Northwestern University and his Ph.D. from the University of Chicago. A professor of English at Cleveland State University, Engle's work has appeared in such publications as *Northern Ohio Live* and *Cleveland* magazine. He also helped edit *The Grotesque Essence: Plays from American Minstrel Style* (1978). In the following selection, Engle begins with a personal dilemma before using inductive reasoning to argue why Superman is such an American legend.

1   When I was young I spent a lot of time arguing with myself about who would win in a fight between John Wayne and Superman. On days when I wore my cowboy hat and cap guns, I knew the Duke would win because of his pronounced superiority in the all-important matter of swagger. There were days, though, when a frayed army blanket tied cape-fashion around my neck signaled a young man's need to believe there could be no end to the potency of his being. Then the Man of Steel was the odds-on favorite to knock the Duke for a cosmic loop. My greatest childhood problem was that the question could never be resolved because no such battle could ever take place. I mean, how would a fight start between the only two Americans who never started anything, who always fought only to defend their rights and the American way?

2   Now that I'm older and able to look with reason on the mysteries of childhood, I've finally resolved the dilemma. John Wayne was the best older brother any kid could ever hope to have, but he was no Superman.

3   Superman is *the* great American hero. We are a nation rich with legendary figures. But among the Davy Crocketts and Paul Bunyans and Mike Finks and Pecos Bills and all the rest who speak for various regional identities in the pantheon of American folklore, only Superman achieves truly mystic stature, interweaving a pattern of beliefs, literary conventions, and cultural traditions of the American people more powerfully and more

accessibly than any other cultural symbol of the twentieth century, perhaps of any period in our history.

4   The core of the American myth in *Superman* consists of a few basic facts that remain unchanged throughout the infinitely varied ways in which the myth is told—facts with which everyone is familiar, however marginal their knowledge of the story. Superman is an orphan rocketed to Earth when his native planet Krypton explodes; he lands near Smallville and is adopted by Jonathan and Martha Kent, who inculcate in him their American middle-class ethic; as an adult he migrates to Metropolis where he defends America —no, the world! no, the Universe!—from all evil and harm while playing a romantic game in which, as Clark Kent, he hopelessly pursues Lois Lane, who hopelessly pursues Superman, who remains aloof until such time as Lois proves worthy of him by falling in love with his feigned identity as a weakling. That's it. Every narrative thread in the mythology, each one of the thousands of plots in the fifty-year stream of comics and films and TV shows, all the tales involving the demigods of the Superman pantheon—Super-boy, Supergirl, even Krypto the superdog—every single one reinforces by never contradicting this basic set of facts. That's the myth, and that's where one looks to understand America.

5   It is impossible to imagine Superman being as popular as he is and speaking as deeply to the American character were he not an immigrant and an orphan. Immigration, of course, is the overwhelming fact in American history. Except for the Indians, all Americans have an immediate sense of their origins elsewhere. No nation on Earth has so deeply embedded in its social consciousness the imagery of passage from one social identity to another: the Mayflower of the New England separatists, the slave ships from Africa and the subsequent underground railroads toward freedom in the North, the sailing ships and steamers running shuttles across two oceans in the nineteenth century, the freedom airlifts in the twentieth. Somehow the picture just isn't complete without Superman's rocketship.

6   Like the peoples of the nation whose values he defends, Superman is an alien, but not just any alien. He's the consummate and totally uncompromised alien, an immigrant whose visible difference from the norm is underscored by his decision to wear a costume of bold primary colors so tight as to be his very skin. Moreover, Superman the alien is real. He stands out among the host of comic book characters (Batman is a good example) for whom the superhero role is like a mask assumed when needed, a costume worn over their real identities as normal Americans. Superman's powers—strength, mobility, x-ray vision and the like—are the comic-book equivalents of ethnic characteristics, and they protect and preserve the vitality of the foster community in which he lives in the same way that immigrant ethnicity has sustained American culture linguistically, artistically,

economically, politically, and spiritually. The myth of Superman asserts with total confidence and a childlike innocence the value of the immigrant in American culture.

7   From this nation's beginnings Americans have looked for ways of coming to terms with the immigrant experience. This is why, for example, so much of American literature and popular culture deals with the theme of dislocation, generally focused in characters devoted or doomed to constant physical movement. Daniel Boone became an American legend in part as a result of apocryphal stories that he moved every time his neighbors got close enough for him to see the smoke of their cabin fires. James Fenimore Cooper's Natty Bumppo spent the five long novels of the Leatherstocking saga drifting ever westward, like the pioneers who were his spiritual offspring, from the Mohawk valley of upstate New York to the Great Plains where he died. Huck Finn sailed through the moral heart of America on a raft. Melville's Ishmael, Wister's Virginian, Shane, Gatsby, the entire Lost Generation, Steinbeck's Okies, Little Orphan Annie, a thousand fiddlefooted cowboy heroes of dime novels and films and television—all in motion, searching for the American dream or stubbornly refusing to give up their innocence by growing old, all symptomatic of a national sense of rootlessness stemming from an identity founded on the experience of immigration.

8   Individual mobility is an integral part of America's dreamwork. Is it any wonder, then, that our greatest hero can take to the air at will? Superman's ability to fly does more than place him in a tradition of mythic figures going back to the Greek messenger god Hermes or Zetes the flying Argonaut. It makes him an exemplar in the American dream. Take away a young man's wheels and you take away his manhood. Jack Kerouac and Charles Kurault go on the road; William Least Heat Moon looks for himself in a van exploring the veins of America in its system of blue highways; legions of gray-haired retirees turn Air Stream trailers and Winnebagos into proof positive that you can, in the end, take it with you. On a human scale, the American need to keep moving suggests a neurotic aimlessness under the surface of adventure. But take the human restraints off, let Superman fly unencumbered when and wherever he will, and the meaning of mobility in the American consciousness begins to reveal itself. Superman's incredible speed allows him to be as close to everywhere at once as it is physically possible to be. Displacement is, therefore, impossible. His sense of self is not dispersed by his life's migration but rather enhanced by all the universe that he is able to occupy. What American, whether an immigrant in spirit or in fact, could resist the appeal of one with such an ironclad immunity to the anxiety of dislocation?

9   In America, physical dislocation serves as a symbol of social and psychological movement. When our immigrant ancestors arrived on America's

shores they hit the ground running, some to homestead on the Great Plains, others to claw their way up the socioeconomic ladder in coastal ghettos. Upward mobility, westward migration, Sunbelt relocation—the wisdom in America is that people don't, can't, mustn't end up where they begin. This belief has the moral force of religious doctrine. Thus the American identity is ordered around the psychological experience of forsaking or losing the past for the opportunity of reinventing oneself in the future. This makes the orphan a potent symbol of the American character. Orphans aren't merely free to reinvent themselves. They are obliged to do so.

10   When Superman reinvents himself, he becomes the bumbling Clark Kent, a figure as immobile as Superman is mobile, as weak as his alter ego is strong. Over the years commentators have been fond of stressing how Clark Kent provides an illusory image of wimpiness onto which children can project their insecurities about their own potential (and, hopefully, equally illusory) weaknesses. But I think the role of Clark Kent is far more complex than that.

11   During my childhood, Kent contributed nothing to my love for the Man of Steel. If left to contemplate him for too long, I found myself changing from cape back into cowboy hat and guns. John Wayne, at least, was no sissy that I could ever see. Of course, in all the Westerns that the Duke came to stand for in my mind, there were elements that left me as confused as the paradox between Kent and Superman. For example, I could never seem to figure out why cowboys so often fell in love when there were obviously better options: horses to ride, guns to shoot, outlaws to chase, and savages to kill. Even on the days when I became John Wayne, I could fall victim to a never-articulated anxiety about the potential for poor judgment in my cowboy heroes. Then, I generally drifted back into a worship of Superman. With him, at least, the mysterious communion of opposites was honest and on the surface of things.

12   What disturbed me as a child is what I now think makes the myth of Superman so appealing to an immigrant sensibility. The shape-shifting between Clark Kent and Superman is the means by which this mid-twentieth-century, urban story—like the pastoral, nineteenth-century Western before it—addresses in dramatic terms the theme of cultural assimilation.

13   At its most basic level, the Western was an imaginative record of the American experience of westward migration and settlement. By bringing the forces of civilization and savagery together on a mythical frontier, the Western addressed the problem of conflict between apparently mutually exclusive identities and explored options for negotiating between them. In terms that a boy could comprehend, the myth explored the dilemma of assimilation—marry the school marm and start wearing Eastern clothes or saddle up and drift further westward with the boys.

14   The Western was never a myth of stark moral simplicity. Pioneers fled civilization by migrating west, but their purpose in the wilderness was to rebuild civilization. So civilization was both good and bad, what Americans fled from and journeyed toward. A similar moral ambiguity rested at the heart of the wilderness. It was an Eden in which innocence could be achieved through spiritual rebirth, but it was also the anarchic force that most directly threatened the civilized values America wanted to impose on the frontier. So the dilemma arose: In negotiating between civilization and the wilderness, between the old order and the new, between the identity the pioneers carried with them from wherever they came and the identity they sought to invent, Americans faced an impossible choice. Either they pushed into the New World wilderness and forsook the ideals that motivated them or they clung to their origins and polluted Eden.

15   The myth of the Western responded to this dilemma by inventing the idea of the frontier in which civilized ideals embodied in the institutions of family, church, law, and education are revitalized by the virtues of savagery: independence, self-reliance, personal honor, sympathy with nature, and ethical uses of violence. In effect, the mythical frontier represented an attempt to embody the perfect degree of assimilation in which both the old and new identities came together, if not in a single self-image, then at least in idealized relationships, like the symbolic marriage of reformed cowboy and displaced school marm that ended Owen Wister's prototypical *The Virginian,* or the mystical masculine bonding between representatives of an ascendant and a vanishing America—Natty Bumppo and Chingachgook, the Lone Ranger and Tonto. On the Western frontier, both the old and new identities equally mattered.

16   As powerful a myth as the Western was, however, there were certain limits to its ability to speak directly to an increasingly common twentieth-century immigrant sensibility. First, it was pastoral. Its imagery of dusty frontier towns and breathtaking mountainous desolation spoke most affectingly to those who conceived of the American dream in terms of the nineteenth-century immigrant experience of rural settlement. As the twentieth century wore on, more immigrants were, like Superman, moving from rural or small-town backgrounds to metropolitan environments. Moreover, the Western was historical, often elegiacally so. Underlying the air of celebration in even the most epic and romantic of Westerns—the films of John Ford, say, in which John Wayne stood tall for all that any good American boy could ever want to be—was an awareness that the frontier was less a place than a state of mind represented in historic terms by a fleeting moment glimpsed imperfectly in the rapid wave of westward migration and settlement. Implicitly, then, whatever balance of past and future identities the frontier could offer was itself tenuous or illusory.

17   Twentieth-century immigrants, particularly the Eastern European Jews who came to America after 1880 and who settled in the industrial and mercantile centers of the Northeast—cities like Cleveland where Jerry Siegel and Joe Shuster grew up and created Superman—could be entertained by the Western, but they developed a separate literary tradition that addressed the theme of assimilation in terms closer to their personal experience. In this tradition issues were clear-cut: Clinging to an Old World identity meant isolation in ghettos, confrontation with a prejudiced mainstream culture, second-class social status, and impoverishment. On the other hand, forsaking the past in favor of total absorption into the mainstream, while it could result in socioeconomic progress, meant a loss of the religious, linguistic, even culinary traditions that provided a foundation for psychological well-being. Such loss was particularly tragic for the Jews because of the fundamental role played by history in Jewish culture.

18   Writers who worked in this tradition—Abraham Cahan, Daniel Fuchs, Henry Roth, and Delmore Schwarz, among others—generally found little reason to view the experience of assimilation with joy or optimism. Typical of the tradition was Cahan's early novel *Yekl,* on which Joan Micklin Silver's film *Hester Street* was based. A young married couple, Jake and Gitl, clash over his need to be absorbed as quickly as possible into the American mainstream and her obsessive preservation of their Russian-Jewish heritage. In symbolic terms, their confrontation is as simple as their choice of headgear—a derby for him, a babushka for her. That the story ends with their divorce, even in the context of their gradual movement toward mutual understanding of one another's point of view, suggests the divisive nature of the pressures at work in the immigrant communities.

19   Where the pressures were perhaps most keenly felt was in the schools. Educational theory of the period stressed the benefits of rapid assimilation. In the first decades of this century, for example, New York schools flatly rejected bilingual education—a common response to the plight of non-English-speaking immigrants even today—and there were conscientious efforts to indoctrinate the children of immigrants with American values, often at the expense of traditions within the ethnic community. What resulted was a generational rift in which children were openly embarrassed by and even contemptuous of their parents' values, setting a pattern in American life in which second-generation immigrants migrate psychologically if not physically from their parents, leaving it up to the third generation and beyond to rediscover their ethnic roots.

20   Under such circumstances, finding a believable and inspiring balance between the old identity and the new, like that implicit in the myth of the frontier, was next to impossible. The images and characters that did emerge from the immigrant communities were often comic. Seen over and over in

the fiction and popular theater of the day was the figure of the *yiddische Yankee*, a jingoistic optimist who spoke heavily accented American slang, talked baseball like an addict without understanding the game, and dressed like a Broadway dandy on a budget—in short, one who didn't understand America well enough to distinguish between image and substance and who paid for the mistake by becoming the butt of a style of comedy bordering on pathos. So engrained was this stereotype in popular culture that it echoes today in TV situation comedy.

21   Throughout American popular culture between 1880 and the Second World War the story was the same. Oxlike Swedish farmers, German brewers, Jewish merchants, corrupt Irish ward healers, Italian gangsters—there was a parade of images that reflected in terms often comic, sometimes tragic, the humiliation, pain, and cultural insecurity of people in a state of transition. Even in the comics, a medium intimately connected with immigrant culture, there simply was no image that presented a blending of identities in the assimilation process in a way that stressed pride, self-confidence, integrity, and psychological well-being. None, that is, until Superman.

22   The brilliant stroke in the conception of Superman—the sine qua non that makes the whole myth work—is the fact that he has two identities. The myth simply wouldn't work without Clark Kent, mild-mannered newspaper reporter and later, as the myth evolved, bland TV newsman. Adopting the white-bread image of a wimp is first and foremost a moral act for the Man of Steel. He does it to protect his parents from nefarious sorts who might use them to gain an edge over the powerful alien. Moreover, Kent adds to Superman's powers the moral guidance of a Smallville upbringing. It is Jonathan Kent, fans remember, who instructs the alien that his powers must always be used for good. Thus does the myth add a mainstream white Anglo-Saxon Protestant ingredient to the American stew. Clark Kent is the clearest stereotype of a self-effacing, hesitant, doubting, middle-class weakling ever invented. He is the epitome of visible invisibility, someone whose extraordinary ordinariness makes him disappear in a crowd. In a phrase, he is the consummate figure of total cultural assimilation, and significantly, he is not real. Implicit in this is the notion that mainstream cultural norms, however useful, are illusions.

23   Though a disguise, Kent is necessary for the myth to work. This uniquely American hero has two identities, one based on where he comes from in life's journey, one on where he is going. One is real, one an illusion, and both are necessary for the myth of balance in the assimilation process to be complete. Superman's powers make the hero capable of saving humanity; Kent's total immersion in the American heartland makes him want to do it. The result is an improvement on the Western: an optimistic myth of assimilation but with an urban, technocratic setting.

24   One must never underestimate the importance to a myth of the most minute elements which do not change over time and by which we recognize the story. Take Superman's cape, for example. When Joe Shuster inked the first Superman stories, in the early thirties when he was still a student at Cleveland's Glenville High School, Superman was strictly beefcake in tights, looking more like a circus acrobat than the ultimate Man of Steel. By June of 1938 when *Action Comics* no. 1 was issued, the image had been altered to include a cape, ostensibly to make flight easier to render in the pictures. But it wasn't the cape of Victorian melodrama and adventure fiction, the kind worn with a clasp around the neck. In fact, one is hard-pressed to find any precedent in popular culture for the kind of cape Superman wears. His emerges in a seamless line from either side of the front yoke of his tunic. It is a veritable growth from behind his pectorals and hangs, when he stands at ease, in a line that doesn't so much drape his shoulders as stand apart from them and echo their curve, like an angel's wings.

25   In light of this graphic detail, it seems hardly coincidental that Superman's real, Kryptonic name is Kal-El, an apparent neologism by George Lowther, the author who novelized the comic strip in 1942. In Hebrew, *el* can be both root and affix. As a root, it is the masculine singular word for God. Angels in Hebrew mythology are called *benei Elohim* (literally, sons of the Gods), or *Elyonim* (higher beings). As an affix, *el* is most often translated as "of God," as in the plenitude of Old Testament given names: Ishma-el, Dani-el, Ezeki-el, Samu-el, etc. It is also a common form for named angels in most Semitic mythologies: Israf-el, Aza-el, Uri-el, Yo-el, Rapha-el, Gabri-el and—the one perhaps most like Superman—Micha-el, the warrior angel and Satan's principal adversary.

26   The morpheme *Kal* bears a linguistic relation to two Hebrew roots. The first, *kal*, means "with lightness" or "swiftness" (faster than a speeding bullet in Hebrew?). It also bears a connection to the root *hal*, where *h* is the guttural *ch* of *chutzpah*. *Hal* translates roughly as "everything" or "all." *Kal-el*, then, can be read as "all that is God," or perhaps more in the spirit of the myth of Superman, "all that God is." And while we're at it, *Kent* is a form of the Hebrew *kana*. In its *k-n-t* form, the word appears in the Bible, meaning "I have found a son."

27   I'm suggesting that Superman raises the American immigrant experience to the level of religious myth. And why not? He's not just some immigrant from across the waters like all our ancestors, but a real alien, an extraterrestrial, a visitor from heaven if you will, which fact lends an element of the supernatural to the myth. America has no national religious icons nor any pilgrimage shrines. The idea of a patron saint is ludicrous in a nation whose Founding Fathers wrote into the founding documents the fundamental if not eternal separation of church and state. America, though, is

pretty much as religious as other industrialized countries. It's just that our tradition of religious diversity precludes the nation's religious character from being embodied in objects or persons recognizably religious, for such are immediately identified by their attachment to specific sectarian traditions and thus contradict the eclecticism of the American religious spirit.

28   In America, cultural icons that manage to tap the national religious spirit are of necessity secular on the surface and sufficiently generalized to incorporate the diversity of American religious traditions. Superman doesn't have to be seen as an angel to be appreciated, but in the absence of a tradition of national religious iconography, he can serve as a safe, nonsectarian focus for essentially religious sentiments, particularly among the young.

29   In the last analysis, Superman is like nothing so much as an American boy's fantasy of a messiah. He is the male, heroic match for the Statue of Liberty, come like an immigrant from heaven to deliver humankind by sacrificing himself in the service of others. He protects the weak and defends truth and justice and all the other moral virtues inherent in the Judeo-Christian tradition, remaining ever vigilant and ever chaste. What purer or stronger vision could there possibly be for a child? Now that I put my mind to it, I see that John Wayne never had a chance.

Discussion Questions

1.   Evaluate the effectiveness of Engle beginning his argument with a personal remembrance. Would it have been any less effective had he omitted it and started the argument with the third paragraph? Explain your answer.

2.   Engle uses inductive reasoning to argue his claim. Evaluate the effectiveness of his choice of method.

3.   Which of Engle's supporting evidence do you find most persuasive? Which is least persuasive? Explain your responses.

4.   Explain how Engle establishes his credibility.

5.   Do you find it unusual that Engle thinks Superman, a cartoon, movie, and television character, is more of an American hero than John Wayne, a real person? What does this say about the characters Americans find venerable?

Our Way of Life
Makes Us Miserable

Erich Fromm

> Erich Fromm was born in 1900 in Germany and died in 1980. Educated at universities in Heidelberg and Munich and at the Psychoanalytic Institute in Berlin, Fromm emigrated to the United States in 1934 and subsequently became a citizen. A famous psychoanalyst, social critic, and philosopher, Fromm taught at Yale University and Columbia University. His books include *Escape from Freedom* (1941), *Man for Himself* (1947), *The Forgotten Language* (1951), *The Sane Society* (1955), *Sigmund Freud's Mission* (1956), *Life without Illusions* (1961), *Beyond the Chains of Illusion* (1962), *The Heart of Man* (1964), and *Anatomy of Human Destructiveness* (1973). Fromm is best known for *The Art of Loving* (1964) and is recognized for applying psychoanalytic theory to social and cultural problems. In the following selection, which first appeared in the *Saturday Evening Post* in 1964, Fromm argues that our "consumption-happy, fun-loving, jet-traveling" way of life creates anxiety, unhappiness, and stress in our lives.

1   Most Americans believe that our society of consumption-happy, fun-loving, jet-traveling people creates the greatest happiness for the greatest number. Contrary to this view, I believe that our present way of life leads to increasing anxiety, helplessness and, eventually, to the disintegration of our culture. I refuse to identify fun with pleasure, excitement with joy, business with happiness, or the faceless, buck-passing "organization man" with an independent individual.

2   From this critical view our rates of alcoholism, suicide and divorce, as well as juvenile delinquency, gang rule, acts of violence and indifference to life, are characteristic symptoms of our "pathology of normalcy." It may be argued that all these pathological phenomena exist because we have not yet reached our aim, that of an affluent society. It is true, we are still far

from being an affluent society. But the material progress made in the last decades allows us to hope that our system might eventually produce a materially affluent society. Yet will we be happier then? The example of Sweden, one of the most prosperous, democratic and peaceful European countries, is not very encouraging: Sweden, as is often pointed out, in spite of all its material security has among the highest alcoholism and suicide rates in Europe, while a much poorer country like Ireland ranks among the lowest in these respects. Could it be that our dream that material welfare per se leads to happiness is just a pipe dream? . . .

3   Certainly the humanist thinkers of the eighteenth and nineteenth centuries, who are our ideological ancestors, thought that the goal of life was the full unfolding of a person's potentialities; what mattered to them was the person who *is* much, not the one who *has* much or *uses* much. For them economic production was a means to the unfolding of man, not an end. It seems that today the means have become ends, that not only "God is dead," as Nietzsche said in the nineteenth century, but also man is dead; that what is alive are the organizations, the machines; and that man has become their slave rather than being their master.

4   Each society creates its own type of personality by its way of bringing up children in the family, by its system of education, by its effective values (that is, those values that are rewarded rather than only preached). Every society creates the type of "social character" which is needed for its proper functioning. It forms men who *want* to do what they *have* to do. What kind of men does our large-scale, bureaucratized industrialism need?

5   It needs men who cooperate smoothly in large groups, who want to consume more and more, and whose tastes are standardized and can be easily influenced and anticipated. It needs men who feel free and independent, yet who are willing to be commanded, to do what is expected, to fit into the social machine without friction; men who can be guided without force, led without leaders, prompted without an aim except the aim to be on the move, to function, to go ahead.

6   Modern industrialism has succeeded in producing this kind of man. He is the "alienated" man. He is alienated in the sense that his actions and his own forces have become estranged from him; they stand above him and against him, and rule him rather than being ruled by him. His life forces have been transformed into things and institutions, and these things and institutions have become idols. They are something apart from him, which he worships and to which he submits. Alienated man bows down before the works of his own hands. He experiences himself not as the active bearer of his own forces and riches but as an impoverished "thing," dependent on other things outside of himself. He is the prisoner of the very economic and political circumstances which he has created.

7 Since our economic organization is based on continuous and ever-increasing consumption (think of the threat to our economy if people did not buy a new car until their old one was really obsolete), contemporary industrial man is encouraged to be consumption-crazy. Without any real enjoyment, he "takes in" drink, food, cigarettes, sights, lectures, books, movies, television, any new kind of gadget. The world has become one great maternal breast, and man has become the eternal suckling, forever expectant, forever disappointed.

8 Sex, in fact, has become one of the main objects of consumption. Our newsstands are full of "girlie" magazines; the percentages of girls having premarital sexual relations and of unwed mothers are on a steep incline. It can be argued that all this represents a welcome emancipation from Victorian morality, that it is a wholesome affirmation of independence, that it reflects the Freudian principle that repression may produce neurosis. But while all these arguments are true to some extent, they omit the main point. Neither independence nor Freudian principle is the main cause of our present-day sexual freedom. Our sexual mores are part and parcel of our *cult of consumption*, whose main principle was so succinctly expressed by Aldous Huxley in *Brave New World*: "Never put off till tomorrow the fun you can have today." Nature has provided men and women with the capacity for sexual excitement; but excitement in consumption, whether it is of sex or any other commodity, is not the same as aliveness and richness of experience.

9 In general, our society is becoming one of giant enterprises directed by a bureaucracy in which man becomes a small, well-oiled cog in the machinery. The oiling is done with higher wages, fringe benefits, well-ventilated factories and piped music, and by psychologists and "human-relations" experts; yet all this oiling does not alter the fact that man has become powerless, that he does not wholeheartedly participate in his work and that he is bored with it. In fact, the blue- and the white-collar workers have become economic puppets who dance to the tune of automated machines and bureaucratic management.

10 The worker and employee are anxious, not only because they might find themselves out of a job (and with installment payments due); they are anxious also because they are unable to acquire any real satisfaction or interest in life. They live and die without ever having confronted the fundamental realities of human existence as emotionally and intellectually productive, authentic and independent human beings.

11 Those higher up on the social ladder are no less anxious. Their lives are no less empty than those of their subordinates. They are even more insecure in some respects. They are in a highly competitive race. To be promoted or

to fall behind is not only a matter of salary but even more a matter of self-esteem. When they apply for their first job, they are tested for intelligence as well as for the right mixture of submissiveness and independence. From that moment on they are tested again and again—by the psychologists, for whom testing is a big business, and by their superiors, who judge their behavior, sociability, capacity to get along, etc., their own and that of their wives. This constant need to *prove* that one is as good as or better than one's fellow-competitor creates constant anxiety and stress, the very causes of unhappiness and psychosomatic illness.

12   The "organization man" may be well fed, well amused and well oiled, yet he lacks a sense of identity because none of his feelings or his thoughts originates within himself; none is authentic. He has no convictions, either in politics, religion, philosophy or in love. He is attracted by the "latest model" in thought, art and style, and lives under the illusion that the thoughts and feelings which he has acquired by listening to the media of mass communication are his own.

13   He has a nostalgic longing for a life of individualism, initiative and justice, a longing that he satisfies by looking at Westerns. But these values have disappeared from real life in the world of giant corporations, giant state and military bureaucracies and giant labor unions. He, the individual, feels so small before these giants that he sees only one way to escape the sense of utter insignificance: He identifies himself with the giants and idolizes them as the true representatives of his own human powers, those of which he has dispossessed himself. His effort to escape his anxiety takes other forms as well. His pleasure in a well-filled freezer may be one unconscious way of reassuring himself. His passion for consumption—from television to sex—is still another symptom, a mechanism which psychiatrists often find in anxious patients who go on an eating or buying spree to evade their problems.

14   The man whose life is centered around producing, selling and consuming commodities transforms himself into a commodity. He becomes increasingly attracted to that which is man-made and mechanical, rather than to that which is natural and organic. Many men today are more interested in sports cars than in women; or they experience women as a car which one can cause to race by pushing the right button. Altogether they expect happiness is a matter of finding the right button, not the result of a productive, rich life, a life which requires making an effort and taking risks. In their search for the button, some go to the psychoanalyst, some go to church and some read "self-help" books. But while it is impossible to find the button for happiness, the majority are satisfied with pushing the buttons of cameras, radios, television sets, and watching science fiction become reality.

15   One of the strangest aspects of this mechanical approach to life is the widespread lack of concern about the danger of total destruction by nuclear weapons; a possibility people are consciously aware of. The explanation, I believe, is that they are more proud of than frightened by the gadgets of mass destruction. Also, they are so frightened of the possibility of their personal failure and humiliation that their anxiety about personal matters prevents them from feeling anxiety about the possibility that everybody and everything may be destroyed. Perhaps total destruction is even more attractive than total insecurity and never-ending personal anxiety.

16   Am I suggesting that modern man is doomed and that we should return to the preindustrial mode of production or to nineteenth-century "free enterprise" capitalism? Certainly not. Problems are never solved by returning to a stage which one has already outgrown. I suggest transforming our social system from a bureaucratically managed industrialism in which maximal production and consumption are ends in themselves (in the Soviet Union as well as in the capitalist countries) into a humanist industrialism in which man and the full development of his potentialities—those of love and of reason—are the aims of all social arrangements. Production and consumption should serve only as means to this end, and should be prevented from ruling man.

17   To attain this goal we need to create a Renaissance of Enlightenment and of Humanism. It must be an Enlightenment, however, more radically realistic and critical than that of the seventeenth and eighteenth centuries. It must be a Humanism that aims at the full development of the total man, not the gadget man, not the consumer man, not the organization man. The aim of a humanist society is the man who loves life, who has faith in life, who is productive and independent. Such a transformation is possible if we recognize that our present way of life makes us sterile and eventually destroys the vitality necessary for survival.

18   Whether such transformation is likely is another matter. But we will not be able to succeed unless we see the alternatives clearly and realize that the choice is still ours. Dissatisfaction with our way of life is the first step toward changing it. As to these changes, one thing is certain: They must take place in all spheres simultaneously—in the economic, the social, the political and the spiritual. Change in only one sphere will lead into blind alleys, as did the purely political French Revolution and the purely economic Russian Revolution. Man is a product of circumstances—but the circumstances are also his product. He has a unique capacity that differentiates him from all other living beings: the capacity to be aware of himself and of his circumstances, and hence to plan and to act according to his awareness.

Discussion Questions

1. Identify some generalizations Fromm makes and the ways in which he supports them.

2. Does Fromm's argument appeal to logic, emotion, or ethics? Do you think his choice is effective? Why or why not?

3. To what extent does Fromm address the opposing perspective in his argument? Explain your answer.

4. Fromm wrote his argument over thirty years ago. Do you think it remains valid today? Explain your response.

5. How convincing is Fromm's idea of a Renaissance of Enlightenment and of Humanism as a solution? Explain your answer.

Writing Topics

1. Choose an emotion that typically has a bad reputation. Write a paper in which you make a case for it being a valuable emotion, as Ellen Goodman did with guilt.

2. Write a paper in which you examine the issue of privacy. For example, should gays come out of the closet? Should prospective students or workers be required to identify their disabilities (e.g., dyslexia) on application forms? Why are people so intent on invading others' privacy?

3. From whom do you think people acquire their beliefs and values: parents? other family members? friends? teachers? religious leaders? Ask people from your own generation and those from previous generations where they acquired their beliefs and values. Write a paper that examines not only where their beliefs and values come from, but where you think they *should* be derived.

4. Much has been written in the last decade or so stating that people's values have eroded. Do you agree with this assessment? What has contributed to the downfall or strengthening of values? Write a paper in which you discuss the research on this topic as well as your own perspective.

5. Select some of the current heroes of American youth. What do these heroes say about today's youth? Make a case that they are bad and detrimental or good and healthy role models.

6. Are people naturally competitive/jealous/curious/trusting (take your pick), or do you think it is an acquired trait? Consult the research conducted by psychologists, sociologists, and educators on the topic of innate versus learned behavior. Write a paper that supports your stand, using others' research to back up your own ideas.

7. Think about the role that peer pressure has on teenagers. Do you see a contradiction in teens wanting to be seen as individuals and yet succumbing to peer pressure, thereby canceling out any chance of being individuals? Examine this seeming contradiction in a paper.

8. In "What Are Our Real Values," Nicols Fox asks who should be responsible for "determin[ing] our values and decid[ing] how our society is going to work." In a paper that examines your own ideas, answer that question.

9. In "The Missing Element: Moral Courage," Barbara Tuchman discusses the role of education in helping to teach, encourage, and support standards and values. Do you see education as the culprit in what many perceive as an increasingly valueless society? In a paper that uses Tuchman's as a springboard, support your own perspective on this issue.

10. Gary Engle's essay examines the ways in which Superman is "so darned American." Choose another cultural icon that you think accurately reflects the American spirit, and write a paper in which you discuss how that icon represents what Americans value.

CHAPTER 12

THE POWER AND POLITICS OF LANGUAGE

Time to Reflect on
Blah-Blah-Blah

Frank Trippett

Frank Trippett was born in 1926. He is the author of
Child Ellen (1975), *The First Horseman* (1974), and *The
States: United They Fall* (1987). In the 1980s, Trippett
was one of *Time* magazine's "Essay" columnists. In the
following viewpoint, which first appeared in *Time,*
Trippett offers his reflections on the useless chatter that
pervades American society.

1   Late in his career, Announcer Bill Stern made an endearing confession
about his vocal ways as the Christopher Columbus of television sportscasting. Said he: "I had no idea when to keep my big, fat, flapping mouth shut."
The insight dawned too late to be of much use to Stern, but it might have
been of value as a guide for his heirs. Unfortunately, nobody in the broadcast booth was listening. The result is the TV sports event as it is today: an
entertainment genre in which an athletic game must compete for attention with the convulsive concatenations of blah-blah-blah that passes for
commentary.

2   Television sportscasters, in short, are still a long way from mastering the
art of the zipped lip. It is this familiar fact that has legions of sports fans ea-
gerly looking forward to a special telecast of a football game that NBC has
promised for Saturday, Dec. 20. The teams and site (Jets *vs.* Dolphins at
Miami) are of little importance compared with the radical innovation that
will be the main attraction: the absence of the usual game commentary.
Thus the telecast will offer—and here Sports Columnist Red Smith leads
the cheers—"no banalities, no pseudo-expert profundities phrased in coach-
ly patois, no giggles, no inside jokes, no second-guessing, no numbing prat-
tle." Just one announcer will be on hand, says NBC to offer only the sort of
essential information (injuries, rulings) that a stadium announcer traditionally provides. The prospect is engaging, even if it may be shocking to see
a game presented merely for the sake of the drama on the field.

3   This blabber-proof telecast looms as far too rare an occasion to waste
only in joy over a trial separation from the stream of half-consciousness

that usually accompanies athletic endeavors on the tube. While sports fans will surely relish the moment, it should also be seized for grander purposes, for awareness may just be dawning in the Age of Communication that silence is indeed often golden. President-elect Ronald Reagan has so far, often to the chagrin of the press, shown an admirable reluctance to grab all of the many chances he gets to sound off on just about anything. Given the possible alternatives, Yoko Ono's fiat that John Lennon's passing be marked with ten minutes of silence around the world was inspired. In truth, the day of the telecast experiment would be a perfect time for the nation to reflect generally—and silently—on the whole disgruntling phenomenon of superfluous talk.

4   The American tendency to unchecked garrulity is most conspicuous in the realm of TV sports, but it does not begin or end there by a long shout. The late-evening TV news, for example, is aclutter with immaterial chatter. "Hap-py talk, keep talkin' hap-py talk . . ." Rodgers and Hammerstein offered that lyrical advice to young lovers, but a great many TV news staffers have adopted it as an inviolable rule of tongue. Hap-py talk is not reprehensible, but should it be force-fed to an audience looking for the news? Surely not, no more than a sports fancier tuning in football should be obliged to endure Tom Brookshier and Pat Summerall happily going over their personal travel schedules.

5   Admittedly, there is not likely to be universal agreement on precisely what talk is superfluous when. The judgment is aesthetic, and tastes vary. Some Americans might regard all sermons, lectures and political speeches as superfluous. Such testiness, however, can be shrugged off as a symptom of hyperactive intelligence. The criteria for talk should be appropriateness and pertinency. The essential question is: Does it subtract from or enhance the moment into which it falls? The deeper reason that sports commentary is annoying is that it so often ruptures the flow of the main event. The effect is easier to see when one imagines it occurring in the middle of a true drama. *Othello,* say:

6   *"Now here's the video tape again with still another angle on Iago as he evilly fingers Desdemona's hanky. And look! Iago is curling the old lip just a trifle. Nice curl too, eh, Chuck? This chap was learning lip curling when the rest of that cast couldn't find the proscenium arch with both hands. Incidentally, about that hanky—you know, the star himself bought that hanky for 79¢ at Lamston's just before opening when it turned out the prop man used the real thing as a dustcloth. Now back to the action onstage . . ."*

7   Existence today often means escaping from the latest Oscar award acceptance speech only to be trapped within earshot of a disc jockey who considers it a felony to fall silent for a second. Some 5,000 radio and TV

talk shows fill the air with an oceanic surf of gabble, a big fraction of it as disposable as a weather-caster's strained charm. It is easy to snap off and tune out, but it is not so simple to elude real-life blather. Try to get away from it all, and soon a stage-struck airline captain will be monologuing about terrain miles below and half-obscured by the cloud cover. Go to the dentist, and the procedure is all but ordained: thumbs fill the mouth, the drill starts to whine, and a voice begins to express all those unpalatable political opinions.

8   At the movies, it is usually the couple two rows back who turn out to be practitioners of voice-over chic, tenderly broadcasting all the half-baked thoughts they ever half-understood about Fellini. Dial a phone number and the absent owner's talking machine coughs a set piece of cuteness before granting a moment for you to interject a brief message. As for bridge players, the typical foursome hardly finishes the play of a hand before the air burbles with a redundant rehashing of it all.

9   Personality, roles and situations all work in the chemistry that induces excessive chatter. And certain subjects pull the stopper on even temperate people. Food, for example, instigates a preposterous quantity of repetitious chat. Sex? It has already provoked such as excess of discussion—functional and gynecological—that it is fair to rule all future comment on the subject may be surplus.

10   Cabbies and barbers have long been assailed for marathon talking, but it is unjust that they so often wind up at the top of the list of nuisances. Indeed, cabbies are often mute and sullen, and ever since barbers became stylists they have felt sufficiently superior to clients that their urge to talk has diminished.

11   To be nettled by untimely yakking does not imply the advocacy of universal silence. A rigorous discipline, silence is practiced by certain monks and others who believe that it heightens the soul's capacity to approach God. For ordinary people, a bit of silence may occasionally seem golden, but what they mostly need is the conversation that keeps them close to others. Those who do not get enough talk tend to wither in spirit.

12   Says Linguistics Scholar Peter Farb in *Word Play:* "Something happened in evolution to create Man the Talker." And a talker man remains, with speech his most exalting faculty. Talk is the tool, the toy, the comfort and joy of the human species. The pity is that talkers so often blurt so far beyond the line of what is needed and desired that they have to be listened to with a stiff upper lip.

Discussion Questions

1. Does Trippett provide a sufficient number of examples to support his main idea? Why or why not?

2. What do you think the people Trippett criticizes would say in their own defense? How does Trippett address potential attacks of his ideas? Explain your answers.

3. Describe the tone or voice of Trippett's viewpoint. Do you think it complements his perspective? Why or why not?

4. In the next to last paragraph, Trippett discusses the implication of an end to meaningless chatter. Does this paragraph seem a reasonable and thorough alternative or solution? Explain your response.

5. If you think that some professions' "unnecessary" talk is justified, identify them and support your reasoning. Do you think Trippett would defend their (over)use of talk? Explain your answer.

Bards of the Internet

Philip Elmer-DeWitt

Philip Elmer-DeWitt was born in Boston and received his education at Oberlin College, Columbia University's School of Journalism, and the University of California at Berkeley. Since 1982, Elmer-DeWitt has written about science and technology for *Time* magazine. As a staff writer for that publication, he has launched two new sections in the magazine: in 1982, "Computers" and in 1987, "Technology." In 1993, Elmer-DeWitt also spearheaded *Time* Online, the interactive edition of the magazine. Elmer-DeWitt has produced over four hundred news and feature stories on subjects ranging from in-vitro fertilization to computer sex. His *Time* magazine cover stories include "Computer Viruses" (1988), "Supercomputers" (1988), "Curing Infertility" (1991), "Cyberpunk" (1993), "Info Highway" (1993), "Video Games" (1993), "Human Cloning" (1994), "The Internet" (1994), and "Sex in America" (1994). In the following selection, Elmer-DeWitt questions why the quality of writing found on the Internet is so poor.

1   One of the unintended side effects of the invention of the telephone was that writing went out of style. Oh, sure, there were still full-time scribblers—journalists, academics, professional wordsmiths. And the great centers of commerce still found it useful to keep on hand people who could draft a memo, a brief, a press release or a contract. But given a choice between picking up a pen or a phone, most folks took the easy route and gave their fingers—and sometimes their mind—a rest.

2   Which makes what's happening on the computer networks all the more startling. Every night, when they should be watching television, millions of computer users sit down at their keyboards; dial into CompuServe, Prodigy, America Online or the Internet; and start typing—E-mail, bulletin-board postings, chat messages, rants, diatribes, even short stories and poems. Just when the media of McLuhan were supposed to render obsolete the

medium of Shakespeare, the online world is experiencing the greatest boom in letter writing since the 18th century.

3   "It is my overwhelming belief that E-mail and computer conferencing is teaching an entire generation about the flexibility and utility of prose," writes Jon Carroll, a columnist at the San Francisco *Chronicle*. Patrick Nielsen Hayden, an editor at Tor Books, compares electronic bulletin boards with the "scribblers' compacts" of the late 18th and early 19th centuries, in which members passed letters from hand to hand, adding a little more at each turn. David Sewell, an associate editor at the University of Arizona, likens netwriting to the literary scene Mark Twain discovered in San Francisco in the 1860s, "when people were reinventing journalism by grafting it onto the tall-tale folk tradition." Others hark back to Tom Paine and the Revolutionary War pamphleteers, or even to the Elizabethan era, when, thanks to Gutenberg, a generation of English writers became intoxicated with language.

4   But such comparisons invite a question: If online writing today represents some sort of renaissance, why is so much of it so awful? For it can be very bad indeed: sloppy, meandering, puerile, ungrammatical, poorly spelled, badly structured and at times virtually content free. "HEY!!!1!" reads an all too typical message on the Internet, "I THINK METALLICA IZ REEL KOOL DOOD!1!!!"

5   One reason, of course, is that E-mail is not like ordinary writing. "You need to think of this as 'written speech,'" says Gerard Van der Leun, literary agent based in Westport, Connecticut, who has emerged as one of the preeminent stylists on the Net. "These things are little more considered than coffeehouse talk and a lot less considered than a letter. They're not to have and hold; they're to fire and forget." Many online postings are composed "live" with the clock ticking, using rudimentary word processors on computer systems that charge by the minute and in some cases will shut down without warning when an hour runs out.

6   That is not to say that with more time every writer on the Internet would produce sparkling copy. Much of the fiction and poetry is second-rate or worse, which is not surprising given that the barriers to entry are so low. "In the real world," says Mary Anne Mohanraj, a Chicago-based poet, "it takes a hell of a lot of work to get published, which naturally weeds out a lot of the garbage. On the Net, just a few keystrokes sends your writing out to thousands of readers."

7   But even among the reams of bad poetry, gems are to be found. Mike Godwin, a Washington-based lawyer who posts under the pen name "mnemonic," tells the story of Joe Green, a technical writer at Cray Research who turned a moribund discussion group called rec.arts.poems into a

real poetry workshop by mercilessly critiquing the pieces he found there. "Some people got angry and said if he was such a god of poetry, why didn't he publish his poems to the group?" recalls Godwin. "He did, and blew them all away." Green's *Well Met in Minnesota*, a mock-epic account of a face-to-face meeting with a fellow network scribbler, is now revered on the Internet as a classic. It begins, "The truth is that when I met Mart I was dressed as the *Canterbury Tales*. Rather difficult to do as you might suspect, but I wanted to make a certain impression."

8   The more prosaic technical and political discussion groups, meanwhile, have become so crowded with writers crying for attention that a Darwinian survival principle has started to prevail. "It's so competitive that you have to work on your style if you want to make any impact," says Jorn Barger, a software designer in Chicago. Good writing on the Net tends to be clear, vigorous, witty and above all brief. "The medium favors the terse," says Crawford Kilian, a writing teacher at Capilano College in Vancouver, British Columbia. "Short paragraphs, bulleted lists and one-liners are the units of thought here."

9   Some of the most successful netwriting is produced in computer conferences, where writers compose in a kind of collaborative heat, knocking ideas against one another until they spark. Perhaps the best examples of this are found on the WELL, a Sausalito, California, bulletin board favored by journalists. The caliber of discussion is often so high that several publications—including the *New York Times* and the *Wall Street Journal*—have printed excerpts from the WELL.

10   Curiously, what works on the computer networks isn't necessarily what works on paper. Netwriters freely lace their prose with strange acronyms and "smileys," the little faces constructed with punctuation marks and intended to convey the winks, grins and grimaces of ordinary conversations. Somehow it all flows together quite smoothly. On the other hand, polished prose copied onto bulletin boards from books and magazines often seems long-winded and phony. Unless they adjust to the new medium, professional writers can come across as self-important blowhards in debates with more nimble networkers. Says Brock Meeks, a Washington-based reporter who covers the online culture for *Communications Daily*: "There are a bunch of hacker kids out there who can string a sentence together better than their blue-blooded peers simply because they log on all the time and write, write, write."

11   There is something inherently democratizing—perhaps even revolutionary—about the technology. Not only has it enfranchised thousands of would-be writers who otherwise might never have taken up the craft, but it has also thrown together classes of people who hadn't had much direct

contact before: students, scientists, senior citizens, computer geeks, grass-roots (and often blue-collar) bulletin-board enthusiasts and most recently the working press.

12   "It's easy to make this stuff look foolish and trivial," says Tor Books' Nielsen Hayden. "After all, a lot of everyone's daily life is foolish and trivial. I mean, really, smileys? Housewives in Des Moines who log on as VIXEN?"

13   But it would be a mistake to dismiss the computer-message boards or to underestimate the effect a lifetime of dashing off E-mail will have on a generation of young writers. The computer networks may not be Brook Farm or the Globe Theatre, but they do represent, for millions of people, a living, breathing life of letters. One suspects that the Bard himself, confronted with the Internet, might have dived right in and never logged off.

Discussion Questions

1.   Who do you think would be the most sympathetic audience for Elmer-DeWitt's viewpoint? How does he gear his ideas toward that audience?

2.   Explain how the sources Elmer-DeWitt quotes in his viewpoint strengthen his ideas.

3.   What do you think the "second-rate" writers to whom Elmer-DeWitt refers would say in their own defense?

4.   How well do you think Elmer-DeWitt addresses this question: Does anonymity afford computer network writers certain privileges or liberties not found in other writing arenas? Explain your answer.

5.   In what ways does the last paragraph soften Elmer-DeWitt's thesis? Evaluate its effectiveness.

ARGUMENT

Why Good English
Is Good for You

John Simon

John Simon was born in 1925. He started his career teaching at the Massachusetts Institute of Technology and Harvard University before becoming a drama and film reviewer. He has also worked as a language columnist for *Esquire* magazine. A theater critic for *New York* magazine, Simon is the author of *Paradigms Lost* (1980), a collection of essays on language and literacy he wrote while at *Esquire*. In the following article from that book, Simon argues the importance of people using correct English.

1   What's good English to you that . . . you should grieve for it? What good is correct speech and writing, you may ask, in an age in which hardly anyone seems to know and no one seems to care? Why shouldn't you just fling bloopers, bloopers riotously with the throng, and not stick out from the rest like a sore thumb by using the language correctly? Isn't grammar really a thing of the past, and isn't the new idea to communicate in *any* way as long as you can make yourself understood?

2   The usual, basic defense of good English (and here, again, let us not worry about nomenclature—for all I care, you may call it "Standard English," "correct American," or anything else) is that it helps communication, that it is perhaps even a *sine qua non* of mutual understanding. Although this is a crude truth of sorts, it strikes me as, in some ways, both more and less than the truth. Suppose you say, "Everyone in their right mind would cross on the green light" or "Hopefully, it won't rain tomorrow," chances are very good that the person you say this to will understand you, even though you are committing obvious solecisms or creating needless ambiguities. Similarly, if you write in a letter, "The baby has finally ceased it's howling" (spelling *its* as *it's*), the recipient will be able to figure out what was meant. But "figuring out" is precisely what a listener or reader should not have to do. There is, of course, the fundamental matter of courtesy to the other person, but it goes beyond that: why waste time on unscrambling simple meaning when there are more complex questions that should receive our

undivided attention? If the many cooks had to worry first about which out of a large number of pots had no leak in it, the broth, whether spoiled or not, would take forever to be ready.

3   It is, I repeat, only initially a matter of clarity. It is also a matter of concision. Space today is as limited as time. If you have only a thousand words in which to convey an important message it helps to know that "overcomplicated" is correct and "overly complicated" is incorrect. Never mind the grammatical explanations; the two extra characters and one space between words are reason enough. But what about the more advanced forms of word-mongering that hold sway nowadays? Take redundancy, like the "hopes and aspirations" of Jimmy Carter, quoted by Edwin Newman as having "a deeply profound religious experience"; or elaborate jargon, as when Charles G. Walcutt, a graduate professor of English at CUNY, writes (again as quoted by Newman): "The colleges, trying to remediate increasing numbers of . . . illiterates up to college levels, are being highschoolized"; or just obfuscatory verbiage of the pretentious sort, such as this fragment from a letter I received: "It is my impression that effective interpersonal verbal communication depends on prior effective intra-personal verbal communication." What this means is that if you think clearly, you can speak and write clearly—except if you are a "certified speech and language pathologist," like the writer of the letter I quote. (By the way, she adds the letters Ph.D. after her name, though she is not even from Germany, where *Herr* and *Frau Doktor* are in common, not to say vulgar, use.)

4   But except for her ghastly verbiage, our certified language pathologist (whatever that means) is perfectly right: there is a close connection between the ability to think and the ability to use English correctly. After all, we think in words, we conceptualize in words, we work out our problems inwardly with words, and using them correctly is comparable to a craftsman's treating his tools with care, keeping his materials in good shape. Would you trust a weaver who hangs her wet laundry on her loom, or lets her cats bed down in her yarn? The person who does not respect words and their proper relationships cannot have much respect for ideas—very possibly cannot have ideas at all. My quarrel is not so much with minor errors that we all fall into from time to time even if we know better as it is with basic sloppiness or ignorance or defiance of good English.

5   Training yourself to speak and write correctly—and I say "training yourself" because nowadays, unfortunately, you cannot depend on other people or on institutions to give you the proper training, for reasons I shall discuss later—training yourself, then, in language, means developing at the very least two extremely useful faculties: your sense of discipline and your memory. Discipline because language is with us always, as nothing else is: it follows us much as, in the old morality play, Good Deeds followed Everyman,

all the way to the grave; and, if the language is written, even beyond. Let me explain: if you can keep an orderly apartment, if you can see to it that your correspondence and bill-paying are attended to regularly, if your diet and wardrobe are maintained with the necessary care—good enough; you are a disciplined person.

6   But the preliminary discipline underlying all others is nevertheless your speech: the words that come out of you almost as frequently and—if you are tidy—as regularly as your breath. I would go so far as to say that, immediately after your bodily functions, language is first, unless you happen to be an ascetic, an anchorite, or a stylite; but unless you are a sty*lite*, you had better be a sty*list*.

7   Most of us—almost all—must take in and give out language as we do breath, and we had better consider the seriousness of language pollution as second only to air pollution. For the linguistically disciplined, to misuse or mispronounce a word is an unnecessary and unhealthy contribution to the surrounding smog. To have taught ourselves not to do this, or—being human and thus also imperfect—to do it as little as possible, means deriving from every speaking moment the satisfaction we get from a cap that snaps on to a container perfectly, an elevator that stops flush with the landing, a roulette ball that comes to rest exactly on the number on which we have placed our bet. It gives us the pleasure of hearing or seeing our words—because they are abiding by the rules—snapping, sliding, falling precisely into place, expressing with perfect lucidity and symmetry just what we wanted them to express. This is comparable to the satisfaction of the athlete or ballet dancer or pianist finding his body or legs or fingers doing his bidding with unimpeachable accuracy.

8   And if someone now says that "in George Eliot's lesser novels, she is not completely in command" is perfectly comprehensible even if it is ungrammatical, the "she" having no antecedent in the nominative (*Eliot's* is a genitive), I say, "Comprehensible, perhaps, but lopsided," for the civilized and orderly mind does not feel comfortable with that "she"—does not hear that desired and satisfying click of correctness—unless the sentence is restructured as "George Eliot, in her lesser novels, is not . . ." or in some similar way. In fact, the fully literate ear can be thrown by this error in syntax; it may look for the antecedent of that "she" elsewhere than in the preceding possessive case. Be that as it may, playing without rules and winning—in this instance, managing to communicate without using good English—is no more satisfactory than winning in a sport or game by accident or by disregarding the rules: which is really cheating.

9   The second faculty good speech develops is, as I have mentioned before, our memory. Grammar and syntax are partly logical—and to that extent they are also good exercisers and developers of our logical faculty—but

they are also partly arbitrary, conventional, irrational. For example, the correct "compared to" and "contrasted with" could, from the logical point of view, just as well be "contrasted to" and "compared with" ("compared with," of course, is correct, but in a different sense from the one that concerns us here, namely, the antithesis of "contrasted with"). And, apropos *different*, logic would have to strain desperately to explain the exclusive correctness of "different from," given the exclusive correctness of "other than," which would seem to justify "different than," jarring though that is to the cultivated ear.

10   But there it is: some things are so because tradition, usage, the best speakers and writers, the grammar books and dictionaries have made them so. There may even exist some hidden historical explanation: something, perhaps, in the Sanskrit, Greek, Latin, or other origins of a word or construction that you and I may very easily never know. We can, however, memorize; and memorization can be a wonderfully useful thing—surely the Greeks were right to consider Mnemosyne (memory) the mother of the Muses, for without her there would be no art and no science. And what better place to practice one's mnemonic skills than in the study of one's language?

11   There is something particularly useful about speaking correctly and precisely because language is always there as a foundation—or, if you prefer a more fluid image, an undercurrent—beneath what is going on. Now, it seems to me that the great difficulty of life lies in the fact that we must almost always do two things at a time. If, for example, we are walking and conversing, we must keep our mouths as well as feet from stumbling. If we are driving while listening to music, we must not allow the siren song of the cassette to prevent us from watching the road and the speedometer (otherwise the less endearing siren of the police car or the ambulance will follow apace). Well, it is just this sort of bifurcation of attention that care for precise, clear expression fosters in us. By learning early in life to pay attention both to what we are saying and to how we are saying it, we develop the much-needed life skill of doing two things simultaneously.

12   Put another way, we foster our awareness of, and ability to deal with, form and content. If there is any verity that modern criticism has fought for, it is the recognition of the indissolubility of content and form. Criticism won the battle, won it so resoundingly that this oneness has become a contemporary commonplace. And shall the fact that form *is* content be a platitude in all the arts but go unrecognized in the art of self-expression, whether in conversation or correspondence, or whatever form of spoken or written utterance a human being resorts to? Accordingly, you are going to be judged, whether you like it or not, by the correctness of your English as much as by the correctness of your thinking; there are some people to whose ear bad English is as offensive as gibberish, or as your

picking your nose in public would be to their eyes and stomachs. The fact that people of linguistic sensibilities may be a dying breed does not mean that they are wholly extinct, and it is best not to take any unnecessary chances.

13   To be sure, if you are a member of a currently favored minority, many of your linguistic failings may be forgiven you—whether rightly or wrongly is not my concern here. But if you cannot change your sex or color to the one that is getting preferential treatment—Bakke case or no Bakke case—you might as well learn good English and profit by it in your career, your social relations, perhaps even in your basic self-confidence. That, if you will, is the ultimate practical application of good English; but now let me tell you about the ultimate impractical one, which strikes me as being possibly even more important.

14   Somewhere in the prose writings of Charles Péguy, who was a very fine poet and prose writer—and, what is perhaps even more remarkable, as good a human being as he was an artist—somewhere in those writings is a passage about the decline of pride in workmanship among French artisans, which, as you can deduce, set in even before World War I, wherein Péguy was killed. In the passage I refer to, Péguy bemoans the fact that cabinetmakers no longer finish the backs of furniture—the sides that go against the wall—in the same way as they do the exposed sides. What is not seen was just as important to the old artisans as what is seen—it was a moral issue with them. And so, I think, it ought to be with language. Even if no one else notices the niceties, the precision, the impeccable sense of grammar and syntax you deploy in your utterances, you yourself should be aware of them and take pride in them as in pieces of work well done.

15   Now, I realize that there are two possible reactions among you to what I have said up to this point. Some of you will say to yourselves: what utter nonsense! Language is a flexible, changing, living organism that belongs to the people who speak it. It has always been changed according to the ways in which people chose to speak it, and the dictionaries and books on grammar had to, and will have to adjust themselves to the people and not the other way around. For isn't it the glory of language that it keeps throwing up new inventions as surf tosses out differently polished pebbles and bits of bottle glass onto the shore, and that in this inexhaustible variety, in this refusal to kowtow to dry-as-dust scholars, lies its vitality, its beauty?

16   Others among you, perhaps fewer in number, will say to yourselves: quite so, there is such a thing as Standard English, or purity of speech, or correctness of expression—something worth safeguarding and fostering; but how the devil is one to accomplish that under the prevailing conditions: in a democratic society full of minorities that have their own dialects or linguistic preferences, and in a world in which television, advertising, and

other mass media manage daily to corrupt the language a little further? Let me try to answer the first group first, and then come back to the questions of the second.

17   Of course language is, and must be, a living organism to the extent that new inventions, discoveries, ideas enter the scene and clamor rightfully for designations. Political, social, and psychological changes may also affect our mode of expression, and new words or phrases may have to be found to reflect what we might call historical changes. It is also quite natural for slang terms to be invented, become popular, and, in some cases, remain permanently in the language. It is perhaps equally inevitable (though here we are on more speculative ground) for certain words to become obsolescent and obsolete, and drop out of the language. But does that mean that grammar and syntax have to keep changing, that pronunciations and meanings of words must shift, that more complex or elegant forms are obliged to yield to simpler or cruder ones that often are not fully synonymous with them and not capable of expressing certain fine distinctions? Should, for instance, "terrestrial" disappear entirely in favor of "earthly," or are there shades of meaning involved that need to remain available to us? Must we sacrifice "notwithstanding" because we have "in spite of" or "despite"? Need we forfeit "jettison" just because we have "throw overboard"? And what about "disinterested," which is becoming a synonym for "uninterested," even though that means something else, and though we have no other word for "disinterested"?

18   "Language has *always* changed," say these people, and they might with equal justice say that there has always been war or sickness or insanity. But the truth is that some sicknesses that formerly killed millions have been eliminated, that some so-called insanity can today be treated, and that just because there have always been wars does not mean that someday a cure cannot be found even for that scourge. And if it cannot, it is only by striving to put an absolute end to war, by pretending that it can be licked, that we can at least partly control it. Without such assumptions and efforts, the evil would be so widespread that, given our current weaponry, we would no longer be here to worry about the future of language.

19   But we are here, and having evolved linguistically this far, and having the means—books of grammar, dictionaries, education for all—to arrest unnecessary change, why not endeavor with might and mind to arrest it? Certain cataclysms cannot be prevented: earthquakes and droughts, for example, can scarcely, if at all, be controlled; but we can prevent floods, for which purpose we have invented dams. And dams are precisely what we can construct to prevent floods of ignorance from eroding our language, and, beyond that, to provide irrigation for areas that would otherwise remain linguistically arid.

20   For consider that what some people are pleased to call linguistic evolution was almost always a matter of ignorance prevailing over knowledge. There is no valid reason, for example, for the word *nice* to have changed its meaning so many times—except ignorance of its exact definition. Had the change never occurred, or had it been stopped at any intermediate stage, we would have had just as good a word as we have now and saved some people a heap of confusion along the way. But if *nice* means what it does today—and it has two principal meanings, one of them, as in "nice distinction," alas, obsolescent—let us, for heaven's sake, keep it where it is, now that we have the means with which to hold it there.

21   If, for instance, we lose the accusative case *whom*—and we are in great danger of losing it—our language will be the poorer for it. Obviously, "The man, whom I had never known, was a thief" means something other than "The man who I had never known was a thief." Now, you can object that it would be just as easy in the first instance to use some other construction; but what happens if *this* one is used incorrectly? Ambiguity and confusion. And why should we lose this useful distinction? Just because a million or ten million or a billion people less educated than we are cannot master the difference? Surely it behooves us to try to educate the ignorant up to our level rather than to stultify ourselves down to theirs. Yes, you say, but suppose they refuse to or are unable to learn? In that case, I say, there is a doubly good reason for not going along with them. Ah, you reply, but they are the majority, and we must accept their way or, if the revolution is merely linguistic, lose our "credibility" (as the current parlance, rather confusingly, has it) or, if the revolution is political, lose our heads. Well, I consider a sufficient number of people to be educable enough to be capable of using *who* and *whom* correctly, and to derive satisfaction from this capability—a sufficient number, I mean, to enable us to preserve *whom*, and not to have to ask "for who the bell tolls."

22   The main problem with education, actually, is not those who need it and cannot get it, but those who should impart it and, for various reasons, do not. In short, the enemies of education are the educators themselves: miseducated, underpaid, overburdened, and intimidated teachers (frightened because, though the pen is supposed to be mightier than the sword, the switchblade is surely more powerful than the ferrule), and professors who—because they are structural linguists, democratic respecters of alleged minority rights, or otherwise misguided folk—believe in the sacrosanct privilege of any culturally underprivileged minority or majority to dictate its ignorance to the rest of the world. For, I submit, an English improvised by slaves and other strangers to the culture—to whom my heart goes out in every human way—under dreadfully deprived conditions can

nowise equal an English that the best literary and linguistic talents have, over the centuries, perceptively and painstakingly brought to a high level of excellence.

23   So my answer to the scoffers in this or any audience is, in simplest terms, the following: contrary to popular misconception, language does not belong to the people, or at least not in the sense in which *belong* is usually construed. For things can rightfully belong only to those who invent or earn them. But we do not know who invented language: is it the people who first made up the words for *father* and *mother*, for *I* and *thou*, for *hand* and *foot*; or is it the people who evolved the subtler shadings of language, its poetic variety and suggestiveness, but also its unambiguousness, its accurate and telling details? Those are two very different groups of people and two very different languages, and I, as you must have guessed by now, consider the latter group at least as important as the former. As for *earning* language, it has surely been earned by those who have striven to learn it properly, and here even economic and social circumstances are but an imperfect excuse for bad usage; history is full of examples of people rising from humble origins to learn, against all kinds of odds, to speak and write correctly—even brilliantly.

24   *Belong*, then, should be construed in the sense that parks, national forests, monuments, and public utilities are said to belong to the people: available for properly respectful use but not for defacement and destruction. And all that we propose to teach is how to use and enjoy the gardens of language to their utmost aesthetic and salubrious potential. Still, I must now address myself to the group that, while agreeing with my aims, despairs of finding practical methods for their implementation.

25   True enough, after a certain age speakers not aware of Standard English or not exceptionally gifted will find it hard or impossible to change their ways. Nevertheless, if there were available funds for advanced methods in teaching; if teachers themselves were better trained and paid, and had smaller classes and more assistants; if, furthermore, college entrance requirements were heightened and the motivation of students accordingly strengthened; if there were no structural linguists and National Councils of Teachers of English filling instructors' heads with notions about "Students' Rights to Their Own Language" (they have every right to it as a *second* language, but none as a *first*); if teachers in all disciplines, including the sciences and social sciences, graded on English usage as well as on specific proficiencies; if aptitude tests for various jobs stressed good English more than they do; and, above all, if parents were better educated and more aware of the need to set a good example to their children, and to encourage them to learn correct usage, the situation could improve enormously.

26   Clearly, to expect all this to come to pass is utopian; some of it, however, is well within the realm of possibility. For example, even if parents do not speak very good English, many of them at least can manage an English that is good enough to correct a very young child's mistakes; in other words, most adults can speak a good enough four-year-old's idiom. They would thus start kids out on the right path; the rest could be done by the schools.

27   But the problem is what to do in the most underprivileged homes: those of blacks, Hispanics, immigrants from various Asian and European countries. This is where day-care centers could come in. If the fathers and mothers could be gainfully employed, their small children would be looked after by day-care centers where—is this asking too much?—good English could be inculcated in them. The difficulty, of course, is what to do about the discrepancy the little ones would note between the speech of the day-care people and that of their parents. Now, it seems to me that small children have a far greater ability to learn things, including languages, than some people give them credit for. Much of it is indeed rote learning, but, where languages are concerned, that is one of the basic learning methods even for adults. There is no reason for not teaching kids another language, to wit, Standard English, and turning this, if desirable, into a game: "At home you speak one way; here we have another language," at which point the instructor can make up names and explanations for Standard English that would appeal to pupils of that particular place, time and background.

28   At this stage of the game, as well as later on in school, care should be exercised to avoid insulting the language spoken in the youngsters' homes. There must be ways to convey that both home and school languages have their validity and uses and that knowing both enables one to accomplish more in life. This would be hard to achieve if the children's parents were, say, militant blacks of the Geneva Smitherman sort, who execrate Standard English as a weapon of capitalist oppression against the poor of all races, colors, and religions. But, happily, there is evidence that most black, Hispanic, and other non–Standard English–speaking parents want their children to learn correct English so as to get ahead in the world.

29   Yet how do we defend ourselves against the charge that we are old fogeys who cannot emotionally adjust to the new directions an ever-living and changing language must inevitably take? Here I would want to redefine or, at any rate, clarify, what "living and changing" means, and also explain where we old fogeys stand. Misinformed attacks on Old Fogeydom, I have noticed, invariably represent us as people who shudder at a split infinitive and would sooner kill or be killed than tolerate a sentence that ends with a preposition. Actually, despite all my travels through Old Fogeydom, I have yet to meet one inhabitant who would not stick a preposition onto the tail of a sentence; as for splitting infinitives, most of us O.F.'s are perfectly

willing to do that, too, but tactfully and sparingly, where it feels right. There is no earthly reason, for example, for saying "to dangerously live," when "to live dangerously" sounds so much better; but it does seem right to say (and write) "What a delight to sweetly breathe in your sleeping lover's breath"; that sounds smoother, indeed sweeter, than "to breathe in sweetly" or "sweetly to breathe in." But infinitives begging to be split are relatively rare; a sensitive ear, a good eye for shades of meaning will alert you whenever the need to split arises; without that ear and eye, you had better stick to the rules.

30   About the sense in which language is, and must be, alive, let me speak while donning another of my several hats—actually it is not a hat but a cap, for there exists in Greenwich Village an inscription on a factory that reads "CRITIC CAPS." So with my drama critic's cap on, let me present you with an analogy. The world theater today is full of directors who wreak havoc on classic plays to demonstrate their own ingenuity, their superiority, as it were, to the author. These directors—aborted playwrights, for the most part—will stage productions of *Hamlet* in which the prince is a woman, a flaming homosexual, or a one-eyed hunchback.

31   Well, it seems to me that the same spirit prevails in our approach to linguistics, with every newfangled, ill-informed, know-nothing construction, definition, pronunciation enshrined by the joint efforts of structural linguists, permissive dictionaries, and allegedly democratic but actually demagogic educators. What really makes a production of, say, *Hamlet* different, and therefore alive, is that the director, while trying to get as faithfully as possible at Shakespeare's meanings, nevertheless ends up stressing things in the play that strike him most forcefully; and the same individuality in production design and performances (the Hamlet of Gielgud versus the Hamlet of Olivier, for instance—what a world of difference!) further differentiates one production from another, and bestows on each its particular vitality. So, too, language remains alive because each speaker (or writer) can and must, *within the framework of accepted grammar, syntax, and pronunciation*, produce a style that is his very own, that is as personal as his posture, way of walking, mode of dress, and so on. It is such stylistic differences that make a person's—or a nation's—language flavorous, pungent, alive, and all this without having to play fast and loose with the existing rules.

32   But to have this, we need, among other things, good teachers and, beyond them, enlightened educators. I shudder when I read in the *Birmingham* (Alabama) *Post-Herald* of October 6, 1978, an account of a talk given to eight hundred English teachers by Dr. Alan C. Purves, vice-president of the National Council of Teachers of English. Dr. Purves is quoted as saying things like "We are in a situation with respect to reading where . . . ," and culminating in the following truly horrifying sentence: "I am going to

suggest that when we go back to the basics, I think what we should be dealing with is our charge to help students to be more proficient in producing meaningful language—language that says what it means." Notice all the deadwood, the tautology, the anacoluthon in the first part of that sentence; but notice especially the absurdity of the latter part, in which the dubious word "meaningful"—a poor relation of "significant"—is thought to require explaining to an audience of English teachers.

33   Given such leadership from the N.C.T.E., the time must be at hand when we shall hear—not just "Don't ask for who the bell rings" (*ask not* and *tolls* being, of course, archaic, elitist language), but also "It rings for you and I."

Discussion Questions

1.   Simon begins his argument with a series of questions. Do you think that he satisfactorily answers them in the rest of his paper? Why or why not?

2.   In what ways can Simon's argument be seen as classist, elitist, and one that privileges certain groups of people? To what extent does he defend his ideas against such a reaction in discussing opposing perspectives? Explain your responses.

3.   How convincing is Simon when he claims that "the preliminary discipline underlying all others . . . is your speech"? To what extent does the strength of his argument rest on his audience agreeing with that warrant? Support your answer.

4.   Simon claims that one of the benefits of good speech is a better memory. Does his logic persuade you of this claim? Why or why not?

5.   Are the people and institutions Simon blames for the problem of incorrect use of language responsible? Are others also to blame? Support your response.

Censorship in the Arts

Kymberli Hagelberg

Born in 1957, Kymberli Hagelberg was a student at the University of Akron before becoming a contributing editor to Scene, the largest entertainment weekly in Ohio. Currently an assistant editor at that magazine, she has published articles and reviews in such newspapers as the Cleveland *Plain Dealer* and the *Akron Beacon Journal,* as well as regional entertainment papers in Virginia and Pennsylvania. In the following selection, which originally appeared in *Scene,* Hagelberg takes a personal stand against censorship in the arts, entertainment, and the news media.

1   To paraphrase the headline of a recent full-page ad that appeared in both the *Akron Beacon Journal* and the *Cleveland Plain Dealer,* "I Am Outraged!" but for very different reasons than those listed by Donald Wildmon's American Family Association (the group which sponsored the advertisement).

2   I am outraged because of a growing trend toward supporting censorship of the arts, entertainment and news media. In this ad, the blame for the social ills of teen-age pregnancy, violence, drug abuse and crime is placed not with a neglectful, absent and sometimes abusive family unit, but "Where we [Wildmon and the AFA] think it belongs: with the members of the Boards of Directors of every major TV network, film, music and record company."

3   The arguments against this kind of cultural stormtrooping are as old as your high school civics teacher, but bear repeating. What individual or group among us has the right to choose what we see, read, listen to and talk about? Who among us is qualified to draw that line? For a society to be free, it must express itself freely.

4   How long might the Vietnam War have continued had we not been fed a steady diet of its horrors on the evening news? Would you really have believed it possible for a *United States citizen* to be brutally beaten by a gang of police officers if someone had not caught the act on video and made the image public? How many countless works of now cherished art would have

been lost if we would have heeded the first voices who claimed the work was sacrilegious or vulgar? How many nudes do you think might have survived the Victorians?

5   But you know all of this, and in a world that has become increasingly violent, exploitative and ugly, the lines between First Amendment Rights and good taste and community standards can admittedly seem a little gray at times. The truth is one man's trash is another man's art. As corny as it sounds, when one guy gets the job of choosing for the masses, that choice is often small-minded, petty and humorless, reflecting only the desires of the most vocal among us. And in case you haven't been listening, for the last twelve years it's been the voices belonging to Wildmon, Pat Buchanan, Jessie Helms, Dan Quayle and Tipper Gore and the PMRC who are most often heard above the din.

6   Though Gore and Helms are the easiest to spot, Wildmon is no less dangerous. You may remember him from his earlier success pressuring PepsiCo to withdraw their financial support from Madonna's "Like A Prayer" Pepsi commercial and its accompanying international tour.

7   Long before Dan Quayle decided to lambast "Murphy Brown" for her lack of family values, it was Wildmon who worked behind the scenes to dissuade advertiser backing of the series on the grounds that a single mother was an improper and immoral role model. The kind of piousness inferred by that kind of "my God/family/race/gender/religion is better than yours" posturing is the foundation upon which all the race/sex/etc. "isms" are built. The fact that Wildmon and the AFA can, under the guise of "protecting our children," incite a generation of adults to lay blame rather than face responsibility, is something for which we should all be outraged.

8   Among the evils that Wildmon currently seeks to rid us of are the television series "Saturday Night Live" (shown long after the bedtime of any child with an attentive/responsible parent), the R-rated (no one under 17 admitted without an adult) movie *Basic Instinct,* the NC-17 rating and any number of music videos and cable programs for which subscribers pay—programs that can be locked out of the home of the concerned viewer upon request. It is beyond dispute that some of these programs are adult entertainment, but since they are either shown at times or with restrictions that should ensure adult viewing, for whom are these self-appointed censors hoping to choose?

9   The answer, I'm afraid, is for all of us. For that, you bet I am outraged, both personally and professionally.

10   What gives Wildmon, the AFA, the PMRC and, by extension, even CSU's J. Taylor Simms the power to pressure companies and schools to censor what they exhibit or support through advertising is not an army of zealots bent on suppressing the First Amendment rights of a few shocking

performance artists funded by NEA grant money. *It is the tacit agreement of all of us who sit silently and, by our silence, give the impression that only Wildmon is outraged.*

11   What makes the call to censor so dangerous as well as outrageous is the widely-held notion that it seems to make so much sense, at first.

12   Under the banner of political correctness, even liberals agree that the line should be drawn somewhere. But again, where?

13   Foolishly, we all hope to silence anything that would insult or embarrass us. Women across the country wanted to ban the misogynist novel *American Psycho.* Gays reviled their depiction in *Basic Instinct,* and every male I know hated the way men were portrayed in *Thelma and Louise.*

14   It is natural for thinking men and women to want to deny racism, shout down those who would glorify abuse and sensationalize sex and violence in their most explicit and aberrant forms. That is human nature and Wildmon's strength.

15   If you believe in the First Amendment, it's important to remember that what most censors really want is to silence *your* voice, not theirs. Why else would a lot of the same people who think the comic book violence of *The Terminator* too explicit for children not object to commercials showing an aborted fetus to those same children during the "family hour?"

16   The only safe or sane place to draw a line is in the heart and mind of every individual.

17   As surely as it is Wildmon's right to express *his* view, it's our responsibility to express *ours.*

18   Speak out. Fight censorship. If you believe in free expression, offer your support to the same television networks, movie studios and record labels that will receive their protests.

19   The only real outrage would be if the voice of censorship were the only voice heard.

Discussion Questions

1.   Hagelberg centers her argument around two questions: What individual or group among us has the right to choose what we see, read, listen to, or talk about? Who among us is qualified to draw the line? Discuss how well she answers those questions.

2.   What do you think Hagelberg's opponents (for example, Donald Wildmon, Pat Buchanan, Jesse Helms, Dan Quayle, and Tipper Gore) would find as the main flaw in her argument?

3. Which of Hagelberg's ideas in support of her argument do you find most convincing? Which are the least convincing? Why?

4. Does Hagelberg's argument appeal to reason, emotion, or ethics? Cite specific examples to support your answer.

5. Hagelberg poses many questions in her argument, some of which are statements in the guise of questions. Identify some and explain how effective you find her use of rhetorical questions.

In Defense of the N Word

J. Clinton Brown

> Born in 1959, J. Clinton Brown earned his B.A. degree
> from the University of Virginia. His work has appeared
> in such publications as *Advertising Age, USA Week-
> end,* and the *Richmond Times-Dispatch.* Currently,
> Brown manages advertising and public relations for a
> national medical products distributor. The following
> selection first appeared in a 1993 issue of *Essence*
> magazine. In it, Brown makes a case for not totally ban-
> ning the use of the word *nigger.*

1 I was casually talking to a friend on the phone when she interrupted me. "Define that," she said in a serious tone. "What?" I asked, completely confused. "That word you just used, define it."

2   The conversation ground to a halt as I, panic-stricken, searched my short-term memory for some sexist remark I might have let slip. I was relieved, if a little exasperated, to find that the problem was not gender, but jargon: I had spoken the *N* word: nigger. Girlfriend wasn't having it!

3   She suggested that I look up the "definition." I quickly resumed my story before we got bogged down in Funk & Wagnalls.

4   I'm seeing this scene played out more and more. Conversation is flowing, somebody's laughing, then, uh-oh, there it is—that word. And the music stops as someone steps onstage to strut their "consciousness."

5   When they indignantly ask for a definition, I know they've missed the point. Slang does not define, it evokes—or provokes. It does not denote, it connotes. It resists literalism and cares little for etymology. When the word in Webster's can't contain your idea, stretch it around both ends and put a pin in the middle. Let it snap back on the unsuspecting. If someone throws a word at you, grab it, transform it, make it your own.

6   African-Americans have a talent for this. So I find it sad that among the most privileged and best educated generation are many who believe that being politically correct means being culturally stilted.

7   Banning the *N* word from our conversations with one another should not be a high priority. Even if we all agreed to the prohibition, the effect

would be nil. Crack dealers wouldn't run for cover. That ugly virus would not mutate into something harmless. David Duke wouldn't change his ideology because we tightened our terminology.

8   Some armchair psychologists drop theories about damage to self-image. In my book, such shallow intellectualizing ignores the complexity and subtlety of African-American thought and speech. I have heard the word "niggah" (note the spelling, dig the sound) all of my life. Many of my elders and friends use it with phenomenal eloquence. They say it to express amusement, incredulity, disgust or affection. There people are very much about being themselves—proudly, intensely, sometimes loudly.

9   Others argue that we cannot expect "them" to stop using it until we do. Wake up! The racists in white America will use whatever derogatory term suits them. They do not care about our intracommunity resolutions. That reasoning seems to spring from the same adolescent urge that gave us "It's a Black thang. You wouldn't understand." Did I miss that meeting? Who started the rumor that white people are trying to "understand"?

10   This N word debate is another symptom of our condition. The discussion of "Black" versus "African-American" reflects the same struggle for self-determination, an effort sustained by the hard, luminous spirit that has survived every evil from the Middle Passage to the Los Angeles Police Department.

11   Here, too, some people lose the point in the fog of their passion. Lately many of us have started using "African-American" with much clenched-fist attitude, but some people have been using it interchangeably with "Black" for years. After all, the term is not so much political as it is simple anthropology. How else can you accurately describe that portion of the African diaspora living in the United States? Even that quiet realization has the power to change people.

12   Still, there may be one more step in this evolution. A decade ago, a sister I know decided to cut it to the bone and call herself African—no modifier, no qualifier, no middleman. African. Lawd, you should'a heard the Black folks gasp.

13   So a humble suggestion for those of us who disapprove of the N word: Chill. The next time someone as "cullud" as I uses it in your presence, don't raise your eyebrows or try to raise their consciousness with some jive science. Just politely express your objection. I, for one, will sincerely apologize, substitute an inoffensive term and continue my discourse. It's a courtesy thang. We should all understand.

Discussion Questions

1. Brown wrote "In Defense of the *N* Word" for *Essence*, a magazine whose audience is primarily African American. Given his audience, what assumptions do you think he made when writing his argument? Do they strengthen or weaken the overall effect?

2. Which of Brown's supporting ideas seem the most convincing to you? Which the least? Explain your answers.

3. What do you think opponents to Brown's argument would say to defend their position? Explain how well Brown addresses his opposition.

4. Do you think that words have the power to create or reinforce racism or are they a byproduct of it? From having read his argument, how do you think Brown would respond? Explain your answer.

5. Do you think Brown is being unusually naive or simplistic in his thinking? Why or why not?

If Black English Isn't a Language, Tell Me, What Is?

James Baldwin

James Baldwin was born in 1924 and died in 1987. He began his writing career in Paris in 1948. A prolific novelist and playwright, Baldwin's most famous works include *Go Tell It on the Mountain* (1953), *Notes of a Native Son* (1955), *The Fire Next Time* (1963), *No Name in the Street* (1972), and *The Price of the Ticket* (1985). In the following essay, which first appeared in *The New York Times* in 1979, Baldwin discusses the political ramifications of language, focusing on the ways in which black English has represented the perennial struggle between blacks and whites.

1   The argument concerning the use, or the status, or the reality, of black English is rooted in American history and has absolutely nothing to do with the question the argument supposes itself to be posing. The argument has nothing to do with language itself but with the *role* of language. Language, incontestably, reveals the speaker. Language, also, far more dubiously, is meant to define the other—and, in this case, the other is refusing to be defined by a language that has never been able to recognize him.

2   People evolve a language in order to describe and thus control their circumstances, or in order not to be submerged by a reality that they cannot articulate. (And, if they cannot articulate it, they *are* submerged.) A Frenchman living in Paris speaks a subtly and crucially different language from that of the man living in Marseilles; neither sounds very much like a man living in Quebec; and they would all have great difficulty in apprehending what the man from Guadeloupe, or Martinique, is saying, to say nothing of the man from Senegal—although the "common" language of all these areas is French. But each has paid, and is paying, a different price for this "common" language, in which, as it turns out, they are not saying, and cannot be saying, the same things: They each have very different realities to articulate, or control.

3   What joins all languages, and all men, is the necessity to confront life, in order, not inconceivably, to outwit death: The price for this is the

acceptance, and achievement, of one's temporal identity. So that, for example, though it is not taught in the schools (and this has the potential of becoming a political issue) the south of France still clings to its ancient and musical Provençal, which resists being described as a "dialect." And much of the tension in the Basque countries, and in Wales, is due to the Basque and Welsh determination not to allow their languages to be destroyed. This determination also feeds the flames in Ireland for among the many indignities the Irish have been forced to undergo at English hands is the English contempt for their language.

4   It goes without saying, then, that language is also a political instrument, means, and proof of power. It is the most vivid and crucial key to identity: it reveals the private identity, and connects one with, or divorces one from, the larger, public, or communal identity. There have been, and are, times, and places, when to speak a certain language could be dangerous, even fatal. Or, one may speak the same language, but in such a way that one's antecedents are revealed, or (one hopes) hidden. This is true in France, and is absolutely true in England: The range (and reign) of accents on that damp little island make England coherent for the English and totally incomprehensible for everyone else. To open your mouth in England is (if I may use black English) to "put your business in the street": You have confessed your parents, your youth, your school, your salary, your self-esteem, and, alas, your future.

5   Now, I do not know what white Americans would sound like if there had never been any black people in the United States, but they would not sound the way they sound. *Jazz*, for example, is a very specific sexual term, as in *jazz me, baby*, but white people purified it into the Jazz Age. *Sock it to me*, which means, roughly, the same thing, has been adopted by Nathaniel Hawthorne's descendants with no qualms or hesitations at all, along with *let it all hang out* and *right on! Beat to his socks*, which was once the black's most total and despairing image of poverty, was transformed into a thing called the Beat Generation, which phenomenon was, largely, composed of *uptight*, middle-class white people, imitating poverty, trying to *get down*, to get *with it*, doing their *thing*, doing their despairing best to be *funky*, which we, the blacks, never dreamed of doing—we *were* funky, baby, like *funk* was going out of style.

6   Now, no one can eat his cake, and have it, too, and it is late in the day to attempt to penalize black people for having created a language that permits the nation its only glimpse of reality, a language without which the nation would be even more *whipped* than it is.

7   I say that this present skirmish is rooted in American history, and it is. Black English is the creation of the black diaspora. Blacks came to the United States chained to each other, but from different tribes: Neither could

speak the other's language. If two black people, at that bitter hour of the world's history, had been able to speak to each other, the institution of chattel slavery could never have lasted as long as it did. Subsequently, the slave was given, under the eye, and the gun, of his master, Congo Square, and the Bible—or, in other words, and under these conditions, the slave began the formation of the black church, and it is within this unprecedented tabernacle that black English began to be formed. This was not, merely, as in the European example, the adoption of a foreign tongue, but an alchemy that transformed ancient elements into a new language: A *language comes into existence by means of brutal necessity, and the rules of the language are dictated by what the language must convey.*

8   There was a moment, in time, and in this place, when my brother, or my mother, or my father, or my sister, had to convey to me, for example, the danger in which I was standing from the white man standing just behind me, and to convey this with a speed, and in a language, that the white man could not possibly understand, and that, indeed, he cannot understand, until today. He cannot afford to understand it. This understanding would reveal to him too much about himself, and smash that mirror before which he has been frozen for so long.

9   Now, if this passion, this skill, this (to quote Toni Morrison) "sheer intelligence," this incredible music, the mighty achievement of having brought a people utterly unknown to, or despised by "history"—to have brought this people to their present, troubled, troubling, and unassailable and unanswerable place—if this absolutely unprecedented journey does not indicate that black English is a language, I am curious to know what definition of language is to be trusted.

10   A people at the center of the Western world, and in the midst of so hostile a population, has not endured and transcended by means of what is patronizingly called a "dialect." We, the blacks, are in trouble, certainly, but we are not doomed, and we are not inarticulate because we are not compelled to defend a morality that we know to be a lie.

11   The brutal truth is that the bulk of the white people in America never had any interest in educating black people, except as this could serve white purposes. It is not the black child's language that is in question, it is not his language that is despised: It is his experience. A child cannot be taught by anyone who despises him, and a child cannot afford to be fooled. A child cannot be taught by anyone whose demand, essentially, is that the child repudiate his experience, and all that gives him sustenance, and enter a limbo in which he will no longer be black, and in which he knows that he can never become white. Black people have lost too many black children that way.

12   And, after all, finally, in a country with standards so untrustworthy, a
country that makes heroes of so many criminal mediocrities, a country unable to face why so many of the nonwhite are in prison, or on the needle, or
standing, futureless, in the streets—it may very well be that both the child,
and his elder, have concluded that they have nothing whatever to learn
from the people of a country that has managed to learn so little.

Discussion Questions

1. Baldwin claims that black English is a bona fide language.
    Which of his reasons in support of his argument are the
    strongest? Which are the weakest? Explain your answers.

2. What do you think Baldwin's opponents would say in their
    own defense? How well does Baldwin rebut opposing perspec-
    tives? Explain your answers.

3. Describe the tone or voice of Baldwin's argument. How does it
    complement his ideas?

4. Why do you think Baldwin regards the term *dialect* as patroniz-
    ing? How does this idea affect the strength of his argument?
    Explain your response.

5. Discuss how do you think J. Clinton Brown would respond to
    Baldwin's argument.

WRITING TOPICS

1. Although some writers in this chapter (Frank Trippett, Philip
    Elmer-DeWitt, and John Simon) criticize people's use of lan-
    guage, do you think they are being too critical and finding fault
    with something of little substance? Is there another way of ana-
    lyzing people's use of language, perhaps as more interesting and
    reflective of the speaker and writer? In other words, why has
    people's use of language become such an issue? Examine this
    topic in a paper that focuses on language use and whose audi-
    ence is Trippett, Elmer-DeWitt, and Simon.

2. In "Why Good English Is Good for You," John Simon indicates
    that people who speak correctly are "cultivated," "civilized,"
    "orderly," and "educated" and that some minorities speak the

way they do because of ignorance. Write a paper in which you take the opposing stance, arguing that the cause and effect relationships Simon offers are erroneous.

3.   Research the First Amendment, which supports free speech. Do you support the First Amendment unequivocally, or do you think it needs to be modified as we approach the twenty-first century? Write a paper that addresses these questions.

4.   Do you or the people with whom you associate use ethnic slurs or sexist language? If your answer is yes, explain why you use them. Imagine your audience as members of the ethnic groups or gender you are insulting. If your answer is no, explain why you don't use them. Imagine your audience as people who do, and your goal is to persuade them to stop.

5.   In a paper, discuss the following question: Does language have the power to influence people's thinking? Cite specific examples to support your stance.

6.   As an African American, J. Clinton Brown takes a surprising stance in "In Defense of the *N* Word." Can you think of other words you think should or should not be banned? What are they? Support your position to an audience who disagrees with your position. Be sure to address the ideas that support their stance.

7.   Explain what you see as the relationship between language and politics. Use the arguments posed by the authors in this chapter to help you analyze the relationship.

8.   Some school systems have banned certain books from their curricula and libraries. Research the books that have been banned, and write a paper in which you support or refute the banning of the specific books in question.

9.   Think of certain types of dialects (or languages) that are widely used (for example, southern, creole, black English). Make a case that these variations enrich language and help to facilitate the speaker's meaning. Imagine your audience as people who disagree with your point of view. Consult the work of linguists to provide support for your ideas.

10. To what extent does a person's choice of language and style of writing have an influence on his or her thinking? In other words, is language a medium by which ideas are expressed or does a person's use of language help to create thought? Write a paper in which you take a stand and support it.

CHAPTER 13

MATTERS OF EQUALITY

Sizism—One of the Last "Safe" Prejudices

Sally E. Smith

Sally E. Smith was born in 1958 and earned a B.A. degree from the University of California/Santa Cruz. Her work has appeared in such magazines as *Radiance* and *Dimensions*. Smith is the executive director of the Sacramento-based National Association to Advance Fat Acceptance. In "Sizism—One of the Last 'Safe' Prejudices," which originally appeared in *The California Activist* in 1990, Smith discusses the ways in which overweight people are the victims of stereotyping and discrimination in employment, education, medical care, and public transportation.

1   As obscene as it sounds, a generation or two ago, Black people were considered to be inherently ugly, stupid, unsanitary, lazy, and enslaved by creature comforts. Today, fat people are assumed to be inherently ugly, stupid, unsanitary, lazy, and enslaved by creature comforts. Such stereotypes are reinforced by both the media and the public. Even in "politically correct" circles, where one would never hear derogatory remarks about people of color, gays and lesbians, or people with disabilities, one continues to hear disparaging remarks about fat people.

2   Stereotypes, and the resulting prejudice, develop from a belief that a group of people share common characteristics. This belief is almost always grounded in myth. The central myth surrounding the prejudice against fat people is that, if fat people really wanted to, they could lose weight. It doesn't seem to matter that research indicates that fat people are fat because of heredity and metabolic factors; that 95–98 percent of all diets fail within three to five years; that much of the $33 billion that the diet industry earns annually comes at the expense of the health and well being of fat people; that more people will die from weight loss surgery than died in the Vietnam War; that yo-yo dieting makes a person fatter; that most fat people have no more choice in their size than a person does in the color of their skin. Our society, which accepts that in the bell curve of the human

species, some people will be shorter or taller than average, and some people will be thinner than average, cannot accept that some people will be fatter than average.

3   This climate of nonacceptance creates a "blame the victim" mentality, wherein myths and stereotypes are used to justify treating fat people as second-class citizens. This has a devastating effect on the quality of life for fat people. Fat people are discriminated against in employment, in that they are denied employment, denied promotions and raises, denied benefits, and sometimes fired, all because of their weight. Fat people are discriminated against in education, in that they are not accepted into graduate programs, and are harassed and expelled because of their weight. Fat people cannot adopt children, solely because of their weight. Fat people are denied access to adequate medical care, in that they are denied treatment, misdiagnosed, harassed, and treated as though every medical condition, from a sore throat to a broken bone, is a weight-related condition. Fat people are denied access to public accommodations, such as public transportation, airline travel, theatres, and restaurants because seating is not available for them.

4   Because fat people are fair game for ridicule and public humiliation, they face substantial social discrimination. Epithets are screamed at fat people; ice cream cones are snatched out of the hands of fat people "for their own good"; fat people are run off of public beaches and out of health spas, because they do not look "acceptable."

5   This discrimination takes an enormous toll on a fat person's self-esteem, particularly when the person is a child. Unlike children in many other oppressed groups, fat children get little support from parents, teachers, or peers; instead of receiving support from her parents or teachers when other children make sizist remarks, a fat child will often be told, "If only you lost weight, you wouldn't have this problem."

6   Research has documented that women are most often the victims of size discrimination. Perhaps this is because men have traditionally garnered credibility through the power and wealth they accumulate, and women have garnered credibility through how closely they conform to society's ideals of beauty. Size discrimination is therefore linked to sexism. Because women of certain ethnic groups tend to be fatter than white women, size discrimination is linked to racism. Because women get fatter as they get older (a physiological phenomena), size discrimination is linked to ageism. Because lower income women tend to be fatter than higher income women, size discrimination is linked to classism. There should be no doubt that size discrimination is a feminist issue.

7   In most places, discrimination against fat people is perfectly legal. Currently, there is only one state, Michigan, which has a statute prohibiting size discrimination. And there are only a few cities which have ordinances

prohibiting discrimination based on personal appearance. When a fat person decides to fight size discrimination, she most often has to litigate using disability rights laws. But the truth is, while some fat people are disabled, most fat people aren't disabled, leading some courts to create a Catch-22 for fat people. There was a case in Pennsylvania, for example, where the court said that even though the employer didn't want to hire the person because of their physical problems, those problems were not a handicap, and therefore the fat person was not protected by the handicap law. Can you have it both ways? "We're not hiring you because you're physically inadequate, but you're not protected because you are physically adequate."

8   Fat people desperately need statutory protection, both to raise their quality of life, and to ensure an avenue of redress should they be discriminated against. The words "height and weight" should be added as a protected category, so that an employer cannot arbitrarily dismiss a candidate or an employee because of her size. Schools and universities should not receive state or federal funding if they discriminate against fat people. High school curriculum dealing with civil rights movements should include the size acceptance movement. Training for teachers should include material to raise sensitivity about size issues, and school health care professionals should have accurate information about fat and health, and the self-esteem issues of fat children. There should be a mandate that every public building, from jury boxes in courtrooms to desks in schools, be accessible to fat people.

9   Neither the California Legislature nor Congress has taken an interest in size discrimination issues. A Congressional subcommittee is holding a series of informational hearings on regulating the diet industry. Legislation coming out of these hearings may give fat people some consumer protection, but will do nothing for problems of size discrimination.

10   Because this is a feminist issue, NOW should take a public stance against size discrimination. An anti-size discrimination resolution, first passed by California NOW at our 1988 Conference, will be considered at the 1990 National NOW Conference in San Francisco.

Discussion Questions

1. Smith likens people's thinking about overweight people to the way people once thought about blacks. How believable is this analogy?

2. Smith refers to overweight people as "fat." Do you think her choice of words was intentional? Why or why not? What effect does her choice of words have on the impact of her viewpoint?

3. Discuss which of Smith's supporting reasons seems the most convincing to you. Which is the least?

4. Smith links size discrimination to sexism, racism, ageism, and classism and concludes that it is a feminist issue. How credible do you find these connections, and what impact do they have on the strength of her viewpoint?

5. What do you think people opposing Smith's main idea would say in their own defense? Does Smith adequately address conflicting perspectives? Explain your answers.

Marriage as a Restricted Club

Lindsy Van Gelder

Born in 1944, Lindsy Van Gelder earned her B.A. degree from Sarah Lawrence College. She has worked as a reporter for United Press International and the *New York Post*. Van Gelder's many articles have appeared in such publications as *Esquire, Redbook, New York, Rolling Stone,* the *Village Voice,* and *Ms.* magazine, in which the following selection first appeared. Van Gelder is a freelance writer. The following selection examines the inequities of gays and lesbians not being able to marry.

1 Several years ago, I stopped going to weddings. In fact, I no longer celebrate the wedding anniversaries or engagements of friends, relatives, or anyone else, although I might wish them lifelong joy in their relationships. My explanation is that the next wedding I attend will be my own—to the woman I've loved and lived with for nearly six years.

2 Although I've been legally married to a man myself (and come close to marrying two others), I've come, in these last six years with Pamela, to see heterosexual marriage as very much a restricted club. (Nor is this likely to change in the near future, if one can judge by the recent clobbering of what was actually a rather tame proposal to recognize "domestic partnerships" in San Francisco.) Regardless of the *reason* people marry—whether to save on real estate taxes or qualify for married students housing or simply to express love—lesbians and gay men can't obtain the same results should they desire to do so. It seems apparent to me that few friends of Pamela's and mine would even join a club that excluded blacks, Jews, or women, much less assume that they could expect their black, Jewish, or female friends to toast their new status with champagne. But probably no other stand of principle we've ever made in our lives has been so misunderstood, or caused so much bad feeling on both sides.

3 Several people have reacted with surprise to our views, it never having occurred to them that gay people *can't* legally marry. (Why on earth did they think that none of us had bothered?) The most common reaction, however, is acute embarrassment, followed by a denial of our main point—

that the about-to-be-wed person is embarking on a privileged status. (One friend of Pamela's insisted that lesbians are "lucky" not to have to agonize over whether or not to get married.) So wrapped in gauze is the institution of marriage, so ingrained the expectation that brides and grooms can enjoy the world's delighted approval, that it's hard for me not to feel put on the defensive for being so mean-spirited, eccentric, and/or politically rigid as to boycott such a happy event.

4   Another question we've fielded more than once (usually from our most radical friends, both gay and straight) is why we'd want to get married in the first place. In fact, I have mixed feelings about registering my personal life with the state, but—and this seems to me to be the essence of radical politics—I'd prefer to be the one making the choice. And while feminists in recent years have rightly focused on puncturing the Schlaflyite myth of the legally protected homemaker, it's also true that marriage does confer some very real dollars-and-cents benefits. One example of inequity is our inability to file joint tax returns, although many couples, both gay and straight, go through periods when one partner in the relationship is unemployed or makes considerably less money than the other. At one time in our relationship, Pamela—who is a musician—was between bands and earning next to nothing. I was making a little over $37,000 a year as a newspaper reporter, a salary that put me in the 42 percent tax bracket—about $300 a week taken out of my paycheck. If we had been married, we could have filed a joint tax return and each paid taxes on half my salary, in the 25 or 30 percent bracket. The difference would have been nearly $100-a-week in our pockets.

5   Around the same time, Pamela suffered a months'-long illness which would have been covered by my health insurance if she were my spouse. We were luckier than many; we could afford it. But on top of the worry and expense involved (and despite the fact that intellectually we believe in the ideal of free medical care for everyone), we found it almost impossible to avoid internalizing a sense of personal failure—the knowledge that *because of who we are, we can't take care of each other*. I've heard of other gay people whose lovers were deported because they couldn't marry them and enable them to become citizens; still others who were barred from intensive-care units where their lovers lay stricken because they weren't "immediate family."

6   I would never begrudge a straight friend who got married to save a lover from deportation or staggering medical bills, but the truth is that I no longer sympathize with most of the less tangible justifications. This includes the oft-heard "for the sake of the children" argument, since (like many gay people, especially women) I *have* children, and I resent the implication that some families are more "legitimate" than others. (It's important to safeguard

one's children's rights to their father's property, but a legal contract will do the same thing as marriage.)

7   But the single most painful and infuriating rationale for marriage, as far as I'm concerned, is the one that goes: "We wanted to stand up and show the world that we've made a *genuine* commitment." When one is gay, such sentiments are labeled "flaunting." My lover and I almost never find ourselves in public settings outside the gay ghetto where we are (a) perceived to be a couple at all (people constantly ask us if we're sisters, although we look nothing like each other), and (b) valued as such. Usually we're forced to choose between being invisible and being despised. "Making a genuine commitment" in this milieu is like walking a highwire without a net—with most of the audience not even watching and a fair segment rooting for you to fall. A disproportionate number of gay couples do.

8   I think it's difficult for even my closest, most feminist straight women friends to empathize with the intensity of my desire to be recognized as Pamela's partner. (In fact, it may be harder for feminists to understand than for others; I know that when I was straight, I often resented being viewed as one half of a couple. My struggle was for an independent identity, not the cojoined one I now crave.) But we are simply not considered *authentic*, and the reminders are constant. Recently at a party, a man I'd known for years spied me across the room and came over to me, arms outstretched, big happy-to-see-you grin on his face. Pamela had a gig that night and wasn't at the party; my friend's wife was there but in another room, and I hadn't seen her yet. "How's M——?" I asked the man. "Oh, she's fine," he replied, continuing to smile pleasantly. "Are you and Pam still together?"

9   Our sex life itself is against the law in many states, of course, and like all lesbians and gay men, we are without many other rights, both large and small. (In Virginia, for instance, it's technically against the law for us to buy liquor.) But as gay couple, we are also most likely to be labeled and discriminated against in those very settings that, for most heterosexual Americans, constitute the most relaxed and personal parts of life. Virtually every tiny public act of togetherness—from holding hands on the street to renting a hotel room to dancing—requires us constantly to risk humiliation (I think, for example, of the two California women who were recently thrown out of a restaurant that had special romantic tables for couples), sexual harassment (it's astonishing how many men can't resist coming on to a lesbian couple), and even physical assault. A great deal of energy goes into just expecting possible trouble. It's a process which, after six years, has become second nature for me—but occasionally, when I'm in Provincetown or someplace else with a large lesbian population, I experience the *absence* of it as a feeling of virtual weightlessness.

10   What does all this have to do with my friends' weddings? Obviously, I can't expect my friends to live my life. But I do think that lines are being drawn in this "pro-family" Reagan era, and I have no choice about what side I'm placed on. My straight friends do, and at the very least, I expect them to acknowledge that. I certainly expect them to understand why I don't want to be among the rice-throwers and well-wishers at their weddings; beyond that, I would hope that they would commit themselves to fighting for my rights—preferably in personally visible ways, like marching in gay pride parades. But I also wish they wouldn't get married, period. And if that sounds hard-nosed, I hope I'm only proving my point—that not being able to marry isn't a minor issue.

11   Not that my life would likely be changed as the result of any individual straight person's symbolic refusal to marry. (Nor, for that matter, do all gay couples want to be wed.) But it's a political reality that heterosexual live-to-gether couples are among our best tactical allies. The movement to repeal state sodomy laws has profited from the desire of straight people to keep the government out of *their* bedrooms. Similarly, it was a heterosexual New York woman who went to court several years ago to fight her landlord's demand that she either marry her live-in boyfriend or face eviction for violating a lease clause prohibiting "unrelated" tenants—and whose struggle led to the recent passage of a state rent law that had ramifications for thousands of gay couples, including Pamela and me.

12   The right wing has seized on "homosexual marriage" as its bottom-line scare phrase in much the same way that "Would you want your sister to marry one?" was brandished twenty-five years ago. They see marriage as their turf. And so when I see feminists crossing into that territory of respectability and "sinlessness," I feel my buffer zone slipping away. I feel as though my friends are taking off their armbands, leaving me exposed.

Discussion Questions

1. Do Van Gelder's personal references strengthen or weaken her viewpoint? Explain your answer.

2. Explain which of the reasons Van Gelder provides for wanting to marry her female lover seem to be the most and the least convincing to you.

3. Does Van Gelder use reason, emotion, or ethics as a way to advance her viewpoint? Identify specific examples that support your response.

4. What do you think people holding opposing views would find as the main flaw in Van Gelder's thinking?

5. Describe the tone or voice of Van Gelder's viewpoint. How does it contribute to the believability of her thinking?

CLAIMING THE SELF

Leonard Kriegel

Leonard Kriegel was born in 1933 and educated at Hunter College, Columbia University, and New York University. A professor of English at City College of the City University of New York, Kriegel is the author of *The Long Walk Home* (1964), *Edmund Wilson* (1971), *Working Through: A Teacher's Journey in the Urban University* (1972), *Notes for the Two Dollar Window* (1976), *Of Man and Manhood* (1979), *Quilting Time* (1982), and *Falling into Life* (1989), from which the following selection is taken. In it, Kriegel examines the ways in which "cripples are second-class citizens."

1 I am not a physician; I am not a psychologist; I am not a sociologist; indeed, I do not work in any aspect of health care. But I am a man who has lived all but eleven of his years here on earth as a cripple, a word I prefer to the euphemistic "handicapped" or "disabled," each of which does little more than further society's illusions about illness and accident and the effects of illness and accident. For to be "disabled" or "handicapped" is to deny oneself the rage, anger, and pride of having managed to survive as a cripple in America. If I know nothing else, I know that I have endured—and I know the price I have paid for that endurance.

2 As a writer and as a teacher of literature, I believe that the essence of what we like to call the human condition is each individual's struggle to claim a self, to create an *I* stamped with his own distinct individuality. This affirmation of the self is what we seek in biography and autobiography. It may exist beyond our capacity to create it, beyond our habits and virtues and will—but not beyond our need. I have never met a man or woman who did not want to stake a claim to an identifiable *I*.

3 Of course, it is a tentative claim, existing within the confines of a world in which we are never truly at home. Our capacities as individuals are always being tested. Everywhere we go, we seek to affirm the separate self, the identifiable *I* who possesses the strength and courage to withstand whatever tests lie in wait. Although it may be immodest to state it openly, the truth is that no one has a greater right to claim that *I* than a man

who has wrested his sense of a separate identity from the very condition that threatened to declare his life as a man at an end. And however self-conscious and embarrassed I am about saying it, no one has a better right to claim that his sense of himself as a man has been seized from adversity than the cripple does.

4   Cripples are forced to affirm their existence and claim selfhood by pushing beyond those structures and categories their condition has created. On one level, this is what all men and women try to do. But in a culture that places such importance on the physical—however uncomfortable it may be with the actual body—the cripple's insistence on getting beyond the restrictions imposed by physical limitations is the kind of violent joining together of forces pulling in opposite directions that is characteristic of modern life.

5   It would be the most absurd nonsense to suggest that the cripple is envied by other Americans seeking to claim the *I*. No one *wants* to find himself the victim of disease or accident—no one, at least, who is rational. Anyone contemplating the prospect of spending the rest of his life in a wheelchair would exchange that fate for a normal pair of legs without a moment's hesitation. Ask me to give up the most visible symbols of being a cripple—in my case, the braces and crutches on which I walk—and I will jump at the chance. To insist on our capacity, to be willing to face the everyday risks that a cripple must confront simply to meet the world, to enjoy the sense of triumph that an *earned* mobility bestows—we can accept all this and yet hunger after what we lack. We can believe in our capacity to face whatever has to be faced; we can assume that we have paid a price for the existence we claim that others might not have been able to pay; we can think of ourselves as having confronted our fate even with such grandiose metaphors as Jacob wrestling with his angel. The one thing cripples cannot afford to do is to assume the luxury of lying to themselves.

6   Cripples are second-class citizens only because they are conscious of nothing so much as of the barriers the outside world places in their way. My hungers are invariably personal; the joys not tasted are joys not tasted *by me*. However simplistic my desires may seem to others, their significance is multiplied a thousand times by an imagination that knows what they are but has not been able to possess them. However absurd and childish they are as desires, I reach out and touch them in my imagination alone. And they are not abstract. They are available to any of those the distinguished social psychologist Erving Goffman labeled the "normals." That *they* should be able to touch them so easily, so unconsciously, infuriates me. For my life as a cripple tells me that a man should earn the self he claims. However successful I may be in the eyes of the world—and I certainly am, to use a phrase that should be burned out of the vocabulary, a man who has "overcome his

handicap"—I am always measuring what I have against what I want. How do I tell the normals that I still dream about being able to run on the beach with my young sons (both of them long since grown adults), that I sometimes lie awake at night thinking about swinging a baseball bat again, that even as I visualize what I would do were I suddenly given the legs of a normal I know that what I want to do would seem stupid and banal in his normal eyes? I want to kick a football, jump rope, ride a bike, climb a mountain—not a mountain as metaphor but a real honest-to-god mountain—ride a horse. I want to make love differently; I want to drive differently; I want to know my sons differently. In short, I want to know the world as the normal is privileged to know it.

7   These are not great feats, not even for the imagination to conjure up. They do not call for special skills or training. But they are what *I* want—what I have never tasted or else tasted so long ago that the memories have become one with the desire, locked in a permanent embrace. And such memories frame all that is absent from my life.

8   People struggle not only to define themselves but to avoid being defined by others. But to be a cripple is to learn that one can be defined from outside. Our complaint against society is not that it ignores our presence but that it ignores our reality, our sense of ourselves as humans brave enough to capture our destinies against odds that are formidable. Here is where the cripple and society war with each other. If we were satisfied to be held up for compassion, to be infantilized on telethons, we would discover that this America has a great deal of time for us, a great deal of room for us in a heart open to praise for its own generosity. We are not, like Ellison's black man, invisible in America. But the outline of the shadow we cast has been created not by us but by those who will find a way to see what they want to see rather than what is there. In what we call literature, as well as in popular culture, we are what others make of us. In literature as demonic as Shakespeare's Richard III or as wooden as Lawrence's Clifford Chatterley, on television as bathetic as the stream of smiling children paraded before our eyes as if their palsy were Jerry Lewis's reason for living, what we invariably discover is that our true selves, our own inner lives, have been auctioned off so that we can be palatable rather than real. We can serve the world as victim or demon, the object of its charity or its terror. But the only thing we can be certain of is that the world would prefer to turn a blind eye and a deaf ear to our real selves—and that it will do precisely that until we impose those selves on the world.

9   Years ago, this recognition led me to write an essay entitled "Uncle Tom and Tiny Tim: Some Reflections on the Cripple as Negro." But the situation of the cripple in American society today seems to me considerably less grim than I described it in 1969. Tiny Tim is not the only image the cripple calls

forth. The self wrested from adversity is a far more attractive image to be offered to society and ourselves.

10   And yet, society is more than a bit dubious about that image's validity. For if it honors what it sees as our suffering, it retreats before our need to define our inner lives, to speak of who and what we are. Society continues to need the ability to define us if it is to be comfortable with us. In its own eyes, it is society that defines our authenticity. I remember that when I returned at the age of thirteen from a two-year rehabilitation stay in a state home, my mother was immediately asked by the neighborhood chairman of the March of Dimes Campaign (this was in 1946, before the introduction of the Salk vaccine) to go from door to door to collect in the campaign's annual fund drive. It seemed somehow natural: My mother possessed a kind of subaltern authenticity, for she was the mother of a cripple. Her presence at the door was supposed to remind our normal neighbors that their charity had been *earned*. Any other individual going from door to door would not have seemed as believable.

11   And the truth is that my mother *was* more effective, for she, along with our neighbors, assumed her authenticity. For the next forty years, long after the disease that had crippled me had been wiped out as a threat by the development of the Salk and Sabin vaccines, my mother made her annual door-to-door pilgrimage for the March of Dimes. Her "success" as a collector of charity was directly attributable to the sense our neighbors had that she was "the genuine article." Indeed, the kind of fund-raising she was doing mixes the comic and the bathetic, and it remains characteristic of efforts of such groups as the Shriners to support hospitals. The Shriners sponsor an annual all-star college football game that displays the salable talents of college athletes while giving everyone—sponsors, hospital executives, fans, professional football scouts, and players—a substantial charity fix. "Let strong legs run so that weak legs can walk" is the game's slogan. I can think of no better illustration of how society defines cripples as their condition. And it does this through the simple strategy of remaining purposely oblivious to the feelings it inspires in them. A child who thinks of himself or herself as an object for the charity of others has been defined as dependent. Only a considerable act of defiance can possibly save that child from the fate of being permanently dependent. In January, 1968, vacationing in Florida with my wife and two small children, I drove past a large shopping center. Strung out in huge black letters against a white marquee was a sign: "Help Crippled Kids! See Stalin's Limousine! Donation: $1.00."

12   Now, this is the kind of material Nathanael West or Woody Allen might have done justice to, for it is genuinely funny, a most human denial of the human. But it is also a definition of cripples from outside, one that remains

the most formidable obstacle in their path as they push toward defining the self. They want to realize all that they can make out of their situation. Society, in turn, wants them to make it feel good. Even the act of reaching out for a real self is a challenge to what society tells cripples is their proper due. Their task is not only to claim a self but also to refuse to allow their pain to be marketed. The authenticity they must insist on is one that each person alone can create—not the cripple's nurses, not the doctors, not the teachers, not the social workers. For no one knows what his existence costs him as he does. No one has lived with the intimacy of his fears as he has. And no one understands better that the self's reality can be taken from the self's resistance. Better if Stalin's limo were laughed out of existence. Better if "Jerry's kids" forced Jerry to understand the immense psychological destructiveness of his telethons. Better if hospitals were viewed as a right to be paid for, not by charity, but by a rational society.

13   Part of me still hungers to perform those banal tasks that define the normal for all of us. But another part of me—perhaps the braver part—insists that the mark of a man is to acknowledge that he has been formed by the very accidents that have made him what he is. Perhaps the task of those of us who are crippled is to face honestly what the normal can choose to ignore, to take a chance on a conscious existence pulled from the remnants of disease or accident. Our condition is intense, our isolation massive. Society views us as both pariah and victim. We are pitied, shunned, labeled, classified, analyzed, and categorized. We are packed in the spiritual ice of a sanitized society in the hope that we can somehow be dealt with in some even more sanitized society of the future. Society will *permit* us anything, except the right to be what we can become. And yet without that right we cannot extricate ourselves from the role of supplicants for society's largesse.

14   If society is uncomfortable with us, it is not uncomfortable with what it can do for us. That shopping center sign was created for the same audience at whose doors my mother knocked. Those Jerry Lewis telethons are responded to by men and women who believe they are deeply concerned with "Jerry's kids." Those well-meaning Shriners in their silly hats interviewed at halftime do not intend to tamper with the cripple's need to establish a self. Accident and disease bring out the charitable in other men. They also bring out the sanctimonious and self-righteous in other men. What cripples discover they share is not physical condition—the differences among them are far more pronounced than the differences between white and black, Jew and Gentile, German and Italian—so much as it is the experience of having been categorized by the normal world. For the normals, we possess a collective presence. For if cripples prove themselves capable of defining their own lives, then what excuse can normals offer for

their failure? If cripples break with the restrictions placed upon their existence and insist that they will be what they have earned the right to be, then where does that leave the normals?

15   I do not wish to suggest that anyone is "better" for having suffered disease or disability. Nonsense does not cease being nonsense when it is cloaked in metaphysics or theology. All I mean is that cripples have no choice but to attempt to establish the terms and the boundaries of their existence, and that they should recognize that in choosing to do this they are going to offend those normals who have an interest in cripples remaining what they want to perceive. Only by turning stigma into strength can cripples avoid the categorization the normal world insists on thrusting upon them. "This is where I am because here is where I have placed myself." Only through scrupulous self-scrutiny can we hold up the ragged ends of our own existence and insist that the normals match our honesty with their own. In a mendacious time, during which what it really takes to become an authentic self has been buried beneath one or another variation on doing one's own thing, the cripple who chooses to be honest can at least keep faith with his wound.

16   Having already witnessed the power of chance and accident, cripples know that if the reconciliation of their needs with the world's actualities can lead to maturity, it can also lead to madness and despair and even suicide. Under the best of circumstances, maturity is not permanent. But when its necessity is dictated by disease or accident it is not only temporary, it is also what one is condemned to live with. Indeed, it can be said of cripples that they are condemned to adulthood. Every step one takes, every breath one draws, every time one makes love, crosses a street, drives a car, one lives out the terms of the adult's argument with responsibility for the self. The image of what one was or could have been smashes against the reality of what one is. And if one has accepted the rules of the game, then the sin of pride beckons—pride in performance, pride in one's capacity.

17   For there is a point at which the living on an everyday basis with that internal enemy who, as Ernest Becker wrote, unremittingly "threatens danger" leads to a certain haughtiness, perhaps even to a barely concealed sense of superiority to normals who have not been called upon to prove their selfhood. Our dirty little secret is the pride we may feel in a performance designed to impose the self on the world. For someone who has matched his or her will against possible destruction, the normal's frame of reference can seem comic, even banal, in the rhetoric it employs and the strategies it assumes. One who lives his daily life on intimate terms with pain can only listen in amazement to a sportscaster praising the courage of an athlete earning a great deal of money on enduring his "aching" knees.

18   But it is always within the power of the normals to diminish the cripples' sense of their own reality. We are, after all, trapped by the accou-
trements of our existence. An individual may choose to create an
authentic self out of defiance of accident or disease, but he cannot remake
the truth of his condition. It is what it is. No matter what demands he
makes upon himself, dead legs do not run and blind eyes do not see. The
cripple can make of his injury an acquisition; he can transform his handicap into a symbol of endurance; he can formulate his very existence as an
act of defiance. But he cannot change what has happened to him. He
must recognize that his life is to be different in its essentials from the life
of the normal person. He has learned to look on stigmatization itself as
something he has earned. He comes to recognize that he has truly been
set apart.

19   The process of recognition has been beautifully voiced in a poem by
Karl Shapiro. The poem is about a soldier's loss of his leg during the Second World War. At first the soldier struggles to accept the loss of part of
his body. The soldier discovers that he must learn to adapt to life without
the leg even as the life he possesses is transformed into an act of defiance
of the loss.

> Later, as if deliberately, his fingers
> Begin to explore the stump. He learns
>   shape
> That is comfortable and tucked in
>   like a sock.
> This has a sense of humor, this can
>   despise
> The finest surgical limb, the dignity
>   of limping,
> The nonsense of wheelchairs. Now he
>   smiles to the wall:
> The Amputation becomes an acquisition.

20   But the soldier in "The Leg" will ultimately discover that even such
hard-won acquisitions can be taken away by the society that insists on
defining who he is, a society that will remain intent on shrinking his reality by insisting on its right to define the limits of his space, the boundaries of his quest for a self. And the effort to live honestly will pinch his
sense of his own courage and test his ability to live on his own terms. For
what we remember remains embedded in what we are—and in what we
once were.

Discussion Questions

1. At the beginning of his argument, Kriegel describes his expertise and interest in writing about the topic. How effective do you find this opening? Would the argument have been less convincing had you not known anything about Kriegel's background?

2. What exactly is Kriegel arguing in his essay?

3. Where do you first find Kriegel's major claim? Is it in a good place? Why or why not?

4. Identify specific examples of Kriegel using the appeals of reason, emotion, and ethics in his argument.

5. Do you think Kriegel sees his audience as holding the same or opposing views that he has on crippled people? What leads you to your answer?

A Defense of Quotas

Charles Krauthammer

Charles Krauthammer was born in 1950 and holds a B.A. degree from McGill University and an M.D. from Harvard University. He has been an essayist for *Time* magazine since 1983 and a syndicated columnist for the *Washington Post* since 1985. A contributing editor to the *New Republic,* Krauthammer is the author of a book of essays entitled *Making Sense of the Eighties* (1985). In 1987, he was awarded a Pulitzer Prize for commentary from the Columbia University Graduate School of Journalism. The following selection first appeared in the *New Republic* in 1985 during the conservative Reagan administration. In it, Krauthammer argues for the need of affirmative action quotas to "redress . . . the historic injustice done to blacks."

1 As recently as three years ago Nathan Glazer noted with dismay the inability, or unwillingness, of the most conservative American administration in fifty years to do anything about the growing entrenchment, in law and in practice, of racial quotas. It seemed that officially sanctioned race consciousness was becoming irrevocably woven into American life.

2 Glazer's pessimism was premature. In the last two years a revolution has been brewing on the issue of affirmative action. It is marked not by the pronouncements of Clarence Pendleton, or the change in composition and ideology of the United States Commission on Civil Rights. That is for show. It is marked by a series of court rulings and administration actions that, step by step, will define affirmative action out of existence.

3 How far this process had gone was dramatized by the leak of a draft executive order that would outlaw in federal government contracting not only quotas and statistical measures but any "preference . . . on the basis of race, color, religion, sex or national origin . . . with respect to any aspect of employment." Although this appeared as a bolt from a blue August sky, it was, in fact, the culmination of a process that has been building over the last several years. It amounts to a counterrevolution in stages on the issue of race-conscious social policy.

4   The counterrevolution has occurred in what is probably the most crucial domain of affirmative action: employment. Classic affirmative action mandates preference for blacks (and women and other favored groups) at all four steps in the employment process: recruitment, hiring, promotion, and firing. The counterrevolution has attacked such preferences at each step of the way, beginning at the end.

5   The first major breach in the edifice of affirmative action was the Supreme Court's Memphis fire fighters decision of June 1984. The City of Memphis had been under a court-ordered consent decree to increase the number of blacks in the fire department. When layoffs came in 1981, a U.S. District Court ruled that last-hired blacks could not be the first fired, as the seniority system dictated. Three whites were laid off instead. The Supreme Court reversed that decision. It ruled that in a clash between a bona fide seniority system and affirmative action, seniority prevails.

6   You cannot fire by race. But can you promote? Can you hire? The next, more tentative, step in the counterrevolution occurred this past spring in the District of Columbia. A suit originally filed in the waning days of the Carter administration had resulted in mandated preferential hiring and promotions for minorities in the city's fire departments. In March the D.C. fire chief, according to one of the judge's directives in the case, ordered that five black fire fighters be promoted over whites who had scored higher than they had.

7   The union immediately filed suit to block the promotions. And the Justice Department joined the suit on the union's side. The judge in the case then rendered a Solomonic decision prohibiting race consciousness in promotion, but permitting it in hiring.

8   The case is under appeal and no one knows how it will come out. The reason is that no one knows how to interpret *Memphis*. Did this ruling apply only to layoffs, as suggested to civil rights groups trying to limit their losses? Or did it apply also to hiring and/or promotion, the other crucial career choke points? You can read *Memphis* either way, and everyone is waiting for the Court to say.

9   Everyone, that is, except William Bradford Reynolds, head of the Justice Department's Civil Rights Division, and leading *contra*. Reynolds is a conservative in a hurry. Invoking *Memphis* as his authority, he ordered fifty-one jurisdictions from New York to Los Angeles to cleanse existing consent decrees (which mandated goals—quotas—in hiring) of any hint of group or racial preference. Not only would preferences be outlawed from now on, but existing decrees would have to be revised to reflect the new dispensation.

10   Reynolds's target is to root out race consciousness in toto, from firing to promotion to hiring. Everything, it seems, except recruitment. Last June, at

the start of Reynolds's confirmation hearings for the number three job at Justice (he was eventually turned down), he sent a letter to Senator Edward Kennedy stating that he favored affirmative action in recruitment. He argued that it is the only permissible affirmative action; in fact, it is how you determine its success. Its success could be "measured," he wrote, "in the number of persons who are recruited to apply."

11   Recruiting, it seems, would be the last refuge for affirmative action. Or so it seemed, until the final step: draft executive order 11246 revising the affirmative action order that since 1968 has mandated race consciousness and statistical norms (quotas) in employment for government contractors. The draft executive order would repeal it all: goals, timetables, statistical norms, and other forms of racial preference.

12   It appears to do so even for Reynolds's cherished exception, recruitment. Hard to tell, though. The first section of the draft order seems to define affirmative action, as Reynolds likes to, as exclusively applicable to recruitment. "Each government contractor . . . shall engage in affirmative recruitment . . . to . . . expand[ing] the number of qualified minorities and women who receive full consideration for hiring and promotion." But the very next section continues: "Nothing in this executive order shall be interpreted to require . . . any preference . . . on the basis of race . . . with respect to any aspect of employment, including . . . recruitment. . . ."

13   Either the drafters are exceedingly careless, or the internal administration debate over whether to go the very last mile in eradicating race consciousness has yet to be decided. In either case, recruitment poses a logical problem for Reynolds & Company (if race consciousness is in principle unjust, how can it be O.K. for recruitment?). But it is not, in practice, a serious issue. If preferential treatment is outlawed for firing, promotion, and hiring, then recruitment really is the last mile: affirmative action expires long before it is reached. The administration and its civil rights opponents seem to agree that if this program—renegotiating the consent decrees and draft executive order 11246—is enacted, recruitment or not, race-conscious affirmative action is dead.

14   They disagree about whether that would be a good thing. Is race-conscious affirmative action worth saving?

15   There are three arguments in favor. The first, marshaled principally against Reynolds's revisionist consent decree is profoundly conservative. It says that at this late date, things are working out well, whatever the merits. Let well enough alone. The Justice Department would "disturb the acquiescence of the community in the new systems established after much travail and effort under the consent decrees," charged the NAACP. It will "threaten

social peace for the sake of ideology," said *The Washington Post*. "Don't stick your nose in cases that have already been resolved," said Representative Don Edwards, one of five representatives who wrote to the attorney general asking him to cease and desist.

16   The irony here, of course, is that the NAACP is relatively new to the cause of "settledness." Not always has it argued that justice should be deferred so as not to "disturb the acquiescence of the community" in existing social arrangements. That was the segregationist case. And in that case, it was argued, correctly, that although settledness and social peace have some claims to make, they cannot prevail over the claims of justice.

17   It works, argues William H. Hudnut, the Republican mayor of Indianapolis, of his city's consent decree setting aside a quarter of its police and fire fighting slots for minorities. Why fix what ain't broke?

18   Because justice is not interested in what's broke and what's not; it is interested in justice. Hence the second argument for affirmative action, the familiar argument that while color blindness may be a value, remedying centuries of discrimination through (temporary) race consciousness is a higher value.

19   Does the right of the disadvantaged to redress (through preferential treatment) override the right of individuals to equal treatment? *Memphis* and the D.C. fire fighters decision begin to parse the issue. The logic of these decisions is that in layoffs and promotion the aggrieved whites have, by dint of service, acquired *additional* individual claims that outweigh the historical claims of blacks. But what about unadorned individual claims? When hired you bring your citizenship with you and nothing else. Shouldn't that be enough to entitle you to equal, colorblind treatment?

20   It is not clear how to adjudicate the competing claims, that of a historically oppressed community for redress, and of the blameless individual for equal treatment. One side claims the mantle of—indeed, it defines itself as the side of—civil rights. But that is surely a semantic claim. The movement began, of course, as a civil rights movement. But when, for example, the D.C. Office of Human Rights declares that its primary mission is to ensure that blacks end up in city jobs in proportion "equal to their group representation in the available work force," the issue has ceased to be rights. It is group advancement.

21   The other side claims the mantle of individual rights and equal treatment. That is not a semantic claim. But it is not an absolute one either. After all, either by design or default, we constantly enact social policies that favor certain groups at the expense of others, the individuals in neither group having done anything to deserve their fate. One routine, and devastating, exercise in social engineering is the government-induced recession,

periodically applied to the economy to curb inflation. The inevitable result is suffering, suffering that we know well in advance will be borne disproportionately by the poor and working class.

22   Is this discrimination by class? Certainly. It is not admitted to be so, and it is certainly not the primary effect. But it is an inevitable and predictable side effect. Yet in the face of an overriding national priority—saving the currency—we adopt policies that disproportionately injure a recognized class of blameless individuals. (Similarly, the draft discriminates by age, the placement of toxic waste dumps by geography, etc. We continually ask one group or another to bear special burdens for the sake of the community as a whole.)

23   If controlling inflation is a social goal urgent and worthy enough to warrant disproportionate injury to a recognized class of blameless individuals, is not the goal of helping blacks rapidly gain the mainstream of American life? Which suggests a third, and to my mind most convincing, line of defense for affirmative action. It admits that the issue is not decidable on the grounds of justice. It argues instead a more humble question of policy: that the rapid integration of blacks into American life is an overriding national goal, and that affirmative action is the means to that goal.

24   To be sure, affirmative action has myriad effects. They even include such subtle negative psychological effects on blacks as the "rumors of inferiority" studied by Jeff Howard and Ray Hammond (TNR, September 9). The calculation is complex. But, it is hard to credit the argument that on balance affirmative action actually harms blacks. Usually advanced by opponents of affirmative action, this argument is about as ingenuous as Jerry Falwell's' support of the Botha regime out of concern for South African blacks. One needs a willing suspension of disbelief to maintain that a policy whose essence is to favor blacks hurts them. Even the Reagan administration admits (in a report sent to Congress in February) that executive order 11246 has helped skilled black men.

25   The Reagan counterrevolutionaries want to end the breach of justice that is affirmative action. A breach it is, and must be admitted to be. It is not clear, however, that correcting this breach is any more morally compelling than redressing the historic injustice done to blacks. In the absence of a compelling moral case, then, the Reagan counterrevolution would retard a valuable social goal: rapid black advancement and integration. Justice would perhaps score a narrow, ambiguous victory. American society would suffer a wide and deepening loss.

Discussion Questions

1. Explain the importance of Krauthammer providing background information on affirmative action.

2. Where in his argument do you first find Krauthammer's major claim? Do you think it is the best place he could have chosen? Why or why not?

3. What strategies does Krauthammer use in arguing his point? How effective do you find his choice of strategies? Explain.

4. What flaws do you think opponents of affirmative action would find in Krauthammer's argument? How well does he defend his position against counterarguments? Explain your answer.

5. Throughout his argument, Krauthammer poses many questions. What purpose do those questions serve?

Affirmative Action:
The Price of Preference

Shelby Steele

Born in 1946, Shelby Steele earned a B.A. degree from Coe College, an M.A. degree from Southern Illinois University, and a Ph.D. from the University of Utah. Steele is an English professor at San Jose State University in California. His work has appeared in such publications as *The American Scholar, Harper's,* and *The New York Times Magazine.* Steele is also the author of *The Content of Our Character: A New Vision of Race in America* (1990), which won the National Book Critics Circle Award in 1990. The following selection, taken from that book, examines Steele's conservative attitudes regarding affirmative action.

1   In a few short years, when my two children will be applying to college, the affirmative action policies by which most universities offer black students some form preferential treatment will present me with a dilemma. I am a middle-class black, a college professor, far from wealthy, but also well-removed from the kind of deprivation that would qualify my children for the label "disadvantaged." Both of them have endured racial insensitivity from whites. They have been called names, have suffered slights, and have experienced firsthand the peculiar malevolence that racism brings out in people. Yet, they have never experienced racial discrimination, have never been stopped by their race on any path they have chosen to follow. Still, their society now tells them that if they will only designate themselves as black on their college applications, they will likely do better in the college lottery than if they conceal this fact. I think there is something of a Faustian bargain in this.

2   Of course, many blacks and a considerable number of whites would say that I was sanctimoniously making affirmative action into a test of character. They would say that this small preference is the meagerest recompense for centuries of unrelieved oppression. And to these arguments other very obvious facts must be added. In America, many marginally competent or flatly incompetent whites are hired everyday—some because their white

skin suits the conscious or unconscious racial preference of their employer. The white children of alumni are often grandfathered into elite universities in what can only be seen as a residual benefit of historic white privilege. Worse, white incompetence is always an individual matter, while for blacks it is often confirmation of ugly stereotypes. The Peter Principle was not conceived with only blacks in mind. Given that unfairness cuts both ways, doesn't it only balance the scales of history that my children now receive a slight preference over whites? Doesn't this repay, in a small way, the systematic denial under which their grandfather lived out his days?

3   So, in theory, affirmative action certainly has all the moral symmetry that fairness requires—the injustice of historical and even contemporary white advantage is offset with black advantage; preference replaces prejudice, inclusion answers exclusion. It is reformist and corrective, even repentent and redemptive. And I would never sneer at these good intentions. Born in the late forties in Chicago, I started my education (a charitable term in this case) in a segregated school and suffered all the indignities that come to blacks in a segregated society. My father, born in the South, only made it to the third grade before the white man's fields took permanent priority over his formal education. And though he educated himself into an advanced reader with an almost professional authority, he could only drive a truck for a living and never earned more than ninety dollars a week in his entire life. So yes, it is crucial to my sense of citizenship, to my ability to identify with the spirit and the interests of America, to know that this country, however imperfectly, recognizes its past sins and wishes to correct them.

4   Yet good intentions, because of the opportunity for innocence they offer us, are very seductive and can blind us to the effects they generate when implemented. In our society, affirmative action is, among other things, a testament to white goodwill and to black power, and in the midst of these heavy investments, its effects can be hard to see. But after twenty years of implementation, I think affirmative action has shown itself to be more bad than good and that blacks—whom I will focus on in this essay—now stand to lose more from it than they gain.

5   In talking with affirmative action administrators and with blacks and whites in general, it is clear that supporters of affirmative action focus on its good intentions while detractors emphasize its negative effects. Proponents talk about "diversity" and "pluralism"; opponents speak of "reverse discrimination," the unfairness of quotas and set-asides. It was virtually impossible to find people outside either camp. The closest I came was a white male manager at a large computer company who said, "I think it amounts to reverse discrimination, but I'll put up with a little of that for a little

more diversity." I'll live with a little of the effect to gain a little of the intention, he seemed to be saying. But this only makes him a halfhearted supporter of affirmative action. I think many people who don't really like affirmative action support it to one degree or another anyway.

6   I believe they do this because of what happened to white and black Americans in the crucible of the sixties when whites were confronted with their racial guilt and blacks tasted their first real power. In this stormy time white absolution and black power coalesced into virtual mandates for society. Affirmative action became a meeting ground for these mandates in the law, and in the late sixties and early seventies it underwent a remarkable escalation of its mission from simple anti-discrimination enforcement to social engineering by means of quotas, goals, time-tables, set-asides and other forms of preferential treatment.

7   Legally, this was achieved through a series of executive orders and EEOC guidelines that allowed racial imbalances in the workplace to stand as proof of racial discrimination. Once it could be assumed that discrimination explained racial imbalances, it became easy to justify group remedies to presumed discrimination, rather than the normal case-by-case redress for proved discrimination. Preferential treatment through quotas, goals, and so on is designed to correct imbalances based on the assumption that they always indicate discrimination. This expansion of what constitutes discrimination allowed affirmative action to escalate into the business of social engineering in the name of anti-discrimination, to push society toward statistically proportionate racial representation, without any obligation of proving actual discrimination.

8   What accounted for this shift, I believe, was the white mandate to achieve a new racial innocence and the black mandate to gain power. Even though blacks had made great advances during the sixties without quotas, these mandates, which came to a head in the very late sixties, could no longer be satisfied by anything less than racial preferences. I don't think these mandates in themselves were wrong, since whites clearly needed to do better by blacks and blacks needed more real power in society. But, as they came together in affirmative action, their effect was to distort our understanding of racial discrimination in a way that allowed us to offer the remediation of preference on the basis of mere color rather than actual injury. By making black the color of preference, these mandates have reburdened society with the very marriage of color and preference (in reverse) that we set out to eradicate. The old sin is reaffirmed in a new guise.

9   But the essential problem with this form of affirmative action is the way it leaps over the hard business of developing a formerly oppressed people to the point where they can achieve proportionate representation on their

own (given equal opportunity) and goes straight for the proportionate representation. This may satisfy some whites of their innocence and some blacks of their power, but it does very little to truly uplift blacks.

10   A white female affirmative action officer at an Ivy League university told me what many supporters of affirmative action now say: "We're after diversity. We ideally want a student body where racial and ethnic groups are represented according to their proportion in society." When affirmative action escalated into social engineering, diversity became a golden word. It grants whites an egalitarian fairness (innocence) and blacks an entitlement to proportionate representation (power). *Diversity* is a term that applies democratic principles to races and cultures rather than to citizens, despite the fact that there is nothing to indicate that real diversity is the same thing as proportionate representation. Too often the result of this on campuses (for example) has been a democracy of colors rather than of people, an artificial diversity that gives the appearance of an educational parity between black and white students that has not yet been achieved in reality. Here again, racial preferences allow society to leapfrog over the difficult problem of developing blacks to parity with whites and into a cosmetic diversity that covers the blemish of disparity—a full six years after admission, only about 26 percent of black students graduate from college.

11   Racial representation is not the same thing as racial development, yet affirmative action fosters a confusion of these very different needs. Representation can be manufactured; development is always hard-earned. However, it is the music of innocence and power that we hear in affirmative action that causes us to cling to it and to its distracting emphasis on representation. The fact is that after twenty years of racial preferences, the gap between white and black median income is greater than it was in the seventies. None of this is to say that blacks don't need policies that ensure our right to equal opportunity, but what we need more is the development that will let us take advantage of society's efforts to include us.

12   I think that one of the most troubling effects of racial preferences for blacks is a kind of demoralization, or put another way, an enlargement of self-doubt. Under affirmative action the quality that earns us preferential treatment is an implied inferiority. However this inferiority is explained—and it is easily enough explained by the myriad deprivations that grew out of our oppression—it is still inferiority. There are explanations, and then there is the fact. And the fact must be borne by the individual as a condition apart from the explanation, apart even from the fact that others like himself also bear this condition. In integrated situations where blacks must compete with whites who may be better prepared, these explanations may quickly wear thin and expose the individual to racial as well as personal self-doubt.

13   All of this compounded by the cultural myth of black inferiority that blacks have always lived with. What this means in practical terms is that when blacks deliver themselves into integrated situations, they encounter a nasty little reflex in whites, a mindless, atavistic reflex that responds to the color black with alarm. Attributions may follow this alarm if the white cares to indulge them, and if they do, they will most likely be negative—one such attribution is intellectual ineptness. I think this reflex and the attributions that may follow it embarrass most whites today, therefore, it is usually quickly repressed. Nevertheless, on an equally atavistic level, the black will be aware of the reflex his color triggers and will feel a stab of horror at seeing himself reflected in this way. He, too, will do a quick repression, but a lifetime of such stabbings is what constitutes his inner realm of racial doubt.

14   The effects of this may be a subject for another essay. The point here is that the implication of inferiority that racial preferences engender in both the white and black mind expands rather than contracts this doubt. Even when the black sees no implication of inferiority in racial preferences, he knows that whites do, so that—consciously or unconsciously—the result is virtually the same. The effect of preferential treatment—the lowering of normal standards to increase black representation—puts blacks at war with an expanded realm of debilitating doubt, so that the doubt itself becomes an unrecognized preoccupation that undermines their ability to perform, especially in integrated situations. On largely white campuses, blacks are five times more likely to drop out than whites. Preferential treatment, no matter how it is justified in the light of day, subjects blacks to a midnight of self-doubt, and so often transforms their advantage into a revolving door.

15   Another liability of affirmative action comes from the fact that it indirectly encourages blacks to exploit their own past victimization as a source of power and privilege. Victimization, like implied inferiority, is what justifies preference, so that to receive the benefits of preferential treatment one must, to some extent, become invested in the view of one's self as a victim. In this way, affirmative action nurtures a victim-focused identity in blacks. The obvious irony here is that we become inadvertently invested in the very condition we are trying to overcome. Racial preferences send us the message that there is more power in our past suffering than our present achievements—none of which could bring us a *preference* over others.

16   When power itself grows out of suffering, then blacks are encouraged to expand the boundaries of what qualifies as racial oppression, a situation that can lead us to paint our victimization in vivid colors, even as we receive the benefits of preference. The same corporations and institutions that give us preference are also seen as our oppressors. At Stanford University minority students—some of whom enjoy as much as $15,000 a year in financial aid—recently took over the president's office demanding, among other

things, more financial aid. The power to be found in victimization, like any power, is intoxicating and can lend itself to the creation of a new class of super-victims who can feel the pea of victimization under twenty mattresses. Preferential treatment rewards us for being underdogs rather than for moving beyond that status—a misplacement of incentives that, along with its deepening of our doubt, is more a yoke than a spur.

17   But, I think, one of the worst prices that blacks pay for preference has to do with an illusion. I saw this illusion at work recently in the mother of a middle-class black student who was going off to his first semester of college. "They owe us this, so don't think for a minute that you don't belong there." This is the logic by which many blacks, and some whites, justify affirmative action—it is something "owed," a form of reparation. But this logic overlooks a much harder and less digestible reality, that it is impossible to repay blacks living today for the historic suffering of the race. If all blacks were given a million dollars tomorrow morning it would not amount to a dime on the dollar of three centuries of oppression, nor would it obviate the residues of that oppression that we still carry today. The concept of historic reparation grows out of man's need to impose a degree of justice on the world that simply does not exist. Suffering can be endured and overcome, it cannot be repaid. Blacks cannot be repaid for the injustice done to the race, but we can be corrupted by society's guilty gestures of repayment.

18   Affirmative action is such a gesture. It tells us that racial preferences can do for us what we cannot do for ourselves. The corruption here is in the hidden incentive *not* to do what we believe preferences will do. This is an incentive to be reliant on others just as we are struggling for self-reliance. And it keeps alive the illusion that we can find some deliverance in repayment. The hardest thing for any sufferer to accept is that his suffering excuses him from very little and never has enough currency to restore him. To think otherwise is to prolong the suffering.

19   Several blacks I spoke with said they were still in favor of affirmative action because of the "subtle" discrimination blacks were subject to once on the job. One photojournalist said, "They have ways of ignoring you." A black female television producer said, "You can't file a lawsuit when your boss doesn't invite you to the insider meetings without ruining your career. So we still need affirmative action." Others mentioned the infamous "glass ceiling" through which blacks can see the top positions of authority but never reach them. But I don't think racial preferences are a protection against this subtle discrimination; I think they contribute to it.

20   In any workplace, racial preferences will always create two-tiered populations composed of preferreds and unpreferreds. This division makes automatic a perception of enhanced competence for the unpreferreds and of questionable competence for the preferreds—the former earned his way,

even though others were given preference, while the latter made it by color as much as by competence. Racial preferences implicitly mark whites with an exaggerated superiority just as they mark blacks with an exaggerated inferiority. They not only reinforce America's oldest racial myth but, for blacks, they have the effect of stigmatizing the already stigmatized.

21   I think that much of the "subtle" discrimination that blacks talk about is often (not always) discrimination against the stigma of questionable competence that affirmative action delivers to blacks. In this sense, preferences scapegoat the very people they seek to help. And it may be that at a certain level employers impose a glass ceiling, but this may not be against the race so much as against the race's reputation for having advanced by color as much as by competence. Affirmative action makes a glass ceiling virtually necessary as a protection against the corruptions of preferential treatment. This ceiling is the point at which corporations shift the emphasis from color to competency and stop playing the affirmative action game. Here preference backfires for blacks and becomes a taint that holds them back. Of course, one could argue that this taint, which is, after all, in the minds of whites, becomes nothing more than an excuse to discriminate against blacks. And certainly the result is the same in either case—blacks don't get past the glass ceiling. But this argument does not get around the fact that racial preferences now taint this color with a new theme of suspicion that makes it even more vulnerable to the impulse in others to discriminate. In this crucial yet gray area of perceived competence, preferences make whites look better than they are and blacks worse, while doing nothing whatever to stop the very real discrimination that blacks may encounter. I don't wish to justify the glass ceiling here, but only to suggest the very subtle ways that affirmative action revives rather than extinguishes the old rationalizations for racial discrimination.

22   In education, a revolving door; in employment, a glass ceiling.

23   I believe affirmative action is problematic in our society because it tries to function like a social program. Rather than ask it to ensure equal opportunity we have demanded that it create parity between the races. But preferential treatment does not teach skills, or educate, or instill motivation. It only passes out entitlement by color, a situation that in my profession has created an unrealistically high demand for black professors. The social engineer's assumption is that this high demand will inspire more blacks to earn Ph.D.'s and join the profession. In fact, the number of blacks earning Ph.D.'s has declined in recent years. A Ph.D. must be developed from preschool on. He requires family and community support. He must acquire an entire system of values that enables him to work hard while delaying gratification. There are social programs, I believe, that can (and should)

help blacks *develop* in all these areas, but entitlement by color is not a social program; it is a dubious reward for being black.

24   It now seems clear that the Supreme Court, in a series of recent decisions, is moving away from racial preferences. It has disallowed preferences except in instances of "identified discrimination," eroded the precedent that statistical racial imbalances are *prima facie* evidence of discrimination, and in effect granted white males the right to challenge consent decrees that use preference to achieve racial balances in the workplace. One civil rights leader said, "Night has fallen on civil rights." But I am not so sure. The effect of these decisions is to protect the constitutional rights of everyone rather than take rights away from blacks. What they do take away from blacks is the special entitlement to more rights than others that preferences always grant. Night has fallen on racial preferences, not on the fundamental rights of black Americans. The reason for this shift, I believe, is that the white mandate for absolution from past racial sins has weakened considerably during the eighties. Whites are now less willing to endure unfairness to themselves in order to grant special entitlements to blacks, even when these entitlements are justified in the name of past suffering. Yet the black mandate for more power in society has remained unchanged. And I think part of the anxiety that many blacks feel over these decisions has to do with the loss of black power they may signal. We had won a certain specialness and now we are losing it.

25   But the power we've lost by these decisions is really only the power that grows out of our victimization—the power to claim special entitlements under the law because of past oppression. This is not a very substantial or reliable power, and it is important that we know this so we can focus more exclusively on the kind of development that will bring enduring power. There is talk now that Congress will pass new legislation to compensate for these new limits on affirmative action. If this happens, I hope that their focus will be on development and anti-discrimination rather than entitlement, on achieving racial parity rather than jerry-building racial diversity.

26   I would also like to see affirmative action go back to its original purpose of enforcing equal opportunity—a purpose that in itself disallows racial preferences. We cannot be sure that the discriminatory impulse in America has yet been shamed into extinction, and I believe affirmative action can make its greatest contribution by providing a rigorous vigilance in this area. It can guard constitutional rather than racial rights, and help institutions evolve standards of merit and selection that are appropriate to the institution's needs yet as free of racial bias as possible (again, with the understanding that racial imbalances are not always an indication of racial bias). One of the most important things affirmative action can do is to

define exactly what racial discrimination is and how it might manifest it-self within a specific institution. The impulse to discriminate *is* subtle and cannot be ferreted out unless its many guises are made clear to people. Along with this there should be monitoring of institutions and heavy sanc-tions brought to bear when actual discrimination is found. This is the sort of affirmative action that America owes to blacks and to itself. It goes after the evil of discrimination itself, while preferences only sidestep the evil and grant entitlement to its *presumed* victims.

27   But if not preferences, then what? I think we need social policies that are committed to two goals: the educational and economic development of disadvantaged people, regardless of race, and the eradication from our society—through close monitoring and severe sanctions—of racial, ethnic, or gender discrimination. Preferences will not deliver us to either of these goals, since they tend to benefit those who are not disadvantaged—middle-class white women and middle-class blacks—and attack one form of dis-crimination with another. Preferences are inexpensive and carry the glamour of good intentions—change the numbers and the good deed is done. To be against them is to be unkind. But I think the unkindest cut is to bestow on children like my own an undeserved advantage while ne-glecting the development of those disadvantaged children on the East Side of my city who will likely never be in a position to benefit from a preference. Give my children fairness: give disadvantaged children a better shot at de-velopment—better elementary and secondary schools, job training, safer neighborhoods, better financial assistance for college, and so on. Fewer blacks go to college today than ten years ago; more black males of college age are in prison or under the control of the criminal justice system than in college. This despite racial preferences.

28   The mandates of black power and white absolution out of which prefer-ences emerged were not wrong in themselves. What was wrong was that both races focused more on the goals of these mandates than on the means to the goals. Blacks can have no real power without taking responsibility for their own educational and economic development. Whites can have no racial innocence without earning it by eradicating discrimination and help-ing the disadvantaged to develop. Because we ignored the means, the goals have not been reached, and the real work remains to be done.

Discussion Questions

1.   Explain how well you think Steele anticipates the opposing point of view and responds to it.

2. Cite specific instances where Steele uses the appeals of emotion and ethics in his argument. What effect does his choice of appeals have on his claim?

3. Throughout his argument, Steele describes talks with friends and personal experiences. How do these additions strengthen or weaken his argument?

4. How convincing are the alternatives Steele presents in his argument? Explain your answer.

5. On what points do you think Charles Krauthammer and Shelby Steele would agree? On what points would they disagree? Cite specific examples from their arguments to support your response.

ARGUMENT

Women in Combat? Give It a Try and See If It Works

Marianne Means

Marianne Means holds a law degree from George Washington University Law Center. A syndicated national affairs columnist since 1966, Means was the White House Correspondent for the Hearst Newspapers during the Kennedy and Johnson administrations. She has covered every presidential campaign since 1960 and writes primarily about the presidency, politics, and public policy issues. A frequent commentator on television and radio, Means has contributed to "Inside Washington," "Meet the Press," "The Today Show," "The Tonight Show," as well as CBS Radio's "Spectrum" and National Public Radio. Means is a member of the Sigma Delta Chi Hall of Fame and has won the Texas Headliners Club Award and the New York Front Page Award. She is also the author of *The Woman in the White House* (1963). Acting chair of the National Press Federation and a board member of the International Women's Media Foundation, Means is the Washington columnist for the Hearst Newspapers and her thrice-weekly columns are syndicated by King Features Syndicate. The following article was first published in 1990 and argues that women should be allowed to hold "combat jobs" in the military.

1   Next to the overblown specter of unisex toilets, it was the vision of women as potential cannon fodder that did in the Equal Rights Amendment.

2   Yet there they were on the spot in Panama, female soldiers conducting themselves with dignity and honor in real live combat. They were only supposed to capture some dogs, but they killed a few of the enemy and got shot at in return.

3   Manuel Noriega's thugs didn't politely ask "Male or female?" before firing. Nor were the guns aimed by females any less business-like than those fired by men.

4   Does this mean Congress may discover it's time to get real?

5   It would take some doing. Few things terrify politicians more than the prospect of being accused of sending beautiful young women—possible loving mothers, all—off to do battle, even to protect vital American interests.

6   The image of woman as fragile flower dies hard. Even after years of equal rights agitation, little boys are still supposed to play with soldiers while little girls content themselves with tea sets and dolls. Men are born to be warriors; women to be desk-bound bureaucrats.

7   Even after the military brass a decade ago finally got serious about training women and coping with the problems of a dual-sex army, nobody in power wanted to be blamed for females returning home in body bags. They were not deterred in this sentiment by the fact parents also cry inconsolably when males return in body bags.

8   Ratification of the late, lamented ERA would have let Congress off the hook, constitutionally ending sex discrimination in the military as elsewhere. But without that pressure Congress has refused to eliminate the old restrictions that keep women from military jobs considered the most dangerous. Laws forbid women in the Navy, Marines and Air Force from serving in combat; the Army is allowed to perpetuate that policy through its own regulations.

9   This arrangement is inherently artificial in a world of high-technology weapons where there are few distinctions between what's a safe job and what's not. The illusion was stripped away with the invasion of Panama, in which about six hundred women were involved. To be on the scene was to be within range of a bullet.

10   Congress is going to hold hearings soon into this question. Rep. Patricia Schroeder, D-Colo., and others plan to introduce legislation to open up all jobs in the armed forces to women, initially on an experimental basis. But emotions still run high against it.

11   Senate Armed Services Chairman Sam Nunn, the Democrats' chief spear carrier on matters military, says that despite Panama he continues to favor the ban.

12   "The burden is on those who advocate it be changed," he said ominously, citing physical differences and "overall morale of the force."

13   As a practical matter, access to combat jobs is important because they are the prestigious stepping stones for promotion into the highest ranks. Nearly half of all military jobs are closed to women, who make up about 11 percent of the armed forces. By overprotecting women, the military holds them back, condemning them to inferior roles.

14   And more is at stake than individual female careers. Women in general cannot expect to enjoy the full opportunities of society if they do not fully participate in its responsibilities.

15   In peacetime, the question of whether women should fight alongside men has not been a burning issue. But the Panama invasion is a reminder that the purpose of the military is to prepare the troops for a war that everyone hopes won't come. That means all the troops, not just some of them.

16   All recruits of both sexes join of their own choice, knowing that their basic mission—no matter how rarely called upon—is fighting. It is a responsibility they must share equally.

17   Way back in 1978, Secretary of Transportation Brock Adams, speaking in his capacity as head of the Coast Guard, urged that the ban on women in combat be lifted. A civilian and a liberal Democrat at that, Adams was dismissed as a troublemaker.

18   Military women have been quietly pushing into more and more job categories as their numbers grow. At least one female loading supervisor flew on six missions aboard an Air Force transport during the invasion of Grenada. But more visible women such as pilots were not allowed near Grenada until the Marines were in firm control of the island.

19   Yet women in uniform are still primarily curiosities.

20   Much of Capitol Hill regards them as distractions for the men. The idea is that males in battle would be too upset about seeing a wounded female to give their all to fighting the enemy. This oddly assumes that seeing a wounded male is not similarly upsetting.

21   A variation on this theme has male soldiers so tender-hearted they would spend their time protecting female colleagues rather than plotting the enemy's destruction. This harkens back to chivalry, an ancient practice presumed to be popular in the army though long ignored in the civilian world. Has anyone seen a young man give up his seat on a crowded bus to a woman lately?

22   There is also the familiar canard that women will cry and panic in battle. Its credibility depends upon a refusal to admit that all humans, including men, sometimes cry—with a special dispensation for Ronald Reagan, whose sentimental weeping was an art form.

23   Nunn or no Nunn, this stuff is baloney. Women who are physically weak or unwilling to fight don't voluntarily sign up for the military. Those that do are professionals. They should be give the chance to prove it.

Discussion Questions

1.   Means uses statistics and quotes politicians as a way of advancing her argument. How effective are these techniques in helping to prove her points?

2. How effective is Means in refuting her opposition? Cite specific examples.

3. What do you see as Means's most convincing reason for allowing women in combat? Which is the weakest? Why?

4. Describe the tone or voice of Means's writing. Discuss what effect it has on the believability of her argument.

5. Evaluate the cause-effect relationship Means establishes when she states, "Women in general cannot expect to enjoy the full opportunities of society if they do not fully participate in its responsibilities."

WRITING TOPICS

1. Usually when most people think of discrimination, they first conjure up specific racial groups. Think of other less obvious groups who have been the victim of discrimination and write a paper in which you reveal the ways in which they have been treated unfairly. Be sure to research the topic to find sources that will corroborate your perspective.

2. Do you think that discrimination is learned or are people born with it? Research the views of social scientists, psychologists, and journalists and write a paper in which you offer your perspective on this topic.

3. Why do you think discrimination is so pervasive in society? Write a paper that examines your ideas about its presence and power.

4. Who do you think is most responsible for perpetuating discrimination: family, friends, the schools, the media? Write a paper in which you identify who or what you see as the leading proponents of prejudice. Remember that the discrimination can be based on race, ethnicity, gender, sexual orientation, religion, physical appearance, and so on.

5. A case can be made that at some time in their lives, most people have been discriminated against, for one reason or another. Given the pervasiveness of discrimination, do you think it will end in your lifetime or in your children's? Why or why not? Write a paper that supports your stance.

6. To what extent do you think that too much is being made of discrimination—that is, many people, for no real reason, are

claiming discrimination for whatever reasons? Examine this question in a paper that looks carefully at both sides of the issue. Make sure that you offer specific examples to support your claim.

7. Do you think that application or census forms should include a new category—mixed race? Do you think that the categories on such forms privilege one group over another? What purpose(s) do they serve? Examine these questions in a paper that addresses the category of race on questionnaires.

8. In "Affirmative Action: The Price of Preference," Shelby Steele states, "I think that one of the most troubled effects of racial preference for blacks is a kind of demoralization, or put another way, an enlargement of self-doubt. Under affirmative action the quality that earns us preferential treatment is an implied inferiority." Do you think this was the intent of affirmative action? Research the origins of affirmative action legislation, and write a paper in which you support or refute Steele's claim.

9. Write a paper in which you enumerate the burdens society places on certain groups based solely on discrimination. How have such groups been limited or deterred because of the discrimination? How have they risen above it?

10. Choose a statement made in any of the selections in this chapter and write a paper that supports or refutes it. Find research that helps to support your stance. If you support the idea, make sure that you offer your own thinking on the matter; if you refute the idea, make sure that you take into account the opposing point of view.

ACKNOWLEDGMENTS

Armstrong, Grace April Oursler, "Let's Keep Christmas Commercial." From *The Saturday Evening Post*, Dec. 18, 1965. Reprinted with permission from The Saturday Evening Post © 1965 The Curtis Publishing Co.

Baldwin, James, "If Black English Isn't a Language, Then Tell Me, What Is?" From *The New York Times*, July 29, 1979. Copyright © 1979 by The New York Times Company. Reprinted by permission.

Boatright, Claudia, "Mythogyny" from *Northern Ohio Live*, June 1993. Reprinted by permission from *Northern Ohio Live* © Claudia Boatright.

Brown, J. Clinton, "In Defense of the N Word," as appeared in *Essence*, June 1993. Copyright © 1990 by J. Clinton Brown. Reprinted by permission of the author.

Cousins, Norman, "How to Make People Smaller Than They Are," from *The Saturday Review*, 1978. Reprinted by permission.

DeMott, Benjamin, "In Hollywood, Class Doesn't Put Up Much of a Struggle." From *The New York Times*, January 20, 1991. Copyright © 1991 by The New York Times Company. Reprinted by permission.

Douglas, Michael, "Dump Gump" as appeared in *The Beacon Journal*, Sunday, July 31, 1994. Reprinted with permission of the Akron Beacon Journal.

Ehrenreich, Barbara, "Goodbye to the Work Ethic." From *The Worst Years of Our Lives* by Barbara Ehrenreich. Copyright © 1990 by Barbara Ehrenreich. Reprinted by permission of Pantheon Books, a division of Random House, Inc.

Ehrenreich, Barbara, "Oh, Those Family Values" in *Time*, July 18, 1994. Copyright 1994 Time Inc. Reprinted by permission.

Elmer-Dewitt, Philip, "Bards of the Internet" in *Time*, July 4, 1994. Copyright 1994 Time Inc. Reprinted by permission.

Engle, Gary, "What Makes Superman So Darned American?" from *Superman at Fifty!* by Gary Engle. Reprinted by permission.

Ferguson, Sarah, "The comfort of being sad" reprinted from *Utne Reader*, July/August 1994. Copyright © 1994 by Sarah Ferguson. Reprinted by permission of the author.

Footlick, Jerrold, with Elizabeth Leonard, "What Happened to the Family?" from *Newsweek*, Special Issue, Winter/Spring 1991 and © 1991, Newsweek, Inc. All rights reserved. Reprinted by permission.

Fox, Nicols, "What Are Our Real Values?" as appeared in *Newsweek*, February 13, 1989. Copyright © 1989 by Nicols Fox. Reprinted by permission of the author.

Fromm, Erich, "Our Way of Life Makes Us Miserable." Reprinted with permission from *The Saturday Evening Post* © 1964 The Curtis Publishing Company.

Goodman, Ellen, "Putting in a Good Word for Guilt," as appeared in *Redbook*, June 1982. Copyright © 1982, The Boston Globe Newspaper Co./Washington Post Writers Group. Reprinted with permission.

Goodman, Paul, "A Proposal to Abolish Grading" from *Compulsory Miseducation* by Paul Goodman, 1964. Reprinted by permission.

Hagelberg, Kymberli, "Wildmon's censorship crusade should not go unopposed" from *Northeast Scene*, 1992. Reprinted courtesy of Cleveland *Scene* Magazine, © 1992 Northeast Scene Inc.

Halpert, Felicia E., "Heroes Wanted" from *Ms. Magazine*, March 1988. Reprinted by permission of Ms. Magazine, © 1988.

Henry, William A., III, "In Defense of Elitism." From *In Defense of Elitism* by William A. Henry III. Copyright © 1994 by William A. Henry III. Used by permission of Doubleday, a division of Bantam Doubleday Dell Publishing Group, Inc.

Kohn, Alfie, "Incentives Can Be Bad for Business." Copyright 1988 by Alfie Kohn. Reprinted from *Inc. Magazine* with the author's permission.

Krauthammer, Charles, "A Defense of Quotas," from *The New Republic*, September 16/23, 1985. Reprinted by permission of *The New Republic*, © 1985, The New Republic, Inc.

Kriegel, Leonard, "Claiming the Self: The Cripple as American Man" from *Falling Into Life*, essays by Leonard Kriegel. Reprinted by permission of the author.

Leo, John, "Sneer not at 'Ozzie and Harriet'" from *U.S. News & World Report*, September 14, 1992. Copyright, 1992, U.S. News & World Report. Reprinted by permission.

Lewis, C. S., "We Have No 'Right to Happiness'" from *God in the Dock* by C. S. Lewis. Copyright © 1970 by C. S. Lewis Pte Ltd, reproduced by permission of Curtis Brown, London and HarperCollins Publishers Limited.

Love, Steve, "Woodstock lessons are just an illusion" which appeared in *The Beacon Journal*, Thursday, August 11, 1994. Reprinted with permission of the Akron Beacon Journal.

Means, Marianne, "Women in Combat? Give It a Try and See If It Works," Asheville *Citizen-Times*, Jan. 9, 1990, p. 4A. Copyright © 1990 by Hearst Publishing Co., Inc. Reprinted with special permission of King Features Syndicate.

Merullo, Roland, "How Pro Football Was Ruined" as appeared in *Newsweek*, January 23, 1984. Copyright © 1984 Roland Merullo. Reprinted by permission of the author.

Micheli, Lyle J., "Children and Sports" which appeared in *Newsweek*, October 29, 1990. Reprinted by permission of author.

Morrow, Lance, "What is the Point of Working?" from *Fishing in the Tiber* by Lance Morrow. Copyright © 1988 by Lance Morrow. Reprinted by permission of Henry Holt and Co.

Ozersky, Josh, "TV's Anti-Families: Married . . . with Malaise," as appeared in *Tikkun* magazine (January/February 1991). Copyright © 1991 Josh Ozersky. Reprinted by permission.

Pettit, Sarah, "In or Out?" from *Newsweek*, August 22, 1994 and © 1994, Newsweek, Inc. All rights reserved. Reprinted by permission.

Quindlen, Anna, "Evan's Two Moms." From *The New York Times*, February 5, 1992. Copyright © 1992 by The New York Times Company. Reprinted by permission.

Raman, V. V., "Why It's So Important that Our Students Learn More about Science" which appeared in *The Chronicle of Higher Education*, April 4, 1984. Reprinted by permission of the author.

Rollin, Betty, "Motherhood: Who Needs It?" which appeared in *Look* magazine, September 22, 1970. Reprinted with permission from H & C Communications, Inc.

Ross, Murray, "Football Red and Baseball Green," as appeared in the *Chicago Review*, January/February 1971. Reprinted by permission of Murray Ross, all rights reserved.

Salter, Stephanie, "25 Years Later—Forgetting Woodstock" which appeared in *The Beacon Journal* (Akron), Thursday, August 11, 1994. Reprinted with permission from the San Francisco Examiner. © 1994 San Francisco Examiner.

Samuelson, Robert J., "Overworked Americans?" from *Newsweek*, March 16, 1992 and © 1992, Newsweek, Inc. All rights reserved. Reprinted by permission.

Schaap, Dick, "So Much of the Joy is Gone" as appeared in *Forbes*, September 14, 1992. © Dick Schaap 1992. Reprinted by permission of the author.

Simon, John, "Why Good English is Good for You." From *Paradigms Lost* by John Simon. Copyright © 1980 by John Simon. Reprinted by permission of the Wallace Literary Agency, Inc.

Smith, Jonathan Z., "Questions in the Great, Unexplained Aspect of Undergraduate Education: The College Major" from *Change*, v. 15 i.4, pp. 35–42, July/August 1983. Reprinted with permission of the Helen Dwight Reid Educational Foundation. Published by Heldref Publications, 1319 Eighteenth St., N.W., Washington, D.C. 20036–1802. Copyright © 1983.

Smith, Page, "Human Time and the College Student." Excerpted from *Dissenting Opinions*. Copyright © 1984 by Page Smith. Reprinted by permission.

Smith, Sally E., "Sizism—One of the Last 'Safe' Prejudices" from *The California Activist*, July 1990. Reprinted by permission of the author.

Steele, Shelby, "Affirmative Action: The Price of Preference" from *The Content of Our Character* by Shelby Steele. Copyright © 1990 by Shelby Steele. Reprinted by permission of St. Martin's Press, Inc., New York, NY.

Steinberg, Laurence, "It's Time to Ask Whether Teenagers Should Be Working at All" by Laurence Steinberg and Ellen Greenberger. Reprinted by permission of Laurence Steinberg.

Steinem, Gloria, "The Importance of Work" which was published as "Why Do Women Work" in Ms. March, 1979. © Gloria Steinem, Ms. *Magazine* March 1979. Reprinted by permission.

Trippett, Frank, "Time to Reflect on Blah-Blah-Blah" in *Time*, December 22, 1980. Copyright 1980 Time Inc. Reprinted by permission.

Tuchman, Barbara, "The Missing Element: Moral Courage." Reprinted by permission of Russell & Volkening as agents for the author. Copyright © 1978 Barbara Tuchman.

Van Gelder, Lindsy, "Marriage as a Restricted Club" in Ms. *Magazine*, February 1984. Reprinted by permission of Ms. Magazine, © 1984.

Weir, Tom, "Navratilova is ace of all female athletes" from *USA Today*, June 24, 1994. Copyright 1994, *USA Today*. Reprinted with permission.

Williams, Patricia J., "Hate Radio" from Ms. *Magazine*, March/April 1994. Reprinted by permission of Ms. Magazine, © 1994.

SUBJECT INDEX

AUTHOR-TITLE INDEX

INSTRUCTOR'S MANUAL

Commitment, Voice, and Clarity

An Argument Rhetoric and Reader

Janet Marting

University of Akron

NTC Publishing Group
Lincolnwood, Illinois USA

CONTENTS

INTRODUCTION

As composition instructors, many of us have had the opportunity to introduce students to personal experience and expository writing. Part of our teaching consisted of demonstrating the features that contribute to the effectiveness of each type of writing. For some of us, however, teaching another type of nonfiction is a new enterprise that poses new challenges: argumentation. Many of our students also experience new challenges when writing argument papers: while their high school courses addressed personal experience and expository writing, few, if any, of their courses focused exclusively on argumentation and researched writing.

Argumentation and research are at the heart of the academy. Ours is a profession in which ideas are posited, supported, challenged, reshaped, and so on. From such exchanges come the refinement of ideas and the birth of new ones. To avoid teaching students the joys of posing ideas, supporting them, considering opposing perspectives, and even changing their initial positions is to be remiss in our responsibility as teachers.

The aim of this Instructor's Manual is to provide a discussion of the ways in which you can best present *Commitment, Voice, and Clarity* to your students. I want to stress the flexibility of this text: while some of you might prefer to teach the rhetoric portion before the readings, others might prefer to teach the readings in conjunction with the rhetoric. The book accommodates either approach.

This Instructor's Manual offers the following materials to assist you:

- Teaching suggestions for Part 1: A Guide to Writing Viewpoints and Arguments;
- Teaching suggestions for Part 2: Readings for Discussion and Analysis;
- A sample fifteen-week course outline;
- A sample ten-week course outline;
- Possible answers to the discussion questions that follow each reading in Part 2.

I hope that by reading this Instructor's Manual in conjunction with the text, you will approach the teaching of argumentation with new-found interest, energy, and enthusiasm.

Teaching Suggestions for
Part 1:
A Guide to Writing
Viewpoints and Arguments

Chapter 1: Understanding Argument

Because many students are unfamiliar with the terminology that is central to argumentation and that is used in this text, I think it is important to begin by "getting your signals straight"—that is, making sure that all of your students understand what is meant by such terms as *argument*, *viewpoint, opinion,* and *persuasion.* This is especially important since many students are far more familiar with spoken arguments than they are with written ones.

Throughout this text, I have used the term *viewpoint* to connote less formal arguments, often the kind of writing that appears in the op/ed and commentary pages of newspapers, the "My Turn" section of *Newsweek* magazine, the "Essay" section of *Time* magazine, and so on. I am very taken with this kind of writing because it deals with observation of and interaction with one's surroundings. Further, I think it is a natural starting point for students in courses that focus on argumentation. Its familiarity and presence are part of its appeal; it attests to the notion that reactions to an event, phenomenon, or idea are the raw material from which bona fide papers emerge.

Viewpoints are a natural part of people's lives. They are a type of writing that has implications beyond academic requirements; they are what students can write as they make their ideas known in larger, more public venues. Showing students how frequently they come in contact with—and even voice themselves—viewpoints is an important starting point. Viewpoints illustrate that writing about ideas need not be a threatening activity or one to be fearful of.

No doubt you have noticed that one of the ways in which this text differs from many other argument books is that it rejects the notion of asking students to write about exceedingly complex and controversial issues that are based on values: abortion, capital punishment, euthanasia, and the like. When I first started teaching in the 1970s as a graduate teaching assistant, I remember telling my students that they were *not* to write about such topics. (Several semesters of reading papers on those topics cured me of any notion that they were suitable for most first-year students.) My thinking has not changed. I prefer not to read wildly passionate and often ill-informed papers that exhort (as opposed to explore), papers that are about subjects so large that it is virtually impossible for students to adequately cover all the necessary material in the typical eight to fifteen required pages. Further, such topics doom most students to failure by sometimes encouraging them to rehash the obvious, to recycle papers they have written in other classes, and, in the worst cases, to plagiarize.

Such large, complex, controversial issues often give students the impression that researching their topics amounts to little more than finding the required number of sources and filling pages to reach the required number. Not only is the real spirit of original thinking and research lost, but students disappear from their writing: their role becomes that of recorder instead of thinker and commentator. Thus, *Commitment, Voice, and Clarity* offers a new perspective on written argumentation and researched papers.

In this chapter, I have provided a list of myths and misconceptions many people have about argument papers. You can expect that some of your students might have been given opposite instruction in previous writing classes. Further explanation of the myths might be in order. Ask your students if they can offer additional reasons for such myths having developed. Solicit your students' questions and reactions so fewer misunderstandings will occur. The exercises at the end of the chapter can help you discover whether students understand the principles they have read. Although many of the exercises are designed for peer group in-class workshops, they can be assigned as out-of-class homework.

One final note. Some students have taken writing courses in which they had less than positive experiences: they were not allowed to voice their own ideas; they were belittled or criticized for offering their beliefs; they were told that they didn't have any worthwhile opinions; and so on. The net result is that some students (showing a savvy understanding of audience!) quickly learned to be silent and waited for the instructor to tell them what he or she wanted them to believe. In short, they became passive students. One of the assumptions on which this book is based is that for students to improve their writing of argument papers, they need to be active readers and writers, voicing and supporting their own perspectives.

To set a positive tone for a course devoted to the writing of argument papers, I believe that students need to be encouraged to address, question, and examine ideas from all possible angles. Let students know that you have no "hidden agenda," that there are no hard and fast, right or wrong answers to the issues they will be examining. What matters most is a thorough, thoughtful, and well-reasoned examination of what students read and write. In so doing, one of the rewards is that the students' audience will take their positions on issues seriously: people will want to hear what they have to say. That, I think, should be incentive enough.

CHAPTER 2: FROM EXPERIENCE-BASED TO IDEA-BASED WRITING

The aim of this chapter is to distinguish between the two types of writing with which most students are familiar: writing about personal experiences and writing about ideas. In addition, the chapter provides examples of the two kinds of writing. A good class activity is to ask your students to find their own examples of the two types, either from what they have read or from their own writing experiences, and to present their examples to the class. In fact, it is a useful exercise to have students begin searching for examples of viewpoint and argument papers in what they read outside of their required course work; this helps to make them aware of written viewpoints and arguments.

Getting students in the habit of reading critically and analytically—outside of course requirements—will open their eyes (literally and figuratively) to the role that viewpoints and arguments play in society. Moreover, because we usually don't read the same publications as our students, they can make us aware of fascinating examples of idea-based writing.

CHAPTER 3: WRITING VIEWPOINT AND ARGUMENT PAPERS

One of the tenets of writing courses is that learning and improving requires practice. No doubt you have used analogies to sports or music to make this point: you can't learn to swim by reading a book about swimming, so you must jump into the water and start stroking; you can't learn to play the guitar by listening to Eric Clapton or Jimi Hendrix, but rather you must pluck away at your six-string. The same holds true for writing. This chapter is based on that very principle: learning by doing.

Prewriting or Brainstorming

This chapter provides nuts-and-bolts information on ways to generate a draft of a viewpoint or argument paper. It begins by offering students a variety of brainstorming or prewriting activities. For many students, producing such raw material is a way to start to see what they have to work with; for others, prewriting breaks them of the blank-page syndrome or of writer's block.

Throughout the chapter, students are asked to complete exercises that put to use what they have just read. I think it is important to ask students to try their hand at these exercises, either as in-class or out-of-class activities. Not only do the exercises offer students important practice, but students' efforts may well produce a finished piece of writing by the end of the chapter.

I have generated the ten sample questions or topics as examples of nonthreatening, user-friendly writing assignments. If you have others you prefer students to write about, substitute them for the ten that appear in the chapter. You might want to refer to the "Writing Topics" that appear at the end of each chapter in Part 2 of this book and have students begin writing on some of them. Or you might want to ask students what they wish to write about and have them select their own topics. The point is to get students writing.

Audience

This chapter offers important information about audience. More often than not, most students imagine either their instructor or their classmates as their audience—and for understandable reason: their instructor and their peers are probably the only people who read their writing. But this need not be the case. Writing effective viewpoint and argument papers has consequences beyond the classroom. Encourage students to think of audiences wider than you or their peers as potential readers. How about, for example, the readers of local newspapers or magazines? By expanding the range of audience, students can see that their writing can have an impact greater than a good grade from an instructor or a pat on the back from their classmates. Writing can instruct, inform, and persuade others to at least take their ideas seriously. Making students aware of audience shows them the consequences of writing.

Defensive Writing

Related to audience awareness is defensive writing or considering counterarguments. By showing students that they must anticipate and address opposing perspectives, we begin to lift the blinders that handicap many students. This is an ideal time to ask your students to get into pairs and play devil's advocate or Doubting Thomas. Using their own papers, ask your students to reenact a debate.

Another useful activity is to divide the class into three groups: have one group argue one perspective, another group argue the opposing perspective, and the third group evaluate which of the two groups is more convincing. This activity can conceivably last one or two class sessions.

Yet another activity is to have students argue the stance that they actually oppose. This forces them to consider seriously the opposing side's ideas, supporting ideas, and logic. The point is to show students the importance of considering opposing perspectives.

Revision

Because writing is just as much a matter of rewriting as it is composing a first draft, I cannot overemphasize the importance of revision. In argument papers especially, revision plays a crucial role. The sheer act of writing often produces a multitude of ideas; writing begets writing. Ask students to think of the times in which their pens on paper or fingers on the keyboard were unable to keep pace with the ideas they were trying to record. Or remind them of the times they reread what they had written and discovered important ideas missing, ideas that didn't belong in the paper, or an organization to their paper that didn't make much sense. That is what revision attends to. Encourage students to revise as often as is needed: there's no magic number of revisions any paper needs. I often show students drafts of my own writing as a way to assure them that revision is a natural part of the writing process, something that all writers who take their work seriously do.

Voice

Although many students may not know the terminology used when discussing matters involving voice, tone, and style, you can expect quite a few of them to bring up the question of "how a paper sounds." Most students are aware of wanting their papers to sound a "certain way" but are unsure of how to achieve the desired effect. I suspect that their interest in voice is their way of saying they want their papers to sound original. Of course, originality in writing is first established by originality in thinking: writing about an idea that has never been examined before, writing about the idea in new ways, making fresh connections between ideas, and so on. (I like to remind students that the root of the word *authority* is *author*.) Sentence structure, word choice, parentheticals, and the like are also a writer's personal stamp. Although many people consider voice to be principally a matter of style, I think it has further ramifications: voice is a form of argumentation; that is, by virtue of writing demonstrating a particular voice, the writer has achieved *ethos*, credibility as an author.

While the material in this section of Chapter 3 might be too ambitious for some students, it certainly is important for all students to consider. Even if a discussion of voice simply makes students aware of the many choices they have as writers, the aim has been achieved. In addition, a discussion of voice affords students an opportunity to *hear* not only their own but other people's writing; it reinforces the idea that their voices do not have to "disappear" in their papers. Attending to matters concerning voice is to assume control over not only the ideas expressed in writing but the ways in which those ideas are rendered. Such control is authority, and authority is power over the written word.

Interesting Your Audience

One of most students' greatest concerns regarding writing idea-based papers is that they will fail to interest their audience. Often, students will ask, "How can I capture my readers' attention when I'm writing about ideas? What will make them interested in reading what I have to say?" Obviously, part of the answer lies in students being committed to their topics. The solution also involves the ways in which the writers present their ideas. Not surprisingly, then, attending to the opening paragraph(s) of papers takes on special importance. Discussing with your students the most (and least) effective examples in this chapter is a way to address this issue. While not all of the examples will be applicable to all papers, they do provide students with a number of possibilities that they might want to try in their own papers.

A good class activity to reinforce the issue of interesting one's audience is to ask your students to bring to class with them examples of particularly strong (or weak) opening paragraphs in what they read outside of class. Having students read their discoveries is a fine way to share their findings with the entire class. Most importantly, it makes students aware of the ways in which the authors they read have successfully engaged them or turned them off.

Editing and Proofreading

I think it's pretty safe to say that most, if not all, students know that they are supposed to check their writing for mistakes before turning it in to the instructor for a grade; it's just as safe to say that many students do not edit or proofread their writing. Their reasons for not doing so vary. I think it is important to *show* students the many ways in which editing and proofreading can benefit them. Just as important is giving them practice sessions in class. While many instructors might contend that it is the students' responsibility to do this outside of class, I see no harm in giving them the time *and* the necessary instruction once or twice in class during the term to edit and proofread their papers. The aim is to get students into the habit of editing and proofreading. Mostly, I think, students need to be *shown* how to proofread; we need to give them useful techniques that will enable them to see their writing objectively. If proofreading is important enough for students to do, it is important enough for us to spend time teaching.

Final Notes

Just as I think it important to explain to students that writing is a recursive process, so too do I feel the need to reiterate it in this Instructor's Manual. As much as we would like for writing to be a neat and tidy enterprise, it isn't. Reminding students of that fact is probably necessary throughout the term. No doubt we remind ourselves of that fact whenever we boot up the computer or open our notebooks to begin writing.

Reader/Writer Checklist

Because there are so many things to remember when we read and write, I have provided a checklist for readers and writers. I find it useful to duplicate these questions and distribute them to students whenever they are at work on a new paper or whenever they are reading and responding to their classmates' papers. By no means exhaustive (that was not its intent), the checklist nonetheless provides important ideas for students to keep in mind before, during, and after having written a draft of a paper. Ask your students to individualize or personalize the list by adding their own special questions that address specific weaknesses in their own writing. You may want to address such questions when you respond to students' papers or meet with students in conferences.

CHAPTER 4: STRATEGIES OF ARGUMENTATION

This chapter focuses exclusively on the principles of formal argumentation. Although some students may be familiar with terms such as *inductive* and *deductive* reasoning, *logos*, *pathos*, and *ethos*, they may see no connection between those terms and their own writing. Hence the importance of explaining to students how the tools of formal argumentation can aid them in creating more reasoned and more effective papers.

After each principle of formal logic is defined, explained, and illustrated, students are provided with exercises to test their understanding of the material they have just read. These exercises can be in-class or out-of-class assignments; they can be completed individually or in groups of students. Because you know your students better than anyone else, the decision rests with you.

Along with completing the exercises, it is helpful for students to turn to their own writing and to analyze the ways in which they have used the tools of formal argumentation. Ask students to write a one- or two-page paper explaining why they made the choices they did and what effect would be created had they chosen differently. Ask that they also discuss how the use of formal argumentation helped to strengthen their papers. Not only do these questions require students to think about the choices they made, but they help to support the idea that different choices produce different effects.

One final note: I would be remiss if I didn't say that teaching logical fallacies can provide students with a good belly laugh. Despite the commonly held belief that logic is dry and boring, I think that examining logical fallacies disproves this notion. Enjoy the humor that results when looking at the fallacies. After all, the study of writing can be fun.

CHAPTER 5: THE RESEARCHED PAPER

Although the sample ten-week and fifteen-week course outlines that appear later in this Instructor's Manual don't show Chapter 5 appearing until the third and eighth week, respectively, it's important to have your students review this material before those weeks, *especially* before they begin researching their papers. Most of the chapter presents the nuts-and-bolts of correct citations and documentation. However, valuable information on correct summaries, paraphrases, and direct quotations also appears in the chapter. Because these forms of acknowledging outside sources are sometimes difficult for students to understand, let alone use correctly, the more time they can spend on it, the better.

Teaching Suggestions for

Part 2:

Readings for Discussion

and Analysis

One of the ways in which this text is flexible is in the organization of its chapters. I have chosen the order based on what I see as a natural progression of related themes and on the increasing level of the themes' difficulty. Although some of you will want to begin with the first theme, "Education," and proceed theme-by-theme through the text, others may choose to begin with another theme and skip around. Any approach will work; do what you think will work best for your students. Better still, ask your students which themes interest them most and arrange your discussion of the chapters based on their preferences. By doing this, you are tailor-making your courses to fit your students' interests. By providing students with some input into the organization of the class, they are more likely to have a stake in the readings (since they selected them), and class discussions will be more interesting and lively.

What follows are brief discussions of what you can expect when you present the readings to your students. Consider this information helpful hints on anticipating students' reactions; combinations of readings that work especially well; specific readings that students will have difficulty understanding, as well as the ones that tend to be favorites; and class activities to help promote lively class discussion of the issues and the strategies of argumentation.

Chapter 6: Education

Most students have a natural interest in this theme—as well they should. From their own experiences and observations of the system in which they were (and continue to be) educated, they have ideas about what works and what doesn't, changes that could be made to improve the schools, and so on.

The first two selections, by Norman Cousins and V. V. Raman, complement each other because the first makes a case for the importance of studying more humanities courses and the second makes a similar case for studying more in the sciences. While at first glance the two view-points might appear to be at odds with each other, they actually posit surprisingly similar ideas, only through different curricula. As such, the viewpoints demonstrate two different approaches to the same topic.

Perhaps the most controversial reading in this chapter is William A. Henry's "In Defense of Elitism." Some students might already be aware of this argument because the book from which this selection is taken received much publicity. Reactions will be divided: Expect your stronger students to agree with Henry and your weaker students to find his argument blasphemous. Given the powerful reactions this piece elicits, it might prove helpful to spend extra time having students analyze the ways in which Henry attempts to support his claim.

The last three readings in this chapter work together nicely. Students will be surprised (and relieved) to read selections in which the authors take a decidedly pro-student approach by attacking final examinations, the college major, and grading. One warning, however: Students will want to turn the discussion and analysis of these essays into a complaint session in which they relate their personal tales of woe. This might prove to be a good occasion for you to distinguish between personal experience and argument and to discuss the ways in which their experiences can be the jumping-off point for idea-based writing. In any event, try to keep the stories to a minimum and direct students' attention to the ways in which the writers take a stand and defend it.

CHAPTER 7: WORKING FOR A LIVING

There seems to be no escaping the topic of work in our society. Granted, most people have to work for a living, but beyond that, work seems to be a pervasive topic: We begin the day by planning our work schedules, and we end our days talking about what happened "at work." Invariably, television news shows feature segments on work-related issues, as do newspapers and magazines. And that doesn't even take into account the many publications devoted exclusively to the workplace and the workforce (for example, *Inc.*, *Forbes*, and so on).

An informal survey of your students will reveal that an overwhelming majority of them see their formal education as a means to an end—that is, they are in school to get a "better" job. Because many students have part-time jobs in addition to their college classes (or have worked in the summer), their experiences can prove helpful when they discuss the selections in this chapter and when they write about work-related issues.

The first two selections, by Lance Morrow and Barbara Ehrenreich, are a good pair to teach together because they both address the work ethic. Because Ehrenreich's piece is decidedly cynical and cutting, it serves as a good contrast to Morrow's far different voice. These two readings are effective examples for an examination of voice and tone in writing.

Of all the readings in this chapter, Laurence Steinberg and Ellen Greenberger's piece on teenagers and work will cause the most interest, if not furor. Expect students to disagree vehemently with the authors' characterization of teenagers who work (and those who don't) after school and on weekends. Encourage students to move beyond their own experiences and observations to refute the selection's thesis. You might want to have students work individually or in small groups to generate lists of counterarguments. In any event, watch out for the fireworks!

Gloria Steinem's "The Importance of Work" addresses gender-related issues regarding the meaning of work. Putting the selection in its historical and cultural context might be necessary, but an intriguing discussion can emerge from examining to what extent this article is specific to women—that is, what would happen if we were to change the female pronouns to male pronouns? Read a few passages making such changes, and students' reactions will help to demonstrate one of Steinem's point.

Alfie Kohn's "Incentives Can Be Bad for Business" addresses the issue of motivation. Students, not surprisingly, will voice a wide range of opinions regarding what motivates workers. Again, you might need to direct students away from just expressing what incentives motivate them to analyzing what their choices are saying about them as workers.

Robert J. Samuelson's "Overworked Americans" provides an example of an argument whose structure is derived from the writer addressing another writer's perspective on an issue. Pointing out to students that good writing is often generated as a reaction to or in response to what has been read shows them one of the ways in which topics originate. In fact, students themselves might want to write their own papers in response to one or several readings in this book.

CHAPTER 8: SPORTS AND LEISURE

The theme of sports and leisure provides a counterpoint to the previous themes of education and work. Because sports and leisure are often as much a part of students' life as education and work, students have much to contribute to class discussions. Don't be surprised if they are even more knowledgeable about statistics than you!

Murray Ross's viewpoint on football and baseball might prove a bit challenging for some students, but it is nonetheless a fine example of the power of analogy to create ideas. His viewpoint also demonstrates thinking about a topic beyond the obvious. Roland Merullo's viewpoint on instant replay is more direct and clear-cut than Ross's piece, but it shows students how an idea-based paper can emerge from a strong dislike of something. As John Milton wrote, "opinions are but ideas in the making."

The remaining selections in this chapter are especially timely and will no doubt spur the interest of students. In "So Much of the Joy Is Gone," Dick Schaap examines how players' inflated salaries have affected sports. Because many students keep abreast of such information, they may be able to use their knowledge of sports figures and statistics to inform their stance on the debate. Felicia E. Halpert's "Sports Heroes Wanted" argues that young girls need female sports heroes in much the same way that young boys have always had male sports heroes. The reading addresses both issues related to sports and issues about gender differences.

Tom Weir's selection on Martina Navratilova demonstrates the importance of refuting potential counterarguments as a way of supporting a claim. It also provides students with an excellent example of how they can generate a topic for an argument paper: select a sports figure (or team) that they deem the best (or most overrated, underappreciated, etc.) and defend their position. Not only does this topic feed into their interest, it forces them to use the tools of argumentation to prove their claim. This assignment is especially effective for students who struggle to find suitable topics or who have trouble adequately backing up their ideas.

Lyle J. Micheli's "Children and Sports" rounds out the chapter by looking at the ways in which children in sporting events can be harmed by seemingly well-meaning adults. From their own experiences, many students will have strong reactions to the selection.

CHAPTER 9: POPULAR CULTURE

No matter where we turn, popular culture invades our lives. From the radio stations we listen to and the television shows we follow to the movies we see at the theater and the advertisements we read in newspapers and magazines, popular culture is a pervasive influence on our lives. This is especially true for children, teens, and young adults who are reported to listen to radio and watch more television than the older generations. Moreover, what with the influence of popular music and television shows, popular culture has a significant presence in students' lives. As such, it is a fitting theme for students to examine.

The first two viewpoints present topics with which many students are very familiar: In "Hate Radio," Patricia J. Williams discusses the popular radio and television talk shows of Howard Stern and Rush Limbaugh, offering the perspective that they represent a microcosm of popular sentiment. Then, in "The Comfort of Being Sad," Sarah Ferguson explores the grunge culture's appeal to young people. Not only will these two viewpoints pique students' interest and reactions, but they will show students how viewpoints can be based on ideas that are derived from critical analysis of what they hear and observe.

In "TV's Anti-Families: Married...with Malaise," Josh Ozersky presents two television shows that reflect what he sees as antifamily sentiments: *Married with Children* and *The Simpsons*. His essay proves to be an effective example of the ways in which analysis can form the basis of an argument paper. So too does Claudia Boatright's "Mythogyny," which examines the danger of advertisements that give young women the impression that beauty means being 5'10" tall and weighing 110 pounds. In "In Hollywood, Class Doesn't Put Up Much of a Struggle," Bemjamin DeMott argues that, despite their popularity and appeal, movies do not accurately represent minorities. All of these readings will spawn much student debate. They also serve as excellent models of argument papers that originate from a close analysis of what people watch and read daily. Further, the selections demonstrate that possible topics for argument papers can very well be related to students' own interests.

The final reading in this chapter differs from the preceding selections because it takes a position that many people oppose: in "Let's Keep Christmas Commercial," Grace April Oursler Armstrong says that she does not object to the commercialization of Christmas. Thus, students can see how arguments can be based on a stand that is strongly opposed to popular thinking.

One of the exciting features of this chapter is that the selections address issues that are central to most students' lives. Not only will students be interested in the topics about which the authors write, but they will read models of how good argument is structured and supported. Not surprisingly, this may well be a chapter on which you want to spend more than one week.

CHAPTER 10: THE AMERICAN FAMILY

In previous composition classes, students probably learned about the importance of choosing topics they were interested in and committed to—and for understandable reason: students will not tire of thinking about, writing, and revising the paper if they care about the topic. Besides, if they aren't interested in the topic, why should their audience be interested in reading about it? Not surprisingly, then, when students are asked to write descriptions or narratives, a prime source of material is the family, a theme they are familiar with and interested in. This chapter also deals with the family, but from a different angle: the selections examine what has happened to the American family in recent years. Much attention in the press has been given to the the health—or, as some would have it, the purported lack of health—of the family. The issue has proven ripe for journalists, sociologists, psychologists, and others.

The first two selections raise the central issue of the chapter: what has happened to the American family. Jerrold Footlick's article provides an overview of the changes in the American family, offering the viewpoint that the American family per se does not exist but has been replaced by American families that reflect the diversity now found in the nation. Barbara Ehrenreich uses former Vice President Dan Quayle's attack on the new types of families (using the popular television show *Murphy Brown*, which cast an unmarried professional in the role of mother) as a springboard for her viewpoint on the American family: Given the sharp rise in reported cases of incest and murder among family members, we must question whether "family values" are what we need. Many students will find this issue exciting because they are in the midst of seeing, if not experiencing for themselves, the changes discussed in the readings.

The next four readings address the issue of marriage and motherhood. Whereas Anna Quindlen, in "Evan's Two Moms," argues that lesbians and gay men are viable parents for children, John Leo's "Snear Not at 'Ozzie and Harriet'" takes a decidedly more conservative view in claiming that a return to the traditional family, as demonstrated by the 1950s television show *Ozzie and Harriet*, is needed. These two readings provide arguments that support differing perspectives on the current topic of new versus traditional parents in the family.

Class discussion of this theme will generally lead students to state that "happiness" is an essential part of the family picture. C. S. Lewis's "We Have No 'Right to Happiness'" addresses this often-held notion when he argues that the "right to happiness" is an ill-founded concept. Students may have difficulty with this reading, not only because of its complex structure, but because its stance is different from what many students believe. Although many students may also take issue with the last reading by Betty Rollin, which questions the myth and role of motherhood that is perpetuated by society, the way in which she argues her thesis is easier for students to understand. Rollin's "Motherhood: Who Needs It?" was written twenty-five years ago and provides an excellent opportunity for students to analyze the validity of her perspective, claim, and supporting evidence. Thus, the added benefit of this reading is a lesson in the timelessness of some issues.

CHAPTER 11: VALUES AND HUMAN NATURE

Part of what shapes our world are the values we bring to it. Influenced by family, friends, education, religion, and the like, values are a fascinating topic because they are seemingly ever changing. Our values reflect who we are as human beings. To know a person's heroes and role models is to know something important about that person. Just as interesting, too, is the study of human nature or "what makes people tick."

In the first selection, Ellen Goodman offers her viewpoint that, despite its bad reputation, guilt is a good emotion. This is an effective example of how viewpoints can originate from a hunch, and thoughtful reflection on the hunch can produce a paper. Encourage your students to find possible paper topics in this manner.

On a more serious note, the next viewpoint by Sarah Pettit, "In or Out: To Tell or Not to Tell," discusses whether lesbians and gay men should come out of the closet and the ramifications of their decisions. Point out to students that Pettit does not explicitly state that lesbians and gay men should or should not come out of the closet; rather she examines the difficult decision that faces people whose sexual orientation is not widely accepted.

The next two selections complement each other, thus teaching well as a pair. In "What Are Our Real Values?" Nicols Fox argues that people's actions differ from what they claim to value, and in "The Missing Element: Moral Courage," Barbara Tuchman focuses on the need for people to stand up for their beliefs. Expect many of your students to agree strongly with Fox. For some students, however, Tuchman's piece will prove more challenging and will take more time to analyze than Fox's. It is well worth the effort.

Gary Engle's selection on Superman will pique students' interest because it deals not only with the theme of values but uses a popular culture icon as its focus. Engle's reading is an especially good model of a piece of writing that thoroughly examines and supports its claim. Moreover, it provides a good example of the ways in which students can find topics for arguments by identifying, describing, and then supporting their beliefs. An effective class exercise is to ask students to choose a figure in the arts (or popular culture) and to examine the ways in which he or she exemplifies what they value.

The final selection in this chapter is sure to elicit strong reactions from students. Erich Fromm argues that the choices we make in our lives have a direct relationship to our (lack of) happiness. As such, Fromm's reading provides an excellent example of valid cause-effect relationships. You can expect students to have a stake in this issue: many will argue that the Baby Boomer generation is to blame for Generation Xers' inability to achieve all that they want (or deserve). Such reactions provide an opportunity to discuss the dangers of the *ad hominem* fallacy. Remind students to attack the issues or the ideas, not to take potshots at people who are not present to defend themselves. You might also want to return briefly to C. S. Lewis's reading in Chapter 10, which addresses whether we have a "right to happiness."

CHAPTER 12: THE POWER AND POLITICS OF LANGUAGE

Students seem to be increasingly aware of the power and politics of language. Most students are cognizant of what is politically correct and incorrect (e.g., the use of the term *African American* instead of *black*, *Native American* instead of *Indian*, *women* instead of *girls*, and so on). Many students understand the ways in which language is used to sway people (through commercials and political speeches, for example). Even in the papers they write for their classes, most students have faced the consequences of the incorrect use of language (for instance, sentences that do not achieve their intended meaning and grammar errors). Although the topic of language was perhaps once considered the territory of "English teachers," many people now see language-related issues as having a direct relationship to and impact on their lives.

The first two viewpoints discuss topics most students can relate to: Frank Trippett's "Time to Reflect on Blah, Blah, Blah" offers his reactions to the needless talk that pervades our lives. By listening to the use of language around him, Trippett has discovered an idea worthy of examination. All the more reason to go about our lives with our ears open. Point out to students the word *reflect* in his title: viewpoints are occasions on which to reflect (or ponder, muse, ruminate) on issues. In "Bards of the Internet," Philip Elmer-DeWitt looks at the less-than-satisfactory quality of writing he reads on the Internet. Much like Trippett, Elmer-DeWitt discovers his viewpoint from observing what might previously have gone unnoticed and unsaid. This, too, is good reason to go about our lives with our eyes open.

The next two essays largely concern the matter of censorship. John Simon, in "Why Good English Is Good for You," denounces the incorrect use of language he reads and hears; thus, he argues for the correct use of language. Many students, not surprisingly, will vehemently disagree with Simon's stance. To emphasize the importance of counterarguments, ask students (either as an in-class or out-of-class assignment) to write a letter to Simon detailing their disagreements and rebutting the points he makes in his argument. This can form the basis of class discussion of Simon's reading.

Next, Kymberli Hagelberg denounces John Wildmon's attempt to censor the popular forms of art that many students enjoy. Expect many students to agree with Hagelberg's stance. You might want to ask them to play devil's advocate and to generate counterarguments. This, too, could become the basis of class discussion of Hagelberg's paper.

The most surprising selection in this chapter is J. Clinton Brown's "In Defense of the N Word": not only does it go against popular sentiment, it flirts with overtones of racism. Ask students what difference it makes that Brown is African American. Would those students who agree with Brown's argument have the same viewpoint if he were white? If nothing else, Brown's selection provides an excellent example of the power of specific word choice: the use of just one word—in this case, the *n* word—can cause quite a stir.

The last reading in this chapter looks at variations of language, specifically Black English. Making a case that Black English is indeed a bona fide language, James Baldwin examines an issue that is still misunderstood by many people. If some students disagree with Baldwin's stance, ask them to define what they think a language is and how Black English fails to fulfill the criteria. How does Baldwin anticipate people's objections? One of the added bonuses of this reading is that it asks students to think about what we mean when we call something a *language*; thus, students are the recipients of an introduction to linguistics.

CHAPTER 13: MATTERS OF EQUALITY

When most people think about equality, chances are they conjure up images of different races and genders. While those issues of equality are examined in the last three selections of this chapter, other less apparent forms of discrimination are discussed in the first three readings.

In "Sizism—One of the Last 'Safe' Prejudices," Sally E. Smith offers her viewpoint that discrimination against overweight people is an often unacknowledged bias. The next selection, by Lindsy Van Gelder, "Marriage as a Restricted Club," posits the viewpoint that lesbian couples are discriminated against because they are not allowed to marry legally, thus preventing them from enjoying the privileges offered to those couples who can (such as health benefits). In "Claiming the Self," Leonard Kriegel argues that disabled people are second-class citizens. These three selections will open many students' eyes—and minds—to three forms of discrimination they might not otherwise have been aware of. An interesting class discussion can ensue on other less apparent forms of discrimination that students may have witnessed. These too might be excellent topics for viewpoint and argument papers.

The next two readings teach well as a pair because they both deal with affirmative action. Charles Krauthammer's "A Defense of Quotas" argues that affirmative action quotas are warranted, while Shelby Steele's "Affirmative Action: The Price of Preference" argues that affirmative action has not worked in favor of the people for whom it was intended. Before you discuss the readings, ask students to share their own views of affirmative action. After they read the two selections, ask them which perspective they find more convincing. What in Krauthammer's and Steele's arguments influenced their choice?

The final reading in this chapter deals with women in the military. "Women in Combat: Give It a Try and See If It Works," by Marianne Means, argues that women should be allowed in combat. Some students will no doubt disagree with Means' stance. Ask all of your students to generate a list of reasons why women should not be allowed to fight in combat. Using Means' reading as ammunition (excuse the pun) to support women in combat, have students debate the issue in class. Ask the students who do not feel strongly one way or the other to be the jury that decides which side offers more convincing reasoning. This exercise allows students to discuss a timely issue and analyze the strategies of argumentation.

AFTERTHOUGHTS

The readings in Part 2 of *Commitment, Voice, and Clarity* serve several functions. First, they deal with topics most students are interested in and have a stake in. As such, you can anticipate lively class discussions. You can also expect students to write papers that mean something to them because of the appealing themes and because they have something to say about those topics. Second, the selections are models of the ways in which writers posit a viewpoint, take a stand, or argue a position. Instead of offering cut-and-dry, pro-or-con approaches to argumentation, the authors muse on a topic, show their audience how they came to adopt a particular perspective, discuss supporting evidence, and address differing points of view. The readings attest to there being no "formula" for the writing of convincing viewpoints and arguments; rather, writers have to establish themselves as credible thinkers, and their arguments have to demonstrate sound, logical, and compelling evidence. I believe that the forty-eight selections do just that—and in a variety of rich and interesting ways.

Sample Fifteen-Week Course Outline

This fifteen-week course outline is meant to be flexible. Because some topics might prove especially difficult (or easy) for your students, it might be best to accommodate their needs by spending more (or less) time on specific chapters in both the rhetoric and the reader. In Part 2, the chapters can be taught in whatever order you prefer.

Week 1   Chapter 1, "Understanding Argument"

Week 2   Chapter 2, "From Experience-Based to Idea-Based Writing"

Week 3   Chapter 3, "Writing Viewpoint and Argument Papers"

Week 4   Chapter 4, "Strategies of Argumentation"

Week 5   Discussion and analysis of Chapter 6, "Education"

Week 6   Discussion and analysis of Chapter 7, "Working for a Living"

Week 7   Discussion and analysis of Chapter 8, "Sports and Leisure"

Week 8   Chapter 5, "The Researched Paper"

Week 9   Discussion and analysis of Chapter 9, "Popular Culture"

Week 10   Discussion and analysis of Chapter 10, "The American Family"

Week 11   Discussion and analysis of Chapter 11, "Values and Human Nature"

Week 12   Discussion and analysis of the Chapter 12, "The Power and Politics of Language"

Week 13   Discussion and analysis of Chapter 13, "Matters of Equality"

Week 14   This week can be used as a "catch-up" time for discussion and analysis of readings not fully examined in preceding weeks. Because some of the themes will elicit more student reactions than others, either returning to them or spending a few extra days on them when they appear on the course outline is appropriate.

Week 15   This week, too, can be spent on topics from the rhetoric or the readings not fully covered in the preceding weeks. Another option is to have student conferences sometime in the middle of the semester—preferably before students begin library research on their topics so you can make sure the students have a clear, well-focused direction, answer any of their specific questions, or discuss their writing with them.

SAMPLE TEN-WEEK

COURSE OUTLINE

Given the time limitations of a ten-week term, it might be best to ask your students which of the chapters in Part 2 interest them the most and design your course outline according to their preferences and yours. Students, of course, can be instructed to read the chapters they did not select. Because the themes are independent of one another, you can change the order in which you discuss them. The course outline that follows includes all of the readings on all of the themes. To secure valuable information on library research, students should read and then periodically review the material in Chapter 5, "The Researched Paper."

Week 1   Chapter 1, "Understanding Argument"
            Chapter 2, "From Experience-Based to Idea-Based Writing"

Week 2   Chapter 3, "Writing Viewpoint and Argument Papers"

Week 3   Chapter 4, "Strategies of Argumentation"
            Chapter 5, "The Researched Paper"

Week 4   Discussion and analysis of Chapter 6, "Education"

Week 5   Discussion and analysis of Chapters 7 and 8, "Working for a Living" and "Sports and Leisure"

Week 6   Discussion and analysis of Chapter 9, "Popular Culture"

Week 7   Discussion and analysis of Chapter 10, "The American Family"

Week 8   Discussion and analysis of Chapter 11, "Values and Human Nature"

Week 9   Discussion and analysis of Chapter 12, "The Power and Politics of Language"

Week 10   Discussion and analysis of Chapter 13, "Matters of Equality"

POSSIBLE ANSWERS TO
DISCUSSION QUESTIONS

What follows are possible answers to the "Discussion Questions" that follow each reading. These represent what you *might* expect from your students. They are not intended to be the *only* answers to the questions; nor are they meant to be thorough. Because many of the "Discussion Questions" ask for students' own understandings or interpretations, these answers are meant to assist you in your discussion of the ways in which the authors employ the strategies of argumentation to help make their viewpoints and arguments convincing.

CHAPTER 6: EDUCATION

Norman Cousins, "How to Make People Smaller than They Are"

1. The title refers to the ways in which not emphasizing the humanities can diminish people's powers to reason, see connections between ideas, and engage in creative endeavors. By schools becoming prejob-training centers, students are not being given the opportunity to "enlarge" their minds.

2. Cousins's audience is any group that does not believe that humanities should be the central focus of the schools' curriculum. Thus, his viewpoint could be directed to any or all of the groups mentioned in the question.

3. Paragraph 7 is the focal point regarding this question. Depending on how convincing people find it, the warrant will prove beneficial or damaging to Cousins's argument.

4. Student responses will vary.

(N.B. No matter how students answer the question, make sure that they support their idea by citing exactly what in the text prompted their reaction. This advice also applies to all other answers in which "student responses will vary" appears.)

5. Professionals in other fields might try to claim that studying the humanities does not necessarily make people more thoughtful, creative, analytical, etc. They also might claim that training for jobs and focusing on the practicalities to which Cousins alludes also teaches people what the humanities claim to teach them. Finally, they might claim that equal attention to both areas of inquiry are necessary to provide students with a broad-based, well-rounded education.

V. V. Raman, "Why It's So Important that Our Students Learn More about Science"

1. Raman poses the idea that instead of science being perceived as a mass of facts and figures, its importance lies in the way it can teach people to question, analyze, and interpret phenomena in the world. He supports his viewpoint by first defining what he does not mean by *science*, what he does mean when he uses the term, and examples of the ways in which the study of science has enlarged our understanding of the world.

2. Raman sees science differently from most people, who probably think of it as just an accumulation of facts and figures. He, on the other hand, sees it as "a mode of inquiry" and "an intellectual framework" that can help people to think, analyze, and understand. Defining his terms is central to his thesis.

3. Raman was most likely directing his viewpoint to people who think that studying science is memorizing useless facts and figures. Because he carefully defines the way he sees science and distinguishes between his definition and the more popular one, he paves the way to examine his perspective.

4. Citing such famous scientists as Copernicus, Galileo, Newton, and Edison provides examples of Raman's claim. Most people know the tremendous contributions these scientists made to the field of science and to our lives.

5. Cousins would probably agree with Raman because of the ways in which Raman defines the term *science*. Both writers support education's emphasis on the importance of mindful inquiry, analysis of ideas, and values. Whereas Cousins finds these emphases in the humanities, Raman locates them in the sciences.

William A. Henry, III, "In Defense of Elitism"

1. Henry's tone can be described as no-nonsense, direct, and stinging. He probably could have made the same points in a more mild-mannered tone, but the effect would not have been as eye-opening and striking.

2. Student responses will vary.

3. Henry uses specific data from surveys, facts, and reports both as springboards and support for his ideas. Some examples include the Department of Commerce's *Statistical Abstract of the United States* and the U.S. Labor Department's Bureau of Labor Statistics. Because these are governmental documents that report researched statistics, their credibility cannot be questioned. Henry's analysis of them, however, can be disputed by people who believe that *all* students, not just the most intelligent and accomplished ones, should be allowed, if not encouraged, to go to college.

4. In varying degrees, Henry uses all three appeals in his argument: principally, reason and emotion, and, to a lesser extent, ethics. By appealing to people's sense of reason (by providing statistics and indisputable facts), emotion (by inciting people's feelings), and ethics (by showing his direct, no-nonsense approach), Henry has a greater chance of reaching—and persuading—a larger audience than if he had used just one kind of appeal.

5. Henry probably envisioned his audience as those people who agree *and* disagree with him: the former as a way to document what they might have thought themselves and the latter as a way to convince them of his perspective.

Page Smith, "Human Time and the College Student"

1. The descriptive opening paragraph serves to catch readers' attention and interest; it puts them in the room, struggling along with the students. The paragraph helps to put readers on the students' (and Smith's) side.

2. Instead of listing all of the reasons against final exams, Smith offers major and minor premises to reach his conclusion. He probably could have reached it by inductive logic as well.

Students might see either form of reasoning as an effective means by which Smith could argue the point.

3. Student responses will vary.

4. Smith probably targeted fellow professors and university administrators as his audience because they have a vested interest in the issue.

5. At the end of his argument, Smith mentions better pacing of instruction and testing and a different weighting of paper and exam grades. Student reactions to these alternatives will vary, as will their own suggestions on ways to improve the current situation.

Jonathan Z. Smith, "Questioning the Great, Unexplained . . . College Major"

1. Because college majors are offered by departments, the two are inextricably related. Student responses to this question, however, will vary.

2. Student responses will vary.

3. Smith establishes his credibility by showing he has researched the topic (e.g., he presents secondary sources as background information on the history of the college major). He also meticulously examines his thesis and supports it with clear, thorough logic.

4. Although Smith uses one example to illustrate his claim, it is a major offered at all universities. The one example supports his thesis. Students may disagree on the degree to which his argument is successful.

5. Proponents of the college major and academic department may cite the longevity of majors and departments as their defense. They might also claim that the individual courses students take in their majors really do connect to each other and give students an enlarged view of the field and that, given the limited number of courses students can take in their college degrees, the major is a sound way to focus on one specific discipline. They might also claim that no better alternative has ever been proposed in the history of academic departments and majors.

Paul Goodman, "A Proposal to Abolish Grading"

1. Goodman's assumption weakens his claim if readers believe that grading serves purposes other than the ones he cites.
2. Student responses will vary. An *ad hominem* logical fallacy appears in paragraph 8 where Goodman dismisses parents when he states, "The parents should be simply disregarded; their anxiety has done enough damage already."
3. Student responses will vary.
4. Student responses will vary.
5. Student responses will vary.

CHAPTER 7: WORKING FOR A LIVING

Lance Morrow, "What Is the Point of Work?"

1. The historical overview provides background information so readers can compare current attitudes toward the meaning of work with previous generations'. It helps to put Morrow's viewpoint in context.
2. Morrow waits until paragraph 4 to pose the question, "Has the American work ethic really expired?" In paragraph 10, he explicitly states his viewpoint that "the work ethic is not dead, but it is weaker now." By waiting until he discusses previous generations' concepts of the meaning of work and their work ethic, he builds up to his main idea, providing a necessary context for current attitudes.
3. Student responses will vary.
4. The two questions in paragraph 4 set the stage for Morrow not only to answer them but to state his position on the work ethic.
5. If readers disagree with Morrow's ideas concerning the meaning found in work, they are less inclined to agree with his viewpoint. His definition of the meaning of work provides the background for his perspective.

Barbara Ehrenreich, "Good-bye to the Work Ethic"

1. Ehrenreich's describing the yuppie as a "pathetic creature" is one example of her use of charged language. Depending on whether readers agree with such descriptions, her use of language can draw readers into the essay or turn them off. No matter if they agree or disagree, however, Ehrenreich captures readers' attention. Her appeal to emotion adds to the flavor of her viewpoint and, for readers who agree with her ideas, to its believability.

2. Student responses will vary.

3. Student responses will vary.

4. Although student responses will vary on the plausibility of Ehrenreich's distinction between a work ethic and a job ethic, the difference is vital: the last paragraph's success depends on it. In fact, Ehrenreich's viewpoint leads up to that final idea.

5. Yuppies might claim that they "abused" the work ethic because they enjoyed their work; competition necessitated them working hard; their lifestyles dictated their working the way they did to earn extra income; they wanted a better lifestyle than their parents had. Some might even claim that what Ehrenreich sees as "abuse" is actually what they see as diligent work. Ehrenreich does not directly address these ideas.

Laurence Steinberg and Ellen Greenberger, "Teenagers and Work"

1. Steinberg and Greenberger paint a negative picture of teenagers, characterizing them as less than conscientious students who are interested in working only to earn the disposable income to buy cars, clothing, stereos, and drugs. If readers agree with their characterization of teens, Steinberg and Greenberger's audience will be sympathetic to their thinking. If, on the other hand, readers disagree with the characterization, Steinberg and Greenberger will have a difficult time winning over people who hold differing perspectives on teens and work.

2. Steinberg and Greenberger seem to assume that teens who do not work after school place a high value on education, go

home directly after school, and study on weekdays and weekends. For students who do work after school, the opposite can
be inferred.

3. Student responses will vary.

4. Steinberg and Greenberger allude to studies and government
    statistics to support their claims. However, no names of specific
    studies or statistics are cited.

5. Student responses will vary.

Gloria Steinem, "The Importance of Work"

1. Although student responses will vary, Steinem's argument still
    has relevance today because, despite the growing numbers of
    women in the workforce, many of them are not the main in-
    come earners in the family. Steinem poses important ideas
    about the meaning people find in work (aside from the finan-
    cial). That alone can contribute to its timeliness.

2. Student responses will vary.

3. Opponents to Steinem's argument might claim that women
    should find value in raising children and in housework; that
    the menial jobs women have cannot provide them with the
    challenge and pleasure higher-level employment affords; that
    work does not necessarily provide people with the benefits
    Steinem describes; that the economy is dramatically altered by
    women joining the workforce. Throughout her argument,
    Steinem addresses these claims.

4. Given the thorough discussion of the "womenworkbecausewe-
    haveto" idea, Steinem's argument is targeted primarily at
    women as a way to encourage them to stand up for reasons to
    work other than "becausewehaveto." Moreover, this piece orig-
    inally appeared in Ms. magazine, whose main readership is
    women, thus giving added evidence that Steinem was directing
    her ideas toward women.

5. Because Morrow finds inherent value in work, he would proba-
    bly agree with Steinem's thesis. In his viewpoint, Morrow men-
    tions women's entrance into the workforce as "a powerful
    source of ambition and energy." Morrow's other statements
    seem to mesh with Steinem's thinking (e.g., "Work is the most
    thorough and profound organizing principle in American life"

and "Work is the way we tend to the world. The way that people connect").

Alfie Kohn, "Incentives Can Be Bad for Business"

1. Student responses will vary.

2. Because Kohn's article first appeared in *Inc.* magazine, a publication read by middle- and upper-management, it is safe to assume that Kohn saw that group of people as his audience. Additional evidence is the number of business studies Kohn cites to support his thinking.

3. Student responses will vary.

4. Possible answers include giving employees the power to make important decisions, independence to work on projects, and responsibility. The Saturn automobile plants, modeled after German and Swedish car companies, advertise that teams of workers build entire cars, taking total responsibility for the finished product. This differs markedly from other car manufacturers, which use the assembly-line approach to building automobiles. The key to Saturn's thinking is to give workers the freedom, responsibility, and power to see a project through from start to finish, thus showing them the fruits of their labor.

5. Because Morrow believes in the intrinsic value of work, he would tend to agree with Kohn. The work ethic is faltering because workers do not see enough meaning in what they do. All the more reason, Kohn suggests, to make work as meaningful as possible for workers by showing them the importance of what they are doing, even if the work is boring.

Robert J. Samuelson, "Overworked Americans"

1. Samuelson argues his case by refutation. In other words, he cites one of Juliet Schor's ideas and offers counterarguments to it. Along with doing this throughout the entire essay, he discusses other studies that support his ideas. Even if people disagree with his stance, they can see that Samuelson has seriously and thoroughly thought out his claim.

2. By beginning his argument with a narrative, Samuelson can interest his audience, show the more personal side of himself

(establishing his credibility as a writer), and indirectly make his audience think about their own experiences of feeling overworked.

3. Although student responses will vary, Samuelson's organization shows how he is methodically building his case by refuting an opposing perspective.

4. By conceding certain points to Schor, Samuelson establishes himself as someone who has an open mind (as opposed to a narrow, blinders-on type of perspective). This contributes to his credibility as a writer.

5. De Tocqueville's quote is not only timeless, but Samuelson's use of it makes it timely. The quote is very fitting. Ending with a quote over 150 years old gives added emphasis to the importance of the topic that Samuelson examines. It also leaves his audience thinking about the perspective he has presented.

Chapter 8: Sports and Leisure

Murray Ross, "Football Red and Baseball Green"

1. Although student responses will vary, Ross does not merely mention that sports are like the drama found in popular theater and football is like war and the space program. He examines the analogies he offers as a way of adding to their credibility.

2. While some will believe that Ross has offered a fascinating analysis of baseball and football, others will claim that he over-intellectualizes two simple games. The responses to this question will vary.

3. Because most Americans are at least slightly familiar with football and baseball, a case can be made that Ross envisioned his audience both as avid fans and those who aren't interested in sports. Given his attention to detail (e.g., the spatial arrangement of the baseball diamond), however, a stronger case can be made that he was directing his viewpoint to readers who are knowledgeable about and interested in the two sports.

4. Ross offers a complete discussion of baseball before he discusses football. Each of the sports is analyzed in reference to the myth Ross attaches to the sport.

5. Quoting William Carlos Williams supports Ross's idea that baseball provides a respite from the chaotic pace of life. Also, by quoting Williams, a poet, Ross reinforces the idea of the beauty in such a sport. Quoting Jerry Kramer and Mike Garrett, both professional athletes, supports Ross's claims by offering experts' proof.

Roland Merullo, "How Pro Football Was Ruined"

1. Using the first-person point of view helps to personalize Merullo's viewpoint. It sounds as though Merullo is talking to his audience.

2. Merullo's main point is not explicitly stated until paragraph 4. By delaying its appearance, Merullo is able to set the mood of the viewpoint and allow his audience to put the point he will be making into context.

3. Although student responses will vary, given the brevity of the viewpoint, a case can be made that Merullo drags out the idea of play-by-play carpentry.

4. Opponents of Merullo's perspective might claim that many points are interesting enough to warrant multiple reshowings or that, with the help of technology, it is revealing to see the plays reshown from various angles, in slow motion, etc. Opponents might also claim that no one is forced to watch the replays and that the viewers' time can be spent getting a snack in the kitchen.

5. Merullo states in paragraph 4 that instant replay isn't bad; it's just that too much of it is unnerving. Further attention to the specific situations when instant replay should be used might help to support his perspective.

Dick Schaap, "So Much of the Joy Is Gone"

1. Student responses will vary.

2. Between Schaap's discussion of professional sports and college sports is a confession of his own guilt. Before discussing college sports, however, he cites the "glamoriz[ation] . . . of hypocrisy and deception and corruption." These three elements are also

prevalent in college sports and thus provide a smooth transition into Schaap's discussion of them in college sports.

3.   Schaap appeals to reason with the abundance of factual information he presents. When he confesses to "shar[ing] the guilt" in his transition into college sports, he also appeals to ethics. Because his argument is about a topic that spurs people's emotions, a case can be made that he employs the appeal of pathos.

4.   Owners might say that they have to pay the "going price" for talent; that athletes are also entertainers who deserve the salaries they are paid; that the playing life of an athlete is short, so he or she deserves the money he or she is paid; and that sports are "big business."

5.   This statement provides a moment of reflection in Schaap's argument for readers to consider whether sports deserve the price tag attached to them. Because sports are not known for teaching "heroic lessons," "positive values," etc., the statement can be seen as strengthening Schaap's argument.

Felicia E. Halpert, "Sports Heroes Wanted"

1.   By beginning her essay with a specific example, Halpert sets the scene for her thesis. The example serves not only as background information, but it engages the audience into learning what point Halpert is trying to make.

2.   Student responses will vary.

3.   Student responses will vary.

4.   If Halpert were writing for a male audience, she might have explained how male sports heroes have influenced young boys. Such a discussion would have helped to show that the issue is not restricted to one gender, and it would help to strengthen her idea that women also need sports heroes of their own gender.

5.   The personal reference at the conclusion of Halpert's argument demonstrates the ways in which the issue of role models in sports affects young women. It personalizes the argument and encourages readers to think about who *they* wanted to be when they were young.

Tom Weir, "Navratilova Is Ace of All Female Athletes"

1. Because he acknowledges the achievements of top female athletes before explaining why he doesn't think they are the best female athlete of the century, Weir probably envisioned as his audience people who might disagree with his choice of Navratilova.

2. Weir methodically cites athletes others might consider for the honor of top female athlete and then explains their shortcomings. Thus, one of the ways he supports his claim is by defusing any counterarguments.

3. The facts and figures Weir presents are indisputable. Student responses will differ.

4. In the first paragraph, Weir states his claim. Then he addresses potential opposing reactions before discussing his reasons for choosing Navratilova as the top female athlete of the century.

5. Student responses will vary.

Lyle J. Micheli, "Children and Sports"

1. Micheli's personal reference establishes his credibility as an authority on the topic. Although writers who are not sports physicians can write convincingly on the issue, Micheli's expertise contributes to the appeal of ethos.

2. Student responses will vary.

3. Volunteer coaches might claim that children are naturally competitive and that injuries result despite the coaches' warnings. They might also state that if children's sports were adequately funded, professional trainers could be hired. In addition, most coaches try to the best of their ability to help young athletes and cannot be faulted on their performance. They might say professional trainers are no guarantee that the number of sports-related injuries will decline and that it is the parents' responsibility to enroll students in the safest sports program.

4. Micheli uses reason or logic to make his case when he cites statistics of sports-related injuries. He also uses the appeal of

ethos when he cites his own experience as cofounder of the first pediatric sports-medicine clinic. Because the issue draws on some people's emotions (e.g., parents, coaches, trainers), a case can be made that he uses the appeal of emotion.

5. Since Micheli cites his credentials and offers statistics on sports-related injuries, he was probably addressing those people involved in youth athletic programs: coaches, trainers, and parents.

CHAPTER 9: POPULAR CULTURE

Patricia J. Williams, "Hate Radio"

1. By introducing personal narrative into her viewpoint, Williams engages her readers, personalizes the topic, and helps to establish a basis for her credibility as an author.

2. Williams's questions force her readers to consider their own reactions or answers to her queries. They also demonstrate that she herself is carefully considering her topic by posing questions that emerge from the points she is examining.

3. Williams appeals to emotions when she discusses a controversial issue, one that many people have strong reactions to. She also appeals to ethics when she introduces her own experiences and reactions when she listens to the radio shows about which she writes.

4. Radio personalities would probably cite First Amendment rights as their first defense. Talk-show personalities would probably also say that if people don't like their shows, they don't have to listen. They also might claim that, given the huge popularity of their shows, their views must represent those of many Americans. Finally, they might claim that Williams is making too much of or overintellectualizing the topic.

5. Williams's thought-provoking last question asks her audience to consider the future of "hate radio." As such, it is a powerful ending because it makes her readers think of the long-term consequences of such talk shows.

Sarah Ferguson, "The Comfort of Being Sad"

1. Because the grunge culture has identified Kurt Cobain and Pearl Jam as their heroes, Ferguson's choice is appropriate and sufficient.

2. Readers' attitudes toward twelve-step meetings might influence whether they find Ferguson's analogy convincing: if they see twelve-step meetings as beneficial and comforting (as opposed to boring and repetitive), they might find her analogy an effective one that helps to strengthen her viewpoint.

3. Student responses will vary.

4. Ferguson makes a point of revealing that she has conducted primary research on the grunge culture. This helps to contribute to the appeals of reason and ethics: her viewpoint reflects her research findings and her sense of character.

5. Members of the grunge culture might claim that *every* generation has its particular concerns. They also might argue that the depression and anger they experience is warranted because of the world their parents left for them. They might offer the idea that music is supposed to reflect personal concerns. Further, because they are not yet adults, they are not responsible for seeing the greater truths in life. Finally, they might state that Williams is overintellectualizing a topic that should be of no concern to her.

Josh Ozersky, "TV's Anti-Families: Married...with Malaise"

1. Ozersky makes his claim at the end of paragraph 4 and beginning of paragraph 5 when he explicitly states his claim about the "decline of the family" and the "anti-family." He uses inductive reasoning as his method of argumentation.

2. Cadow is a psychologist whose ideas add credibility to Ozersky's argument because of her experience analyzing behavior.

3. Student responses will vary.

4. Student responses will vary.

5. Ozersky states that "the TV screen is neither a mirror, reflecting ourselves paralyzed in chairs in front of it, nor a window, through which we observe the antics of distance

players. . . . TV seeks only to impose its own values. . . ."
Thus, television is not responsible for accurately reflecting
any group of people.

Claudia Boatright, "Mythogyny"

1. Boatright's use of three vivid descriptions of advertisements
   immediately engages the curiosity of her readers and illustrates
   examples of the issue she addresses in her argument.
2. Student responses will vary.
3. Boatright uses logic and reason in her argument (describing
   the advertisements and citing critics). She also uses emotion to
   advance her ideas (the topic is controversial, with most people
   having strong opinions). Because she includes her experiences
   as a teacher and reveals herself to be a concerned adult, she
   also appeals to ethics.
4. Boatright probably envisioned advertisers who market their
   products as a possible audience because she discusses the effect
   the ads have on young women. For the same reason, she might
   have imagined teenagers as her audience as a way to instruct
   them about the danger of the ads perpetuating falsehoods.
5. The unstated "plan of action" is obviously to ban the advertisements and educate students about the dangers that such advertising has on women's self-image.

**Benjamin DeMott, "In Hollywood, Class Doesn't Put Up Much of a
Struggle"**

1. Student responses will vary.
2. Because DeMott has selected well-known, successful movies,
   his position is strengthened. Readers are most likely familiar
   with the movies, and their popularity lends added urgency to
   the problem DeMott discusses.
3. Readers will be more inclined to believe DeMott's thesis if
   they have seen the movies about which he writes because they
   will be able to visualize for themselves the problems DeMott
   claims exist. Readers who have not yet seen the films, however, can only go on DeMott's analysis of them.

4. DeMott methodically analyzes one film after another as a way to support his claim. The result is a convincing argument.

5. Student responses will vary.

Grace April Oursler Armstrong, "Let's Keep Christmas Commercial"

1. Student responses will vary.

2. Armstrong uses the appeal of logic in her argument when she describes the history of gift giving and the real meaning of Christmas, which cannot be bought or sold. She also uses the appeal of emotion because the topic is fraught with strong feelings on both sides. When she describes her experiences shopping at Christmas, she might invoke the appeal of ethics as she reveals herself as a trustworthy person.

3. Armstrong probably envisioned people who denounce the commercialization of Christmas as her audience. If she were addressing people who are not bothered by Christmas's commercialization, she would be writing to the already converted.

4. Student responses will vary.

5. Student responses will vary.

CHAPTER 10: THE AMERICAN FAMILY

Jerrold Footlick, "What Happened to the Family?"

1. Although responses may differ, the seeming contradiction in Footlick's first two sentences emphasizes the idea that the traditional American family is being replaced by new kinds of families. Footlick's observation spurs his audience to continue reading to discover the outcome of his perspective.

2. Footlick supports his viewpoints by citing statistics, quoting demographers and sociologists, and presenting a history of the family. Student responses will vary on which pieces of evidence seem most convincing.

3. Footlick's brief history of the family provides information about the development of the family over time and puts the contemporary family into context, thus making readers better understand and appreciate families in the 1990s.

4. Throughout his viewpoint, Footlick discusses how the concept of family is deeply rooted in people's psyches, memories, values, and even dreams. People are "sensitive" to the topic: whether Americans try to return to the traditional family of the 1950s or continue to enlarge the ways in which we define family, in a very important way, family is a part of our future.

5. No support is really needed because Footlick's observation can be construed as common knowledge, which does not require supporting evidence. The word *family* connotes the sustenence and love to which Footlick refers.

Barbara Ehrenreich, "Oh, *Those* Family Values"

1. Ehrenreich offers a sarcastic view of the current interest in "family values" and "pro family" when the families that are current in the news are those in which murder, rape, incest, and dismemberment have occurred.

2. While Ehrenreich bases her observations on highly publicized news stories, they can be seen as representative of the growing, and pervasive, violence in the country. If nothing else, Ehrenreich's examples call attention to the "hellish side of family life."

3. Student responses will vary.

4. Ehrenreich's tone is no-nonsense, cutting, cynical, and sarcastic. Some examples appear in paragraph 2 ("We live in a culture that fetishizes the family as the ideal unit of human community, the perfect container for our lusts and love") and paragraph 10 ("We may be stuck with the family—at least until someone invents a sustainable alternative—but the family, with its deep, impacted tensions and longings, can hardly be expected to be the moral foundation of everything else").

5. People disagreeing with Ehrenreich's viewpoint might point out that she is discussing the exception to the rule and that most families do not reflect the publicized examples on which she bases her viewpoint.

Anna Quindlen, "Evan's Two Moms"

1. Quindlen employs deductive reasoning in her viewpoint. Her major premise is that marriage is a demonstration of the loving

commitment between two adults; the minor premise is that those two adults may be gay partners; and the conclusion is that gay partners make good parents. Quindlen's sound logic contributes to the strength of her viewpoint.

2. By discussing the reservations of some religious communities, Quindlen addresses opposing perspectives.

3. Quindlen's uses the appeal of logic in her argument. She discusses the facts and the reasoning that support her stance.

4. Quindlen probably had in mind people who object to gay couples marrying because she uses clear and logical reasoning to argue her point. She also rebuts opposing perspectives.

5. Student responses will vary.

John Leo, "Sneer Not at 'Ozzie and Harriet'"

1. Student responses will vary.

2. Leo quotes sociologists, the Rockefeller Commission, a well-known journalist, and the *New York Times* to advance his argument. These respected sources provide not only ideas that confirm his beliefs but data from which he infers new thinking.

3. Opponents to Leo's argument might claim that society has changed so much in the thirty or forty years since "Ozzie and Harriet" was the norm that his perspective is unrealistic. They might also claim that the new types of families are not necessarily as unhealthy as he suggests they are. They might find fault with Leo's contention that feminism "arose as a reaction to the traditional family, and the other movements fed into the antifamily mood." Also, they might claim that the current composition of families is not necessarily "antifamily" but just a different type of family.

4. Leo's tone is direct, hard hitting, and no-nonsense. He states his understanding of issues without elaborate clarification. The opening paragraph of his argument is one such example.

5. Barbara Ehrenreich would probably find fault with Leo's definition of terms (e.g., family values) and his reading of social movements (e.g., feminism). She would probably find fault with Leo not adequately considering current social conditions that are responsible for the breakdown of the family. She

would question whether Leo is romanticizing the whole notion of family values and his disregard of the violence, incest, and other ills that have occurred in a time in which so-called family values are *de riguer*.

C. S. Lewis, "We Have No 'Right to Happiness'"

1. Student responses will vary.
2. Because he first states what a "right to happiness" isn't, what other rights are, what Clare actually meant, the ways in which he agrees and disagrees with Clare, and repeated definitions of various terms, Lewis uses an involved and complex method by which to argue his stance.
3. Given Lewis's careful attention to defining his terms and explaining his agreements and disagreements with Clare's beliefs, Lewis anticipates opposing perspectives.
4. Student responses will vary.
5. Student responses will vary.

Betty Rollin, "Motherhood: Who Needs It?"

1. In her argument, Rollin attacks the commonly held belief that women's desire for motherhood is instinctive, and she rebuts the Motherhood Myth.
2. Although not as totally relevant today as it was twenty-five years ago (due, in large part, to the lessons feminism taught us), Rollin's article is still relevant. It will remain so until people abandon their belief that motherhood is instinctive in women and their acceptance of other facets of the Motherhood Myth.
3. Student responses will vary.
4. An answer to this question must take into account the year in which Rollin's selection was written. In 1970, the women's movement was in its infancy, and many (if not most) women hadn't yet fully analyzed and responded to the myths they had previously accepted and lived by. Thus, Rollin probably considered women as her audience. She

probably did not exclude men from her targeted audience be-cause men were responsible for helping to perpetuate (if not create) the myths Rollin examines.

5. Throughout her argument, Rollin's careful attention to logic accounts for her effective attention to opposing perspectives.

Chapter 11: Values and Human Nature

Ellen Goodman, "Putting in a Good Word for Guilt"

1. Because of the light, sometimes whimsical, and humorous topic Goodman has chosen to explore, the first person is a jus-tified and effective choice. Had she used the third person, the viewpoint might have lost some of its personal, jocular effect.

2. Student responses will vary.

3. For situations in which guilt *does* serve a useful purpose, you can expect students to cite obvious situations when people have broken rules that are punishable in the courts (stealing, acts of violence, and the like). Because these are such obvious reasons, Goodman does not have to address them in her view-point. Examples in which guilt serves a useful purpose will vary from student to student.

4. By citing the thinking of psychiatrists, sociologists, and the clergy, Goodman adds a serious dimension to an otherwise light-hearted viewpoint. Their contributions add substance and depth to her ideas.

5. Because all people, at some times in their lives, feel guilty (whether it is warranted or not), Goodman was probably not targeting any particular audience. Added support for this re-sponse is the fact that she wrote this viewpoint for the *Boston Globe*, a metropolitan newspaper with a wide range of readers. A case can be made, however, that because many of her exam-ples are about mothers and their children, she might have viewed her audience as women.

Sarah Pettit, "In or Out: To Tell or Not To Tell"

1. By beginning and ending her viewpoint with a personal story, Pettit brings the issue of outing to a personal level, one that

involves real people and not just a group of anonymous people. Employing such a technique is very engaging.

2. Although she does not explicitly state that people should or should not come out of the closet, Pettit discusses the difficulty and ramifications of the choice lesbians and gays face in their choice to stay in or come out of the closet.

3. Pettit carefully considers *both* sides of the issue, taking into account the problems caused by the choices people make.

4. Because this viewpoint was submitted to and published in *Newsweek* magazine, whose readership is both men and women, gays and straights, it is safe to assume that Pettit envisioned a wide range of readers. Also, because of her meticulous attention to the difficult choices both closeted and out gays and lesbians face, her viewpoint was probably not directed at either group.

5. Pettit's clear, nonjudgmental, and frank tone contributes to the overall effectiveness and believability of her viewpoint. She handles a complex and difficult topic honestly, fairly, and convincingly.

Nicols Fox, "What Are Our Real Values?"

1. By using the first person plural *we*, Fox engages her audience, placing them in the position of having to reflect on and answer the question she poses in the title of her argument. If she had used the third person, she would have forfeited the sense of immediacy and direct address that the first-person plural creates.

2. Fox argues that despite what people *say* they value, their actions indicate otherwise; that is, there exists a significant disparity between what people say and what they do.

3. Student responses will vary.

4. Fox offers numerous examples of what people say they value and what their actions indicate they value, thus pointing to the differences between what they say and what they do. The repetition of the questions, "What are our values?" and "What are the real American values?" reinforces the idea that people's actions contradict their claims.

5. The questions Fox raises throughout her argument not only strengthen her argument that "actions speak louder than

words," but they invite her audience to consider for themselves what their own "real values" are.

Barbara Tuchman, "The Missing Element: Moral Courage"

1. Tuchman's historical background of instances in which moral courage was at issue helps to put into context the current situation she addresses in her argument. Her audience learns that the issue is not peculiar to the time about which she writes.

2. Given Tuchman's analysis of the many examples in which moral courage was (and is) not displayed, her principal method of appeal is logic and reason.

3. Tuchman cites people who hold positions of leadership (e.g., parents, teachers, educators, and writers) as being responsible for distinguishing between good and bad, right and wrong.

4. Because examples of the absence of moral courage persist (some might say the number of examples has become epidemic) in the 1990s, Tuchman's argument is as relevant now as it was twenty-five years ago.

5. Nicols Fox and Barbara Tuchman certainly would agree that there exists an abnegation of responsibility: people refuse to take a stand and demonstrate responsibility for their beliefs. However, whereas Fox would say that people's actions differ from their statements, Tuchman would say that people go so far as to refuse to even claim responsibility, let alone act responsibly. Thus, the picture Tuchman paints is bleaker than Fox's.

Gary Engle, "What Makes Superman so Darned American"

1. Engle's personal remembrance draws his audience into his essay. It allows his readers to see the way this issue has its roots in early childhood and is one that has persisted. Readers might also ask themselves who *they* think might win: John Wayne or Superman.

2. Starting with paragraph 3, Engle discusses his many reasons for claiming that Superman is "*the* great American hero." His reasoning is convincing.

3. Student responses will vary.

4. Engle establishes his credibility by his careful, thorough, and well-reasoned discussion of his supporting evidence. Examining other authors such as Cooper, Melville, Wister, Steinbeck, Kerouac, and Moon, he provides evidence of having carefully researched the topic. His discussion of popular culture and language creates the same impression.

5. Student responses will vary.

Erich Fromm, "Our Way of Life Makes Us Miserable"

1. One example of a generalization that Fromm supports is that material affluence will not make people happy. He supports this statement with the example of Sweden, a country that has both "material security" and the highest suicide and alcoholism rates.

2. Fromm's method of appeal is logic: he provides well-reasoned and carefully considered evidence to support his claim.

3. Student responses will vary.

4. Because of the relatively new terminology that describes workers today (e.g., *stressed out, burned out, workaholics,* etc.), because of the high suicide rate (especially among teens), and because of the increased incidence of drug abuse and spousal abuse, a case can be made that Fromm's argument is as valid today as it was thirty years ago (if not more so).

5. Student responses will vary.

CHAPTER 12: THE POWER AND POLITICS
OF LANGUAGE

Frank Trippett, "Time to Reflect on Blah, Blah, Blah"

1. Trippett offers a wide range of examples: sportscasters, politicians, numerous radio and talk shows, moviegoers, cabdrivers, and barbers.

2. Television sportscasters, for example, might claim that they offer interesting and pertinent information for their viewers. They also might say that "color commentary" fills potential

"dead air" and replaces the excitement of attending the sports events. They finally might claim that no one is forcing people to listen to them: viewers can always turn down the volume on their television sets.

3. Trippett's tone is frank, no-nonsense, and even sarcastic. As a striking contrast to the excess verbiage Trippett condemns, the tone is very fitting.

4. Student responses will vary.

5. Student responses will vary.

Philip Elmer-Dewitt, "Bards of the Internet"

1. The most sympathetic audience would probably be people who value precision, correctness, well-rendered ideas, and even elegance in language. Elmer-Dewitt contrasts the writing he reads on the Internet with writers in past centuries who took great pains with both the content and correctness of their writing.

2. Elmer-Dewitt's sources provide background material for his ideas and demonstrate that he has incorporated pertinent research into his topic, thus adding to the credibility of his perspective.

3. The writers to whom Elmer-Dewitt refers would probably say that he is overintellectualizing the issue and that writing on the Internet should not be judged by the same standards of other writing. They might also claim that, for their audience, the writing is appropriate, if not well-written.

4. Student responses will vary.

5. Elmer-Dewitt's last paragraph does retreat from his earlier attack on the quality of writing found on the Internet. He may criticize it, but he backs off before writing it off (excuse the pun).

John Simon, "Why Good English Is Good for You"

1. Student responses will vary.

2. Simon's argument privileges people who speak and write Standard English or Edited American English. He fails to take into account other forms of English that have their own rules of

"correct" grammar (e.g., Black English). Simon defends his position by claiming that there is a correct English and an incorrect English, and the former is better than the latter.

3. Student responses will vary.

4. Student responses will vary.

5. No one seems to be immune from blame for the poor English usage Simon discusses: teachers, parents, writers, even the vice-president of the National Council of Teachers of English! Simon seems to blame everyone who does not conform to his standard.

Kymberli Hagelberg, "Censorship in the Arts"

1. Student responses will vary.

2. Hagelberg's opponents would probably claim that the First Amendment right guaranteeing free speech does not include pornography and obscenity. Furthermore, pornography and obscenity contribute to the moral decline of the country.

3. Student responses will vary.

4. By addressing the issue of free speech and censorship, Hagelberg draws on people's emotions, and by her use of analogies and logic, she appeals to reason.

5. One example of a rhetorical question appears in paragraph 3: "What individual or group among us has the right to choose what we see, read, listen to and talk about?" Most people would answer with a vehement, "No one has the right!"

J. Clinton Brown, "In Defense of the N Word"

1. Brown's assumption is that African Americans would take offense at anyone using the word *nigger*. Without this assumption, Brown would not have a thesis to argue.

2. Student responses will vary.

3. Brown's opponents would probably claim that African Americans should not perpetuate the use of language that demeans their race. African Americans should be role models for people. If they themselves use such terms, it might be seen as license for others to do so as well. In paragraph 5,

however, Brown contends that language "does not define, it evokes—or provokes."

4. While many people would probably claim that language is a by-product of racism, and because language reflects ideas, some might claim that language creates thoughts or ideas. Brown would probably side with the former belief because he claims that if people are already prejudiced, language is not going to change their attitudes.

5. Because Brown cites an incident in which he uses the word *nigger* in the company of fellow African Americans, his argument is believable. He also makes an important point when he claims that African Americans have "higher" priorities. Perhaps the situation is analagous to a person being able to insult his or her family, but that privilege is not extended to anyone else.

James Baldwin, "If Black English Isn't a Language, Then Tell Me, What Is?"

1. Student responses will vary.

2. People disagreeing with Baldwin might claim that the issue *is* a matter that deals solely with language and that there is one "correct" language and that any others are weak variations. Baldwin rebuts this perspective by explaining what all languages have in common and the ways in which Black English has contributed to the language white Americans take for granted.

3. Baldwin's tone is direct, forceful, and full of passion. The tone effectively fits the importance and urgency of the issue Baldwin presents, not to mention his interest in it.

4. Dialects are variations of languages and technically not considered languages themselves. Dialects denote a subcategory of language. Thus, for people to refer to Black English as a dialect is tantamount to saying it is a lesser language or not a language at all.

5. J. Clinton Brown would most likely agree with Baldwin. Language is a political tool, and those who use specific words such as *nigger* are articulating their particular perspective.

CHAPTER 13: MATTERS OF EQUALITY

Sally E. Smith, "Sizism—One of the Last 'Safe' Prejudices"

1. Some people may object to Smith's analogy because blacks cannot change the color of their skin, but most overweight people are capable of losing weight. In essence, although both ways of thinking involve prejudice, the recipients of the prejudice cannot be compared.

2. Given Smith's occupation, her choice of words was most likely intentional. Using the term *fat* indicates that Smith is not embarrassed by or regretful about people being overweight, even if other people are bothered by it.

3. Student responses will vary.

4. Student responses will vary.

5. People who oppose Smith's claim might say that overweight people must be accommodated in ways that affect other people: the space in restaurants, theaters, airplanes, and so on and that, despite Smith's claim, most people are capable of losing weight.

Lindsy Van Gelder, "Marriage as a Restricted Club"

1. Van Gelder's personal references certainly show the impact on individual people of the issue she presents. They also provide specific examples of the prejudice about which she writes. Some readers, however, may be put off when Van Gelder states that she no longer attends her friends' weddings or celebrates their wedding anniversaries.

2. Student responses will vary.

3. Van Gelder uses the appeal of logic to argue her stance when she cites the ways in which gay people are not eligible for health benefits, despite their willingness to commit to their partner. When Van Gelder discusses in paragraph 7 the "*genuine* commitment" as "flaunting" in the straight community, she appeals to emotions. As a carefully considered and rendered viewpoint, she appeals to ethics as she establishes herself as a reputable spokesperson.

4. Those who disagree with Van Gelder's viewpoint would probably point to their moral values and state that religious and governmental agencies do not approve of gay men and lesbians marrying.

5. Van Gelder approaches her topic clearly, strongly, and directly. She expresses anger at the unfairness of the laws that prevent gay and lesbian couples from marrying. The tone contributes to the power and effectiveness of her viewpoint.

Leonard Kriegel, "Claiming the Self"

1. Kriegel's opening is very engaging because he first clarifies what expertise he does and does not have to argue his claim. Although his thesis could have been argued by someone who is not crippled, his background adds interest, emotion, and credibility to his argument.

2. In his essay, Kriegel is arguing that in a world where physical capability is valued, crippled people are "second-class citizens" who are always being challenged and tested.

3. Kriegel first introduces his claim in paragraph 3: "Our capacities as individuals are always being tested." In paragraph 4, he continues, "Cripples are forced to affirm their existence and claim selfhood by pushing beyond those structures and categories their conditions have created." By first having established his interest in and expertise on the topic, Kriegel's claim is well-positioned.

4. Kriegel uses the appeal of emotion in the first paragraph of his argument by stating that he has been crippled since he was seven years old. He also uses the appeal of reason by the way he logically supports his stance. Because Kriegel proves himself a reliable writer, he demonstrates the appeal of ethics in his argument.

5. Because most people have never given serious thought to the difficulties faced by the disabled, a case can be made that Kriegel probably wrote to an audience that is unaware of the difficulties about which he writes. But because Kriegel's reflections are so thoughtful and thought-provoking, the disabled can also benefit from his understandings about being what he calls a "second-class citizen."

Charles Krauthammer, "A Defense of Quotas"

1. Background information on affirmative action provides an educational backdrop for Krauthammer's audience. It also helps to strengthen Krauthammer's argument because readers will understand the original intent of affirmative action.

2. Krauthammer's claim is first stated in paragraph 15, which is the first of three arguments in favor of saving affirmative action. Although Krauthammer could have stated his thesis earlier, the historical review that precedes his claim provides helpful background information to help put the topic into context.

3. Krauthammer proves his point by carefully examining three principal reasons for saving affirmative action. Student responses to his strategy will vary.

4. Opponents might claim that affirmative action has unfairly promoted the rights of less-qualified employees and students, much to the detriment of more deserving candidates. Krauthammer addresses this counterargument in his discussion of the three arguments in favor of saving affirmative action.

5. Krauthammer asks rhetorical questions as a way of emphasizing the points he has just made (e.g., paragraph 17, "Why fix what ain't broke?" and paragraph 19, "Shouldn't that be enough to entitle you to equal, colorblind treatment?").

Shelby Steele, "Affirmative Action: The Price of Preference"

1. Student responses will vary.

2. Steele uses the appeal of emotion when he discusses the demoralizing effect affirmative action has had on blacks and his own reactions to it as a black man. He employs the appeal of ethics when, throughout his argument, he establishes himself as a credible, reliable observer of black and white responses to affirmative action.

3. The personal conversations Steele relates in his argument add to his credibility as a writer. They also personalize his argument, showing the impact affirmative action has had on individual people and how his beliefs have developed.

4. Student responses will vary.

5. Charles Krauthammer and Shelby Steele might agree that affirmative action was needed when it was first legislated. However, Krauthammer might not concede to Steele that what it has done to African Americans' psyches is reason enough to end the program.

Marianne Means, "Women in Combat? Give It a Try and See If It Works"

1. Means uses statisics to indicate that she has researched her topic; the statistics show the ways in which women are held back in the military. The politicians' quotes serve a similar function.

2. Student responses will vary.

3. Student responses will vary.

4. Means's tone is occasionally cynical and cutting (e.g., paragraph 3, "Manuel Noriega's thugs didn't politely ask 'Male or female?' before firing" and in paragraph 4, "Does this mean Congress may discover it's time to get real?"). Because arguing against such statements is difficult, the tone strengthens her argument. It also demonstrates an urgency to take her thesis seriously and to make changes in the policies that govern women's roles in the military.

5. By linking opportunities to responsibilities, Means is not only furthering the effectiveness of her argument, but she is proving that not taking action has consequences greater than whether women can serve in combat.